T0310924

Modern Principles, Practices, and Algorithms for Cloud Security

Brij B. Gupta
National Institute of Technology, Kurukshetra, India

A volume in the Advances in Information Security,
Privacy, and Ethics (AISPE) Book Series

Published in the United States of America by
IGI Global
Information Science Reference (an imprint of IGI Global)
701 E. Chocolate Avenue
Hershey PA, USA 17033
Tel: 717-533-8845
Fax: 717-533-8661
E-mail: cust@igi-global.com
Web site: http://www.igi-global.com

Copyright © 2020 by IGI Global. All rights reserved. No part of this publication may be reproduced, stored or distributed in
any form or by any means, electronic or mechanical, including photocopying, without written permission from the publisher.
Product or company names used in this set are for identification purposes only. Inclusion of the names of the products or
companies does not indicate a claim of ownership by IGI Global of the trademark or registered trademark.

Library of Congress Cataloging-in-Publication Data

Names: Gupta, Brij, 1982- editor.
Title: Modern principles, practices, and algorithms for cloud security /
  edited by Brij B. Gupta.
Description: Hershey, PA : Information Science Reference, 2019. | Includes
  bibliographical references and index. | Summary: "This book examines the
  principles, algorithms, applications, and practices of security in cloud
  computing"-- Provided by publisher.
Identifiers: LCCN 2019024172 (print) | LCCN 2019024173 (ebook) | ISBN
  9781799810827 (hardcover) | ISBN 9781799810834 (paperback) | ISBN
  9781799810841 (ebook)
Subjects: LCSH: Cloud computing--Security measures.
Classification: LCC QA76.585 .M6434 2019 (print) | LCC QA76.585 (ebook) |
  DDC 004.67/82--dc23
LC record available at https://lccn.loc.gov/2019024172
LC ebook record available at https://lccn.loc.gov/2019024173

This book is published in the IGI Global book series Advances in Information Security, Privacy, and Ethics (AISPE) (ISSN:
1948-9730; eISSN: 1948-9749)

British Cataloguing in Publication Data
A Cataloguing in Publication record for this book is available from the British Library.

The views expressed in this book are those of the authors, but not necessarily of the publisher.

For electronic access to this publication, please contact: eresources@igi-global.com.

Advances in Information Security, Privacy, and Ethics (AISPE) Book Series

Manish Gupta
State University of New York, USA

ISSN:1948-9730
EISSN:1948-9749

Mission

As digital technologies become more pervasive in everyday life and the Internet is utilized in ever increasing ways by both private and public entities, concern over digital threats becomes more prevalent.

The **Advances in Information Security, Privacy, & Ethics (AISPE) Book Series** provides cutting-edge research on the protection and misuse of information and technology across various industries and settings. Comprised of scholarly research on topics such as identity management, cryptography, system security, authentication, and data protection, this book series is ideal for reference by IT professionals, academicians, and upper-level students.

Coverage

- IT Risk
- Security Classifications
- Cookies
- Network Security Services
- Telecommunications Regulations
- Privacy Issues of Social Networking
- Privacy-Enhancing Technologies
- Access Control
- Global Privacy Concerns
- Device Fingerprinting

IGI Global is currently accepting manuscripts for publication within this series. To submit a proposal for a volume in this series, please contact our Acquisition Editors at Acquisitions@igi-global.com or visit: http://www.igi-global.com/publish/.

The Advances in Information Security, Privacy, and Ethics (AISPE) Book Series (ISSN 1948-9730) is published by IGI Global, 701 E. Chocolate Avenue, Hershey, PA 17033-1240, USA, www.igi-global.com. This series is composed of titles available for purchase individually; each title is edited to be contextually exclusive from any other title within the series. For pricing and ordering information please visit http://www.igi-global.com/book-series/advances-information-security-privacy-ethics/37157. Postmaster: Send all address changes to above address. Copyright © 2020 IGI Global. All rights, including translation in other languages reserved by the publisher. No part of this series may be reproduced or used in any form or by any means – graphics, electronic, or mechanical, including photocopying, recording, taping, or information and retrieval systems – without written permission from the publisher, except for non commercial, educational use, including classroom teaching purposes. The views expressed in this series are those of the authors, but not necessarily of IGI Global.

Titles in this Series

For a list of additional titles in this series, please visit: www.igi-global.com/book-series

Security, Privacy, and Forensics Issues in Big Data
Ramesh C. Joshi (Graphic Era University, Dehradun, India) and Brij B. Gupta (National Institute of Technology, Kurukshetra, India)
Information Science Reference • copyright 2020 • 456pp • H/C (ISBN: 9781522597421) • US $235.00 (our price)

Handbook of Research on Machine and Deep Learning Applications for Cyber Security
Padmavathi Ganapathi (Avinashilingam Institute for Home Science and Higher Education for Women, India) and D. Shanmugapriya (Avinashilingam Institute for Home Science and Higher Education for Women, India)
Information Science Reference • copyright 2020 • 482pp • H/C (ISBN: 9781522596110) • US $295.00 (our price)

Advanced Digital Image Steganography Using LSB, PVD, and EMD Emerging Research and Opportunities
Gandharba Swain (Koneru Lakshmaiah Education Foundation, India)
Information Science Reference • copyright 2019 • 201pp • H/C (ISBN: 9781522575160) • US $165.00 (our price)

Developments in Information Security and Cybernetic Wars
Muhammad Sarfraz (Kuwait University, Kuwait)
Information Science Reference • copyright 2019 • 351pp • H/C (ISBN: 9781522583042) • US $225.00 (our price)

Cybersecurity Education for Awareness and Compliance
Ismini Vasileiou (University of Plymouth, UK) and Steven Furnell (University of Plymouth, UK)
Information Science Reference • copyright 2019 • 306pp • H/C (ISBN: 9781522578475) • US $195.00 (our price)

Detection and Mitigation of Insider Attacks in a Cloud Infrastructure Emerging Research and Opportunities
T. Gunasekhar (Koneru Lakshmaiah Education Foundation, India) K. Thirupathi Rao (Koneru Lakshmaiah Education Foundation, India) P. Sai Kiran (Koneru Lakshmaiah Education Foundation, India) V. Krishna Reddy (Koneru Lakshmaiah Education Foundation, India) and B. Thirumala Rao (Koneru Lakshmaiah Education Foundation, India)
Information Science Reference • copyright 2019 • 113pp • H/C (ISBN: 9781522579243) • US $165.00 (our price)

Network Security and Its Impact on Business Strategy
Ionica Oncioiu (European Academy of the Regions, Belgium)
Business Science Reference • copyright 2019 • 289pp • H/C (ISBN: 9781522584551) • US $225.00 (our price)

Exploring Security in Software Architecture and Design
Michael Felderer (University of Innsbruck, Austria) and Riccardo Scandariato (Chalmers University of Technology, Sweden & University of Gothenburg, Sweden)
Information Science Reference • copyright 2019 • 349pp • H/C (ISBN: 9781522563136) • US $215.00 (our price)

701 East Chocolate Avenue, Hershey, PA 17033, USA
Tel: 717-533-8845 x100 • Fax: 717-533-8661
E-Mail: cust@igi-global.com • www.igi-global.com

Dedicated to my wife, Varsha, and daughter, Prisha, for their constant support during the course of this book

   B. B. Gupta

Editorial Advisory Board

Dharma P. Agrawal, *University of Cincinnati, USA*
Nalin A. G. Arachchilage, *University of New South Wales, Australia*
Mohd Anuaruddin Bin Ahmadon, *Yamaguchi University, Japan*
Jin Li, *Guangzhou University, China*
Kuan-Ching Li, *Providence University, Taiwan*
Ahmad Manasrah, *Yarmouk University, Jordan*
Gregorio Martinez Perez, *University of Murcia, Spain*
Nadia Nedjah, *State University of Rio de Janeiro, Brazil*
T. Perumal, *Universiti Putra Malaysia (UPM), Malaysia*
Konstantinos Psannis, *University of Macedonia, Greece*
Seungmin Rho, *Sungkyul University, South Korea*
Michael Sheng, *Macquarie University, Australia*
Shingo Yamaguchi, *Yamaguchi University, Japan*

Table of Contents

Detailed Table of Contents

Chapter 1

  Sayani Sen, Sarojini Naidu College for Women, Dumdum, West Bengal, India
  Sathi Roy, Asian International School, Howrah, West Bengal, India
  Suparna Biswas, Maulana Abul kalam Azad University of Technology, West Bengal, India
  Chandreyee Chowdhury, Jadavpur University, India

Today's computational model has been undergoing a huge paradigm shift from personalized, local processing using local processing unit (LPU) to remote processing at cloud servers located globally. Advances in sensor-based smart applications such as smart home, smart health, smart transport, smart environment monitoring, etc. are generating huge data which needs to stored, pre-processed, analyzed using machine learning and deep learning techniques, which are resource-hungry, to generate results to be saved for future reference, and all these need to be done in real time, with scalability support satisfying user data privacy and security that may vary from application to application. In smart application like remote health monitoring and support, patient data needs utmost privacy besides confidentiality, integrity, and availability.

Chapter 2

  Christos Stergiou, University of Macedonia, Greece
  Kostas E. Psannis, University of Macedonia, Greece

Mobile cloud computing provides an opportunity to restrict the usage of huge hardware infrastructure and to provide access to data, applications, and computational power from every place and in any time with the use of a mobile device. Furthermore, MCC offers a number of possibilities but additionally creates several challenges and issues that need to be addressed as well. Through this work, the authors try to define the most important issues and challenges in the field of MCC technology by illustrating the most significant works related to MCC during recent years. Regarding the huge benefits offered by the MCC technology, the authors try to achieve a more safe and trusted environment for MCC users in order to operate the functions and transfer, edit, and manage data and applications, proposing a new method based on the existing AES encryption algorithm, which is, according to the study, the most relevant encryption algorithm to a cloud environment. Concluding, the authors suggest as a future plan to focus on finding new ways to achieve a better integration MCC with other technologies.

Chapter 3

Pramod P Pillai, VTU Extension Centre, UTL Technologies Ltd,, India
Venkataratnam P., VTU Extension Centre, UTL Technologies Ltd., India
Siva Yellampalli, School of Engineering and Applied Sciences, SRM University AP -
    Amarvati, India

Cloud computing is becoming a de facto standard for most of the emerging technology solutions. In a typical cloud environment, various tenants purchase the compute, storage resource, and would be sharing the resource with other tenants. Sharing of the resources among various tenants is not popular due to the security concerns. There are few solutions that try to solve the security problem of resource sharing among tenants. Having a trusted mediator between multiple tenants is one of the methods. Few research papers have been written, and this chapter attempts to enhance one of the published solutions: Cross-tenant access control model for cloud computing. Most of the existing research papers explore the theoretical way to solve the problem. This project develops a working prototype and proves how resource sharing can be achieved. This research develops the concept of resource sharing activation, where the resource can be shared with multiple cloud tenant and the deactivation where the shared resources can be removed from the shared resource pool.

Chapter 4

Dharavath Ramesh, Indian Institute of Technology (ISM), Dhanbad, India
Rahul Mishra, Indian Institute of Technology (ISM), Dhanbad, India
Damodar Reddy Edla, National Institute of Technology, Goa, India
Madhu Sake, Guru Nanak Institutions Technical Campus, Hyderabad, India

This chapter explains a secure smart cloud framework based on identity-based proxy signature (IDBPS) scheme on Computational Diffie-Hellman (CD-H) assumption and AckIBE for data management. The objective of this chapter is to construct a secure hierarchical structure of homogeneous and heterogeneous cloud centers. This structure gives various types of computing services in the support of data analysis and information management. In this, the authors also introduce a security-related solution based on acknowledgment identity-based encryption (AckIBE), an IDBPS on computational Diffie-Hellman assumption, and identity-based proxy re-encryption to face critical security issues of the proposed framework.

Chapter 5

Pragati Priyadarshinee, CBIT, India

The purpose of this chapter is to develop a cloud computing adoption scale for Indian manufacturing, service, and process industries. The scale development procedure has been followed from the previous studies and is refined further for clear understanding to adopt easily. In the first step, the authors have conducted a qualitative study for item selection. The second step includes pilot testing of 110 responses for measurement scale purification, and finally, they are validating the scale with 660 sample respondents through convergent validity and discriminant validity. The initial result showed very poor threshold values for the items "top management support" and "marketplace establishment," which have strong literature support. This measurement scale will help managers to evaluate the level of cloud adoption to increase the business performance. The study is a first attempt to develop a validated scale for cloud adoption that can be used in Indian industries.

The recent emergence of cloud computing has drastically altered everyone's perception of infrastructure architectures, software delivery, and development models. Projecting as an evolutionary step, cloud computing encompasses elements from grid computing, utility computing, and autonomic computing into an innovative deployment architecture. Cloud computing systems offer a lot of advantages like pay per use and rapid service provisioned on demand, while it suffers for some concerns specially security. In fact, a number of unchartered risks and challenges have been introduced from this new environment. This chapter explores the security issues in cloud computing systems and shows how to solve these problems using a quantitative security risk assessment model.

Chapter 7

The cloud is an appealing innovation that has driven, in record time, an extraordinary interest. It is right now one of the busiest regions of research in IT, due to its adaptability, vigor, and capacity to altogether lessen the expenses of administrations to clients on the web. Additionally, cloud stores all client information in server farms dispersed the world over. In this manner, security has turned into a foremost worry that anticipates numerous organizations to receive its administrations. Clients should store their information, a few of which are ordinarily secret or individual; in this way, the authors are exceptionally mindful to information honesty and classification amid exchange to a cloud server. This exploration chapter plans to build up an investigation on the different security threats engaged with distributed computing along with their recent countermeasures.

Chapter 8

Cloud computing has the potential of adding strategic value to the higher education domain owing to exemplary growth in ubiquitous data and communication services ranging from student access to educational materials to developing teaching and research practices. Despite the wide adoption of CC in HEIs, there is a paucity of research that specifically addresses the issue of trust in cloud adoption in the UK HEI context, as well as identifying smarter and more efficient strategies to overcome the existing CC trust issue in this domain. The authors propose a five-stage strategic roadmap to address the trust issues impacting the uptake of cloud services in UK universities. They conclude that IT and management participation and support are the keys to the success of the strategic framework.

Chapter 9
A Proposal of Improvement for Transmission Channels in Cloud Environments Using the CBEDE
Methodology 184

Reinaldo Padilha França, State University of Campinas (UNICAMP), Brazil

Yuzo Iano, State University of Campinas (UNICAMP), Brazil

Ana Carolina Borges Monteiro, State University of Campinas (UNICAMP), Brazil

Rangel Arthur, State University of Campinas (UNICAMP), Brazil

Sharing, transmitting, and storing data has been one of the great needs of today. In the last years, concepts and developed methodologies of cloud computing systems have been improved. This concept created in the 1960s today is present in daily life from ordinary users to even large companies. The present study aims to develop a method of data transmission based on discrete event concepts. This methodology was named CBEDE (by the acronym). The experiments were matched in the MATLAB software simulation environment, where the memory consumption of the proposed methodology was evaluated. Therefore, the CBEDE methodology presents great potential to intermediate users and computer systems, ensuring speed, low memory consumption, and reliability. Being the differential of this research, the use of discrete events applied in the physical layer of a transmission medium, the bit itself, being this to low-level of abstraction, the results show better computational performance related to memory utilization related to the compression of the information, showing an improvement reaching up to 69.93%

Chapter 10
Meta-Heuristic and Non-Meta-Heuristic Energy-Efficient Load Balancing Algorithms in Cloud
Computing.. 203

Rojalina Priyadarshini, C. V. Raman College of Engineering, India

Rabindra Kumar Barik, KIIT Deemed to be University, India

Brojo Kishore Mishra, GIET University, India

The number of users of cloud computing services is drastically increasing, thereby increasing the size of data centers across the globe. In virtue of it, the consumption of power and energy is a major concern for system designers and developers. Their goal is now to develop power and energy-efficient products at the same time maintaining the quality and cost of products and services. For managing the power and efficiency, several aspects are taken into consideration in cloud computing paradigm. Load balancing, task scheduling, task migration, resource allocation are some of the techniques, which need to be efficiently employed to minimize the energy consumption. This chapter represents the detailed survey of the existing solutions and approaches for energy-efficient load balancing algorithms used in cloud environments. The research challenges as well as future research directions are also discussed in this chapter.

Meta-path is an important concept of heterogeneous information networks (HINs). Meta-paths were used in many tasks such as information retrieval, decision making, and product recommendation. Normally meta-paths were proposed by human experts. Recently, works on meta-path discovery have proposed in-memory solutions that fit in one computer. With large HINs, the whole HIN cannot be loaded in the memory. In this chapter, the authors proposed distributed algorithms to discover meta-paths of large HINs on cloud. They develop the distributed algorithms to discover the significant meta-path, maximal significant meta-path, and top-k meta-paths between two vertices of HIN. Calculation of the support of meta-paths or performing breadth first search can be computational costly in very large HINs. Conveniently, the distributed algorithms utilize the GraphFrames library of Apache Spark on cloud computing environment to efficiently query large HINs. The authors conduct the experiments on large DBLP dataset to prove the performance of our algorithms on cloud.

This author has for the past decade developed a mathematical basis for product languages, at times with colleagues, applying agent crypto-signatures to authenticate business process models. This chapter is the newest application for what is at recent times called block chain. A new algebraic tree based public key cryptography techniques and algorithm for crypto-signatured block chain processing is presented. The techniques apply agent crypto-signatured algebras and block product language signatures for an agenda-based block chain protocol. An algorithm with a new public key computable trust model for signature tree block parties accomplishes the block chain goals.

The CIM, PIM, and PSM models are the main levels of the MDA approach. Model transformation is an important step in the MDA process. Indeed, in MDA there are two elementary transformation kinds: CIM to PIM transformation and PIM to PSM transformation. However, most searches propose approaches transforming PIM to PSM, since there are multiple points in common between PIM and PSM. Nevertheless, transforming CIM to PIM is rarely addressed in research because these two levels are mainly different. However, there is not a synthesis work that makes it possible to carry out a model transformation from CIM to PIM towards PSM until obtaining the code. This synthesis methodology allows controlling models transformation from CIM to PIM to PSM, indeed, up to obtaining code according the MDA. This approach makes it possible to limit the intervention of computer scientists in the life cycle of software development. Indeed, this methodology allows modeling only CIM, the business process, and then obtains the source code through successive semi-automatic transformations.

Preface

Today, Cloud Computing services have become an indispensable part of modern Information and Communication Technology (ICT) systems, and this paradigm has proven to be an incredible technology for providing quickly deployed and scalable Information Technology (IT) solutions with reduced infrastructure costs. Cloud Computing service models include Infrastructure as a Service (IaaS), Platform as a Service (PaaS), and Software as a Service (SaaS). Various other aspects associated with this paradigm are distributed access control, risk management, Cloud architecture, Cloud governance, database security, network security, and so forth. However, use of Cloud technology is raising serious issues associated with security, privacy, latency, inadequate service levels, governance, forensics, data protection, maturity and reliability. These issues prevent Cloud Computing solutions from becoming the prevalent alternative for mission critical systems.

Moving information assets offer Cloud Computing with the potential of reduced costs, on-demand self-service, ubiquitous network access, location independent resource pooling, rapid elasticity, and measurable services for the Cloud users. However, these Cloud Computing services also open a number of security, privacy, and forensics related issues and challenges that are required to be dealt with.

This book contains chapters dealing with different aspects of computer networks and cyber security. These include Cyber-security issues in Clouds, Information revelation and privacy in Cloud computing, Cloud computing security data analysis tools and services, Cloud with User Mobility, Mobile Cloud Computing's Security and Management challenges, Security for Cross Tenant Access Control in Cloud Computing, Secured handling of Extra-scale computational loads on Clouds, Anonymous authentication for privacy preserving in Cloud, Privacy concepts and applications in Cloud Platforms, Cloud Interoperability & Standards, Cloud Ecosystem, Cloud management and virtualization, Security and privacy of cloud user's data, Cyber-attacks and solutions for high fidelity Cloud storage, Cloud Security Risk Management, Distributed access control in Cloud, Secure cloud architecture, Cloud Computing Adoption, Cloud Computing Adoption in Higher Education, Energy Efficient Load Balancing Algorithms in Cloud Computing, Distributed Algorithms for Cloud, Block Chain model for cloud and so on.

Acknowledgment

Many people have contributed greatly to this book on *Modern Principles, Practices, and Algorithms for Cloud Security*. I would like to acknowledge all of them for their valuable help and generous ideas in improving the quality of this book. With my feelings of gratitude, I would like to introduce them in turn. The first mention is the authors and reviewers of each chapter of this book. Without their outstanding expertise, constructive reviews and devoted effort, this comprehensive book would become something without contents. The second mention is the IGI Global staff, especially Courtney Tychinski, development editor and her team for their constant encouragement, continuous assistance and untiring support. Without their technical support, this book would not be completed. The third mention is my family for being the source of continuous love, unconditional support and prayers not only for this work, but throughout my life. Last but far from least, I express my heartfelt thanks to the Almighty for bestowing over me the courage to face the complexities of life and complete this work.

B.B. Gupta

August 25, 2019

Chapter 1
Security– and Privacy– Aware Computing in Cloud With User Mobility:
An Extensive Review

Sayani Sen
Sarojini Naidu College for Women, Dumdum, West Bengal, India

Sathi Roy
Asian International School, Howrah, West Bengal, India

Suparna Biswas
Maulana Abul kalam Azad University of Technology, West Bengal, India

Chandreyee Chowdhury
Jadavpur University, India

ABSTRACT

Today's computational model has been undergoing a huge paradigm shift from personalized, local processing using local processing unit (LPU) to remote processing at cloud servers located globally. Advances in sensor-based smart applications such as smart home, smart health, smart transport, smart environment monitoring, etc. are generating huge data which needs to stored, pre-processed, analyzed using machine learning and deep learning techniques, which are resource-hungry, to generate results to be saved for future reference, and all these need to be done in real time, with scalability support satisfying user data privacy and security that may vary from application to application. In smart application like remote health monitoring and support, patient data needs utmost privacy besides confidentiality, integrity, and availability.

DOI: 10.4018/978-1-7998-1082-7.ch001

Copyright © 2020, IGI Global. Copying or distributing in print or electronic forms without written permission of IGI Global is prohibited.

INTRODUCTION TO SECURITY AND PRIVACY ISSUES OF USER DATA ON CLOUD

The interpretation of 'Cloud Computing' according to the National Institute of Standard and Technology (NIST) is cloud computing is a platform which enables on-demand, universal, convenient network access to a shared pool of configurable computing resources. This can be used for minimal management cost and service provider interaction (Leavitt, 2009). For a Cloud Computing environment, both resources and applications are delivered as services with minimal cost by using the underlying Internet connection. The three most well-known services of cloud computing (depicted in Figure 1) are defined below (Amini et al, 2015).

1. **Software as a service (SaaS):** SaaS represent the largest cloud market, where the software and related data of the software are deployed by the cloud service provider. Most of the SaaS applications can be run directly through the web browser without any installations or download.
2. **Platform as a service (PaaS):** In PaaS the service provider makes services easy to the user to perform a specific task. It makes development, testing, and deployment of software easy and cost-effective.
3. **Infrastructure as a service (IaaS):** IaaS provides storage and virtual machine to improve the business applications of the user (Leavitt, 2009).

Cloud computing has few characteristics like service on-demand, worldwide network access, location independence, resource elasticity, and security. These merits make cloud computing more attractive to both the world industrial and academic research. However, there are few problems to be solved for the

Figure 1. Services of cloud computing

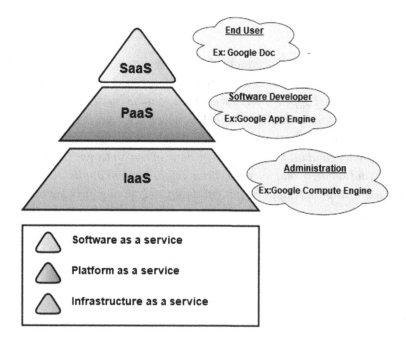

enterprises as well as personal users regarding data storage and deployment of the applications in a cloud computing environment. Data security is one of the most significant barriers in the cloud computing environment. It is consisting of the issues of trust, privacy and legal matters as discussed in (Shah et al, 2008). There are three different accesses to cloud computing which is public, private and hybrid cloud computing environments. The public cloud environment is the service provider's property which can be used by anyone. Private cloud is the property of the company which can be accessed by the authorized user, whereas, combination of private and public cloud is called the hybrid cloud (Leavitt, 2009).

Applications of Cloud Computing

Cloud computing is the key driving force behind most web applications today. Application paradigms, such as e-commerce, m-commerce, banking to IoT to smart city are possible because of the availability of cloud services. This is summarized in Figure 2. Today, most internet users are accessing one or more cloud services for storage, computation and communication. Collaborative applications are developed to encourage working in a group remotely and that has eased application development across the globe. Cloud services such as, storage and remote execution along with its elastic nature has helped small companies to flourish as they do not need to purchase or maintain expensive servers. With mobile and wearable devices communicating over the cloud, data and computation offloading at runtime is possible. This has facilitated complicated games to run on lightweight handheld devices where the devices mostly work as an input-output device but the core application is executed in cloud. Mobile cloud computing is another paradigm that has come up to provide stable performance to mobile users by incorporating optimizations in virtual machine selection in the cloud end. This is important especially to improve user experience for various applications ranging from computer games to stock market transactions.

Figure 2. Potential applications of cloud computing

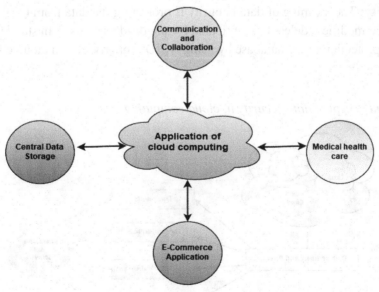

Healthcare industry has also seen a sea change as cloud computing has given a much reliable option for health data storage and management that can survive server crash. Today, in many countries, cloud services are used for many core healthcare applications as it heavily cuts down the operational and maintenance costs. The traditional reactive healthcare system, where a patient would visit a doctor only when some symptoms appear has been changed to proactive mode where the wearable sensing devices can collect health data and send to cloud for storage and analysis. Proactive monitoring is crucial for detecting chronic diseases in their early stages as well as day-to-day monitoring of them. Patient monitoring systems, ambient assisted living systems are instances of cloud enabled healthcare applications that are popularly used for eldercare and for monitoring patients undergoing rehabilitation after surgery etc.

Cloud computing has changed the landscape of e-learning applications as well. M-learning applications utilize the cloud for storage and processing capability to add richer user experiences. But these applications suffer from security threats that are explained in the following sections.

Security Vulnerabilities, Attacks and Threats

Major challenges of cloud computing environments include resource management and monitoring and data security. However, in cloud computing environment there is no such standard protocol available for application deployment in cloud, so there is lack of standardization on controlling the data in cloud. Numerous techniques have been designed to provide security to the data but most of these techniques are not sufficient to provide a comprehensive solution due to the dynamic nature of the cloud computing environment. The foremost issues in data security in cloud computing is privacy of data, protection to the data, reliable and secure data transmission. The security threats in the cloud computing environment include loss of data, service disruption, threats, unreliable data transmission, and malicious attack from outside world. The four most important aspects of data security in cloud computing environment are data Integrity, data Confidentiality, data Availability, and data privacy. These are explained below and summarized in Figure 3.

1. **Data Integrity:** The meaning of data integrity is protecting the data from unauthorized used like data cannot be modified, deleted or fabricated by any third party user. In standalone machine it is easy to give protection to the database by using ACID property. But in cloud computing environ-

Figure 3. Important accept of data security in cloud computing

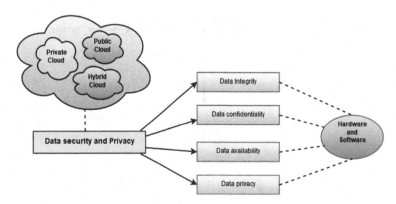

ment integrity means provide the three basic services of cloud computing SaaS, PaaS, IaaS. It can be obtain by using the technique digital signature and RFID.

2. **Data Confidentiality:** Confidentiality is needed to maintain the privacy of the important data. The data confidentiality, authentication, and access control issues in cloud computing environment can be addressed by increasing the cloud reliability and data encryption. However, simple encryption methods suffer from key sharing issues and also cannot support complex application requirements (Rakesh et al, 2012). There are few other encryption strategies to maintain the confidentiality of the user data like Homomorphic Encryption, Encrypted Search and Database, Hybrid Technique, and Deletion Confirmation etc (Sun et al, 2014).

3. **Data Availability:** Data availability means accessing the saved data at anytime from anywhere. Data may be lost due to network failure or hard disk crash. Such user data is needed to be recovered using different verification tools available to test the authenticity of the available data. In that case, the cloud vendor will explain the jurisdiction to the clients and should provide data safety guarantees.

4. **Data Privacy:** In general, data privacy implies the ability of an individual or a group of members to hide their data from outside world and reveal it to the selected one. In the case of privacy which and how is the most important term. Which data to be protected, like present data is more important than past data. The second important term is how, means how the user wants to protect his/her data. It is possible that user wants to get notified manually every time before anyone makes use of the data (sun et al, 2014).

Threat Models

Before taking a closer look to the cloud security here we have discussed about the two main aspects of security- the threats of cloud computing and vulnerability of cloud computing (Amini et al, 2015).

Threats of cloud computing: Cloud Security Alliance (CSA) is a security assurance provider which gives security to the critical data and area of the cloud computing. It helps to understand the security threats and also in managing risks. Few most significant on demand nature related threats are listed below (Leavitt, 2009).

1. **Data Loss:** The most critical and terrifying threats for businesses and consumers point of view is data loss. Any data deletion by the service provider by mistake can lead to loss of consumers' data.

2. **Stealing Credentials:** It may possible that the attackers steal the users credentials and get access to the critical area of the cloud computing services. In that case the organization should prohibit sharing of important data and stronger authentication techniques are required.

3. **Insecure Interface:** Customers of cloud computing environment use Application Programming Interface (API) to interact and manage the cloud services. Authentication, and access control technology is needed to protect the APIs from malicious attacks.

4. **Malicious Insider:** In that case, the data may be damaged by the authorized user while working on a network. Thus, confidentiality, integrity and accessibility may get lost because of such attacks.

5. **Stealing Data:** Stealing private information from private organization by outsiders is not acceptable at any point. Data encryption can help to reduce the risk of data stealing but in that case encryption key is very important. As loosing of encryption key is equivalent to loosing of data itself.

Other than this there are some other treats in cloud computing environment like Denial of services (Lohman et al, 2011) where, attacker prevents the user to reach to the destination. Cloud computing does not provide any strong registration process to get access to the cloud services. So, any user with a valid credit card can access register and access the services. This may lead to attack on the cloud environment.

Vulnerability of Cloud Computing: It is the probability of an asset which will be unable to resist from the action of a threat agent ("Risk Taxonomy et al, n.d.). In cloud computing environment, for moving, organizational, critical or confidential data different types of vulnerabilities should be considered. Here, in this section we have discussed few of the vulnerabilities.

Riding of a Session: It can be defined as sending command to the web applications by the hackers to get the unauthorized access to the data. Hackers can perform malicious activities and even can delete the user data.

Accessing Through VM: This kind of vulnerability allows attackers to run code on virtual machine that may lead to operating system break down of the user machine. In this way, an attacker gets access to the host operating system and other virtual machine directly (Rouse, 2009).

Encryption Method: The developer can use good encryption algorithm with proper key arrangement procedure to protect the data from vulnerability.

Recovery of Data: The developer should use a data recovery procedure to recover the data with proper security (Kenyon, 2010).

There are other vulnerability issues in cloud computing environment like lack in internet protocol design, metering and billing vendor lock in etc (Kenyon, 2010).

AN OVERVIEW OF TOOLS, ALGORITHMS, TECHNIQUES USED IN SECURE CLOUD ARCHITECTURE

In the field of Cloud Computing, security of data is very crucial. The data which is stored on the cloud needs to be secured from unauthorized access (Islam et al, 2017). Thus data security and privacy are the most critical aspect with respect to cloud computing.

When sharing of resources of multiple organizations occur, there is a very high chance for the data to get misused. Hence a risk factor gets involved. Thus enhancing security of data (Dimitrios et al, 2012) and protection of data is a challenge in this field.

As technology advances towards cloud environment, we must be aware regarding the benefits and challenges of Cloud Computing (Kalpana et al, 2012) Among the challenges, Data Security and Privacy is a major concern.

Literature Survey

In the paper (Kanti et al, 2014), the author provides a technique which maintains the integrity of data. Here, at first data is being sent to the server which is saved behind the images. Hence the unauthorized users cannot access as well as cannot perceive the data since it is hidden. Here steganography with image is used for protecting the integrity of data. But the data security during transmission is not there. Though it was a very unique approach but could have been much popular as it could not handle integrity and confidentiality of data while uploading to cloud server.

In the paper (Aparjita et al, 2014), the authors describes a scheme where at first the plain text is converted in hexadecimal format using MD5 algorithm, which was again converted to encrypted cipher text using AES algorithm. Thus it uses two step encryption process one for plain text and another for already encrypted text. This scheme can be easily implemented but the keys are not at all secure that are being used for encryption the data.

In this paper (Bala et al, 2014), a protocol is used for the verification of storing the data and also in retrieving the intact data. The main advantage is assuring integrity by the use of digital signature. The process is a bit complex as data along with key are allowed to encrypt and decrypt accordingly.

In this paper (Singla et al, 2013), the issue of data security is the primary concern for data transmission and to encrypt the data .Here an encryption scheme is accompanied by Extensible Authentication Protocol- Challenge-Handshake Authentication Protocol (EAP-CHAP).

In this paper (Khadilkar et al, 2010), the author shares the data. The problem is regarding the storing data and accessing data. A different technique is described here using Hive and Hadoop for more convenience.

In this paper (Alangar et al, 2013), the author attracts attention towards the problem of data security and data encryption is done to resolve this issue. A list of various encryption techniques such as RSA,DES etc are used.

In this paper (Sahu et al, 2013), when the service providers are not very cooperative with the users. This approach can be modified with the help of third party auditor i.e. an external entity maintains of integrity of data along with the user which provides a better security.

In the paper (Yadav et al, 2014), fingerprint of client is required for encryption and decryption of the data. The approach is a very unique since no two persons can have the same fingerprints. It is not always possible that the person using the cloud services will have fingerprint machine for such situation extra machines are to be purchased and this is how it makes the model.

Security Issues in Cloud Environment:

Challenges/issues related to security in the field of cloud are described below:-

Integrity

We can preserve information that has not been modified by an unauthorized user during data transfer, data storage and data retrieval. This is known as integrity (Islam et al, 2017; Velumadhava et al, 2015). When more than one user can share identical data, application or platform in the cloud which can be

Table 1. Summary of related works

Author's details (Auhor name-Publishing year)	Security Attributes	Security Techniques	Remarks
Mrinal Kanti Sarkar et al, January 2014	Privacy/Confidentiality	Data hiding algorithm is used in Steganography (hiding data within images)	Matlab
Aparjita Sidhu et al, January 2014	Privacy/Confidentiality	AES,MD5,RC4	Java language with IDE Eclipse or Net Beans. Encryption done using hashing
R. Bala Chandar et al, January 2014	Data Integrity, Access Control, Data Authentication	RSA	Provides end to end cloud security
Sanjoli Singh et al, July 2013	Privacy/Confidentiality, Integrity	Rijndael encryption Algorithm	Extensible Authentication Protocol-Challenge Handshake Authentication Protocol (CHAP) is introduced which ensures security
Varsha Alangar et al, October 2013	Authenticity and Integrity	DES,RSA	Loss of data, Data Infection, Key Management Problem, Virtual Machine attacks are the security threats
Ashis Bhagat et al, May 2013	Privacy/Confidentiality, Integrity and Consistency, Client Authentication by password	AES and RSA (decrypt data with Digital Signature)	Implemented in Java, Algorithm ElGamal Digital Signature is implemented using ClouSim and CloudAnalyst with Eclipse
Varsha Yadav et al, May 2014	Confidentiality, Integrity, Recovery	AES(for Encryption) and RSA (for Key Generation)	Implemented in Java, Simulator used: CloudSim

changed by any other unauthorized user (Kalpana et al, 2012). This may cause the integrity failure. Hence maintaining data integrity (Zissis et al, 2012) is our fundamental task. The cloud service providers have to ensure integrity hence making the data secured.

Availability

Cloud Data is stored as a collection of data which resides in various Cloud servers (Zissis et al, 2012). Hence availability becomes the most important legitimate issue (Khan et al, 2014).

Relocatable Data

Data is highly mobile in the Cloud field. The cloud service providers are responsible to ensure data security. They must protect customer's information by providing robust authentication. User can know the location where the data is stored on Cloud. Data may move from one location to another. Cloud Service Provider keep the data initially at an appropriate location (Kalpana et al, 2012). Later it may change its location.

Confidentiality and Privacy

Confidentiality and privacy is the major responsibility of the cloud service provider. There is no personal data (Khan et al, 2014) stored in the cloud such as password. Cloud Service Provider allows to access the cloud data by authorized users and there is no personal data stored in the cloud such as password. Cloud providers must ensure that there is no access to inappropriate data (Zissis et al, 2012) in the cloud. Vulnerabilities are to be checked to protect data (Islam et al, 2017). Security tests (Kalpan et al, 20120 must be done to protect cloud data. Encryption is one of the best solution to confidentiality (Velumadhava et al, 2015).

Algorithms applied for Cloud Security

Symmetric and Asymmetric algorithms are used for security purpose. Encryption provides a protection to cloud data. Figure 4 depicts data security method to control data in Cloud Storage.

Security Algorithms can be broadly classified as:

- Private Key / Symmetric Algorithms
- Public Key / Asymmetric Algorithms
- Hash based Algorithms

Cloud Service Providers does not have any defined algorithm to ensure data security from threats and attacks. They try to secure data using security algorithms. The primary goal of these algorithms is to make the decryption of the generated cipher text harder. The more the length (Chatterjee et al, 2017) of the key the harder it is to decrypt. Thus making the algorithms more efficient.

Figure 4. Security method to control data in cloud storage

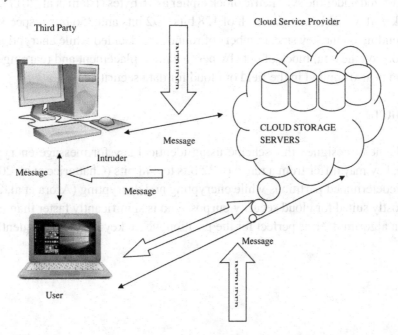

Private Key/Symmetric Algorithm

This algorithm uses identical secret key to encrypt and decrypt data (Bhardwaj et al, 2016). Same Secret key is used by both the sender and receiver.

The main advantage of symmetric/private key algorithm is that it has very high speed while data encryption since it has requires less power for computation (Chatterjee et al, 2017).

There are disadvantages (Bhardwaj et al, 2016) with Symmetric Algorithms:

- Sharing one single secret key to encrypt and decrypt data over the internet is very unsecure. Cloud service providers face very difficulty while communicating with sender and the receiver. Changing the secret key and keeping it secure during the sharing phase is the main concern.
- If the intruder alters the content issues of data integrity and non-repudiation occurs.

Data Encryption Standard Algorithm

DES is symmetric-key block cipher algorithm. Identical secret key is used for the encrypting and decrypting purpose (Chatterjee et al, 2017). The entire plaintext is divided into blocks of 64 bit and key size is taken as 56 bits. The round key size is 48 bits. Multiple permutations and substitutions are done.

There are three phases including the initial and final permutation (Chatterjee et al, 2017)which are taken as the first and last phase respectively for data encryption. Sixteen rounds (Islam et al, 2017) considered as second phase each of which uses a 48-bit key thereby finally producing a 64-bit data in encrypted form.

This algorithm and its overall mechanism is applied in the cloud environment for data security.

Advanced Encryption Standard Algorithm

AES is also categorized under the symmetric block cipher as 16 bytes (Islam et al, 2017). It has a 128 bits of specified block with variable key size each of 128 bits, 192 bits and 256 bits respectively (Chatterjee et al, 2017). Depending on the key size, numbers of rounds are decided while encryption. Instead of using bits, it functions on the total block of data by performing replacement and rearrangement on bytes .

This algorithm is also applied in the field of cloud for data security.

Blowfish Algorithm

In 1993 Bruce Schneier designed this scheme using identical key for message encryption as well as decryption. Here, key may differ from a range of 32 bits to 448 bits (Chatterjee et al, 2017). A message is divided into predetermined partitions while encrypting and decrypting (Arora et al, 2013).

Hence it is mostly suited for cloud security purpose and is significantly faster than most of the symmetric encryption algorithms. It is perfect for the position where key is not so frequently altered.

Asymmetric Algorithm

Here, to encrypt data, public key is used and to decrypt the data and private key is used. Keys are simply large numbers that have been paired together but are asymmetric (not identical) (Bhardwaj et al, 2016). The main asymmetric/public key algorithms are Diffie-Hellman and RSA.

RSA Algorithm

RSA consists of asymmetric keys for message encryption and message decryption (Arora et al, 2013). RSA uses random numbers which are prime in nature to enhance security (Bahrdwaj et al, 2016) The major drawback of RSA is the usage of small values for key (Islam et al, 2017). Here the encryption process becomes fragile. Again if large values of prime numbers drops the performance.

RSA is used for the purpose of generating the key and performing the encryption and decryption of the message. Before encryption, the Key is generated. At the sender end, at first the message is encrypted using Public Key and stored in the Cloud. At the Receiver end the user wants to access the data from the Cloud Service Provider according to requirement. It authenticates the user by verifying and finally delivers the data in encrypted format. User then decrypts to find the original data. Thus, encryption is done by the Cloud service provider and decryption is done by the Cloud user (Kalpana et al, 2012).

Diffie-Hellman Key Exchange Algorithm

In this protocol sender and receiver will exchange the shared secret key for the inter communication using an unsafe channel. The shared key is not for encryption or decryption. Thus attacker thinks that both sender and the receiver exchanged values by transformation of keys (Malik et al, 2015) and now both of them have the same session key. Thus they can evaluate the required session key.

Function of Authentication Module of Diffie Hellman Algorithm

How to Make a New Registration for the Cloud Service

The steps for registration for the cloud service is as follows:-

1. Firstly the user is required to register who needs to access different types of cloud services. During registration, the details of user eg user_id and mobile number is taken as input. The mobile number is used for validating a genuine user (Malik et al, 2015) by sending a message including a key which the user will have to enter for creating the account over the cloud to make a successful registration.
2. When user_id and password is entered, a key is being sent (Malik et al, 2015) that is generated using a Diffie-Hellman Key Exchange Algorithm. This key is valid for a specific time instance and then is destroyed.

Table 2. The comparative study of the cloud security algorithms

Characteristics	AES in Cloud	DES in Cloud	RSA in Cloud
Type of Key used	Uses Symmetric key	Uses Symmetric key	Uses Assymmetric key
Initial Size	128 bits	64 bits	1024 bits
Security	Secured	Secured	Not Secured for provider
Capacity	Used for large data	Use for medium data	Use for small data
Memory required	Less memory is used	More memory is used	Highest memory usage

How to Use Cloud Service

1. Secondly, when a user wants to use the cloud services, they are requested to enter details. Registration is successful only when user details are correct (Malik et al, 2015).The key is then sent to the mobile number of the user.
2. The user then enter the key which was received on mobile .If the key matches with the key generated using the Diffie-Hellman Algorithm, then only data access and all the cloud services (Malik et al, 2015) is provided to the user after authentication is made successful.

Hash based Algorithm

This algorithm uses fixed size data using compression technique.

Message Digest Algorithm

For message encryption public key is used private key is used to decrypt the message. MD5 uses a hash value of 128-bit and a message of varying length. At first the input is divided into blocks of 512 bit. A 128 bit data which is fixed is delivered as output (Chatterjee et al, 2017).

Characteristics and Comparison of Cloud Security Algorithms

The Comparative Study (Arora et al, 2013) of the Cloud Security Algorithms according to their features are as follows:

Simulation Tools for Cloud Based Solutions and Services

Before adopting any cloud services it is always better to test the clouds. For example, some clouds involved in the cloud resources are very costly and the cost of internet for using the cloud resources may cause inconvenience in the budget. Effective resource utilization (Gupta et al, 2016) is not possible in the case of cloud. Through Cloud Simulation Tools, Testing of the clouds is done.

Advantages of Cloud simulation tools (Gupta et al, 2016) are:-

1. No **Capital Investment Involved:-** Simulation tools requires no installation and maintenance cost.
2. **Provides Better Results:** Simulation tools helps user to change input easily as and when required, thus providing better results as an output.
3. **Risks are Assessed:-** Risks are assessed (Gupta et al, 2016) as there is no running cost for simulation tools with respect to capital.

For real time implementation, a cloud computing simulator (Gupta et al, 2016) is required. Simulators are needed mainly required for algorithm execution, security threat analyzing, infrastructure quality and performance measurement.

It is very much challenging and complex to choose the right simulation tool for a given scenario and at the same time also knowing about the features of each tool. Simulators may be free, open source and commercial (Gupta et al, 2016).

Simulators make dynamic and flexible configuration thereby making cloud reliable and scalable (Bala et al, 2014). Easy commands and graphical user interface (Gupta et al, 2016) is provided. Simulators with performance and security enable researchers to simulate cloud environments. These are the main advantages of Cloud Simulators.

The various types of tool kits for the purpose of Simulation are:

CloudSim

CloudSim is a simulation tool kit based on Java (Bala et al, 2014).
The features are listed below:

- The simulation kit supports experiments and application in the cloud.
- Communication between various components and simulation clock are the main functions.

CloudAnalyst

CloudAnalyst is a GUI based simulator. CloudAnalyst provides a powerful simulation framework.
The features are listed below:

- It is very easy to use for viewing results of different experiments.
- Outputs may be viewed with tables and charts.
- Simulation outlines can be saved and can be formed as a loop.
- A series of simulations can be done when parameter is slightly changed.
- Evaluation of social network tools (Bala et al, 2014) is supported by the simulator.

GreenCloud

The GreenCloud is a GUI based open source, user-friendly simulator. It provides simulation for energy-aware cloud computing (Gupta et al, 2016) data centres.
The features are listed below:

- The simulator mainly have a focus in monitoring and energy consumption in cloud computing environment.
- This simulator tries to minimize the electricity consumption by improving power management and dynamic management.

iCanCloud

The iCanCloud is a GUI based open source, user-friendly simulator (Gupta et al, 2016).
The features of iCanCloud are listed below:

- iCanCloud supports the simulation of large storage which is one of the major ojective of this simulator.
- iCanCloud was designed to be a powerful simulator by optimizing flexibility, accuracy, performance and scalability (Gupta et al, 2016).
- Repository of iCanCloud can add new components.

Emusim

Integrated Emulation and Simulation (Emusim) is an open source software.
The features of Emusim are listed below:

- It automatically extracts the information regarding the behavior of an application
- It reduce the cost while running in a cloud based simulation (Gupta et al, 2016).

GroudSim

GroudSim is a Java-based simulator which only requires one simulation thread. GroudSim mainly focuses on the IaaS (Infrastructure as a service) area (Gupta et al, 2016).

DCSim (Data Centre Simulation)

DCSim is an event-driven Java based simulator which gives an easy platform for doing experiments.
The features are listed below:

- DCSim shares the workload.
- DCSim allows quick development and instant response on data centre (Gupta et al, 2016).

ISSUES IN DESIGNING SECURE CLOUD ARCHITECTURE

Cloud computing has been successful with the support of enabling technologies such as Internet of Things, Big data, Machine and Deep Learning among others. Utility of cloud platform in many forms such as Platform as a service (Paas), Storage as a service (Saas), Infrastructure as a service (Iaas) can be exploited over wide range of users ranging from individual to small organization to large ones to offload huge data handling to cloud infrastructure which can be availed without exclusive ownership thus huge monitory investment and also maintenance related hazards can be avoided. As it is popularly known that no lunch is free similarly to avail all these advantages of cloud platform there a question may arise of security compromise of data and application that will be running remotely at public cloud and that is the reason behind not getting preferred over the issue of underlying security principles of cloud platform (Ramchandra et al, 2017). Unauthorized access to any sensitive data at public cloud may jeopardize the security and privacy requirement of a particular application hence cloud must have stringent access control policy (Ramchandra et al, 2017) to assure a minimum level of guaranteed trust between the service lender and end user. Edge computing using smartphones, laptops, Tablet computers etc. got immensely popularized by the backbone support of cloud computing by taking away the computing and storage load from the resource constrained devices thus saving battery power, limited memory etc. along with user mobility support progressing towards new paradigm Mobile cloud Computing (Dinh et al, 2013; Khan et al, 2013).

Secure Functional Cloud Framework

Key characteristics of cloud computing and services designed and developed on this platform are popular due to salient features (Zissis et al, 2012) which also make this framework vulnerable to security attacks and threats compromising security requirements of an application. Some of the key salient features are:

- **Provisioning of Allocation/Deallocation Dynamically:** Cloud computing provides virtual computing platform to the user as per the application demands along with easy and non-hazardous provision of joining and placing demand for resources without taking minimum pain to gain the required support in terms of required computing, memory, energy and application specific security assurance. Similarly if any user wants leave then his/her allocated resources are released without manual intervention and much changes in existing cloud system setup.
- **Location Independence:** Location independence is related to ability to access and utilize cloud framework which is globally placed and the user needs to be least bothered about the location of the cloud server that would be providing service or infrastructure or platform required to execute the particular task submitted by the user.
- **User Mobility Support:** From the emerging point of cloud computing till date, the edge devices have been revolutionarily changed from heavy weight desktop computing to light weight, portable devices such as laptop, tablet computers, smartphone etc. to satisfy with the ever dreamed demand of users to be able to access, update or modify required data, to avail services or to utilize resources (memory, CPU, battery power etc.) existing virtually somewhere in this globe.

- **Integration with Legacy Systems and Advanced Devices and Networks:** Cloud computing started in support of client-server architecture where private or stand-alone server has been replaced with cloud server implemented with several virtual machines (VMs) and now been associated with specialized networks like wireless body area network (WBAN) which is generally used to sense vital health parameters through sensors and analyse data at cloud.
- **Reliability Issue Over Redundancy:** As data ported to the cloud gets copied and executed at several places unknowingly to the user or requiring specific intervention by the user, reliability of computation as well as data saved is ensured by the inherent property of cloud.
- **Scope of Easy Expansion of Resources as Per Demand:** If the scalability issue arises in required infrastructure or capability usage of cloud framework, then expansion and assignment of additional requirements can easily be done.
- **Underlying Security:** As multi-parties are involved in cloud computing framework to access same data, work on same data, sharing computing and storage resources, cloud framework assures a level of security by ensuring access control and authentication along with privacy and availability.

Security requirements of different applications are different. Applications in military or surveillance essentially needs to implement confidentiality along with integrity and availability whereas healthcare applications primarily requires data integrity along with privacy over confidentiality. Additional encryption-decryption algorithms to implement confidentiality, hashing algorithms to ensure integrity can be deployed on top of the inherent security measures provided by the cloud framework. Again, as data generated and offloaded to the cloud mostly are by sensors and forwarded to the cloud platform to store, analyze etc. through edge devices such as smartphone, laptop, Tab etc., computing devices involved in cloud based applications are heterogenous in nature having varying resources, computing and power etc. Moreover, the network or links through which data gets forwarded are also heterogenous in nature e.g. sensors communicate through short range communication links (WiFi, Zigbee, Wimax, Bluetooth etc.), edge devices send data through open wireless internet to cloud thus it gets reflected that communication links in terms of available bandwidth, communication range, speed etc. are also heterogenous. Now the most fundamental question arises when it comes to add any additional security measure to make the data secure then while implementing in whole system, henterogeneity plays a key role. For example, traditional heavyweight asymmetric key cryptography algorithm RSA can be applied between edge devices and cloud servers to make data confidential but not between sensors and edge devices because sensors' limited computing ability and resources do not permit to computer additional computations required to perform RSA, also frequency of sensing is very high, so repeatedly doing encryption makes it next to impossible. In summary, unilaterally no single security technique be applied in Internet of Things and cloud based framework.

User Mobility Support

'AAA', anywhere, anytime, anything services and computing has got immensely popularized as user location is not a factor to prevent someone accessing any infrastructure resource or availing any service. This has been possible with the rapid advancement in semiconductor technology that add miniaturization and portability to the powerful devices, availability of communication bandwidth and enhanced speed, cost reduction leading to affordability of smart devices with internet connectivity, availability of supporting public infrastructure such as WiFi/access points mounted both at indoors and outdoors. Popular exploitation of mobile user carrying smart devices is service discovery e.g. to find nearest health centre or hospital or diagnostic centre or medicine shop, any food hub etc. in any locality or region. If extent or scale of such services increases, then connection with cloud services is required but often physical distance between edge device and cloud framework may add to increased latency degrading quality of service. Concept of Cloudlet (Satyanarayanan et al, 2009). has been introduced to address this issue. Here the authors proposed a concept of cloudlet which is an extended version of real cloud environment towards local end thus reducing physical distance with user to ensure good quality of service. Cloudlet can be formed as a cluster of few computers not so powerful, low cost thus adding low infrastructural expense and these computers are connected or plugged to cloud framework.

Another mobile cloud computing framework is MobiCloud (Huang et al, 2010) that implements secure mobile cloud environment in Mobile Adhoc Network (MANET). This secure framework provides Virtual Trusted and Provisioning Domain (VTaPD) by implementing secure routing for preserving security requirements of information flow. In this framework, uniquely mobile devices having computing and communication ability and available resources act as a service node to act as a service provider virtually along with user mobility support.

Real challenge in mobile cloud computing lies in providing seamless connectivity of mobile users while accessing cloud infrastructure or availing cloud services and for that efficient mobility management is required which has opened a new research wing (Akyidiz et al, 1999).

REFERENCES

Akyildiz, I., McNair, J., Ho, J., Uzunalioglu, H., & Wang, W. (1999). Mobility management in next-generation wireless systems. *Proceedings of the IEEE, 87*(8), 1347–1384. doi:10.1109/5.775420

Alangar, V. (2013). Cloud Computing Security and Encryption. *International Journal of Advance Research in Computer Science and Management Studies, 1*(5), 58-63.

Amini, Jamil, Ahmad, & Z`aba. (2015). Threat Modeling Approaches for Securing Cloud Computing. *Journal of Applied Sciences*, 953-967.

Arora & Parashar. (2013). Secure User Data in Cloud Computing Using Encryption Algorithms. *International Journal of Engineering Research and Applications, 3*(4), 1922-1926.

Bala Chandar, R., Kavitha, M. S., & Seenivasan, K. (2014). A Proficient Model for High End Security in Cloud Computing. *ICTACT Journal on Soft Computing, 4*(2), 698-702.

Bhagat & Sahu. (2013). Cloud Data Security while using Third Party Auditor. *International Journal of Computer Applications, 70*(16), 9-14.

Bhardwaj, Subrahmanyam, Avasthi, & Sastry. (2016). Security Algorithms for Cloud Computing. Elsevier *Procedia Computer Science, 85*, 535 – 542.

Chatterjee & Roy. (2017). Cryptography in Cloud Computing: A Basic Approach to Ensure Security in Cloud. *International Journal of Engineering Science and Computing, 7*(5), 11818-11821.

Dinh, T. H., Lee, C., Niyato, D., & Wang, P. (2013). A survey of mobile cloud computing: Architecture, applications, and approaches. *Wireless Communications and Mobile Computing, 13*(18), 1587–1611. doi:10.1002/wcm.1203

Grobauer, B., Walloschek, T., & Stocker, E. (2011). Understanding cloud computing vulnerabilities. *IEEE Security and Privacy, 9*(2), 50–57. doi:10.1109/MSP.2010.115

Gupta, Beri, & Behal. (2016). Cloud Computing: A Survey on Cloud Simulation Tools. *International Journal for Innovative Research in Science & Technology, 2*(11), 430-434.

Hamza & Omar. (2013). Cloud computing security: Abuse and nefarious use of cloud computing. *Int. J. Comput. Eng. Res.*, 22-27.

Huang, D., Zhang, X., Kang, M., & Luo, J. (2010). MobiCloud: building secure cloud framework for mobile computing and communication. In *2010 fifth IEEE international symposium on service oriented system engineering*, (pp. 27-34). IEEE. 10.1109/SOSE.2010.20

Indu, Anand, & Bhaskar. (2018). Identity and access management in cloud environment: mechanisms and challenges. *Engineering Science and Technology, an International Journal, 21*(4), 574-588.

Islam, N. (2017, July). Analysis of Various Encryption Algorithms in Cloud Computing. *International Journal of Computer Science and Mobile Computing, 6*(7), 90–97.

Kalpana, P., & Singaraju, S. (2012). Data Security in Cloud Computing using RSA Algorithm. *International Journal of Research in Computer and Communication technology, 1*(4), 143-146.

Kenyon, H. (2010). Closing an overlooked vulnerability. *Government Computer News*. Retrieved from https://www.drivesaversdatarecovery.com/images/pdf/GCN+09_06_10.pdf

Khadilkar, V., Gupta, A., Kantarcioglu, M., Khan, L., & Thuraisingham, B. (2010). Secure Data Storage and Retrieval in the Cloud. *COLLABORATECOM Proceedings of the 2010, 6th International Conference on Collaborative Computing: Networking, Applications and Worksharing (CollaborateCom 2010)*, 1-8.

Khan, A. N., Kiah, M. M., Khan, S. U., & Madani, S. A. (2013). Towards secure mobile cloud computing: A survey. *Future Generation Computer Systems, 29*(5), 1278–1299. doi:10.1016/j.future.2012.08.003

Leavitt, N. (2009). Is cloud computing really ready for prime time? Computer, 42(1), 15–25. doi:10.1109/MC.2009.20

Lohman, T. (2011). *DDoS is cloud's security achilles heel*. Retrieved from http://www.computerworld.com.au/article/401127/ddos_cloud_security_achilles_heel/

Malik & Kumar. (2015). Cloud Computing Security Improvement using Diffie Hellman and AES. *International Journal of Computer Applications, 118*(1), 25-28.

Melland & Grance. (2009). The nist definition of cloud computing. National Institute of Standards and Technology.

Muttalib Khan, Haroon Khan, & Ahmad. (2008). Security in Cloud by Diffie Hellman Protocol. *International Journal of Engineering and Innovative Technology, 4*(5), 125-128.

Rai, P. K., & Bunkar, R. K. (2014). Study of security risk and vulnerabilities of cloud computing. *Int. J. Comput. Sci. Mobile Comput., 3*, 490–496.

Rakesh, D. H., Bhavsar, R. R., & Thorve, A. S. (2012). Data security over cloud. *International Journal of Computers and Applications*, (5), 11–14.

Ramachandra, G., Iftikar, M., & Khan, F. A. (2017). A Comprehensive Survey on Security in Cloud Computing. *Procedia Computer Science, 110*, 465–472. doi:10.1016/j.procs.2017.06.124

Rouse, M. (2009). *Virtual machine escape*. Retrieved from http://whatis.techtarget.com/definition/virtual-machine-escape

Sarkar & Chatterjee. (2014). Enhancing Data Storage Security in Cloud Computing Through Steganography. *ACEEE Int. J. on Network Security, 5*(1), 13-19.

Satyanarayanan, M., Bahl, V., Caceres, R., & Davies, N. (2009). The case for vm-based cloudlets in mobile computing. *IEEE Pervasive Computing, 8*(4), 14–23. doi:10.1109/MPRV.2009.82

Shah, M. A., Swaminathan, R., & Baker, M. (2008). Privacy preserving audit and extraction of digital contents. IACR Cryptology EPrint Archive, 186.

Sidhu & Mahajan. (2014). Enhancing Security in Cloud Computing Structure by Hybrid Encryption. *International Journal of Recent Scientific Research, 5*(1), 128-132.

Singla & Singh. (2013). Cloud Data Security using Authentication and Encryption Technique. *International Journal of Advanced Research in Computer Engineering & Technology, 2*(7), 2232-2235.

Soares, L. F. B., Fernandes, D. A. B., Freire, M. M., & Inacio, P. R. M. (2013). Secure user authentication in cloud computing management interfaces. *Proceedings of the IEEE 32nd International Performance Computing and Communications Conference*, 1-2. 10.1109/PCCC.2013.6742763

Sun, Y., Zhang, J., Xiong, Y., & Zhu, G. (2014). Data Security and Privacy in Cloud Computing. *International Journal of Distributed Sensor Networks*, 1–9.

The Open Group. (2009). *Risk Taxonomy*. The Open Group.

Velumadhava Rao, R., & Selvamani, K. (2015). Data Security Challenges and Its Solutions in Cloud Computing. *Elsevier Procedia Computer Science, 48*, 204 – 209.

Yadav, V., & Aggarwal, P. (2014). Fingerprinting Based Recursive Information Hiding Strategy in Cloud Computing Environment. *International Journal of Computer Science and Mobile Computing, 3*(5), 702 – 707.

Zissis, D., & Lekkas, D. (2012). Addressing cloud computing security issues. *Future Generation Computer Systems, 28*(3), 583–592. doi:10.1016/j.future.2010.12.006

Zissis, D., & Lekkas, D. (2012). Addressing cloud computing security issues. *Future Generation Computer Systems, 28*(3), 583–592. doi:10.1016/j.future.2010.12.006

Chapter 2
Recent Advances Delivered in Mobile Cloud Computing's Security and Management Challenges

Christos Stergiou

ⓘD https://orcid.org/0000-0002-7713-3667

University of Macedonia, Greece

Kostas E. Psannis

University of Macedonia, Greece

ABSTRACT

Mobile cloud computing provides an opportunity to restrict the usage of huge hardware infrastructure and to provide access to data, applications, and computational power from every place and in any time with the use of a mobile device. Furthermore, MCC offers a number of possibilities but additionally creates several challenges and issues that need to be addressed as well. Through this work, the authors try to define the most important issues and challenges in the field of MCC technology by illustrating the most significant works related to MCC during recent years. Regarding the huge benefits offered by the MCC technology, the authors try to achieve a more safe and trusted environment for MCC users in order to operate the functions and transfer, edit, and manage data and applications, proposing a new method based on the existing AES encryption algorithm, which is, according to the study, the most relevant encryption algorithm to a cloud environment. Concluding, the authors suggest as a future plan to focus on finding new ways to achieve a better integration MCC with other technologies.

DOI: 10.4018/978-1-7998-1082-7.ch002

Copyright © 2020, IGI Global. Copying or distributing in print or electronic forms without written permission of IGI Global is prohibited.

INTRODUCTION

The need of "*cloud*" support has become inefficient due to the intensive computations, the mass storage, and the security issues. Some examples include limited storage capacity, communication capabilities, energy and processing. Inefficiencies like these have motivated us in order to find a model for the combination of CC and other technologies such as Internet of Things and Big Data. As a "*base*" technology, Cloud Computing consolidates various technologies and applications to get the maximum capacity and performance of the existing infrastructure (Kryftis et al., 2016; Stergiou & Psannis, 2016; Stergiou et al., 2018b).

Mobile Cloud Computing improved through the recent years by a new generation of services based on the concept of the "*cloud computing*", which aims to provide access to the information and the data from anywhere at any time, and simultaneously restrict or eliminate the need for hardware equipment (Rahimi et al., 2014; Stergiou & Psannis, 2016; Stergiou & Psannis, 2017b; Stergiou et al., 2018f). In particular, Mobile Cloud Computing (MCC) could be defined as an integration of Cloud Computing (CC) technology and mobile devices in order to make mobile devices resourceful in terms of computational power, memory, storage, energy, and context awareness (Fremdt et al., 2013; Keskin & Taskin, 2014; Haung, 2011; Stergiou et al., 2018c). As a result of the operations of Cloud Computing, it could be used as useful base for several technologies, such as Internet of Things (IoT), Big Data (BD) and Surveillance Systems, and could provide improvements on their functions.

Therefore, the term mobile cloud is generally referred to in two perspectives: (a) infrastructure based, and (b) ad-hoc mobile cloud. In infrastructure based mobile cloud, the hardware infrastructure remains static, and provides services to the mobile users. Although cloud is useful for computing and storage (Rahimi et al., 2014; Stergiou & Psannis, 2017a; Stergiou et al., 2018d), the traditional computation offloading techniques cannot be used directly for smartphones because these techniques are generally energy-unaware and "*bandwidthhungry*".

Furthermore, the term "*cloud computation*" is defined as "*the use of computing logistical resources by using services transported over the internet*" (Stergiou & Psannis, 2016; Stergiou & Psannis, 2017b). Nowadays, Cloud Computing services constitute one of the world's largest areas of competition between giant companies in the IT sector and software (Mell & Grance, 2011). However, Cloud Computing security is an evolving sub-domain of computer security, network security, and, more broadly, information security. It refers to a broad set of policies, technologies, and controls deployed to protect data, applications, and the associated infrastructure of cloud computing (Rahimi et al., 2014; Mell & Grance, 2011; Haghighat, 2015). Thus, as the MCC is the outcome of CC it faced the same security and privacy challenges and issues.

In addition to this, CC additionally used to be a base technology for other technologies due to its types of services (Stergiou & Psannis, 2016; Stergiou et al., 2018b; Plageraset al., 2017). One of those is the Big Data (BD). BD is a term used to describe the expected, due to the connected to the Internet devices, rapid increase in the volume of data production. Subsequently, these large amounts of data could be defined as "*a broad term for data sets so large or complex that traditional data processing applications are inadequate*" (Stergiou et al., 2018b). Furthermore, BD is often associated to the use of predictive analytics or certain advanced methods to extract knowledge from the data. Rarely, are also related to a particular size of set of data (Hilbert & López, 2011; Fu et al. 2015). Precision in BD could result in more confident decision making, and better decisions may drive in increased operational efficiency, reduced costs, and minimized risk (Hilbert & López, 2011). From this scope, it can be observed that BD is now equally important both for business and internet. This happens because more information drives to more accurate analysis (Stergiou & Psannis, 2016). The real problem is not that the large amounts of data have been obtained, but whether they have any value or not. Hopefully, by predicting that organizations would be able to acquire information from any source, harness the relevant data, and analyze them in a specific way in order to get quick answers, the following should be achieved: 1) reduce costs, 2) reduce time, 3) produce new items and optimize their offerings, and 4) take more ingenious decisions (Stergiou & Psannis, 2017b).

Regarding Security and Privacy issues and challenges in the field of CC and particularly of MCC, and in order to succeed a secure communication over the network, encryption algorithm plays an important role. It is a valuable and fundamental tool for the protection of the data. Encryption algorithm converts the data into scrambled form by using "*a key*" and only the user have the key in order to decrypt the data. Regarding the researches that have been made in the field, an important encryption technique is the Symmetric key Encryption. In Symmetric key encryption, only one key is used to encrypt and decrypt the data. In this encryption technique the most used algorithm is the AES algorithm (Stergiou & Psannis, 2017b; Kumar et al., 2011; Kaur & Kinger, 2014; Negi et al. 2013).

AES (Advanced Encryption Standard) is the high developed encryption standard recommended by NIST aiming to replace the older DES algorithm. Brute force attack is the only effective attack known against it, in which the attacker tries to test all the characters combinations to unlock the encryption. The AES algorithm block ciphers. Also, AES has been carefully tested for many security applications (Huang, 2011; Stergiou et al., 2018d; Singh & Kinger, 2013; Gupta et al. 2016).

The rest of the paper is organized in 6 sections as follows. In section 2 we present previous work that address challenges and solutions related to Mobile Cloud Computing. Section 3 provides a comparative analysis of the previous works which we have studied offering a brief analysis about evolution of the number of researches that have been made through the years. In section 4 we offer a brief literature analysis of CC and MCC. In section 5 we discuss the outcomes of the literature study and additionally we propose an algorithm method as an indicated solution for Security and Management challenges. Final conclusions and future research directions are given in section 6.

BACKGROUND

For the purpose of this paper we study and analyze previous literature which has been studying two aspects, Security and Privacy Management in MCC and Security and Privacy of MCC. In addition to this, we also present some former works of our research group which have been made in field of CC in general. All the papers presented with ascending form, from the older to the newest. The following paragraphs present the papers which contributed significantly in our study.

Security and Privacy Management in MCC

Initially, the papers that deal with the Security and Privacy issues of Management in MCC are illustrated [23-34]. As we can realize there are several works in this field. More particular, Angin et al. (2010) propose an entity-centric approach for an IDM model in Cloud environment. The proposed approach based on two aspects: a) active bundles, and b) anonymous identification. The active bundles include a payload of Personally Identifiable Information, privacy policies and a virtual machine that enforces the policies and additionally the active bundles use a set of protection mechanisms in order to protect themselves. As regard the anonymous identification, they use it with the aim to mediate interactions between the entity and the Cloud services using entity's privacy policies. Moreover, the authors present the main characteristics of the approach which are: a) independent of third party, b) provides minimum information to the Service Provider, and c) provides ability to use identity data on untrusted hosts. Then, Doukas et al. (2010) demonstrate the implementation of a mobile system that enables electronic healthcare data storage, update and retrieval using CC. The proposed mobile application based in Google's Android OS and offers management of patient health records and medical images. This system was evaluated with the use of Amazon's S3 cloud service. Finally, the authors summarize the details of the implementation and then present initial results of the system in practice. Moreover, Dinh et al. (2011) survey the MCC technology, which could help the general readers to have an overview of the MCC including the definition, the architecture, and the applications. Also, this work presents the issues, the existing solutions, and the recent approaches of the MCC technology. At the end, the authors discuss a number of future research directions of the MCC. Through Habib et al. (2011) propose a multi-faceted Trust Management system architecture for a cloud computing marketplace, with the aim to support the customers in reliably identifying trustworthy cloud providers. The proposed system offers means to identify the trustworthy cloud providers in term of different attributes that assessed by multiple sources and roots of trust information. Furthermore, Prasad et al. (2012) presents a sort survey of MCC evolution and additionally explains how CC and Mobile Devices could be combined with good terms for future opportunities, implications and legal issues for developing countries. In another research, Shiraz et al. (2012) try to review the existing Distributed Application Processing Frameworks, also known as DAPFs, for SMDs in MCC domain. The main objective of this work is to highlight issues and challenges to existing DAPFs in developing, implementing, and executing computational intensive mobile applications within MCC domain. Thus, through this work the authors propose a thematic taxonomy of the current DAPFs, and then they review current offloading frameworks by using thematic taxonomy, and analyze the implications and critical aspects of current offloading frameworks. Finally, this work puts forward open research issues in distributed application processing for MCC that remain to be addressed. Also, Kim & Park (2013) proposes a trust management approach by making an analysis of user behavioral patterns for a reliable MCC. So, the authors suggest a method in order to quantify a one-dimensional trusting relation count on the analysis of telephone call data from Mobile Cloud Environment. Subsequently, it is enhanced trustworthiness of data production, management, and overall application. Whaiduzzaman et al. (2014) present a state-of-the-art survey of vehicular Cloud Computing. More detailed, the authors present a taxonomy for vehicular Cloud in which special attention has been devoted to the extensive applications, Cloud formations, key management, inter-Cloud communication systems, and broad aspects of privacy and security problems. Additionally, this work illustrates the design of an architecture for Vehicular Cloud Computing, itemize the properties required in vehicular Cloud which support the proposed model. In order to achieve their goal, authors compare the proposed mechanism with normal Cloud Computing and then discuss about open research issues and the future directions. Additionally, Khalil et al. (2014) discuss the limitations of the state-of-the-art Cloud Identity Managements with respect to mobile clients. In particular, the authors demonstrate that the current IDMs are vulnerable to three attacks. As a result of their research, the authors propose and validate a new IDM architecture dubbed Consolidated IDM that countermeasures these attacks. Through their experimental results the authors illustrates that CIDM offers its clients with better security guarantees and that it has less energy and communication overhead compared to the current IDM systems. Furthermore, Ali et al. (2015) offer a detailed survey of the security issues that arise due to the very nature of Cloud Computing. Furthermore, this work presents a number of recent solutions offered in the literature with the aim to counter the security problems. In addition, there is a brief view of the highlighted security vulnerabilities in the Mobile Cloud Computing. Then, Rittinghouse & Ransome (2009) discuss about the evolution of the computing as regarding the historical perspective, with focus on advances which primarily led to the evolution of the Cloud Computing. Additionally, there is a survey of some of the critical components that are vital in order to make the Cloud Computing paradigm feasible. The authors by addressing a number of particular legal and philosophical problems try to conclude with a hard look at all the successful Cloud Computing vendors. Finally, Mollah et al. (2017) try to present the major security and privacy issues and challenges in the field which have grown much interest among the academia and research community. Also, they try to illustrate reports of recent works of literature. Moreover, they present a comparative analysis of the literature works based on different security and privacy requirements, and concluding they present the open issues in the field.

Security and Privacy of MCC

Subsequently, the papers that deal with the Security and Privacy issues of the MCC are illustrated. Starting from the oldest, a survey of the various security issues that pose a threat to the Cloud as presented by the work of Subashini & Kavitha (2011). The survey that illustrated in this work could be more specific to different security problems which have emanated due to the nature of the service delivery models of a Cloud Computing system. Continuously, Liang et al. (2011) propose a Security Service Admission Model based on Semi-Markov Decision Process in order to model the system reward for the Cloud provider. Initially, through this work try to define the system states by a tuple represented by the numbers of Cloud users and the associated to them security service categories, and the current event type. Then, the authors derive the system steady-state probability and service request blocking probability with the use of their proposed model. Then, Hada et al. (2011) propose a trust model for Cloud architecture which uses mobile agent as security agents to acquire useful information from the virtual machine that the user and the service provider could utilize with the aim to keep track of privacy of their data and virtual machines. In the proposed model the security agents can dynamically move through the network, replicate themselves according to the requirement, and perform the assigned tasks like accounting and monitoring of virtual machines. Also, Popa et al. (2013) propose a framework with the aim to secure the data transmitted between the components of the same Mobile Cloud Application, and with the aim to ensure the integrity of the applications at the installation on the mobile device and when being updated. Furthermore, the proposed framework of this work allows applying different security properties to various kinds of data and not the same properties to all the data processed by the application. In addition to this, the proposed approach takes into account the user's preferences and the mobile device performances. Moreover, Hashizume et al. (2013) discuss and identifies the main vulnerabilities in CC systems, and the most important threats that found in the literature related to CC technology and its environment, as well as to identify and relate vulnerabilities and threats with possible solutions. Suo et al. (2013) with the aim to facilitate the emerging domain of MCC security and privacy, in brief review the advantages and system model of MCC, and pay attention to the security and privacy in the MCC. At the end, the authors provide the current security and privacy approaches, by deeply analyzing the security and privacy problems from the aspects of mobile terminal, mobile network and Cloud. Additionally, Shahzad & Hussain (2013) present a comprehensive literature review of MCC and the security and privacy issues that MCC faced. Also, the authors present a complete understanding analysis of MCC, in where they explain its architecture, advantages and applications. At the end, the authors conclude that their research is significant useful for the mobile service providers, and thus they can improve the security technologies and mechanisms used for Cloud security in order to minimize the user's security concerns. Then, Khan et al. (2013) illustrate particular efforts that have been devoted in research organizations and academia in order to build secure MCC environments and infrastructures. Thus, in the spite of the efforts, there are a number of loopholes and challenges that still exist in the security policies of MCC. The authors through the literature review conclude in three things that discussed in this work. Firstly, they highlight the current state of the art work which proposed to secure MCC infrastructures. Secondly, they identify the potential problems. Finally, they provide taxonomy of the state of the art. Furthermore, Zhang et al. (2017) propose a novel technique that called "match-then-decrypt", in which a matching phase is also presented before the decryption phase. The proposed technique operates by computing special components in ciphertexts, which are used in order to perform the test that if the attribute private key matches the hidden access policy in ciphertexts without decryption. Moreover, in this work there is a proposal of a basic anonymous ABE construction, and then obtain a security-enhanced extension based on strongly existentially unforgeable one-time signatures. More specifically, the authors conclude that the formal security analysis and performance comparisons indicate that their proposed solutions simultaneously ensure attribute privacy and improve decryption efficiency for outsourced data storage in MCC. Finally, Jiang et al. (2018) initially identify that the scheme that proposed in former work of Tsai and Lo, which was privacy aware authentication scheme for distributed MCC services, fails to achieve mutual authentication. The authors of this work conclude to this regarding it is vulnerable to the service provider impersonation attack. In addition to this, the authors state that the former scheme also suffers from some minor design flaws, including the problem of biometric measure, wrong password, and fingerprint login, no user revocation facility when the smart card is lost or stolen. At the end, they offer some a number of suggestions in order to avoid the aforementioned design flaws in future design of authentication schemes.

Research Group's Previous Works in CC and MCC

At this point there will be present a number of former works which deal with problems and solutions in the field of Cloud Computing in general. More particular, some of them deal with problems and solutions in the field of Mobile Cloud Computing. Starting again from the oldest, Stergiou & Psannis (2016) try to combine the MCC and IoT with the Big Data with the aim to examine the common characteristics and in addition to discover which of MCC and IoT benefits improve the operation of BD applications. Also, the authors of this work present the contribution of MCC and IoT individually to Big Data. Moreover, Stergiou et al. (2018a) present a survey of Internet of Things and CC focusing on the security problems of both of them. More particular, the authors try to combine these technologies aiming to examine the common features, and also aiming to discover the benefits of their integration. At the end, there is a presentation of the contribution of Cloud Computing to the IoT. So, this work illustrates how the Cloud Computing improves the functionality of Internet of Things, and additionally, surveys the security challenges of the integration of Cloud Computing and Internet of Things. Continuously, Stergiou & Psannis (2017a) present a survey of Big Data and Cloud Computing, illustrating their basic characteristics, and focusing on the security and privacy problems of both of them. Regarding this, the authors try to combine the functionality of Big Data and Cloud Computing aiming to examine the frequent characteristics, and in addition to this to discover the benefits which are related in security problems of their integration. Furthermore, Stergiou & Psannis (2017b) survey Cloud Computing and Big Data technology, and their major characteristics, focusing on the security and privacy problems of both of them. Particularly, the authors combine the functionality of two technologies aiming to examine the common characteristics, and additionally to discover the benefits related in security issues of their integration. Then, there is a presentation of a novel method of an algorithm that can be used for the purpose of improving Cloud Computing's security through the use of algorithms that can offer more privacy in the data related to Big Data. At the end, there additionally a survey about the challenges of the integration of Cloud Computing and Big Data related to their security level. Also, Stergiou et al. (2018b) in order to achieve a type of network that will offer more intelligent media-data transfer new technologies were studied. Thus, the authors initially studied the use of various open source tools of Cloud Computing analyzers and simulators. So, the authors after they measure the simulated network performance with CloudSim simulator, they use the Cooja emulator of the Contiki OS aiming to confirm and access more metrics and options. In particular, in this work there is an implementation of a network topology from a small section of the script of CloudSim with Cooja, so that the authors could test a single network segment. The results that have been produced of the experimental procedure illustrate that there are not duplicated packets received during the whole procedure. Finally, Stergiou et al. (2018e) propose a novel system for Cloud Computing integrated with Internet of Things as a base scenario for Big Data. Moreover, the authors try to establish an architecture relaying on the security of the network with the aim to eliminate the security issues. The solution proposed in this work installs a security "*wall*" between the Cloud server and the outer Internet, aiming to eliminate the privacy and security problems. As regard the main goal of this paper a sort survey of IoT and Cloud Computing also presented, focusing on the security issues of both of them. Additionally, the authors state that through their study conclude that Cloud Computing could offer a more "*green*" and efficient "*fog*" environment for sustainable computing scenarios.

Literature Comparative Analysis

Taking into account the Related Research Review Section we realized that the study of MCC's Security and Privacy issues become more popular in the research and academic community over the recent years. We have come to the above conclusion counting on our study of several works in the field of Security and Privacy of Mobile Cloud Computing. The main balk of these works presented in Related Research Review Section. Consequently, there is a need for further research in this area as the growing numbers studied indicate.

As we can observe, the last four years the interest of the researchers has increased considerably compared to the previous decade. Figure 1 illustrates the growth of studies in Security and Privacy Management in Mobile Cloud Computing through the years. Equally important Figure 2 represents the growth of studies in Security and Privacy of Mobile Cloud Computing through the years.

The study of previous works motivates us to survey the Security and Privacy challenges and issues of the Mobile Cloud Computing technology. Thus, count on the major works related to Security and Privacy challenges and issues we have tried to figure out them in Table 1.

Table 1 lists the major challenges and issues which we have distinguished from the related works. Through Table 1 we can figure out which are the major issues and challenges of the Mobile Cloud Computing that have been addressed by the literature.

Figure 1. Growth of works made in security and privacy management in mobile cloud computing over the years

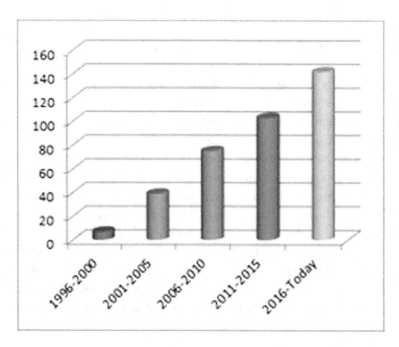

Figure 2. Growth of works made in security and privacy of mobile cloud computing over the years

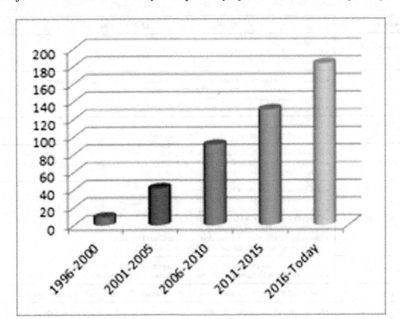

Introducing To Cloud Computing

CC offers abilities and functions such as computing, storage, services, and applications over the Internet. In general, to render smartphones energy efficient and computationally capable, major changes to the hardware and software levels are required. This causes the cooperation of developers and manufacturers (Rahimi et al., 2014).

Features

As all technologies, so the CC technology has a number of characteristics which determine its operation. These characteristics are represented and outlined below.

CC(a): Storage over Internet

Storage over Internet can be defined as "*a technology framework that uses Transmission Control Protocol/Internet Protocol (TCP/IP) networks to link servers and storage devices and to facilitate storage solution deployment*" (Whaiduzzaman et al., 2014; Garg et al., 2013).

CC(b): Service over Internet

The Service over Internet has as major objective is to "*help customers all over the world in order to transform aspirations into achievements by harnessing the Internet's efficiency, speed and ubiquity*" (Whaiduzzaman et al., 2014; Garg et al., 2013).

Table 1. Related research work's challenges and issues of the Mobile Cloud Computing technology

Year	Author	Challenge/Issue
2009-08	J. W. Rittinghouse & J. F. Ransome (2009)	• Cloud reliability to users • Users desired outcomes of the Cloud • Levels of trust in Cloud environment
2010-09	C. Doukas et al (2010)	• Sharing and management of medical information resources through mobile healthcare systems
2010-11	P. Angin et al (2010)	• Entities authentication to service providers • Entities multiple accounts associated with multiple service providers
2011-01	S. Subashini & V. Kavita (2011)	• Cloud environment safety • New Cloud model targeting to improve the existing one
2011-04	H. Liang et al (2011)	• Increased number of Critical and Normal Security service users • Allocate Cloud resource aiming to maximize the system rewards with the considerations of the Cloud resource consumption and incomes generated from Cloud users.
2011-10	H. T. Dinh et al (2011)	• Low bandwidth of Mobile Cloud Computing • Availability of Mobile Cloud Computing • Heterogeneity of Mobile Cloud Computing • Computing offloading of Mobile Cloud Computing • Security of Mobile Cloud Computing • Enhancing the efficiency of data access of Mobile Cloud Computing • Context-aware mobile Cloud services of Mobile Cloud Computing
2011-11	S. M. Habib et al (2011)	• Not consistent descriptions in Service Level Agreements among Cloud providers • Uncertain reliably identifying trustworthy Cloud providers for the customers
2011-12	P. S. Hada et al (2011)	• Major need of bringing reliability, transparency and security in Cloud model for client satisfaction
2012-10	M. R. Prasad et al (2012)	• Cloud Computing challenges: Performance, Security & Privacy, Control, Bandwidth Costs, Reliability • Mobile Cloud Computing legal issues
2012-11	M. Shiraz et al (2012)	• Users expectation to run computational intensive applications on Smart Mobile Devices in the same way as powerful stationary computers • Establishment of distributed application processing platform at runtime which requires additional computing resources on Smart Mobile Devices
2013-01	D. Popa et al (2013)	• Use of MCC increases security risks and privacy invasion • MCC application model not well-defined
2013-06	A. Shahzad & M. Hussain (2013)	• Security and privacy risks faced be MCC uses • Architecture and Cloud service delivery models issues • Mobile Cloud infrastructure issues • Mobile Cloud communication channel issues
2013-07	H. Suo et al (2013)	• Security and privacy issues and challenges in MCC
2013-07	A. N. Khan et al (2013)	• Security threats have become a hurdle in the rapid adaptability of the MCC paradigm
2013-12	M. Kim & S. O. Park (2013)	• MCC architecture, design and implementation need to be improved due to limited computing capability and storage issues • Trust management approach for reliable MCC
2013-12	K. Hashizume et al (2013)	• Risk of outsourcing data to third party Cloud providers • Cloud Computing inherits many technologies security issues
2014-02	M. Ali et al (2014)	• Services provided by third party Cloud providers entail additional security threats • Migration of user's assets outside the administrative control in the Cloud environment escalates the security concerns.
2014-03	I. Khalil et al (2014)	• Mobile devices are easy to be compromised • Mobile users store Personal Identifiable Information in unprotected text files, cookies and applications • Limitations of state-of-the-art Cloud Identity Management Systems with respect to mobile clients
2014-04	Md. Whaiduzzaman et al (2014)	• Traffic management and road safety by instantly using vehicular resources • Vehicular Cloud Computing security challenges: Authentication, Secure location & localization, Securing vehicular communication, Vehicular public key infrastructure, Data security, Network heterogeneity, Access control
2017-02	Y. Zhang et al (2017)	• Each decryption usually requires many pairings and the computation overhead grows with the complexity of the access formula • Existing schemes suffer a serve efficiency drawback and not suitable for MCC where users may be resource-constrained
2017-04	M. B. Mollah et all (2017)	• Data security challenges • Partitioning and offloading security challenges • Virtualization security challenges • Mobile Cloud applications security challenges • Mobile devices security challenges • Privacy challenges
2018-06	Q. Jiang et al (2018)	• A previous proposed scheme of Tsai & Lo fails to achieve mutual authentication and withstands all major security threats

CC(c): Applications over Internet

Cloud Applications, or as scientific known as Applications over Internet, are the programs which have been written to do the job of a current manual task, or virtually anything, and which perform their job on the server through an internet connection (Whaiduzzaman et al., 2014; Garg et al., 2013).

CC(d): Energy Efficiency

Energy Efficiency could be defined as "*a way of managing and restraining the growth in energy consumption*" (Whaiduzzaman et al., 2014; Garg et al., 2013). By delivering more services for the same energy input or for the same services for less energy input may be something more energy efficient (Whaiduzzaman et al., 2014; Garg et al., 2013).

CC(e): Computationally Capable

The services of computational clouds are leveraging the computationally concentrated and ubiquitous mobile applications which have been enabled by the technology of MCC. Thus, a system can be considered as computationally capable when it meets the requirements to offer us the results we want, by making the right calculations.(Whaiduzzaman et al., 2014; Garg et al., 2013).

Security on Cloud Computing

CC security is an evolving sub-domain of computer security, network security and information security. It makes an allusion to a broad set of policies, technologies, and controls deployed to protect data, applications, and the associated infrastructure of CC.

CC technology offers through its storage solutions to users and industries various capabilities with the aim to store and process their data in third-party data centers (Haghighat et al., 2015). Thus, by aiming to offer secure communication through the network, encryption algorithm plays a vital role. As regards the researches that have been made, an important encryption technique is the Symmetric Key Encryption. In Symmetric key encryption, only one key is used to encrypt and decrypt the data. In this encryption technique the most used algorithm is the AES (Kumar et al., 2011; Kaur & Kinger, 2011; Stergiou et al., 2018g; Gupta & Badve, 2017).

AES (Advanced Encryption Standard) is the newest encryption standard and the more reliable, recommended by NIST to replace DES algorithm. The only effective scenario of attacking in AES is the Brute force attack, in which the attacker tries to test all the characters combinations to unlock the encryption. AES encryption model is fast and flexible, and in addition, it can be implemented on different platforms (Singh & Kinger, 2013).

Mobile Cloud Computing Trade Offs

CC has some disadvantages-limitations which should be eliminated over the years in order to achieve a better and more ideal use. Some businesses and especially the smaller ones need to be aware of these limitations before going in for this technology.

CC(I-a): Security

One major issue of the MCC is the security issue. Before someone adopts this technology, they should know that all the company's sensitive information would be surrender to a third-party Cloud service provider. This could potentially put the company in great risk. Hence, someone must be absolutely sure that they would choose the most reliable service provider, who will keep the information completely safe (Stergiou & Psannis, 2016; Viswanathan, 2012; Pfarr et al., 2015; Stergiou et al.,2018g; Gupta et al., 2016).

CC(I-b): Connectivity

Internet connection is critical to CC. Thus, the user should be certain that there is a good result before opting for these services. Since someone owes a mobile device which is connected to the internet has become the norm in the wireless world of today, CC has a very large potential user base (Stergiou & Psannis, 2016; Almrot & Andersson, 2013).

CC(I-c): Performance

Another major concern of the CC pertains to its performance. Some users feel performance is not as good as in native applications. Thus, checking with one service provider and understanding their track record is advisable (Stergiou & Psannis, 2016; Fremdt et al., 2013; GetCloud Services, 2014).

CC(I-d): Latency (Delay)

In CC, latency (sometimes referred as turnaround time) is defined as the time involved in offloading the computation and getting back the results from the nearby infrastructure or cloud (Stergiou & Psannis, 2016; Li et al., 2017).

CC(I-e): Privacy

Data privacy is important and is one of the main bottlenecks that restrict consumers from adopting CC. Therefore, to gain consumers trust in the Cloud, the application models must support application development with privacy protection, and implicit authentication mechanisms (Stergiou & Psannis, 2016; Pfarr et al., 2014; Shi et al., 2010).

Challenges Outcomes by Combining Cloud COMPUTING with Other Technologies

When critical applications, such as the IoT applications, move towards the Cloud Computing technology, concerns arise due to the lack of trust in the service provider or the knowledge about service level agreements (SLAs) and knowledge about the physical location of data. Consequently, new challenges require specific attention as mentioned in surveys (Botta et al., 2016; Bhattasali et al., 2013; Simmhan et al., 2011). Multi-tenancy could also compromise security and lead to sensitive information leakage. Moreover, public key cryptography cannot be applied at all layers due to the computing power constraints imposed by the things. These are examples of topics that are currently under investigation in order to tackle the big challenge of security and privacy in integrating Cloud Computing with other technologies (Botta et al., 2016; Book, 2018; Stergiou et al., 2018g; Gou et al., 2017).

Subsequently, some challenges about the security issue in the integration of Cloud Computing with other technologies are listed below (Botta et al., 2016).

1. **Heterogeneity:** A big challenge in Cloud Computing integration with other technologies is related to the wide heterogeneity of devices, operating systems, platforms, and services available and possibly used for new or improved applications (Grozev & Buyya, 2014).
2. **Performance:** Often Cloud Computing integration with other technologies applications introduce specific performance and QoS requirements at several levels (i.e. for communication, computation, and storage aspects) and in some particular scenarios meeting requirements may not be easily achievable (Rao et al., 2012).
3. **Reliability:** When Cloud Computing integration with other technologies is adopted for mission-critical applications, reliability concerns typically arise. When applications are deployed in resource constrained environments a number of challenges related to device failure or not always reachable devices exists (He et al., 2014).
4. **Big Data:** With an estimated number of 50 billion devices that will be networked by 2020, specific attention must be paid to transportation, storage, access, and processing of the huge amount of data they will produce (Dobre & Xhafa, 2014).
5. **Monitoring:** As largely documented in the literature, monitoring is an essential activity in Cloud environments for capacity planning, for managing resources, SLAs, performance and security, and for troubleshooting (Aceto & Botta, 2013).

Cloud Computing as Base Technology for Big Data

Cloud Computing (CC) is a new generation of services which aims to provide accessibility to information and data from any place at any time. With this kind of novel technology there is no limitation and no further need for hardware equipment. The recent years, Cloud Computing services compose one of the major areas in the world of competition among the giant companies in the field of IT and software (Mell & Grance, 2011; Skourletopoulos et al., 2017; Dorgham et al., 2018).

More specifically, Cloud Computing is consisted of a technology of internet services providing remote use of hardware and software. As a result, the users of Cloud Computing could have access to information and data from any place at any time. In the concept of Cloud Computing there is another technology called Mobile Cloud Computing (MCC) that refers in general concept to in two prospects (Stergiou et al., 2018f): a) infrastructure based, and b) ad-hoc mobile cloud. In the prospect of infrastructure based mobile cloud, the infrastructure of the hardware is still static and delivers services to the mobile users (Stergiou et al., 2018c; Batalla et al. 2016). Particularly, MCC is defined as *"the integration of Cloud*

Computing and Mobile technology in order to make any type of mobile devices resourceful in terms such as computational power, memory, storage and energy" (Stergiou & Psannis, 2017b). Regarding the usage of Cloud services in Mobile devices many types of services could be processed through it. Thus, high quality media could be transmitted through Cloud environment progressed in applications which were installed and operated in Cloud.

Considering this Cloud Computing could be settled as a base technology to operate other technologies such as Big Data and consequently to be accomplished an integration of Cloud and Big Data (Haghighat et al., 2015; Garg et al., 2013). In addition to this, Cloud Computing also used to be a base technology for others technologies due to its type of services (Stergiou & Psannis, 2016; Stergiou et al., 2018d).

As already mentioned, one of those is Big Data (BD). Big Data used to describe the surprisingly rapid increase in volume of data in structured and unstructured form. It is a broad term for data sets so large or complex that traditional data processing applications are inadequate. Furthermore, Big Data often refers to the use of predictive analytics or certain advanced methods to extract value from data. Rarely, it also refers to a particular size of data set (Hilbert & López, 2011; Fu et al., 2016). Precision in Big Data could result in more confident decision making, and better decisions may lead to an increased operational efficiency, reduced costs, and minimized risk [18]. From this scope we realize that the Big Data is now equally important both for business and internet. This happens because more information leads to more accurate analyses (Stergiou & Psannis, 2016). The real problem is not that you have acquired large quantities of data, but whether it has any value or not. Hopefully, by envisaging that the organizations would be able to obtain information from any source, harness the relevant data and analyze it with the aim to get quick answers, we will achieve the following: 1) to reduce costs, 2) to reduce time, 3) to produce new products and to optimize their offerings, 4) to make more intelligent decisions (Stergiou & Psannis, 2017a; Stergiou & Psannis, 2017b).

RESEARCH OUTCOMES & PROPOSED SOLUTIONS

Table 2 presents the challenges that have been addresses by the literature work which we have studied. As we could observe most of the works that we have studied focus on the *"Trusted environment"* which in our opinion is the major issue of the Mobile Cloud Computing, and as a result the *"Security"* issue is most popular in the literature work. Additionally, concerning the rest of the challenges we come to the conclusion that the *"Reliability"* and the *"Management"* are also basic issues that need to be addressed. More detailed, through the number of 22 works that we have stood out the statistic results are the following: Privacy 6 of 22, Security 15 of 22, Trusted environment 15 of 22, Bandwidth 5 of 22, Environment limitations 10 of 22, Management 11 of 22, Reliability 12 of 22, User authentication 9 of 22, Efficiency 5 of 22. Equally important, the less mentioned issues are the *"Bandwidth"* and the *"Efficiency"* which are really vital for the functionality of the Mobile Cloud Computing technology. Regarding this, we could realize that more researches need to be done in the field in order to find better solutions aiming to improve Bandwidth and Efficiency of MCC.

Thus, based on previous works (Stergiou et al., 2018b; Stergiou & Psannis, 2017a; Stergiou et al., 2018f; Stergiou et al., 2018c; Stergiou et al., 2018d; Stergiou & Psannis, 2017b; Plageras et al., 2017; Stergiou et al., 2018a; Stergiou et al., 2018e) the optimal solution in order to achieve a reliable and trusted environment with a more *"safe"* authentication and encryption for the users the MCC system have to adapt the AES encryption algorithm.

Table 2. Literature challenges in the field of Mobile Cloud Computing

Literature work	Challenges								
	Privacy	Security	Trusted environment	Bandwidth	Environment limitations	Management	Reliability	User authentication	Efficiency
Rittinghouse & Ransome, 2009			X			X	X	X	
Doukas et al., 2010			X			X			
Angin et al., 2010	X	X				X		X	
Subashini & Kavitha, 2011		·	X		X	X			
Liang et al., 2011		X	X			X	X	X	
Dinh et al., 2011		X	X	X			X		X
Habib et al., 2011		X	X				X	X	
Hada et al., 2011		X	X				X		
Prasad et al., 2012	X	X		X		X	X	X	
Shiraz et al., 2012					X	X			X
Popa et al., 2013	X	X			X	X			
Shahzad & Hussain, 2013	X	X	X		X		X		
Suo et al., 2013	X	X	X						
Khan et al., 2013		X			X				
Kim & Park, 2013			X	X	X		X		X
Hashizume et al., 2013		X	X				X	X	
Ali et al., 2015		X	X		X	X	X		
Khalil et al., 2014			X		X	X	X	X	
Whaiduzzaman et al., 2014		X				X	X	X	X
Zhang et al., 2017			X	X	X				X
Mollah et al., 2017	X	X		X					
Jiang et al., 2018		X	X		X			X	

The AES algorithm has variable key length of 128, 192, or 256 bits, with default 256 bits. It encrypts data blocks of 128 bits in 10, 12 and 14 round depending on the key size. AES encryption is fast and flexible algorithm, and it can be implemented on various platforms especially in small devices, such as mobile devices. Also, AES has been carefully tested for many security applications (Singh & Kinger, 2013). As a result, the AES algorithm provides the ability to have speed key setup time a good key agility. So, if we use this algorithm we could have a trusted relay method with an encryption of a speed key setup. Therefore, instead the trust relay use we can seize also there no serious weak keys in AES and so we could have a beneficial security use of the encryption in the integrated new model. Similarly, we can take advantage the less memory which AES needs for implementation that makes it for restricted-space environments. Thus, we can seize the transmit power that AES offers and as a result we can have a better and more trusted transmission in a MCC environment (Stergiou & Psannis, 2017b; Singh & Kinger, 2013; Stergiou et al., 2018e; Gupta, 2018).

Count our study and the reliability of AES encryption algorithm for a MCC environment we suggest the following part of pseudocode based on the AES encryption algorithm.

Table 3. Suggested pseudocode based on the AES encryption algorithm

Algorithm 1
input -> byte[]
byte[] + R.Key -> state[]
for 6 to 66
W[i-1] -> T
if i mod 6 = 0
rotate T + 6
W[i-6] / T -> W[i]
R.Key+1
i+1 -> i
Row +1 -> Row
state[] -> output[]

With this proposed method we can extend the advances of MCC, in particular when it integrates with other technologies like IoT and Big Data, by developing a highly innovative and scalable service platform to enable secure and privacy services. Through tour research we can propose the algorithm 1 which extends the security advances of MCC environment, especially when integrates with other technologies. As a proposal of this work could be this part of pseudocode algorithm which uses the original key consists of 128 bits/16 bytes which are represented as a 6x6 matrix.

Experimental Results

Compared our proposed method with the existing one we come to some measurements that have been through time and showing the benefits of our proposed method.

As we can observe by Figure 3 the more often is the combined use of the algorithms, the higher level of security of the data usage we get every time. The upper line represents our proposed model of AES algorithm and the other (down line) represents the existing AES algorithm. Based on Figure 3 we can also figure out that our proposed method is over from the existing model regarding the higher security level of encryption that it can achieve through the time.

CONCLUSION AND FUTURE DIRECTIONS

The MCC technology provides a number of possibilities, but additionally places several challenges and issues that need to be addressed as well. Mobile Cloud Computing refers to an infrastructure where data, applications and information could be processed through a mobile device, but simultaneously outside of the mobile device. The main objective of the use of MCC is to decrease the use of stronger hardware and to have the access to data and applications, and in many times to more computational power, from every place and in any time, through a mobile device.

With our study, in regard on the huge benefits of the Mobile Cloud Computing technology, we try to achieve a more safe and trusted environment for the MCC users in order to operate the functions, and transfer, edit and manage data and applications. This could be achieved proving a novel method count on the AES encryption algorithm, which is, according to our study, the most relevant encryption algorithm to a Cloud environment.

Figure 3. Security level of encryption algorithms of measurement used for the study of AES model algorithm

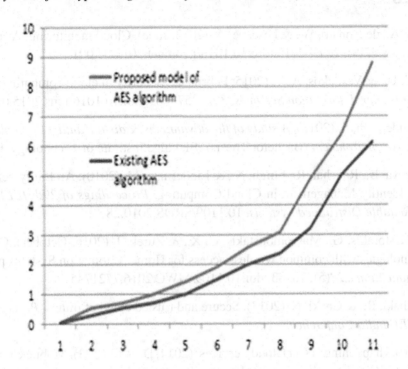

Furthermore, we try to define the most important issues and challenges in the field of Mobile Cloud Computing technology by presenting a number of the most significant works related to MCC through the last eight years.

As a future work, we could focus to find novel ways to achieve a better integration MCC with other technologies, focusing on security algorithms and all the challenges that the technologies faced on security level. Regarding the rapid development of Cloud technology the security issues of Mobile Cloud Computing must be solved or reduced to a minimum in order to have a better and safer model. The security challenges and issues that surveyed in this work could be the sector for further research as a case study, with the goal of minimizing them.

ACKNOWLEDGMENT

The authors would like to thank the anonymous reviewers for their valuable comments and feedback which was extremely helpful in improving the quality of the paper.

REFERENCES

Aceto, G., Botta, A., de Donato, W., & Pescape, A. (2013, June). Cloud monitoring: A survey. *Elsevier, Computer Networks*, *57*(9), 2093–2115. doi:10.1016/j.comnet.2013.04.001

Ali, M., Khan, S. U., & Vasilakos, A. V. (2015, February). Security in cloud computing: Opportunities and challenges. *Elsevier, Information Sciences*, *305*, 357–383. doi:10.1016/j.ins.2015.01.025

Almrot, E., & Andersson, S. (2013). *A study of the advantages & dis-advantages of mobile cloud computing versus native environment* (Bachelor Thesis). Blekinge Institute of Technology, Karlskrona.

Angin, P., Bhargava, B., Ranchal, R., Singh, N., & Linderman, M. (2010). An Entity-centric Approach for Privacy and Identity Management in Cloud Computing. *Proceedings of 29th IEEE International Symposium on Reliable Distributed Systems*. 10.1109/SRDS.2010.28

Batalla, J. M., Mastorakis, G., Mavromoustakis, C. X., & Zurek, J. (2016, October). On cohabitating networking technologies with common wireless access for Home Automation Systems purposes. *IEEE Wireless Communications*, *23*(5), 76–83. doi:10.1109/MWC.2016.7721745

Bhattasali, T., Chaki, R., & Chaki, N. (2013). Secure and trusted cloud of things. *Proceedings of INDICON Annual IEEE India Conference*.

Blog: Follow what's happening at Get Cloud Services. (2014, December 23). Mobile Cloud Com-puting – Pros and Cons. *GetCloud Services*. Available: https://www.getcloudservices.com/blog/mobile-cloud-computing-pros-and-cons/

Botta, A., de Donato, W., Persico, V., & Pescape, A. (2016, March). Integration of Cloud Computing and Internet of Things: A Survey. *Journal of Future Generation Computer Systems*, *56*, 1–54. doi:10.1016/j.future.2015.09.021

Dinh, H. T., Lee, C., Niyato, D., & Wang, P. (2011, October). A survey of mobile cloud computing: Architecture, applications, and approaches. *Wireless Communications and Mobile Computing*, *13*(18), 1587–1611. doi:10.1002/wcm.1203

Dobre, C., & Xhafa, F. (2014, July). Intelligent services for big data science. *Future Generation Computer Systems*, *37*, 267–281. doi:10.1016/j.future.2013.07.014

Dorgham, O., Almonani, A., Alauthman, M., Albalas, F., & Obeidat, A. (2018, April). An Online Intrusion Detection System to Cloud Computing Based on Neucube Algorithms. *International Journal of Cloud Applications and Computing*, *8*(2), 96–112. doi:10.4018/IJCAC.2018040105

Doukas, C., Pliakas, T., & Maglogiannis, I. (2010). Mobile Healthcare Information Management utilizing Cloud Computing and Android OS. *Proceedings of 32nd Annual International Conference of the IEEE EMBS*. 10.1109/IEMBS.2010.5628061

Fremdt, S., Beck, R., & Weber, S. (2013). Does Cloud Computing Matter? An analysis of the Cloud Model software-as-a-service and its impact on operational agility. *Proceedings of 46th Hawaii International Conference on System Sciences*, 1025-1034. 10.1109/HICSS.2013.182

Fu, Z., Ren, K., Shu, J., Sun, X., & Huang, F. (2015, December). Enabling Personalized Search over Encrypted Out-sourced Data with Efficiency Improvement. *IEEE Transactions on Parallel and Distributed Systems*.

Fu, Z., Ren, K., Shu, J., Sun, X., & Huang, F. (2016, September). Enabling Personalized Search over Encrypted Outsourced Data with Efficiency Improvement. *IEEE Transactions on Parallel and Distributed Systems*, 27(9), 2546–2559. doi:10.1109/TPDS.2015.2506573

Garg, S. K., Versteeg, S., & Buyya, R. (2013). A framework for ranking of cloud computing services. *Future Generation Computer Systems*, 29(4), 1012–1023. doi:10.1016/j.future.2012.06.006

Gou, Z., Yamaguchi, S., & Gupta, B. B. (2017). Analysis of Various Security Issues and Challenges in Cloud Computing Environment: A Survey. In *Handbook of Research on Modern Cryptographic Solutions for Computer and Cyber Security* (pp. 221–247). IGI Global.

Grozev, N., & Buyya, R. (2014, March). Inter-cloud architectures and application brokering: Taxonomy and survey. *Software, Practice & Experience*, 44(3), 369–390. doi:10.1002pe.2168

Gupta, B. B., Agrawal, D. P., & Yamaguchi, S. (2016). Handbook of Research on Modern Cryptographic Solutions for Computer and Cyber Security. IGI Global. doi:10.4018/978-1-5225-0105-3

Gupta, B. B., & Badve, O. P. (2017, December). Taxonomy of DoS and DDoS attacks and desirable defence mechanism in a Cloud computing environment. *Springer, Neural Computing and Applications*, 28(12), 3665–3682.

Gupta Brij, B. (2018). *Computer and Cyber Security: Principles, Algorithm, Applications, and Perspectives*. CRC Press, Taylor & Francis.

Habib, S. M., Ries, S., & Muhlhauser, M. (2011). Towards a Trust Management System for Cloud Computing. *Proceedings of IEEE International Joint Conference TrustCom-11/IEEE ICESS-11/FCST-11*. 10.1109/TrustCom.2011.129

Hada, P. S., Singh, R., & Meghwal, M. M. (2011, December). Security Agents: A Mobile Agent based Trust Model for Cloud Computing. *International Journal of Computers and Applications*, 36(12), 12–15.

Haghighat, M., Zonouz, S., & Abdel-Mottaleb, M. (2015, November). CloudID: Trustworthy cloud-based and cross-enterprise biometric identification. *Expert Systems with Applications*, 42(21), 7905–7916. doi:10.1016/j.eswa.2015.06.025

Hashizume, K., Rosado, D. G., Fernandez-Medina, E., & Fernandez, E. B. (2013, December). An analysis of security issues for cloud computing. *Journal of Internet Services and Applications*, 4(5), 1–13.

He, W., Yan, G., & Xu, L. D. (2014, May). Developing vehicular data cloud services in the IoT environment. *IEEE Transactions on Industrial Informatics*, *10*(2), 1587–1595. doi:10.1109/TII.2014.2299233

Hilbert, M., & López, P. (2011). The World's Technological Capacity to Store, Communicate, and Compute Information. *Science*, *332*(6025), 60–65. doi:10.1126cience.1200970 PMID:21310967

Huang, D. (2011, October). Mobile cloud computing. *IEEE COMSOC Multimedia Communications Technical Committee (MMTC). E-Letter*, *6*(10), 27–31.

Jiang, Q., Ma, J., & Wei, F. (2018, June). On the Security of a Privacy-Aware Authentication Scheme for Distributed Mobile Cloud Computing Services. *IEEE Systems Journal*, *12*(2), 2039–2042. doi:10.1109/JSYST.2016.2574719

Kaur, R., & Kinger, S. (2014, March). Analysis of Security Algorithms in Cloud Computing. *International Journal of Application or Innovation in Engineering & Management*, *3*(3), 171–176.

Keskin, T., & Taskin, N. (2014). A pricing model for cloud computing service. *Proceedings of 47th Hawaii International Conference on System Science*, 699-707. 10.1109/HICSS.2014.94

Khalil, I., Khreishah, A., & Azeem, M. (2014, March). Consolidated Identity Management System for secure mobile cloud computing. *Elsevier, Computer Networks*, *99*, 99–110. doi:10.1016/j.comnet.2014.03.015

Khan, A. N., Mat Kiah, M. I., Khan, S. U., & Madani, S. A. (2013, July). Towards secure mobile cloud computing: A survey. *Elsevier, Future Generation Computer Systems*, *29*(5), 1278–1299. doi:10.1016/j.future.2012.08.003

Kim, M., & Park, S. O. (2013, December). Trust management on user behavioral patterns for a mobile cloud computing. *Springer, Cluster Computing*, *16*(4), 725–731. doi:10.100710586-013-0248-9

Kryftis, Y., Mastorakis, G., Mavromoustakis, C., Mongay Batalla, J., Pallis, E., & Kormentza G. (2016). Efficient Entertainment Services Provision over a Novel Network Architecture. *IEEE Wireless Communications Magazine*.

Kumar, Munjal, & Sharma. (2011). Comparison of Symmetric and Asymmetric Cryptography with Existing Vulnerabilities and Countermeasures. *International Journal of Computer Science and Management Studies, 11*(3).

Li, J., Huang, L., Zhou, Y., He, S., & Ming, Z. (2017, January). Computation partitioning for mobile cloud computing in big data environment. *IEEE Transactions on Industrial Informatics*, *11*.

Liang, H., Huang, D., Cai, L. X., Shen, X. S., & Peng, D. (2011). Resource Allocation for Security Services in Mobile Cloud Computing. *Proceedings of IEEE Conference on Computer Communications Workshops INFOCOM WKSHPS 2011*. 10.1109/INFCOMW.2011.5928806

Mell, P., & Grance, T. (2011). NIST Definition of Cloud Computing - Recommendations of the National Institute of Standards and Technology. National Institute of Standards and Technology Special Publication.

Mollah, M. B., Azad, M., & Vasilakos, A. (2017, April). Security and privacy challenges in mobile cloud computing: Survey and way ahead. *Journal of Network and Computer Applications*, *84*, 38–54. doi:10.1016/j.jnca.2017.02.001

Negi, P., Mishra, A., & Gupta, B. B. (2013). Enhanced CBF Packet Filtering Method to Detect DDoS Attack in Cloud Computing Environment. *Cryptography and Security*. arXiv preprint arXiv:1304.7073

Pfarr, F., & Buckel, T. (2014). Cloud Computing Data Protection – A Literature Review and Analysis. *Proceedings of 47th Hawaii International Conference on System Sciences*, 5018-5027. 10.1109/HICSS.2014.616

Plageras, A. P., Stergiou, C. L., & Psannis, K. E. (2017). Solutions for Inter-connectivity and Security in a Smart Hospital Building. *Proceedings of 15th IEEE International Conference on Industrial Informatics (INDIN 2017)*. 10.1109/INDIN.2017.8104766

Popa, D., Cremene, M., Borda, M., & Boudaoud, K. (2013). A Security Framework for Mobile Cloud Applications. *Proceedings of 11th RoEduNet International Conference*. 10.1109/RoEduNet.2013.6511724

Prasad, M. R., Gyani, J., & Murti, P. R. K. (2012, October). Mobile Cloud Computing: Implications and Challenges. *Journal of Information Engineering and Applications*, *2*(7), 7–15.

Rahimi, M. R., Ren, J., Liu, C. H., Vasilakos, A. V., & Venkatasubramanian, N. (2014, April). Mobile Cloud Computing: A survey, State of Art and Future Directions. *Mobile Networks and Applications*, *19*(2), 133–143. doi:10.100711036-013-0477-4

Rao, B. B. P., Saluia, P., Sharma, N., Mittal, A., & Sharma, S. V. (2012). Cloud computing for Internet of Things & sensing based applications. *Proceedings of IEEE 6th International Conference on Sensing Technology (ICST 2012)*, 374–380. 10.1109/ICSensT.2012.6461705

Rittinghouse, J. W., & Ransome, J. F. (2009). *Cloud Computing: Implementation, Management, and Security*. CRC Press.

Shahzad, A., & Hussain, M. (2013). Security Issues and Challenges of Mobile Cloud Computing. *International Journal of Grid and Distributed Computing*, *6*(6), 37–50. doi:10.14257/ijgdc.2013.6.6.04

Shi, E., Niu, Y., Jakobsoon, M., & Chow, R. (2010). Implicit Authentica-tion through Learning User Behavior. *Proceedings of ISC'10 13th International Conference on Information Security*, 99-113.

Shiraz, M., Gani, A., Khokhar, R. H., & Buyya, R. (2012, November). A Review on Distributed Application Processing Frameworks in Smart Mobile Devices for Mobile Cloud Computing. *IEEE Communications Surveys and Tutorials*, *15*(3), 1294–1313. doi:10.1109/SURV.2012.111412.00045

Simmhan, Y., Kumbhare, A. G., Cao, B., & Prasanna, V. (2011). An analysis of security and privacy issues in smart grid software architectures on clouds. *Proceedings of IEEE 4th International Conference on Cloud Computing*, 582–589. 10.1109/CLOUD.2011.107

Singh, G., & Kinger, S. (2013). Integrating AES, DES, and 3-DES Encryption Algorithms for Enhanced Data Security. *International Journal of Scientific & Engineering Research, 4*(7).

Skourletopoulos, G., Mavromoustakis, C. X., Mastorakis, G., Batalla, J. M., & Sahalos, J. N. (2017, August). An Evaluation of Cloud-Based Mobile Services with Limited Capacity: A Linear Approach. *Springer, Soft Computing, 21*(16), 4523–4530. doi:10.100700500-016-2083-4

Stergiou, C., & Psannis, K. E. (2016, May). Recent advances delivered by Mobile Cloud Computing and Internet of Things for Big Data applications: A survey. *International Journal of Network Management*, 1–12.

Stergiou, C., & Psannis, K. E. (2017a). Algorithms for Big Data in Advanced Communication Systems and Cloud Computing. *Proceedings of 19th IEEE Conference on Business Informatics 2017 (CBI2017)*. 10.1109/CBI.2017.28

Stergiou, C., & Psannis, K. E. (2017b, November). Efficient and Secure Big Data delivery in Cloud Computing. *Springer, Multimedia Tools and Applications, 76*(21), 22803–22822. doi:10.100711042-017-4590-4

Stergiou, C., Psannis, K. E., Gupta, B., & Ishibashi, Y. (2018e, June). Security, Privacy & Efficiency of Sustainable Cloud Computing for Big Data & IoT. *Elsevier, Sustainable Computing, Informatics and Systems*.

Stergiou, C., Psannis, K. E., Gupta, B., & Ishibashi, Y. (2018g, September). Security, Privacy & Efficiency of Sustainable Cloud Computing for Big Data & IoT. *Elsevier, Sustainable Computing, Informatics and Systems, 19*, 174–184. doi:10.1016/j.suscom.2018.06.003

Stergiou, C., Psannis, K. E., & Gupta, B. B. (2018f). Advanced Media-based Smart Big Data on Intelligent Cloud Systems. *IEEE Transaction on Sustainable Computing*.

Stergiou, C., Psannis, K. E., Kim, B.-G., & Gupta, B. (2018a, January). Secure integration of IoT and Cloud Computing. *Elsevier, Future Generation Computer Systems, 78*(3), 964–975. doi:10.1016/j.future.2016.11.031

Stergiou, C., Psannis, K. E., Plageras, A. P., Ishibashi, Y., & Kim, B.-G. (2018b, March). Algorithms for efficient digital media transmission over IoT and cloud networking. *Journal of Multimedia Information System, 5*(1), 27–34.

Stergiou, C., Psannis, K. E., Plageras, A. P., Xifilidis, T., & Gupta, B. B. (2018c). Security and Privacy of Big Data for Social Networking Services in Cloud. *Proceedings of IEEE conference on Computer Communications (IEEE INFOCOM 2018)*. 10.1109/INFCOMW.2018.8406831

Stergiou, C. L., Psannis, K. E., Gupta, B. B., & Ishibashi, Y. (2018d). Security, Privacy & Efficiency of Sustainable Cloud Computing for Big Data & IoT. *Elsevier, Sustainable Computing, Informatics and Systems*.

Subashini, S., & Kavitha, V. (2011, January). A survey on security issues in service delivery models of cloud computing. *Journal of Network and Computer Applications*, *34*(1), 1–11. doi:10.1016/j.jnca.2010.07.006

Suo, H., Liu, Z., Wan, J., & Zhou, K. (2013). Security and Privacy in Mobile Cloud Computing. *Proceedings of 9th International Conference on Wireless Communications and Mobile Computing (IWCMC 2013)*. 10.1109/IWCMC.2013.6583635

Viswanathan, P. (2012). *Cloud Computing – Is it Really All That Beneficial?* Available: http://mobiledevices.about.com/od/additionalresources/a/Cloud-Computing-Is-It-Really-All-That-Beneficial.htm

Wang, C., Ren, K., Lou, W., & Li, J. (2010, July). Toward publicly auditable secure cloud data storage services. *IEEE Network*, *24*(4), 19–24. doi:10.1109/MNET.2010.5510914

Whaiduzzaman, Md., & Haque, M. N. (2014, June). A Study on Strategic Provision of Cloud Computing Services. *The Scientific World Journal*, 1–8.

Whaiduzzaman, M., Sookhak, M., Gani, A., & Buyya, R. (2014, April). A survey on vehicular cloud computing. *Journal of Network and Computer Applications*, *40*, 325–344. doi:10.1016/j.jnca.2013.08.004

Zhang, Y., Chen, X., Wong, D. S., Li, H., & You, I. (2017). *Ensuring attribute privacy protection and fast decryption for outsourced data security in mobile cloud computing. Elsevier, Information Sciences*, 379, 42–61.

Zhu, S., & Han, Y. (2018, January). Secure data outsourcing scheme in cloud computing with attribute-based encryption. *International Journal of High Performance Computing and Networking*, *12*(2), 128–136. doi:10.1504/IJHPCN.2018.094363

Chapter 3
Security for Cross-Tenant Access Control in Cloud Computing

Pramod P Pillai
VTU Extension Centre, UTL Technologies Ltd,, India

Venkataratnam P.
VTU Extension Centre, UTL Technologies Ltd., India

Siva Yellampalli
School of Engineering and Applied Sciences, SRM University AP - Amarvati, India

ABSTRACT

Cloud computing is becoming a de facto standard for most of the emerging technology solutions. In a typical cloud environment, various tenants purchase the compute, storage resource, and would be sharing the resource with other tenants. Sharing of the resources among various tenants is not popular due to the security concerns. There are few solutions that try to solve the security problem of resource sharing among tenants. Having a trusted mediator between multiple tenants is one of the methods. Few research papers have been written, and this chapter attempts to enhance one of the published solutions: Cross-tenant access control model for cloud computing. Most of the existing research papers explore the theoretical way to solve the problem. This project develops a working prototype and proves how resource sharing can be achieved. This research develops the concept of resource sharing activation, where the resource can be shared with multiple cloud tenant and the deactivation where the shared resources can be removed from the shared resource pool.

DOI: 10.4018/978-1-7998-1082-7.ch003

Copyright © 2020, IGI Global. Copying or distributing in print or electronic forms without written permission of IGI Global is prohibited.

INTRODUCTION

Security is one of the biggest concerns in today's technology driven world. Security breach, privacy violation has become every day news. With many critical sectors like healthcare, transport, energy embracing the technological innovation in a big way securing the resources used by these sectors becomes critical. The business needs and the financial aspect is forcing many companies to adapt the cloud infrastructure of the business need. In a cloud infrastructure the infrastructure is owned and maintained by 3rd party, and the other unknown application would be executed in the same physical infrastructure. This is not how the legacy application were run. In legacy environment the software application was run in an independent infrastructure and for all practical purpose the application and hardware were owned by same entity. But the cloud paradigm changes this approach and enables faster and cost-effective deployments. But this approach raised many concerns on the security aspect. The question to what extends the 3rd party entities providing the cloud services can be trusted. It would be a beneficial in terms of economics to share resources with other tenants in the cloud environment. But how to trust the resources that are hosted by the other entities in the same cloud environment.

OBJECTIVE

The objective of the chapter is to provide an enhanced and secure solution to share the resources among various tenants in a public cloud infrastructure. The existing solution are studied, and the short comings are understood. This is followed by an analysis to arrive at detailed high-level requirements for the new proposed solution. The requirements are then used to arrive a high-level design which is then prototyped in a public cloud infrastructure.

SCOPE OF THE PROJECT

The scope of the project is to build a porotype to share resources among the various tenants in a cloud environment in a secure way. The prototype version of this project is limited to sharing the resource between two public cloud-based file sharing servers.

PROBLEM DEFINITION

There are many solutions for sharing resources in a public cloud infrastructure with each solution has its own limitation. The design by Quratulain Alamet et al in the paper titled A Cross Tenant Access Control (CTAC) Model for Cloud Computing: Formal Specification and Verification (Alam et al, 2017) proposed many improved in the existing resource sharing mechanism in the public cloud infrastructure. But this paper has few limitations and has opportunities to improvement. The current work improvises on the work conducted by Quratulain Alam et al. The area identified for improvement are as follows

1. Reduce the messaging between the tenants to share given resource.
2. Share the resource only for a predefined time rather than sharing it forever.
3. The resources that are shared are encrypted.

CHAPTER OUTLINE

This chapter provides the detailed description on steps, methods and procedures followed for the execution of the designee, comparison of different parameters and the complete physical design implementation. This chapter has four sections and short description of each section is mentioned below,

Section 1 discusses the Literature survey,

Section 2 details the system architecture of the system and requirement specification.

Section 3 explores the design options that were explored for the various sub-system design.

Section 4 explains the verification aspect.

SECTION 1

Literature Survey

To address the security concern and to obtain an optimum solution for the resource sharing in public cloud environment many theories and practical solutions were proposed in various papers. The notable few areas are listed below,

- Role based access (RBAC)
- Single Sign-On (SSO) techniques are combined with Security Assertion Markup Language (SAML)
- Mediation service.
- Cross-tenant trust model (CTTM)
- Role based cross-tenant trust model (RB-CTTM)

Role based access (RBAC) method discussed in many papers (Ferraiolo et al, 2001), provides granular level of access control. But it has its own limitation since in a cloud environment, either the individual or organization may have more than one tenants and would typically manage separate infrastructure. Therefore, it is very much possible that users do not agree to have a common agreement to manage the access control. RBAC works nicely for the user accounts and not so nicely for some tenants. Nebula Cloud Computing Platform (McKenty et al, nd.) developed by NASA Ames Research Center at Moffett Field, California has integrated RBAC with finer authorization in to private cloud system. But Nebula supports only centralized authority, which is not a feasible solution for the public cloud solution.

Sayler (2013) in the paper described in details autonomous multi-tenant network security framework known as Jobber. Jobber built a solid inter-tenant network policy solution which can automatically allowing optimized communication between trusted tenants while also blocking traffic from untrusted tenants. But some of the security aspect is not demonstrated by the Jobber.

Single Sign-On (SSO) techniques can be combined with Security Assertion Markup Language (SAML) to perform authentication and also simple authorization in cloud environments ("Single Sign-On", 2013), but fine-grained authorization provided by RBAC solutions is not possible.

The Multi-tenant data architecture by IBM ("What is a cloud provider?", n.d.) and Microsoft (Chong et al, nd.) had proposed a resource sharing approach in data-centric cloud using database schema. This solution is applicable to databases solution running on the cloud and not for other shared resources in the cloud.

While these approaches are suitable for specific aspects of cloud computing, there remains need for a general model of cross-tenant access control. Hence it is better to have a trusted entity which can manage the access control of shared resource for all the tenants under a Cloud Service Provider (CSP).

The papers (Chong et al, n.d.; "Single Sign on", 2013; Alam et al, 2017) describes the usage of Mediation service to provide the access control in cloud infrastructure. But every solution has its own limitation. Many of the solution considers the resource sharing aspect, but do not consider the full security aspect in the solution. Quratulain et al (2017) designed a Mediation service considering security into consideration. The solution was not prototyped but proved using simulation models. Also, some of the messaging sequence considered in the paper are not optimal. The resource sharing is done forever or till the originating tenant decides to deactivate the resource sharing but does not account for the cases where the resources has to be shared for a predefined time interval. There is no specification on how the deactivation of the shared resource by an unknown user is handled.

The proposed solution fixes the security pitfall that were identified with the existing solution proposed in paper (Alam et al, 2017). In addition, few enhancements are also identified as part the current research work. The solution is prototyped which can be demonstrated using real world cloud solutions. The message for the resource activation and resource deactivation is simplified without losing the security of the system. A timer based resource activation is implemented to prevent any misuse of the activated resource, and a secure communication TLS is used between all the communication entities.

BACKGROUND

Cloud service providers ("What is a cloud provider?", n.d.) are third party companies that provides cloud-based platform, infrastructure, applications or storage services. The end user would only pay only of the services that they use. The cloud service provider typically provides a web interface where the cloud user can manage resources and perform the customized setting to enable/disable a particular service or implement access control feature on the resources.

Quratulain Alam (2017) in the paper proposed a concept of cloud resource mediation service (CRMS) which acts a mediator between the various tenants and, the cloud users entrust the data to the cloud service provider (CSP). This mediation server, CRMS, acts as a broker between various cloud tenants and the helps to attains the access control over the resources that the tenants share among themselves. The mediation server knows the set of resources that are present in the system, the owner of the resource and the list of tenants with whom the resources can be shared.

The simplified architecture diagram of the concept that was proposed Quratulain Alam (2017) in the paper is as shown in figure (1). The architecture is simplified to suit the current project implementation without losing the overall architecture concept. The entities mentioned in the diagram is as explained below.

Figure 1. Architecture overview of cross tenant access control system

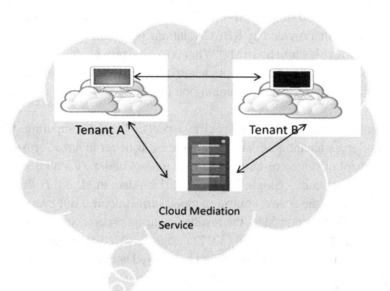

Figure 1 : Architecture overview of Cross Tenant Access Control System.

- Tenant A and Tenant B are cloud services.
- Cloud Mediation Server is the trusted mediation server and is also known as cloud resource mediation service. In the rest of the thesis this entity will be referred to as mediation server.
- Mediation server holds the list of shared resources owned by each tenant that can be accessed other tenant.

Firstly, it is important to know in brief how the system specified by paper (Alam et al, 2017) works before exploring on the architecture and design of the current research work The below sequence diagram shows the message flow associated with the permission request in a cloud environment as described in

In the sequence diagram shown in figure (2) T1 and T2 are the two cloud tenants, with T1 owning a resource to be shared and T2 is the entity which is requesting the resource. CRMS is an entity which perform the authentication and authorization decision based on the security policy provided by T1. The below steps explain the message flow

1. T1 receives access requests from T2 and redirects the request to the CRMS for further processing.
2. The CRMS on receiving the permission-activation request redirected from T1, evaluates the request on the pre-published policies.
3. The user has to authenticates at the parent tenant, T2.
4. Upon successful authentication, the user will be redirected again to CRMS with the attributes requested by the CRMS for cross tenant policy execution.
5. The user's attributes are evaluated against the T1 policy and if the policy criteria are successfully fulfilled, then the user is provided service access at T1; otherwise, the access request is denied.

Figure 2. Message flow of resource activation as proposed by Quratulain Alam (2017) in the paper

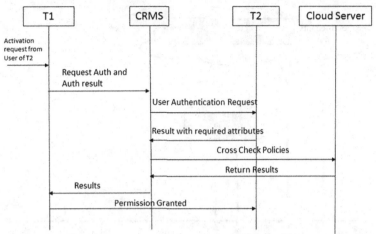

Figure 2:Message flow of resource activation as proposed by Quratulain Alam et al in the paper[1]

SYSTEM ARCHITECTURE

The figure (3) provides the high-level overview of the system in terms of the software usage and its interaction. The figure (3) has the software mapping to the general architecture shown in figure (1).

Cloud Tenants

The cloud tenants Tenant A and Tenant B are implemented using Google Drive and DriveHQ cloud solutions. The Google drive and DriveHQ are free file storage solution that runs on the cloud. These solutions provide multiple options to the end customer, but only the file server option is utilized here. Preconfigured accounts are created for this purpose. For this prototype the resources that are shared among the tenants are files.

Database

The data that must be persistent has to be stored in non-volatile memory. The idea is - even if the process crashes or if the system goes for reboot the data saved in the non-volatile memory can be retrieved by the program and can be used. Some of the examples that require storage in non-volatile memory are user identity and password pair, the key used to encrypt a file, the authorization list etc. In the simplest for the non-volatile storage can be achieved by saving the contents in a plain text file and retrieving/updating it as required. Though this approach is simple it has overhead of book keeping everything that is stored. With technological advancement its easier and preferred solution to use a database developed by third party and use the same to write and retrieve the data. Majority of the database available in the market uses SQL for the purpose of writing and retrieving the data. In the project there are set of variables

Figure 3. High-level overview of the system in terms of the software usage and interaction

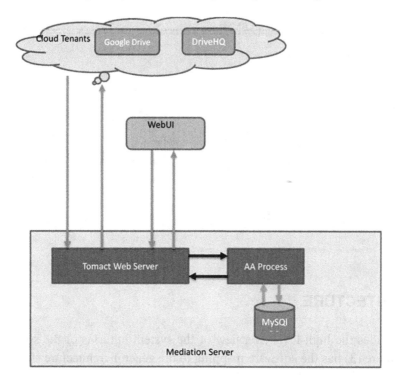

Figure 3 : High-level overview of the system in terms of the software usage and interaction

that has to be stored in a persistent value. User identity and password keypair, the name of the shared resources, the key associated with the username, the session key etc are the few items that has to be stored persistently. There are many popular databases that are available in the market and the prototype version will use MySQL database. The Community Edition of MySQL is free and is licensed under the GPL which make a perfect choice for the project.

Web Interfacing to Manage the Resource

The resource that are shared in this research work are files. It could have been any resource but for the simplicity and reasons explained in next section files are used as shared resources. The trigger to share the resource and usage of the share resource is a manual, which means a user interface has to be provided to share and use the shared resource. For this purpose, a suitable user interface has to be developed. To ensure that the resources are shared by and shared with authorized user alone, there should be sufficient session management implemented in the interface. The interface can be a command line-based interface or a graphical web-based interface. Consider the ease of implementation the project uses the web based graphical user interface approach to manage the shared resources. The web interface would support logging to the mediation server, selecting the resource to shared and selecting with whom the resource should be shared.

Tomcat Web Server

The user interface is web page driven, and this requires a corresponding support on the server side to process the request that are sent from the web page user interface. This is achieved via the webserver, which is a program that uses hypertext transfer protocol (http) and responds to the request that are send from the web page clients. The web page and web server work in client/server model with the web user interface being the client and the webserver acting as the server. There are many web servers available in the market for use. Apache, Internet Information Server (IIS), nginx, Google Web Server (GWS), Domino servers, NetWare server etc. In this project the webserver provided by apache namely Apache Tomcat. The Apache Tomcat software is an open source implementation of the Java Servlet, Java Server Pages, Java Expression Language and Java WebSocket technologies (Apache tomcat, n.d.).

Authentication and Authorization

For security reasons the set of entities that can access any part of the system has to be restricted and for the same reason the access to the user has to be limited to the predefined set of operations. This brings in the concept of authentication and authorization of the users to access the system resource. Authentication in web-based domain in simple term would mean, a user providing a predefined user identification and password to login to the system. The user identity and the password provided by the user is then compared against the prestored values and if they match the user is termed as authenticated user to access the system. Once the login is performed the set of operations that the user can perform defines the authorization aspect. As part of authorization one has to define the set of operation that can be performed by a given user. So, the first step to system access is authentication and its followed by authorization.

In our system the system access is performed via web page and hence the web interface will provide the facility to authorize the user. In fact, no functionality is accessible without successful authentication. The user identity and password pair are stored in the mediation server database and the authentication is performed by the process within Mediation server. Once the mediation server authorizes the user successfully the same is intimated to the user via web access and a web session is created. The authorization part is done via web server. That is the user based on the profile is restricted to access a limited set of operation that can be performed.

MVC Architecture

Model View Controller (MVC) is a popular software architecture which is commonly used to implement user interfaces and hence it is a popular choice for architecting web application. MVC separates out the application logic into three separate parts namely Model, View and Controller. Model represents shape of the data and business logic. View is a user interface. Controller handles the user request. The figure (4) illustrates the interaction between Model, View and Controller.

Figure 4. Model view controller (MVC)architecture

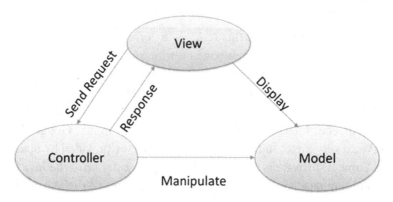

Figure 4 : Model View Controller (MVC)Architecture

Interface Among Various Entities

There are external and internal interfaces that make the system complete. The external interface includes the interface from the mediation server to the file server namely Google one drive and DriveHQ. This interface is not secure due to the practical limitation of the third-party file server. The scope of this project initially was to have a secure TLS session between the mediation server and the external file server (google one drive and the DriveHQ), but it's not achieved. As a mitigation the files that are stored on the external file server are encrypted using AES algorithm and the key used for encryption is known only the tenant that is sharing the resource and to the tenant with whom the resource is shared. Thus, though interface is insecure the resources is shared via this interface is secured. The other external interface is between the web client and the webserver. This is an http interface. There are few internal interfaces with in the mediation server. There is an internal interface between the Tomcat webserver, Authentication and Authorization entity, and between the MySQL database and the Authentication and Authorization entity. Since these are processes internal to the mediation server hence they need not be secure and in this project, they are not secured for the same reason.

REQUIREMENT SPECIFICATION

Based on the literature survey and the further analysis the scope of the project was presented earlier section. For developing a system with quality it's important to have the requirements specified early in the research. The specification will have to specified at multiple levels, with each level capturing the details at different granularity. The specification starts at Level1, aka L1 requirements, which captures the specification as perceived by an end user of the project. This is followed by Level2 specification which captures the system level requirements. Level2 specification details the requirements by splitting the whole system into logical or physical system and specifying what is expected from the combination of sub-systems. This also involves specifying the interfaces between various sub-systems. The third level of requirement specification is known as Level3 specification where each requirement related to each entity are covered. In the project the level3 specification is provided for cloud tenants, the Mediation server and the Graphical User interface.

Level 1 Specification

Level 2 Specification – System Level

Level 3 Specification – Entity Level

Entity Level Specification - Tenant

Entity Level Specification – Graphical User Interface

Entity Level Specification – Mediation Service

DETAIL DESIGN

The requirements and architecture covered in the section 2 forms the basis for the design. While designing attempt is being made to keep the design as generic as possible, but some of the design aspect had to be constrained to the domain of the prototype version of the project. Some of the constraints that had to be looked into were the availability of free software for faster development, cloud services that could be used with ease, with less or no cost. The current project work is an improvement on an existing research paper (Alam et al, 2017), but the scope of paper did not have a design to cover. Hence scope of designing current thesis include design for the original work and the design for the improvement that were identified as part of this research work.

Table 1. Level 1 specification

Requirement Number	Requirement Text
L1_1	As a CSP I want to facilitate secure resource sharing between to cloud tenants on the fly

Table 2. Level 2 - system specification

Requirement Number	Requirement Text
L2_1	System shall enable sharing of resources between two tenants.
L2_2	System shall have a mediator which is trusted by all the tenants.
L2_3	System shall maintain the list of shared resources supported by each tenant and the list who can access them.
L2_4	System shall support logging of the activities to audit the transaction in the system.
L2_5	System shall support secure message exchange between various entities for sharing resources

Table 3. Level 3 specification for tenant

Requirement Number	Requirement Text
L3_T_1	Each tenant shall publish the list of resources that are available for sharing along with the list of tenants that can access the resource.
L3_T_2	Each tenant shall have the capability to request the resources from the peer tenant on need basis.
L3_T_3	The tenant shall be capable of sharing a resource via activation request and release the resource via deactivation request to peer tenant.
L3_T_4	Receiving tenant shall verify the deactivation request is received only from the tenant for which the resource is allocated. This is to prevent rouge tenant from sending deactivation request to remove the resource allocated to genuine tenant.
L3_T_5	All the resource sharing request and resource accessing request shall be forwarded to the mediation server.
L3_T_6	Each tenant system shall rely on the mediation server to authenticate the peer tenant.

Table 4. Level 3 specification for GUI

Requirement Number	Requirement Text
L3_G_1	A GUI interface shall be provided on each tenant so that the tenant can request the shared resource.
L3_G_2	The GUI shall have the option to select the required shared resource and tenant from where shared resourced would be fetched.

WHAT RESOURCE TO BE SHARED?

The first and foremost question to be resolved is to identify what resources are to be shared between various cloud tenants. Since the cloud tenants in the identifiable by its IP address, in theory any computing resources could be shared between the cloud tenants. For example, the one of the cloud tenants may have some resources that could share video conversion technology to other cloud tenant. Or it could be a cloud tenant sharing its computing resources with other cloud tenant. The list can grow to a big number as e various usecases are analyzed and documented. Also cost associated with each of the usecase can

Table 5. Level 3 specification for mediation service

Requirement Number	Requirement Text
L3_M_1	Mediation Service shall maintain the list of supported tenants and track the request that are made by each tenant.
L3_M_2	The mediator shall handle the authorization request while sharing resource. (1) The activation request shall be verified by the Mediation service to check if the requested resources are available for sharing from the tenant. (2) The deactivation request shall be verified by the Mediation service to check if the deactivation request is valid one.
L3_M_3	Mediation service shall accept the deactivation requests if the requesting tenant has already requested for an activation session.
L3_M_4	All the system entities shall support logging to track the transactions happening in the system for verification.

vary. The cost involves the time to design and implement a given usecase and also the cost associated in procuring the shared resource licenses. Also, the time involved in developing a complex usecase for the prototype can be considerably larger. Considering the above factors and based on the feedback with the stakeholders it was decided to make an entity which is cost effective and simple to implement, and do not consume too much time and resource. Based on this decision a file, either ascii or binary, is defined as a shared resource for this prototype. With the file being defined as a shared resource many of the design aspect will have to constrained with this decision.

If the file is treated as a shared resource, then the question comes how it is different from the many network file server solutions that are available in the market. The answer to this comes by the fact that the network file sharing solution are shared with the know set of IP address and in some cases the files shared by the network are exposed directly to the end user, unlike this thesis solution where-in the files sharing happens via a mediator. This kind of resource sharing via a mediator may look like a limitation, but the design is flexible enough to include other shared resource with less changes.

DESIGN INPUTS

The bigger system can be broken down into smaller subsystem and then each subsystem can be designed at individual level and later stitched together to get an overall system. In this section various design options that were explored for important subcomponents are documented along with the reasoning for the design section.

Design Option to Select The Cloud Tenants

With the decision to make a file as a shared resource the next step is to select a design that us suitable to share the file among the cloud tenant. Following design option were explored.

Design 1: Use a Commercial Cloud Tenant

In this design a commercial cloud solution like Microsoft Azure or Amazon web server is selected and then implement a file sharing solution. The design would involve developing solution that is custom made, that provides a authentication framework, and an interface to share files with external entities etc.

Pros

1. Since the solution is custom made it provides enough flexibility in the design.
2. The interface security can be implement as required by the specification.

Cons

1. It's expensive to build a solution from ground zero.
2. It take more time to build a stable solution.
3. The solution is error prone since the amount compared to readymade solution.

Design 2: Cloud Based File Service as Cloud Tenant

In this design a commercial file sharing cloud service is used. The cloud tenants would be file sharing solution like Google drive, DriveHQ, dropbox etc. These solutions provide ready solution for sharing the file and hence it has inbuild mechanism for authentication and would have a standard interface to access the files.

Pros

1. The solution are less expensive especially from the prototype point of view since they are available at almost zero cost.
2. The interfaces to these servers are available in public domain and hence easy to implement.
3. The time to develop is very less.

Cons

1. There is less flexibility in terms of customizing the solution to individual need.
2. Some of the solution do not expose secure interface to the external world. To make the solution secure additional secure mechanism has to be implemented at the mediation server.

Considering the ease of implementation and cost involved in the developing the solution it has been decided to go with design option 2 . For file sharing solution Google drive and DriveHQ has been selected. To overcome the short coming of having insecure interface between the file sharing tenant and external entity the file that is shared is encrypted and the keys are shared using authorized users.

Message Authorization – Manual Versus Automatic

The authorization for the accessing the shared resource is critical in order to avoid unnecessary access. The precondition for these designs is that the resources is already shared by the sharing party. This covers only the authorization aspect.

Design 1: Manual Authorization

In this design option for every step in the overall authorization flow the authorization is done manually by the appropriate user by logging to the web page of the mediation server. This case is explained using Activation of a resource usecase. The message flow is as shown in the figure (5)
    The details associated with the message flow is as explained below.

1.   Tenant-B send the request to access a shared request that is owned by Tenant-A
2.   The Tenant-A on being notified about the request logs into the web portal and seeks the mediation servers to check the authorization of this request.
3.   Mediation server admin on being notified of step 2 logs into the web portal and checks if Tenant-B is authorized to access the request resources. If it is authorized, then it sends a positive response to the Tenant-A
4.   Tenant-A on receiving the authorization result again logs into the web portal and authorizes the Tenant-B to access the shared resource

Figure 5. Message flow for manual authorization

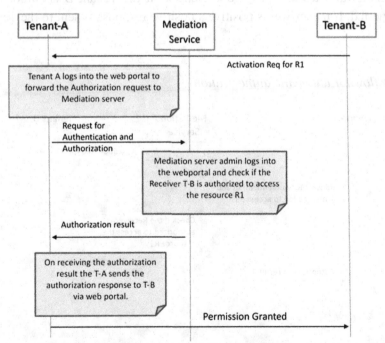

Figure 5 : Message flow for Manual Authorization

Following are the pros and cons with the above approach

Pros:

1. The approach gives every user in the system to get granular access to the authorization.

Cons

1. There are too many manual interventions required to achieve the required activation of a shared resources.
2. Due to the manual effort in every step the sharing of the resources can be delayed.
3. The manual steps are error prone.

Design 2: Automatic Authorization

In this design each entity has the intelligence to forward the request to the next entity for authorization. Each entity performs its job and overall authorization is completed collectively. In this approach the manual intervention is only to request the share resources and the rest of the flow is automated with required logic inbuilt. The message flow for this design approach for an activation request is as shown in figure (6)

The details associated with the message flow is as explained below.

1. Tenant-A shares the resource R1
2. Tenant-B request the mediation server to authorize to access the resource R1
3. Mediation server validates the message and checks if the Tenant-B is authorized to access the resource requested. If the answer is positive a positive response is sent to the Tenant-B

Figure 6. Message flow for automatic authorization

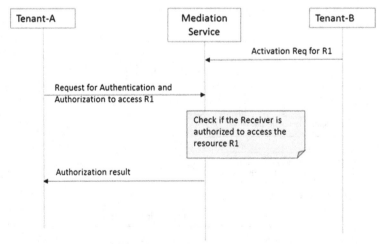

Figure 6 : Message flow for automatic authorization

Following are the pros and cons with the above approach

Pros:

1. The design ensures that there is no manual intervention as part of the shared resource authorization process.
2. The design is modular since the responsibilities of each entities are clearly defined.
3. Due to automatic authorization mechanism there is no delay associated with human factors.

Cons

1. The flow being automated debugging an issue and isolating the fault is cumbersome.

Based on the above analysis it has been decided to follow automatic authorization for the shared resources. Hence design 2 is selected.

Message Exchange Protocol Between Various Entities

There are various entities in the system and a proper communication is required for the working of end to end system. This point to point communication should be done via protocol that is common across various entities in the system. Following options were explored.

Option 1: Develop a custom-made messaging mechanism to enable the point to point communication. This would include developing the specification for the protocol, implement it and also verify the same. The library that implements the protocol should be made available for the all the hardware variant, the operating system and the programming language that is used on this project.

Option 2: Use the standard messaging like HTTP and API calls. This approach would require a standard set of libraries that are available in the market. This approach would require identifying the standard tools and library that are readily available for use and also understand the licensing terms and the monetary cost of using such tools.

Based on the factors like ease of development and time to develop it has been decided to pursue option 2.

Persistency of User Credentials

The mediation server is the entity that stores all the credentials of the system. This include the access details of the cloud tenants, the user who would login to the web portal to access the resources. These credentials have to be stored forever since they are required as long as the system is live. There are multiple ways to store the credentials and below section explain the possible ways.

Option 1: The credentials can be stored in the text file either in clear text format or in encrypted format. This will require developing logic to retrieve and write the credentials to the file when required.

Option 2: This option is using MySQL database to store the credentials in a predefined table. Since the database take care of storage and retrieval aspect, the logic of implementation is limited to the few set of APIs exposed by MySQL.

Both the options are good with equal merits. Since MySQL database is used by the project for other purposes too, its deemed advantage to continue to use the MySQL database for storing the credentials.

Log Maintenance

Logs form an important aspect for debugging the issue and also for forensic investigation. One of the options is to dump the log on to the standard console or to a file. Second option is to store the logs into a standardized location from where the logs can be retrieved. Since there are variety of logs that are present in the system like one used for debugging during development and testing phases and another set of logs for production phase and for forensic investigation. Hence it has been decided to support both the options of logging.

USER SCENARIOS

This section covers the message flow of the various user scenarios that are possible.

Registration of a User Account

Precondition: Mediation server is configured, and the web portal is up and running.
Actor: Web client, Web server, Mediation server.

Description:

1. User access the web portal of mediation server by proving the appropriate URL.
2. User clicks on the registration button.
3. User enters the following details on the web page.
   a. Username
   b. Email id to be associated with the user account
   c. Password for the account
   d. Selects the tenant to which the user has to be associated with. The choice is either google drive or DriveHQ
   e. Selects the access policy for the account. The access policy can be student, Professor, or researcher.
   f. Phone number associated with the account. This value is not used in the current implementation.
4. Web client form the registration request message and send the details to the webserver running on the mediation server.
5. Mediation server fetches the parameters sent by the web page and stored into local variables.
6. The username is checked for uniqueness by comparing the username presented by the web page against all the username present in the table reg in MySQL database.
7. Mediation server creates a random security key and links the security key to the new account.
8. The random key is then sent to the email id of the registered user.
9. A successful registration notification is sent to the web page client.

Post Condition

A user account is created in the mediation server

Sequence Diagram

Login to the System

Precondition: The user account is created, and the security key associated with the user is available with the user.

   Actors: Mediation server, Web portal, User

Figure 7. User registration message flow

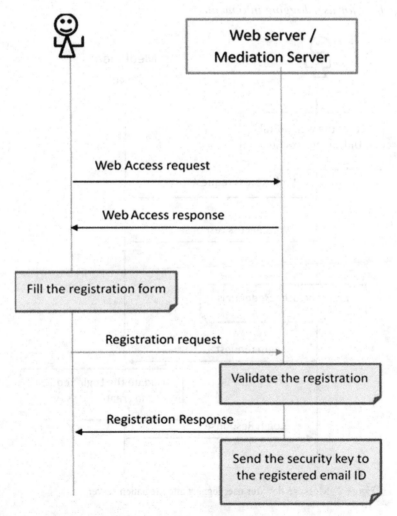

Figure 7 : User Registration message flow

Description:

1. The user opens the web portal to login to the Mediation server
2. User enters the user credentials and the secret key
3. User clicks the submit button.
4. Web client builds the login message with the parameters - username, password and security key and sends it to the web server running on the Mediation server.
5. Mediation server checks if the user with the given credentials exists, by querying the database (table reg).
6. On getting a positive response from the query the mediation server sends a positive response to the web client and creates a session for the login session.
7. The session attributes include the following
   a. User name

Figure 8. Message flow for user logging into mediation server

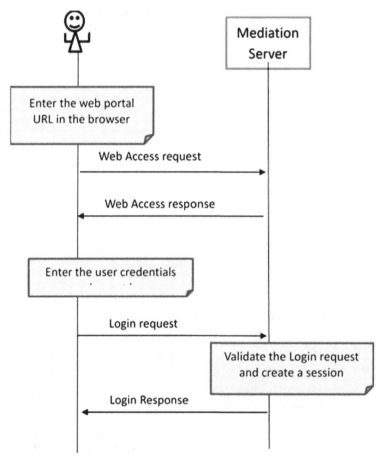

Figure 8 : Message flow for user logging into mediation server

    b.   Associated tenant Name
    c.   Email Id of the user
    d.   Security Key of the user
    e.   Upload Policy of the user

Post Condition: User establishes a web session with the mediation server.

Sequence Diagram:

Activation of the Resource

The resource that is used for sharing is file and hence the activation of the resource maps to uploading the file to the file sharing server.

    Precondition: The users are configured on the mediation server with valid credentials. Here tenant-A is the entity that owns the resource.

    Actors: Tenant-A, Mediation server, Web portal.

Description:

1.   User logs into the mediation server web portal using username, password and the unique security key.
2.   User Selects
    a.   The file to be shared
    b.   File access policy which are student, professor and researcher.
    c.   And enters the file access key, which is used to encrypt the file.
3.   The web portal sends the details of the user name, file name, file access key, file access policy details to the mediation server.
4.   Mediation server on receiving the activation request fetches the name of the file, file access policy, file access key and the username.
5.   Mediation server uses the file access key to encrypt the file using AES encryption.
6.   Mediation server uses the username to identify the associated tenant. The tenant can be Google drive or DriveHQ.
7.   Based on the tenant type mediation server uses appropriate APIs to upload the file to the cloud file server.
8.   Mediation server stores the values to identify the file and its ownership into the table (table upload) to identify the file.

Post Condition

The selected resource is shared with the given access group.

Sequence Diagram

Setting the Duration for Which the Resource can be Shared

Precondition: The resource that is to be shared is activated and available for sharing.
  Actors: Mediation server, Web portal.

Description:

1. The user logs on to the web portal.
2. The user selects the menu to set the timer associated the shared resource
3. User sets the start time and end time indicating the time duration for which the resource is to be shared and clicks the submit button.
4. The web client sends the filename, start time and end time details to the web server running on the mediation server.
5. The mediation server update the database with the time start time and end time details.

Figure 9. Message flow for resource activation or sharing

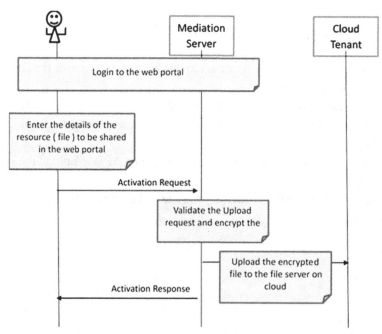

Figure 9 : Message Flow for resource activation or sharing

Post Condition:

The duration for which the resources are shared is set in the database.

Sequence Diagram:

Deactivation of the Resource

Precondition: The resource that is to be shared is activated and available for sharing.
   Actors: Mediation server, Web portal.

Figure 10. Message flow for setting the deactivation timer

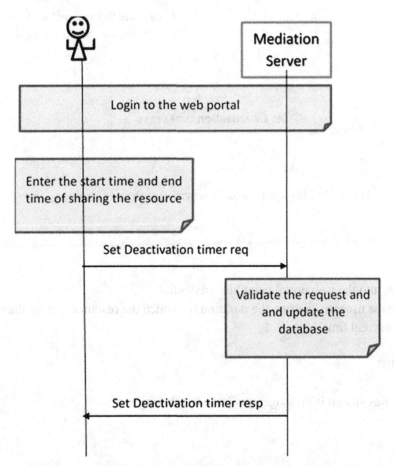

Figure 10 : Message flow for setting the deactivation timer

Figure 11. Message flow for deactivation of shared resource

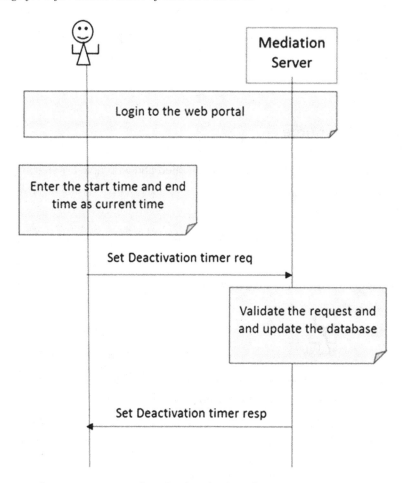

Figure 11 : Message flow for deactivation of shared resource

Description:

1. The user logs into the web portal using the credential.
2. User execute the usecase "Setting the duration for which the resource can be shared" with the end value as the current time.

Post Condition:

The resource that was shared is no longer available for sharing.

Figure 12. Message flow for accessing shared resource

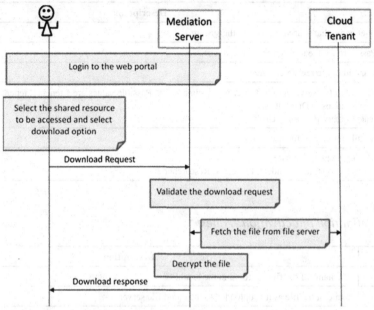

Figure 12 : Message flow for accessing shared resource

Sequence Diagram

Access Shared Resource

Precondition:

1.   The resource that is to be shared is activated and available for sharing.
2.   The user has access to the shared resources and is in possession of the secret key associated with the shared resource.

Actors: Mediation server, Web portal.
Description:

1.   User logs into the web portal using the credentials.
2.   User clicks on the menu to check the shared resources.
3.   Web Portal displays only the resources that the user is authorized to access.
4.   User clicks on the download option and provides the security key associated with the resource.
5.   User sends the tenant name, name of the file to be download, the security key of the file, username who has logged into the web portal to web server running on the mediation server.
6.   The mediation server check if the filename and the associated key matches the value stored in the database.

Table 6. Messsage defination of Registration Request

Name	Description
uname	User name that is used to login to the system
pass	Password for the user to login to web portal
email	email id of the registered user
tenent	The cloud file server to which user is associated with. Possible values are { tenent1, tenent2} tenent1 maps to DriveHQ tenent2 maps to Google Drive
mno	Mobile number of the user
policy	The hierarchy of the user. Possible values are { student, Professor, Researcher }

Table 7. Messsage defination of activation request

Name	Description
file	The name of the file as stored in the local PC
fname	Name of the file as it is uploaded to the cloud file server
fkey	The key to encrypt the file
policy	The policy of the user Possible values are { student, Professor, Researcher }

Table 8. Messsage defination of download request

Name	Description
fname	Name of the file as it is uploaded to the cloud file server
fkey	The key used to decrypt the file
uname	The owner of the file

Table 9. Message defination of Login Request

Name	Description
uname	User name used to login
pass	password of the user
skey	Secrect key of the user

7. The mediation server checks if the resource that is shared is still allowed to be shared. This is done by checking the current time against the time when the sharing of the resources has to be stopped. If the resource sharing is allowed the usecase continue with the next step else the usecase ends after sending an error response to web portal.

8. The mediation server connects to the file server cloud tenant and downloads the file locally.
9. The mediation server uses the security key and decrypts the file that is downloaded.
10. The content of the files are displayed to the user on the web browser.

Post Condition:

The shared resources is available with the authorized user.

Sequence Diagram:

INTERFACE DEFINITION – MESSAGE STRUCTURE

The message exchanged between the web client and the web server is via http protocol. Here the GET or POST methods are used for the message exchange. For both the type the message will contain name and value pairs. Since the name value pair is used the web client and the web server should use the same name to identify a give parameter. This forms the interface definition between the web client and the web server. The interface definition for the messages exchanged between the web client and web server are captured below.

Registration Request

This the message sent from web client to web server as part of user registration process. The message exchanged between web client and web server is as shown below.

Activation Request

This is the message sent from web portal to web server to share a resource

Download Request

This message is sent from the web portal to the web server to download the shared resource.

Login Request

This message is sent from the web portal to the web server while logging into the Web Server.

VERIFICATION

The implementation is always prone to human error. The error could be due to misinterpretation of requirements, or due to bad design or it could be because of flaw in implementation logic. Hence it is important to check if the product that is developed is meeting the expectation of the original specification. This is achieved in the verification stage. This verification can be done are different stages. These can be classified as Component verification, Integration verification and System Verification.

Component Verification

In this approach a specific module/function or program is verified in isolation. This typically involves writing the stubs for the given module. In this project this aspect was achieved using print statements at the relevant places. This was performed for the code written in all the sub-system.

Integration Verification

In integration verification the functionally across two sub-systems are verified. Typically test stubs and drivers are used to perform this testing. The interface definition document is mandatory for performing this kind of testing. Understanding of the messages that are expected to flow between the sub-systems, the handshakes between the subs-system. The kind of verification typically done via log verification or using tools that can capture the message between two entities followed by checking the contents of the captured logs.

System Verification

The system verification involves the checking the correctness of the system, the software delivered, the documents that are delivered. The system verification is done by integrating all the sub-systems used in the product. In this current project the scope of verification is limited to the verification of the implementation and the verification is done by checking the correctness of the implementation against the requirement. In some cases, it was found during the verifications that the requirements is no feasible to be met and hence it was decided to change the requirement to align with the ground reality

TEST PLAN

To cover the test scope, test environment, test strategy a test plan has to be in place along with the specification. This is important to ensure that proper planning is in place with adequate test resource.

Test Planning Assumption

The test plan covers the system and integration level of verification. The component and unit level testing are expected to be completed as part of the implementation. The expectation is the code implemented in completeness and the required executables are available for verification. The specification is assumed to frozen and no changes are expected. Any change in the requirement has to be treated as a failure point in the requirement.

Testing Environment

The test bed for the integration and system verification is done on end to end set up compromising of the mediation server and the two cloud-based file servers. As mentioned in the architecture section the resource to be shared is a file and hence the verification will be performed on the same. In usual cases the integration testing is performed in a simulated environment. Creating simulation tools is not possible within the given time frame and hence the end-to-end environment is used for integration test verification too. The system verification assumes the entities as black boxes and verifies that the end to end scenarios are as per the L2 specification.

The figure (13) depicts the actual test environment.

The Mediation server id hosted on a laptop/desktop. The file server is hosted on remote server namely the google drive and DriveHQ. The credentials to these are not configurable from the entities that are under testing and hence only criteria is to ensure that these servers are reachable from the mediation server. The web portal of the mediation server is accessed via standard web browser like Internet explorer or Google Chrome. To check the message that flows between the various external entities Wireshark tool is used.

Figure 13. Test environment

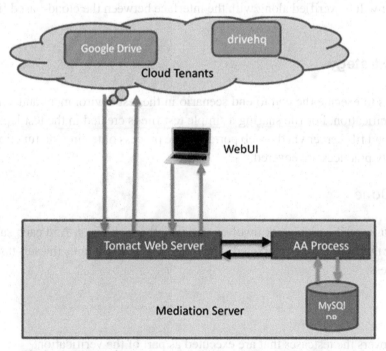

Figure 13 : Test environment

Table 10. Defination of completion

Sub-Task	Evidence for completeness
Test planning	The test plan is ready
Testing cases	The testcases with description are available
Testcase to requirement mapping	The test case to requirement mapping in tabular format
Test execution completeness	All the testcases are executed and all the testcases are marked as PASS

Tools for Testing

For the verification following tools are used

1. Web Browser
2. Standard laptop/desktop with internet access
3. Wireshark

Verification Entities

For system verification the verification entity is the Mediation server which provides the cross-tenant access functionality along with host the web server. The web user interface is also verified to check the user interface specification. For the integration verification the interfaces between the web portal and the web server will be verified along with the interface between the cloud-based file server and the mediation server.

General Test Strategy

The test strategy is to execute the end to end scenario in the test environment and verify that they are aligned to the specification. For file sharing a simple test file is created in the test laptop and uploaded the same to the cloud file server via the web portal. In the process of testing the functionality verify that the general security practices are covered.

Definition of Done

The complete feature verification work involves various other sub-tasks. And each sub-task requires a definition to mark that sub-task as completed. The following table captures the sub-tasks and its definition of completeness.

Testcases

Following table covers the testcases that are executed as part of the verification.

Table 11. Testcase with test description

Test #	Testcase Title	Description
T1	Registration of a user	**Input:** Connect to the web portal via a browser Click on the registration option. Provide the required details necessary in the form Submit the Form **Expected Output:** The user should be registered in the mediation server User secret key should be available in the registered email id
T2	Authentication of a user by the mediation server	**Input:** Connect to the web portal via a browser Click on the Login option. Enter username, password and secret key. Submit the form **Expected Output:** The user should be able to login to the mediation server
T3	Sharing of the resource by a registered user	**Input:** Login to the mediation server Select the resource that must be shared. Share the resource **Expected Output:** The resource is shared and is available for the user with the same profile.
T4	Deactivation of the resource	**Input:** Login to the mediation server Select the resource that was shared. Set the deactivation time as current time. Click the submit **Expected Output:** The resource is no longer available for sharing
T5	Each tenant requesting resource from peer	**Input:** Login to the mediation server Select the resource that was shared earlier. Provide the file security key Click on the download option **Expected Output:** The share resource is available for the end user.
T6	Deactivation of resource only from authorised peer	**Input:** Login to the mediation server with policy student. Select the resource that was shared earlier with policy professor. Click on the download option. **Expected Output:** The share resource is not available for the end user.
T7	Tenant publishing the list of resource available for sharing	**Input:** Login to the mediation server Select the resource that must be shared. Share the resource **Expected Output:** The resource is shared and is available for the user with the same profile. Verify by logging as another user to see the resources are available for download

continued on the following page

Table 11. Continued

Test #	Testcase Title	Description
T8	GUI should provide the option to select the shared resource and tenant from where the shared resource can be fetched	**Input:** Login to the mediation server In the user interface there should be a option to select the shared resource **Expected Output:** The shared resources are available in the GUI
T9	The mediation server maintains the list of supported tenants	**Input:** There is no direct way to verify this. This testcase has to be executed by checking the database (MySQL) Login to the mediation server Connect to the MySQL database. Check the entries present in table tenant by executing the sql command in the database. **Expected Output:** The list of shared resources are available in the database present in the mediation server.
T10	Logging of the message request is supported	**Input:** Login to the mediation server Perform the activation of resource operation. **Expected Output:** The operation that are performed are available in the log file.
T11	Resource sharing and Resource accessing handling by Mediation server	**Input:** Login to the mediation server Select the resource that has to be shared. Share the resource Input: Login to the mediation server and different user Select the resource that was shared earlier. Provide the file security key Click on the download option **Expected Output:** The user is able to share the resource via mediation server and the resource can also be accessed via mediation server.

Testcase to Requirement Mapping

The following table covers the testcase to requirement mapping.

Test Results

All the testcases mentioned above were passed. Below is the list of issues that were identified as part of testing, and the resolution column capture the resolution for the issue.

Communication Matrix

The communication matrix captures the TCP/IP ports that are open on a given device. This is important to know the open ports from security point of view.

Table 12. Testcase to requirement mapping

Test #	Testcase Title	Requirement Number
T1	Registration of a user	L3_M_5
T2	Authentication of a user by the mediation server	L3_T_6
T3	Sharing of the resource by a registered user	L3_T_3, L3_M_2
T4	Deactivation of the resource	L3_T_3, L3_M_2, L3_M_3
T5	Each tenant requesting resource from peer	L3_T_2, L3_M_3, L3_G_1
T6	Deactivation of resource only from authorised peer	L3_T_4, L3_M_3
T7	Tenant publishing the list of resource available for sharing	L3_T_1
T8	GUI should provide the option to select the shared resource and tenant from where the shared resource can be fetched	L3_G_2, L3_G_1
T9	The mediation server maintains the list of supported tenants	L3_M_1
T10	Logging of the message request is supported	L3_M_4
T11	Resource sharing and Resource accessing handling by Mediation server	L3_T_5

Table 13. Issues identified as part of testing along with the resolution

Sl No	Issue Description	Resolution
1	As per requirement the receiving tenant shall redirect the request to the Mediation service for checking the share resources.	The requirement was modified as "All the resource sharing request and resource accessing request shall be forwarded to the mediation server."
2	As per the requirement the mediator shall forward the authorization request to the peer node. But no such option exists in the system design	The requirement was changed to align with the design. The requirement was reworded as " The mediator shall handle the authorization request while sharing resource".
3	Deactivation of the resource was not working. There is no option in the GUI to deactivate the resource	The deactivation of the resource has to be done by setting the deactivation timer to current time.

Table 14. Communication matrix of mediation server

Application	Open Port
MySQL	3306
Apache Tomcat	8084

FUTURE RESEARCH DIRECTIONS

As part of testing and post project analysis following area were identified for future research.

- The cloud solutions are tied to google drive and hardhq solutions and this can be enhanced to make the solution generic by providing the user to configure the cloud server as needed.
- The password aging, password complexity, account locking feature can be implemented for the user accounts that are used.
- Deactivation of the shared resource. Currently this is achieved indirectly by setting the timer to appropriate value, instead there should be an option to deactivate the resource with a click of a button.
- The current prototype implementation is restricted to file as a shared resource. This can be enhanced to share any feasible computable entity as a shared device. This would be of greater usefulness for machine to machine communication which would be the tread in the 5G communication era.
- A set of APIs can be developed to sharing the resource and requesting for shared resource. This will enable programmatic way to share the resource and seek the shared resource in run time. Current implementation is driven by humans via web interface. APIs development will enable automated resource sharing, which will is a key enabler for machine to machine communication.

CONCLUSION

The research concludes that

- security is an important and key factor in the cloud computing world since the physical resources are shared among various tenants. It become more important in the emerging era of machine to machine communication where the more resources are shared among various entities.
- message optimization should be considered wherever feasible. As the number of entities participating in the communication network increases even a minor improvement will have a positive impact in terms of performance.
- it is feasible to share the resource between two cloud entities via a mediation sever in a secure way.
- using standardized security libraries and tools are essential in building secure software solution, since building inhouse security solution from scratch is time consuming and also error prone.

REFERENCES

Alam, Q., Malik, S. U. R., Akhunzada, A., Choo, K.-K. R., Tabbasum, S., & Alam, M. (2017). A Cross Tenant Access Control (CTAC) Model for Cloud Computing:Formal Specification and Verification. *IEEE Transactions on Information Forensics and Security, 12*(6), 1259–1268. doi:10.1109/TIFS.2016.2646639

ApacheT. (n.d.). Retrieved from: http://tomcat.apache.org/

Chong, F., Carraro, G., & Wolter, R. (n.d.). *Multi-tenant data architecture*. Retrieved from http://ramblingsofraju.com/wp-content/uploads/2016/08/Multi-Tenant-Data-Architecture.pdf

Chong, R. F. (n.d.). *Designing a database for multi-tenancy on the cloud*. Retrieved from https://developer.ibm.com/tutorials/dm-1201dbdesigncloud/

Ferraiolo, D. F., Sandhu, R., Gavrila, S., Kuhn, D. R., & Chandramouli, R. (2001, August). Proposed NIST standard for role-based access control. *ACM Transactions on Information and System Security, 4*(3), 224–274. doi:10.1145/501978.501980

Foster, I., Zhao, Y., Raicu, I., & Lu, S. (2008). Cloud computing and grid computing 360-degree compared. In *Grid Computing Environments Workshop (GCE)*, (pp. 1–10). IEEE. 10.1109/GCE.2008.4738445

McKenty, J. (n.d.). *Nebula's implementation of role based access control (RBAC)*. Retrieved from http://nebula.nasa.gov/blog/2010/06/03/nebulas-implementation-role-based-access-control-rbac/,2010

Sayler, A., Keller, E., & Grunwald, D. (2013). Jobber: Automating inter-tenant trust in the cloud. *5th USENIX Workshop Hot Topics Cloud Comput.*

Single Sign-On with SAML on force.com. (2013). Retrieved from http://wiki.developerforce.com/page/SingleSign-OnwithSAMLonForce.com

What is a Cloud Provider? (n.d.). Retrieved from: https://azure.microsoft.com/en-in/overview/what-is-a-cloud-provider/

KEY TERMS AND DEFINITIONS

Authentication: It is a process of verifying a user's identity. In simple mechanism, this involves using a username and password to prove one identity. In complex system, certificates, images can be used to prove one's identity.

Authorization: In computing world authorization refers to specifying access rights/privileges to computing resources.

Cloud Computing: It defined as on demand availability of computing resources, like data storage and computing power, without direct active management by the user.

CSP (Cloud Service Provider): Is a company that offers some component of cloud computing—typically infrastructure as a service (IaaS), software as a service (SaaS), or platform as a service (PaaS)—to other businesses or individuals.

HTTP (Hypertext Transfer Protocol): Is an application protocol for distributed, collaborative, and hypermedia information systems. HTTP is the foundation of data communication for the world wide web.

RBAC (Role-Based Access Control): Is a method of limiting access to computing resource based on the roles of individual users within an organization.

SAML (Security Assertion Markup Language): Is an open standard for exchanging authentication and authorization data between parties, in particular, between an identity provider and a service provider.

SFTP: Secure file transfer protocol.

Chapter 4
Secure Identity–Based Proxy Signature With Computational Diffie–Hellman for Cloud Data Management

Dharavath Ramesh

https://orcid.org/0000-0003-3338-6520

Indian Institute of Technology (ISM), Dhanbad, India

Rahul Mishra

Indian Institute of Technology (ISM), Dhanbad, India

Damodar Reddy Edla

National Institute of Technology, Goa, India

Madhu Sake

Guru Nanak Institutions Technical Campus, Hyderabad, India

ABSTRACT

This chapter explains a secure smart cloud framework based on identity-based proxy signature (IDBPS) scheme on Computational Diffie-Hellman (CD-H) assumption and AckIBE for data management. The objective of this chapter is to construct a secure hierarchical structure of homogeneous and heterogeneous cloud centers. This structure gives various types of computing services in the support of data analysis and information management. In this, the authors also introduce a security-related solution based on acknowledgment identity-based encryption (AckIBE), an IDBPS on computational Diffie-Hellman assumption, and identity-based proxy re-encryption to face critical security issues of the proposed framework.

DOI: 10.4018/978-1-7998-1082-7.ch004

Copyright © 2020, IGI Global. Copying or distributing in print or electronic forms without written permission of IGI Global is prohibited.

INTRODUCTION

Smart models improve reliability, efficiency and substantiality of computing services in comparison with traditional power grids in the form of smart grids (Farhangi et al, 2010). There are various benefits given by smart grids to electrical related grids, but their presence and accuracy is confined to smaller locations. Due to several challenges, there is a necessity of deployment of the smart grids in larger capacities. Information management is associated with the management that gathers, stores, and processes the information (Bojkovic et al, 2012; Duff et al, 2009; Fan et al, 2012). A suitable framework is required to manage huge sets of data, i.e. to select the data, deploy and include the data, monitor the data and analyze the data of smart cloud models in a heterogeneous environment. In the scenario of smart models, several sources create and generate different type of data in a large quantity which is termed as big data. These sources denote the consumption activities of the customers; phase-wise data for storage and retrievals; energy consumption of the data used by several smart location meters; to manage, maintain and to control the data. Data related to a network taken by operational devices like virtual machines, servers, etc., can also serve as other parameters. These data are widely used in decision making. Big data are measured exponentially in terms of power utilities. Countries like China, US, and Europe are estimated to install and utilize about 450 million smart meters by that date. Also, predictions show that the number of smart operational meters of different models of cloud will touch the range of 650 million by the year 2020. Sometimes, processing the tasks in real time become more important since it usually has strict deadlines. Any delay may cause harmful and destructive results of the whole system.

ID Based Proxy Signature Scheme Based on CDH Problem

Proxy signature has attracted significant attention from scholars as well as researchers (Baek et al, 2015; Schuldt et al, 2008; Wang et al, 2015; Cao et al, 2016; Wei et al, 2014; Zhang et al, 2011; Boldyreva et al, 2012; Gu et al, 2013). But, in order to bind between user's corresponding identity and the public key (usually taken as a "*random*" string) as a proxy signature, a certificate service is needed. This certificate is constructed by a trusted third party known as CA (Certificate Authority) in a *PKI*. Thus, two verifications are required to be made by the receiver: for the user's certificate and for the signature. Shamir, in 1984, introduced the concept related to identity-based cryptography (*IDB*), which solves the above problem. In IDB cryptography, the public key generator (*PKG*) constructs the private key, whereas the public key is the identity of the user such as an email etc.

Recently, certain Identity based proxy signature schemes (IDBPS) have been built in the standard model. But these contain loose security reductions, where, they cannot prevent the delegator attacks. Also, their computational efficiency is very low. To accommodate this constraint, in this chapter, we construct an efficient IDBPS and prove its security based on computational Diffie-Hellman assumption. As compared with other schemes, we have two main advantages; tight security reduction and more complete security that includes resistance of the delegator attack. Also, our scheme provides efficient performance, including less computational cost and shorter signature size as compared to other existing similar IDBPS schemes. In addition to this, in our scheme, secure channels are not required for transferring delegation keys, where other identity-based proxy signature schemes need this environment.

Support of Cloud Environment

The cloud computing model is a remarkable and a well-known platform for different computing scenarios that provides different measured services and benefits over traditional computational models. It is energy efficient, scalable, agile, flexible and cost saving (Hayes et al, 2008). It provides energy saving mechanisms and platform of saving the cost. Cloud computing as a smart model addresses the problem related to information at large scale. This is exploited in two folds: it is highly scalable and able to deal with the amount of information being processed. Also, it efficiently utilizes the resources concerned with the data centers. In order to handle huge amount of data, the cloud environment yields better and faster computation facility of parallel and distributed computing with efficient storage. In order to process the huge amount of data which is termed as big data, new algorithms to perform with data analysis and new approaches used for handling the unexpected amount of big data are required. It is possible for a cloud service provider (*CSP*) to provide cheaper, more reliable and better cloud services for the users, with the help of lower and under managed cloud infrastructure. To handle these modalities, many smart grid and cloud computing properties in the form of different cloud models have been analyzed. This analysis proved the validity of the relationship between the smart grid and cloud computing (Rusitschka et al, 2010).

By keeping these constraints into consideration and with the motivation of the work presented in (Lim et al, 2011), in this manuscript, a secure smart cloud framework is proposed as a ***smart model*** based AckIBE for the management of large amounts of data (big data) in homogeneous and heterogeneous cloud data centers. This chapter has threefold contributions:

- Design of smart model: A framework that supports cloud computing for processing information management related to big data, also termed as smart model, provides reasonable scalability and security.
- A security solution supported by an identity-based encryption (IBE), ID based proxy signature scheme (IDBPS-CDH) on computational Diffie-Hellman problem and identity based proxy re-encryption is introduced for the proposed smart model to provide secure communication between heterogeneous and homogeneous entities.
- Additionally, acknowledgments (AckIBE) are introduced and it is shown that how messages along with signatures and the acknowledgments are sent in a hierarchical cloud environment from one level to another.

The main contributions regarding IDBPS-CDH scheme is as follows:

- We propose and model a tight security IDBPS-CDH scheme which has more complete security and can withstand the delegator attack.
- The proposed scheme IDBPS-CDH is more efficient and it reduces the computational cost as compared to other similar existing IDBPS schemes.
- Other schemes need secure channels to transfer secret delegation keys produced during the delegation procedure of proxy signer, whereas the proposed scheme just requires ordinary channels i.e., the proposed scheme is comparatively secure and lower in cost.

The rest of this chapter is organized as follows. **Section 2** reviews the related work. **Section 3** and **Section 4** presents the proposed *Smart model* with possible security solutions. In a particular manner, **Section 3** emphasizes the proposed *Smart model* architecture whereas **Section 4** explains related solutions based on *AckIBE*. Finally, we demonstrate the security analysis in **Section 5** followed by the validation and in **Section 6**. And finally, we conclude in **Section 7**.

RELATED LITERATURE

Smart Model: Information Management

Gathering, processing and storing of information are the three important factors of management of a smart model. Various solutions have been introduced and proposed for addressing the issues related to the collection of large quantities of data. The issue of interoperability is managed by standardizing the data structures that are introduced in smart grids (Bojkovic et al, 2012; Fan et al, 2012; Wang et al, 2011).

Approaches for Security

In the literature, various security vulnerabilities have been detected (Li et al, 2009), where the smart grid deployment is huge. In order to process the information on smart meters, various methodologies have been introduced to capture certain security issues (Efthymiou et al, 2010; Kalogridis al, 2010; Li et al, 2010; chu et al, 2013). As mentioned by Wei et al. (2010), smart models are protected against cyber-attacks. Some frameworks for the security have been introduced to control the consistent factors related to the security requirements of smart model components. Rogers et al. (2010) used digital signatures and time stamps to provide the authentication among communication entities participated in the network. To have a secure computing in the cloud environment, identity based cryptography serves a good purpose as explained in (Shamir et la, 1984; Ateniese et al, 2006; Green et al, 2007; Shao et al, 2011). Coates et al. (2016) introduced the architecture of smart model's security in a specific environment. In public cloud environment, verification of remote data integrity is a major security concern. Because, after outsourcing the data, user's data can be corrupted by malicious CSP. In order to deal with security concerns, some dynamic PDP models are designed (Wang et al, 2013; Zhang et al, 2014). In (Khurana et al, 2010), general grid has an identity-based key agreement while our work emphasizes on providing a framework of security which is based on identity-based encryption, identity based proxy signature scheme and identity-based proxy re-encryption schemes to the proposed smart model.

Identity Based Cryptographic Scheme

Shamir proposed identity based cryptography that removes the requirement to detect whether certificates are valid in traditional public key scenario (Rusitschka et al, 2010). The generator of the private key (*P_KG*) is the reliable party that produces a secret key *msk* which is called the master key and also the public parameter known as *params*. The private keys are distributed in the same manner as the digital certificates are issued in any normal public key cryptography scheme. The *P_KG* authenticates users and distributes private keys in correspondence with their identities. An encryption algorithm is executed by a sender, who has *IDrec* that encrypts an original plain text message *M*. The receiver deciphers cipher-text *C* by executing the decryption algorithm in taking as the *KIDrec*, which is the private key received from the generator *P_KG*. In (Gentry et al, 2002), a methodology named hierarchical identity-based cryptography (HIBC) is introduced. HIBC is the extension of identity based cryptography, which is used in such a manner that the root *P_KG* produces private keys and authentication of identity to other users that are lower level P_KGs (Rusitschka et al, 2010).

Identity Based Proxy Re-Encryption and Other Security Encryptions

Proxy re-encryption permits a proxy to change the ciphertext created using the public key of Alice so that the changed ciphertext can be deciphered with the help of the private key of another party Bob. Green and Ateniese proposed an identity based proxy re-encryption scheme which is much closer to the framework of our proposed smart model (Green et al, 2007). Ateniese et al. (2006) proposed the first full functional proxy re-encryption scheme to perform the encryption based on related parameters. It is based on the pairing like IBE encryption scheme proposed by Boneh et al. (2008). Xiaming Hu et al. (2016) introduced secure and efficient identity-based proxy signature scheme in the standard model based on Computational Diffie-Hellman problem with proxy signature scheme. Ramesh et al. (2017) introduced an e-Stream cipher-based secure and dynamically updating policy for secure cloud storage. It examined a stream cipher called *ChaCha20* for providing security and efficient storage.

Proxy Signature Scheme

Proxy signature has attracted significant attention from scholars as well as researchers (Baek et al, 2015; Schuldt et al, 2008; Wang et al, 2015; Cao et al, 2016; Wei et al., 2014; Zhang et al, 2011; Boldyreva et al, 2012; Gu et al, 2013). But, in order to bind the flow between user's corresponding identity and the public key (usually taken as a "random" string), in proxy signature, a certificate is needed. This certificate is constructed by a trusted third party known as CA (*Certificate Authority*) in PKI. Thus, two verifications are required to be made by the receiver: for the user's certificate and for the signature. Shamir introduced the concept related to identity-based cryptography (IDB), which solves the above problem (Shamir et al, 1984). In IDB cryptography, the public key generator (*PKG*) constructs the private key, whereas the public key is the identity of the user such as an email etc.

IDB signature is combined with proxy signature to obtain a new signature type called as IDBPS (Gu et al, 2015; Zhang et al, 2003; Gu et al, 2006; Wu et al, 2007). It simplifies key management procedure in setting on the certificate. Cao and Cao (2010) were the first to propose direct construction of an IDBPS without random oracle model that was secure. But, since it was an incomplete model, it could not withstand the delegator attacks (Cao et al, 2010; Sun et al, 2013). Gu et al. (2015) introduced a detailed framework which is a security model of IDBPS. But, it could not withstand the delegator attacks. All these schemes had loose security reductions. The security proof modeled in (Katz et al, 2003)proved that an adversary may include their own constructs in different ways. Hu et al. (2015) proposed another

IDBPS scheme in the standard model. This IDBPS has security reduction and better computational efficiency. But, this scheme required a lot of system parameters. And the security reduction (2015) were not tight i.e. (a reduction is called tight if). The methodology presented in (Hu et al, 20150 also could not withstand the delegator attacks. Wang and Wei introduced an improved proxy signature scheme (Wang et al, 2016). However, their scheme also was not based on the identity. Therefore, it is still a challenge to build an IDBPS-CDH scheme secured in a complete security model in the standard model with tight security reduction. On the other hand, some of the works related to the security mechanisms have been propagated in order to make the application domain massive in various fields. By keeping the above mentioned works in consideration, in this chapter, we address the related IDBPS schemes to fill the negative overlaps occurred in the smart model security (Tewari et al, 2017; Hai et al, 2018; Zkik et al, 2017; Gou et al, 2017; Ibithal et al, 2017; Gupta et al, 2018; Gupta et al, 2016).

SECURE SMART MODEL

Smart model is an information management framework that provides scalability, flexibility and security. Management of data is designed according to these models. Also, these models use the cloud computing technology to perform the data related operations. The basic strategy we opt and follow is that the framework is constructed at three different levels of hierarchy: *top, regional and end-user* levels. The first and second level contains the entities as cloud computing centers. The lowermost level contains end-user intelligent devices.

The top level cloud is responsible to manage general devices and to collect the data taken across several regional centers of cloud environment. These regional devices of cloud are responsible for the management of lower hierarchical level, which contains various front end intelligent and thus the regional cloud, of any specific region, processes the huge amount of data occurring from such devices. In smart grids, leakage of information should be avoided because smart grids are vulnerable to insecurity and illegal breach, and it may result in fatal consequences. We further propose a security solution which makes use of IBE and IBS (Boneh et al, 2001; Green et al, 2007) and identity based proxy re-encryption (IDBPRE). The benefit of using IBE when compared with traditional public key encryption scheme is explained when identity based encryption uses identities instead of digital certificate that depends upon public key infrastructure. A lot of resources are saved for performance of computation and communication. Also, the scalability issue is resolved. Additionally, to ensure that data are received successfully by the receiver and there is no loss of data in the cloud environment. To preserve this instance, an acknowledgement is introduced, which is sent by receivers to the intended senders. These acknowledgements are sent in encrypted form so that the user deciphers it after receiving. The architecture used is depicted in **Figure. 1**. A detailed IDBPS security model that includes self-proxy and proxy private key exposure. The tight security under the new security model which is based on CDH assumption is introduced. The proposed model has complete and tight security and can resist the delegator attack. On the other hand, the proposed scheme is more efficient in the sense that its computational cost is reduced than most of the present similar IDBPS schemes. Also, our scheme requires only ordinary channels for transferring the secret delegation keys. These keys were created during the delegation procedure for the proxy signer. If we compare it with other IDBPS schemes, then we find that these other schemes need secure channels to transfer secret delegation keys. So, the proposed scheme is low in cost and more secure.

Figure 1. Architecture used in the system

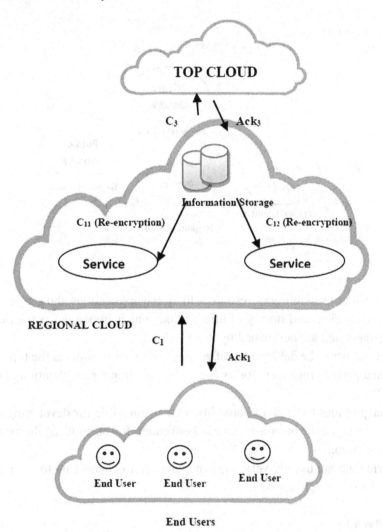

Smart Model: General Architecture

The proposed *smart model* architecture is depicted in **Figure. 2**. This contains a grid which is partitioned into various regions. A cloud computing center manages these regions. The cloud computing center can be a multi cloud environment of the form of public or private. The primary responsibility of any regional cloud center is to manage the end-user devices belonging to the region. It also to provide a processing of initial level of the information that arrive from such intelligent devices. The computing center situated at the topmost level is accountable for managing and processing the data for the whole grid. Every computing center is accountable for the deployment of these services mentioned as follows.

Figure 2. Architecture of the smart frame

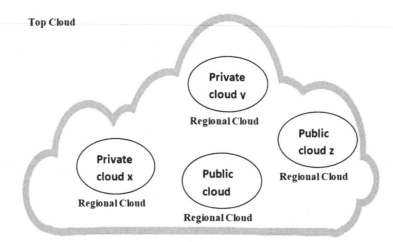

IaaS: This layer makes availability of resources to all the applications and services deployed in the system. Gathering, processing, and storing of information, which are known as the three main tasks of information management and are performed by this service.

SaaS: This layer performs the deployment of services of a smart-model at the top of the system. For example, services that permit consumers for saving and optimizing their utilization of energy (Ateniese et al, 2006) e.g. GPM.

PaaS: This layer provides tools and related libraries accountable for developing cloud computing services and applications. Platform-as-a-service is convenient for in-built requirements for the implementation of the applications.

DaaS: Smart grid data are usually very large in quantity. It is beneficial to offer statistics services related with data for service consumers.

Component Views

In this section, we introduce four basic functional clusters in our *Smart model* framework. These services are illustrated in **Figure. 3**.

Information Storage: Main information storages contain all the information accumulated from the front end intelligent devices. These storages are used in various modes of transportation using wired channel as well as wireless channel. The related statistics exist in the corresponding cluster.

General User Services: Services consumed by electricity user are general user services. Examples are to control, to monitor, and to optimize their electric utilization. This sort of service includes most of the SaaS and also PaaS services that provide libraries utilized for user services.

Control and Management Services: All services with respect to system management like governance service, monitor, task scheduling and security fall under this category.

Electricity Distribution Services: The services related to electricity distribution fall under this category. Examples include optimization service, measuring quality of service measurement, services pertaining to distribution.

Figure 3. Functionality of cloud service clusters

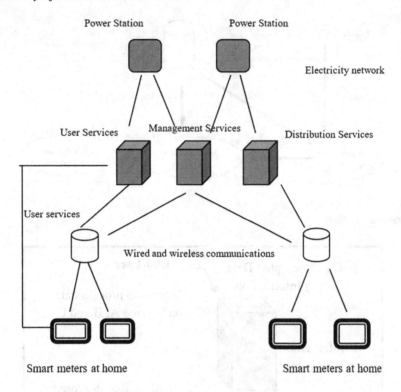

Flow of Information Management

Handling the information flow in any system is a big challenge because, the smart grid handles huge amounts of data. There exists a centralized service that is responsible for the management of information flows. The inputs are collected from various parameters such as amount of information, time of arrival, and service clusters using which a schedule related to information flow are constructed. This schedule explains the processing of information as well as the beginning and end of the flow. The centers of information and service clusters go through this schedule. The schedules created have an expiry time as well, post which new schedule need to be created. **Figure. 4** illustrates the information flow schedule.

SECURITY SOLUTIONS

As shown in **Figure. 5**, in the smart model framework, we make the following assumptions.

Figure 4. Information flow schedule

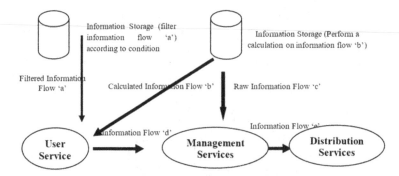

Figure 5. Proxy re-encryption

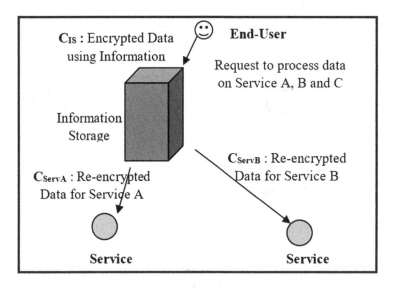

Model Description

We assume the following points while realizing the security framework.

- A generator of private key *PK_G* issues private key for the entities involved in participation, as soon as they register. *PK_G* is responsible and is reliable and holds the responsibility at the national level.
- In order to recognize the top cloud, the regional clouds and the end users, the unique strings in the form of *IDs* are used. These are used for verification as well as for signature.
- Each entity in participation gets a *PK_G* in correspondence with its identity so that the cipher-text that contains the sensitive data can be decrypted.

- Every entity in participation sends the encrypted information to the entity present only a level above. An end user sends the encrypted information to the regional cloud entities while the regional cloud entities send encrypted information to the top cloud only.
- Every entity in participation can authenticate data using the private key obtained from the *PK_G*.

The ID based proxy signature scheme is used for more security.

- Every receiver level of the information can send the acknowledgement to the sender.

Figure. 6 depicts the main idea that is framed. The top cloud is responsible for managing regional clouds. In the hierarchy, the top cloud contains distribution services, management services and power stations. The regional clouds have basic user services and information storages. The lowest hierarchy is of smart (intelligent) end-user devices.

Key Generation

Setup: Through the parameter $\psi > 1$ of security, the *PK_G* creates a secret key, also termed as the master (secret) key *mskey* and a parameters's set *params*. This parameter *params* is distributed among end users and all the clouds. Say, in case of Top cloud, procedure is followed as:

Figure 6. Hierarchical architecture

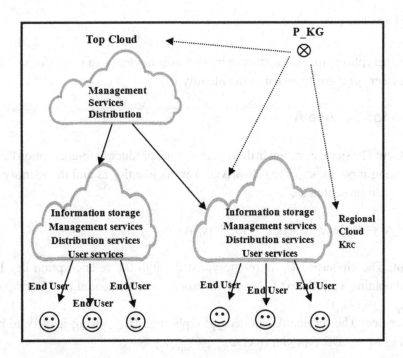

Extract_TC_Key: Once the identity TC of top cloud is obtained, the generator *PK_G* creates κ_{TC}, a private key by executing **Extract()**, the extraction algorithm of the private key which intakes identity TC as the input. It is represented as:

$\kappa_{TC} \leftarrow$ Extract_TC_Key(params, mskey, TC).

Similarly, using the identities for information storage as *IS*, service A as *Serv_A*, end user as *EndU*, the corresponding private keys are produced.

Encryption to Top Cloud

1. Encrypt_to_TC: An original message *M* can be encrypted into a ciphertext C_{TC} by any information storage on the execution of the Extract() IBE extraction algorithm.

We depict the encryption task as follows:

$C_{IS} \leftarrow$ Encrypt_to_TC (params, TC, M).

2. 2. Decrypt_TC: The ciphertext obtained is decrypted by top cloud into a decrypted message M on performing the execution algorithm called as Decrypt using the private key κ_{TC} using the identity TC. We depict the encryption task as follows:

$M \leftarrow$ Decrypt_TC(params, $\kappa_{TC,}$ C_{TC}).

Similarly, the encryption process on storage by end-user devices can be performed with the help of the **Encrypt** and **Decrypt** algorithms using the identity IS.

Re-encryption for Service A

1. **Re_enc_KGen:** The storage present in the regional cloud produces a re-encryption key Re_encK$_{IS}$ → Serv_A intaking input as κ_{IS}, the self-private key its identity *IS* and the identity of service A as *Serv_A*. This is represented as:

RencK$_{IS}$ → Serv_A ← Re_enc_KGen($\kappa_{IS,}$ IS, Serv_A).

2. **Re_Encrypt:** The ciphertext C_{IS} is re-encrypted through the re-encryption key Re_enc_K$_{IS}$ → Serv_A and obtains a ciphertext C_{Serv_A}. This process is represented by CServ$_A$ ← Re_encrypt (Re_enc_K$_{IS->Serv\_A}$, C_{IS}).
3. **Decrypt_Service:** The service A can decrypt ciphertext C_{ServA} using its private key κ_{ServA}. It is represented as M ← Decrypt_Service($\kappa_{ServA,}$ C_{ServA}).

Acknowledgement (e.g. by Regional Cloud): Any level whether topmost cloud, regional cloud or end-user can send the acknowledgement to any sender level. It is also sent in an encrypted form so that the recipient can decrypt it. The same encryption procedure is used.

ID based Proxy Signature Scheme: An identity based proxy signature scheme is constructed and used for authentication purpose by the participating entities. The procedure is described in the following section.

Security Transformation

The security framework discussed below uses IBE scheme proposed by Boneh and Franklin (2001) and Green and Ateniese's (2010) identity-based proxy re-encryption scheme. Both the schemes use the bilinear pairing e: G X G -> G_T, is a bilinear pairing. Here, the groups G and G_T are of prime order, which has the following properties:

- **Bilinear:** $\forall$ r, s $\in Z_p^*$, e(g^r, h^s) = $e(g,h)^{rs}$.
- **Non-Degeneracy:** It follows: $e(g,h) \neq 1$.
- For all g, h $\in$ G, e(g, h) can be efficiently computable.

In other words, let us infer, E_p be an elliptic curve over field F_w, $w = v^n$ where v be a large prime. Then, $E_p[\phi] = [M \in E_p | M \cdot \phi = O]$, assign the ϕ torsion sub-group of E_p for a large prime. Further, the mapping for weil–pairing generates; e: $E_p[\phi] \times E_p[\phi] \rightarrow F_{w^\beta}^*$ (where $\beta \in Z^+$ and ϕ divides ($\phi^\beta - 1$)).

Maintaining Confidentiality

This happens in three phases as (i) Key Generation, (ii) Encryption to top cloud (iii) Proxy Re-Encryption to Information Storage. The Key generation phase happens in the below manner.

- **Key_setup:** The party PKG takes G and G_T, two multiplicative cyclic groups of prime order p and an admissible pairing e: G x G $\rightarrow$ G_T, a generator g $\in$ G and hash functions $H_1:\{0,1\}^* \rightarrow$ G and $H_2:G_T \rightarrow \{0,1\}^n$, n $\in Z_p^+$ where n is the size of the plaintext. We then take random $u \in Z_p^*$ and calculate a $\in g^u$. The top cloud sets secret master secret key *mskey* = u and a set of public parameters params = (G,G_T,e,g,a,H_1,H_2). The parameters params is distributed to top, regional and end-users by key generator *PubKG*.
- **Extract_TC_Key:** On obtaining the identity of top cloud TC, the generator PubKG computes H1 $(TC)^u \in$ G and produces the private key κ_{TC} = H1(TC) ^{u}.

Similarly, private keys of Information Storage (*IS*), Service A (*Serv_A*), End User (*EU*) are produced using the extract algorithm.

Encryption to Top Cloud

- **Extract_to_TC:** A regional cloud entity can encipher an original message M with the help of params parameter and the identity TC of top cloud using following calculations. Take random value v where, $v \in Z_p^*$. Calculate $C_1 = g^v$ and $C_2 = M \cdot e(a, H1(TC))^u$. Later, we get output ciphertext as $C_{TC} = (C_1, C_2)$.
- **Decrypt_TC:** With the help of private key $\kappa_{TC} = H1(TC)^v$, the top cloud can decrypt a received ciphertext $C_{TC} = (C_1, C_2)$ into M, where $M = C_2/(e(C_1, \kappa_{TC}))$.

Similarly, encryption to information storage located in regional clouds can be performed by the end user devices, where identity *IS* is used for information storage.

Proxy Re-Encryption to Information Storage

- **Re_enc_KGen:** A re-encryption key is received by information storage possessing identity as *IS* by calculating $Re\_enc\_K_{IS \to ServA} = (Rk_1, Rk_2, Rk_3)$. Here we compute $Rk_1 = g^x$ and $Rk_2 = L \cdot e(a, H_1(Serv\_A))^x$ and $Rk_3 = K_{IS}^{-1} \cdot H_2(T)$. We take random $x \in Z_p^*$. and $L \in G_T$.
- **Re_encrypt:** We have the re-encryption key $Re\_enc\_K_{IS \to ServA} = (Rk_1, Rk_2, Rk_3)$. The ciphertext $C_{IS} = (C_1, C_2)$ is re-encrypted by service A and a new ciphertext is calculated as $C_{Serv\_A} = (C_1, C_2, e(C_1, Rk3), Rk1, Rk2)$.
- **Decrypt_Service:** Let $C_{servA} = (C_1', C_2', Rk_1', Rk_2') = (C_1, C_2 \cdot e(C_1, Rk3), Rk_1, Rk_2)$.

Since we have $K_{servA} = H1(Serv\_A)^u$, the service A calculates $L = RK_2' / e(K_{serv\_A}, Rk_1')$. Later, we calculate $M = C_2' / e(C_1', H_2(L))$.

Authentication Service

CDH Problem and CDH Assumption: We have a three tuple (f, f^i, f^j), where f is a generator of G_0 and i, j are random numbers from Z_p, the CDH problem is to find f^{ij}. It is said that $(\in, t)$ CDH assumption holds if there is no algorithm that executes with the time at most t and with the probability at least $\in$ is able to solve the given CDH problem.

ID based Proxy Signature Scheme (IDBPS): An ID based Proxy Signature Scheme is used. It contains five components: *P_Setup*, *P_Extract*, *P_Delegate*, *Proxy Sign* and *P_Verify*.

P_Setup: The generator *P_KG* randomly take $g' \in G_0$ and $b \in Z_p^*$ and calculates $g_1 = g'^b$. Then at random we pick $g_0, g_2, g_3, g_4, g_5 \in G_0$ and $t_0, t_1 \in Z_p^*$ and then set $e(g', g') = S$. Additionally, we define three collision resistant hash functions $H_0: \{0,1\}^* \to Z_p$; $H_1: \{0,1\}^* \times \{0,1\}^* \times G_0 \to G_0$; $H_2: \{0,1\}^* \times \{0,1\}^* \times G_0 \times G_0 \to Z_p$. The public parameter is $(G_0, G_T, e, g_0, g_2, g_3, g_4, g_5, S, H_0, H_1, H_2)$ and the master key is g_2^b.

P_Extract: *P_KG* produces a private key for a given identity $ID \in Z_p^*$ by using the following procedure:

- Random elements y_0, $y_1 \in Z_p^*$ and a random $D \in G_0$ are selected
- Calculate $k=e(D, g_4 g'^{ID} g_5^{y0})$. The value k is checked $k = S$ then $\psi = 1$. And $t\psi$ denotes t1, or if $k \neq S$ then $\psi = 0$ and $t\psi$ denotes t0.
- Calculate $d_{ID} = (d_1, d_2) = (g_2^b (g_0 g_2 t_\psi g_3^{ID})^{y1}, g'^{y1})$. The private key of ID is (d_1, d_2, y_0, D).

P_Delegate: We assume ID_o as identity of original signer (Osigner) and private key is d_{IDo}, and the ID_p is the identity of proxy signer (Psigner) and private key is d_{IDp}. For delegating the signing capability of Osigner to Psigner, a warrant $Wr \in Z_p^*$ is first defined by Osigner which includes the Osigner's identity and Psigner's identity as well, and the relation of delegation. Then it does as follows.

1. Osigner calculates $So=H_1(Wr, T, d_{IDo})$. Here T is a time stamp. Sends *(So, W, T)* to Psigner.
2. If the delegation of Osigner is accepted by the Psigner, then Psigner calculates $s_p=H_2(Wr, T, S_o, d_{IDp})$. Sends *(Wr, T, s_p)* to PubKG. However, if the delegation request is rejected by Psigner, then it is aborted.
3. After PubKG receives *(Wr, T, s_p)*, it calculates $S_o' = H_1(Wr, T, d_{IDo})$ and verification is done if $s_p = H_2(Wr, T, S_o', d_{IDp})$. If the equation does not hold, then it is aborted. Else, *W* is made as a delegation identity by PubKG and uses the PExtract algorithm to calculate a private key $d_{Wr} = (d_{Wr1}, d_{Wr2})$ of the identity *Wr*.
4. Then, PubKG calculates $S_{Wr}=d_{Wr1} +H_1(Wr, T, d_{IDp})$ and *(S_{Wr}, d_{Wr2})* is sent to Psigner.
5. After receiving *(S_{Wr}, d_{Wr2})*, Psigner calculates $d_{Wr1} = S_{Wr} - H_1(Wr, T, d_{IDp})$.

In the end, Psigner receives the proxy private key $d_{wr} = (d_{wr1}, d_{wr2})$ of the delegation *Wr*. It is to be noted that since H_1 and H_2 are both collision resistant hash functions, all the transmission of above information do not need secure channel. It is important to use ordinary channel.

Proxy_Sign: Psigner uses the following algorithm. We have $ID \in Z_p^*$, (d_1, d_2, y_0, D) of ID and msg $\in \{0,1\}^*$ which is the message that is being signed. The signature is calculated by the signer as follows:

- Select at random $y_2 \in Z_p^*$.
- Calculate $\partial 1 = d1 . (g_4 g_5^{H0(msg)})^{y2}$, $\partial 2 = d2 = g'^{y1}$, $\partial 3 = g'^{y2}$, $\partial 4 = D$.
- The signature is $\partial = (y_0, \partial 1, \partial 2, \partial 3, \partial 4)$.

P_Verify: We have the signature $(y_0, \partial 1, \partial 2, \partial 3, \partial 4)$ on ID and the msg. Using these, the algorithm is explained as:

- Calculates $e(\partial 4, g_4 g'^{ID} g_5^{y0})$ to get the value of ψ.
- Calculate: $e(\partial 1, g') = e(g_2, g_1) e(g_0 g_2 t_\psi g_3^{ID}, \partial 2) e(g_4 g_5^{H_0(msg)}, \partial 3)$.

The signature is accepted if the above equation holds true.

SECURITY ANALYSIS

IBE scheme

The IBE scheme's correctness can be proven easily. The correctness of *IDBPS* scheme is proved as follows. Let $C_{Serv\_A} = (C_1', C_2', Rk_1', Rk_2') = (C_1, C_2, e(C_1, Rk_3), Rk_1, Rk_2)$.

$Rk_2'/e(K_{serv\_A}, Rk_1') = Rk_2'/e(H_1(Serv\_A)^u, Rk_1)$

$= L \cdot e(a, H_1(Serv\_A))^x / e(H_1(Serv\_A)^u, Rk_1)$

$= L \cdot e(g^u, H_1(Serv\_A))^x / e(H_1(Serv\_A)^u, Rk_1)$

$= L \cdot e(H_1(Serv\_A)^u, g^x)/e(H_1(Serv\_A)^u, Rk_1)$

$= L$

$C_2'/e(C_1', H_2(L)) = C_2.e(C_1, Rk_3)/e(C_1, H_2(L))$

$= C_2.e(C_1, K_{IS}^{-1}. H_2(L)) / e(C_1, H_2(L))$

$= C_2 . e(C_1, K_{IS}^{-1})$

$= M.e(a, H_1(IS))^v . e(C_1, K_{IS}^{-1})$

$= M.e(g^v, H_1(IS)^u).e(C_1, K_{IS}^{-1})$

$= M$

For ID Based Proxy Signature Scheme

The correctness of IDBPS scheme can be proved as:

$e(\partial 1, g') = e(g_2^b(g_0 g_2 t_\psi g_3^{ID})^{y1} e(g_4 g_5^{H_0(msg)})^{y2}, g')$.

$= e(g_2^b, g') e(g_0 g_2 t_\psi g_3^{ID}, g'^{y1}) e(g_4 g_5^{H_0(msg)}, g'^{y2})$.

$= e(g_2, g_1) e(g_0 g_2 t_\psi g_3^{ID}, \partial 2) e(g_4 g_5^{H_0(msg)}, \partial 3)$.

Security Analysis

In this section, we analyze the security aspects related to IDPSE-CDH. The proposed methodology restricts the delegator attacks without random oracles completely (Fang et al, 2009). On the other hand, there may be a possibility of attacks with random oracle restrictions. In order to restrict the random oracle instances, a related scenario has been framed to give constant overlay. These factors are analyzed in the below manner.

Section 1: Preliminaries and definitions

Group G_1 belongs to a cyclic additive group. It maps to a cyclic multiplicative group G_2 by Weil pairing. The order of G_1 and G_2 is not necessarily prime. In this chapter, we consider the case where the order q of G_1 and G_2 is a product of some large primes.

Definition 1: *(CDH problem) Let a; b be chosen from* Z_q *at random and P be chosen from* G_1 *at random. Given (P; aP; bP), compute* $abP \in G_1$. G_1 is referred to as a gap Diffie-Hellman (*GDH*) group if DDHP can be solved in polynomial time and no polynomial algorithm can solve *CDHP* with non-negligible advantage within polynomial time (IEEE et al, 2011; Chu et al, 2013; Wei et al, 2010).

Definition 2: Let a polynomial time probabilistic algorithm Υ be a *GDH* parameter generator. Taking a security parameter ℓ, $\Upsilon(1^\ell)$ generates two cyclic group G_1 and G_2. For a sufficiently large ℓ an algorithm A has advantage $\in(\ell)$ in solving the *CDHP* problem for Υ, if ℓ is sufficiently large,

$$Adv_\gamma = \Pr[A(G_1, G_2, \hat{e}, P, aP, bP)$$
$$= abP \mid (G_1, G_2, \hat{e}) \leftarrow \gamma(1^\ell), P \in G_1, a, b \in Z_q] > \in(\ell)$$

Setup of a Proxy key: Assume that Alice is the original signer and Bob is her proxy. Alice delegates a signing right to Bob by issuing a proxy tuple containing a proxy signing key. A sound proxy signature protocol must meet the following requirements.

- A proxy signature recipient is convinced of the authenticity of a proxy, i.e., the proxy signer Bob is authorized for proxy signing on behalf of the original signer Alice.
- Alice cannot sign on behalf of Bob.

Setup: (Alice) Run $\Upsilon(1^\ell)$ with the input $\ell \in Z$ and set $(G_1, G_2, \hat{e})$ as the output. Pick strong hash functions $H_1: \{0, 1\}^* \rightarrow G_1$, $H_2: \{0, 1\}^* \times G_1 \times G_1 \rightarrow G_2$.

KeyGen1: (Alice) Choose $s \in Z_q$ as Alice's secret key and then compute the associated public key $P' \leftarrow sP$, where $P \in G_1$ is public.

Extract: (Alice) Input: the $ID_A \in \{0,1\}^*$ of Alice and the $ID_B \in \{0,1\}^*$ of Bob.

Output: $Q_{ID_A} \leftarrow H_1(ID_A), Q_{ID_B} \leftarrow H_1(ID_B)$, and $Q_{ID} = Q_{ID_A} + Q_{ID_B}$.

KeyGen2: (Bob) Input: $x \in Z_q$ and Q_{ID}. Output: $X \leftarrow xQ_{ID}$. X is sent to Alice.

KeyGen3: (Alice) Input: $u \in Z_q$, s, Q_{ID}, a, where $a \in \{0,1\}^*$ is the proxy agreement.

Output: proxy public key $U \leftarrow uP'$, $v \leftarrow H_2(a, U, X)$ and proxy signing key $K \leftarrow s(uX + vQ_{ID})$. The proxy tuple consists of (ID_A, ID_B, a, X, K). Send the tuple to Bob. Make U public.

Lemma 1. *If algorithm A_0 is defined for an adaptively chosen message and ID attack to our proxy signature protocol with running time t_0 and advantage $\in_{01}$. Then, there is an algorithm A_1, for adaptively chosen message attack and a given ID, that has the running time $t_1 \leq t_0$ and advantage $\in_1 \geq \frac{\in_{01}}{q_{H2}}(1 - 1/\phi)$ where ϕ_{H1} denotes the number of queries to random oracle H_1 asked by A_0.*

Proof: Now, we infer that for any ID, algorithm A_0 queries G(ID) and Extract(ID) at maximum once, with none lack of generality. Our algorithm A_1;

- Selects a random $s \in \{1, 2, \ldots, q_{H_2}\}$, further algorithm A_0 asked the ith query to hash function H_2 and denote it by ID_i. Let $ID_i^!$ be a ID, if it holds $i=s$ and ID_i else, $H_2(ID_i^!)$, Extract($ID_i^!$), Proxy_sign($ID_i^!$, msg) respectively.
- Then, execute algorithm A_0 with the given system parameters; algorithm A_1 responds to A_0 queries to H_1, H_2, Extract and Proxy_sign by computing $H_1^!, H_2^!$, Extract$^!$, Proxy_sign$^!$ respectively. Now, the output of algorithm A_0 is $(ID_{out}, msg, \partial)$.
- If it holds $ID_{out} = ID$ and $(ID_{out}, msg, \partial)$ is valid, then the output values would be $(ID_{out}, msg, \partial)$ else reject.

However, the allocations produced through hash function, $H_2^!$, Extract[!] and Proxy_sign[!] are distinct from those produced by H_2, Extract and Proxy_sign of proposed model. Further, algorithm A_0 doesn't extract any knowledge from queries result. So,

Pr [(ID$_{out}$, msg, ∂) is valid] $\gtrsim \in_0$.

As H_2 represents a random oracle functionality, the output of probability from algorithm A_0 is valid without the help of any queries from $H_2^!(ID_{out}) = ID_i$ is insignificant. Especially,

Pr[ID$_{out}$ = ID$_i$ for some i |(ID$_{out}$, msg, ∂) is valid] $\gtrsim 1 - 1\backslash\phi$

As, s is randomly chosen, so we have;

Pr [ID$_{out}$ = ID$_s$| ID$_{out}$ =ID$_i$ for some i] $\gtrsim 1/q_{H_2}$, on associating all these values together,

Pr [ID$_{out}$ = ID$_s$ = ID and (ID$_{out}$, msg, ∂) is valid] $\gtrsim \in_{01} (1 - 1/\phi) \cdot (1/q_{H_2})$ as wanted.

With this we state that the algorithm A_1 may be regarded as an adversary to the non-ID based method obtained by using solving an ID in ID based proxy signature scheme, that is allowed to get right of entry to the extraction oracle to achieve secret keys related to identities specific from the fixed one in addition to the signing oracle and hash features.

Lemma 2: *If A_1 launches an adaptively chosen message attack with a fixed ID against our scheme for a running time t1 by querying random oracle H_2 and the signer at most ϕ_{H2}, and ϕ S times, respectively, and advantage $\in_1 \geq 10(\phi_S + 1)(\phi_S + \phi_{H_2})/\phi$, then the CDHP can be solved with probability $\in_2$ $\geq 1/9$ with running time $t_2 \leq 23\phi_{H2}t_1/\in_1$.*

Theorem 1: An adaptively chosen message attack and an *ID* attack can be launched by an algorithm A_0 against our system by querying random oracles H_1, H_2 and the signer at most ϕ_{H_1} , ϕ_{H_2} , and and ϕ_S times, respectively, and has running time t_0 and advantage $\in_1 \geq 10(\phi_S + 1)(\phi_S + \phi_{H_2})/(\phi - 1)$, then Computational Diffie-Hellman Problem can be solved with probability $\geq 1/9$ and with running time

$$\leq \frac{23\phi_{H1}\phi_{H2}t_0}{\in_{01} (1 - 1/\phi)} \equiv T_1.$$

Proof of security for our protocol: We now prove security of our proxy signature scheme based on the lemmas above. Assume that there present an original signer in the Regional Cloud (Alice), a proxy in the Regional Cloud (Bob), and a signature recipient in the top cloud (Chris). There exist three possible attacks against our protocol.

Scenario 1: Proxy Signer Against Original Signer

Proxy signer plays a game with original signer and tries to extract Original Signer's secret key that can be used to authorize proxy signers. The proxy signing key is constructed by using a variant of Schnorr's signature algorithm. Actually, both *a* and *X* (see '*Setup of a Proxy key*' explained in **Section 1** as preliminaries) are signed by Alice using her private key $sQID$. The attack by algorithm A_0 should now be an adaptively chosen message plus adaptively chosen ID_A and IDB. We now denote A_0 by A_0'. Therefore, in the implementation of query, A_0'has to ask random oracle H_1, qH_1 querying questions for each of chosen ID_A and ID_B. A_1 needs to randomly replace an adaptively chosen ID in each of two separate sets of queries. This game is referred as Game B. As a result a new security proof and a lemma has been generated.

Lemma 3: Assume that A_0' queries H_1 for ID_A and ID_B with running time t_0 respectively, and has advantage $\in_{02}$. Then, there is an algorithm A_1, for adaptively chosen message attack and the given ID_A and ID_B, which has the running time $t_1 \leq t_0$ and advantage, where $\in_1 \geq \dfrac{\in_{02}}{\phi_{H_1}\phi_{H'_1}}(1-1/\phi)^2$ where $(\phi_{H_1}, \phi_{H'_1})$ are the numbers of queries to H_1 w.r.t (ID_A and ID_B) asked by A_0', respectively. It can be proven straightforward from **Lemma 1**, by noting that the queries for ID_A and ID_B are independently processed. Accordingly, we need to amend **Theorem 1** in the below manner.

Theorem 2: An algorithm A_0' can launch an adaptively chosen message and ID attack against our system by querying H_1 for ID_A and ID_B at most qH_1, qH_1' times, and H_2 and the signer at most qH_2, and q_S times, with running t_0 respectively and advantage $\in_{02} \geq \dfrac{10(\phi_S+1)(\phi_S+\phi_{H_2})\phi_{H_1}\phi_{H'_1}}{\phi(1-1/\phi)^2}$, then CDHP can be solved with probability $\geq 1/9$ and with running time $\leq \dfrac{23\phi_{H_1}\phi_{H'_1}\phi_{H_2}t_0}{\in_{02}(1-1/\phi)} \equiv T_2$.

The algorithm A_0' gives the output as a proxy tuple $(ID_{out}, ID'_{out}, a, X, K)$. If (ID_{out}, ID'_{out}) happens to be (ID_A, IDB) and it satisfies Verify 1, then the proxy tuple is valid. According to Forking Lemma (Cha et al, 2003; Pointcheval et al, 2000), we can obtain two valid proxy tuples, $(ID_{out}, ID'_{out}, a, X, K)$ and $(ID_{out}, ID'_{out}, a', X, K')$, where uX in K, K' is treated as a signature commitment. As a result, A_1 finds two equations $K = s(uX + vQID)$ and $K' = s(uX+v'QID)$, with the probability and time described in **Theorem 2**. The secret key can be found: $sQID = (K–K')/(v – v')$. This implies the correctness of **Theorem 2** in this security proof.

Scenario 2: Original Signer Against Proxy Signer

Original signer plays a game with Proxy signer with an aim on extracting Proxy signer's secret key xQ_{ID}. The success in this game will gain the right to sign on behalf of Proxy Signer. The game is played on the *SKP*. We can still apply the proof model that has been used in Game B. **Lemma 3** and **Theorem 2** are still correct to the *SKP*. As a result, A_0' outputs a proof tuple, $(ID_{out}, ID'_{out}, m, X, \Theta, C)$, which is valid if $(ID_{out}, ID'_{out}) = (ID_A, ID_B)$ and it satisfies Verify 2. Again, based on Forking Lemma, A_1 can find two valid proofs, $(ID_A, ID_B, m, X, \Theta, C)$ and $(ID_A, ID_B, m', X, \Theta, C')$, with the probability and running time, described in **Theorem 2**. The equations w.r.t the proofs are $C=(\theta - cx)Q_{ID}$ and $C' = (\theta - c'x)Q_{ID}$, from which we can find the secret key xQ_{ID}.

Scenario 3: Signature Recipient Against Proxy Signer

Signature recipient plays a game with Proxy signer to extract Proxy signer's secret proxy key. Our proxy signature is more secure than a normal signature, because to break our scheme, Signature Recipient needs to extract two secret keys K and xQ_{ID}. A_0' and A_1 should now play two separate games against K and xQ_{ID}, respectively. The game against K is the same as that proposed by Cha and Cheon (2003) as summarized in the preceding subsection. The game against xQ_{ID} is the same as that of **Scenario 2**.

Remark$_1$: Scenario 3 can be considered as an attack which is carried out through two independent attacks or two independent approaches to solve two CDHPs respectively. From Theorems **1 and 2**, in **Scenario 3** if there are A_0 *and* A_0' satisfying the conditions in **Theorems 1 and 2** then the probability of solving two Computational Diffie-Hellman Problems respectively is at least 1/81 with running time $\leq \max(T_1, T_2)$.

Lemma 4: *If there may be an algorithm A_1, for an adaptively chosen message attack and given ID attack to our proposed model, which queries H_1, H_2, Proxy_sign and Extract at maximum* q_{H_1}, q_{H_2} and q_E *times respectively and has execution time* t_1 *and advantage* $\in_{01} \gtrsim 10(q_s + 1)(q_s + q_{H_2})/(\phi)$ *then CDHP may be solved within desired time* $\gtrsim (12068\, q_{H_1} t_1)/\in_{01}$.

Lemma 5: *If there may be an algorithm A_0, for an adaptively chosen message attack and given ID attack to our proposed model, which queries H_1, H_2, Proxy_sign and Extract at maximum* q_{H_1}, q_{H_2} and q_E *times respectively and has execution time* t_0 *and advantage* $\in_{01} \gtrsim 10(q_s + 1)(q_s + q_{H_2})/(\phi - 1)$ *then CDHP may be solved within desired time* $\gtrsim (12068\, q_{H_1} t_0)/\in_{01}(1 - (1/\phi))$.

VALIDATION AND PLATFORM USAGE

In this section, we provide a particular scenario through the usage of platform. We have participating entities as ***Top cloud***, entities in the ***Regional Cloud*** and ***End-user***. The scenario shows private key generation of the entities, Signature Generation and Encryption, Decryption and Signature Verification, Acknowledgment sent by a sender and received by the receiver. Let the confidential message be ***"SM8||75KW||Kolkata"***. The below mentioned executed scenarios illustrate the operational possibilities w.r.t the message applied at various services. All the considered operations are depicted in **Figure. 7 (a, b, c, d, and e)**.

1. **Figure. 7 (a) -First Step**: The entities of top and regional cloud and the end users are registered and their private keys are generated.
2. **Figure. 7 (b) -Second Step**: The smart meter makes use of the regional center identity to encipher its confidential message with respect to the daily consumption of electricity. Along with this, a signature is also generated based on IBS scheme and both the encrypted message (cipher text) and the signature are sent to the Regional center (server).
3. **Figure. 7(c) -Third step:** The received message is decrypted by the regional center using its generated private key and also verified for authentication using verification process of IDBPSE scheme.
4. **Figure. 7(d) -Fourth Step:** The regional center sends an encrypted acknowledgement to the sender (here smart meter).The encryption and decryption process is done by using the same IBE scheme.

Figure 7(a). Registration of entities in Regional Cloud, Top Cloud, End-user, Service A

....................Confidentiality Services....................

Key Generation:

Private Key of TC :
29745781920769038953095469878117538328272777619124352313125521694475111662299529777096127753070215866234 6240Private Key of IS :
26668310566844142170634802648243445688027826915030839302045913457618782658874658145988115292858240121250 3684Private Key of EU :
3797612680421135477354293808941257924858924313616449400659868345356362279500640257900642673697299666592 54453

Private Key of Serv_A :
53027653833315927028183302836687205668398808162458352172494050947257143825605397537205517374083945472798 8161

Figure 7(b). Signature Generation and Encryption by sender

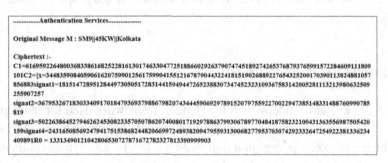

....................Authentication Services....................

Original Message M : SM9||45KW||Kolkata

Ciphertext :-
C1=6169592264800368338616825228161301746330477251886602926379074745189274265376879376599157228460911180 9101C2={x=3448359084059061620759901256175990415512167879044322418151902688922765432520017039011382488105 7856883signat1=18151472895128449730505172831441594944726523883073474523231093675831420052811132139806325 09255907257
signat2=3679532671830334091701847936937988679820743444590692978915207975592270022947385148331488760990785
819
signat3=5022638645279462624530823357050786207400801719297886379930678977048418758232100431363556987505420
159signat4=2431650856924794175153868244820669972489382094795593130068277953703074292332647254922381336234
409891R0 = 13313490121042806530727871672782327813390999903

Figure 7(c). Decryption and signature verification by the receiver

Decrypted Message :-
SM9||45KW||Kolkata
Accepted: Signature Verified.

Figure 7(d). Acknowledgment sent by the receiver to the sender

Original Message M :
Acknowlegment:
TC: Message Received.

Ciphertext:
C1=6583866038307379107164993997887034085567491960313622423218838112096020273590817112834730733985371299124131041 2720C2={x=26458511347635550420353636241167339698212171382090861128029086996289005282885027889026700917346199688870 391069signat1=171073132477026242171936072794604401799324665806127485355007700099382381186152279969854529785501835 7502526448signat2=455841986920210150314919169431365645704270638156268494358013388235141665242037567170325134658406 5968636837086signat3=43178936926019118909329161565772468893520933135632564030011630682307093790510714183130989457 50048836481993684signat4=849469018633824660618105786422057190010866430989906113373582170049406736973494625874120319 620651120089874697R0 = 4405332112479901315836414639093418065649504485502

5.   **Figure. 7(e) -Final Step:** The smart meter receives the acknowledgment by decrypting the received data.

Performance

We may observe that the verification process is most expensive and the signing procedure is less expensive by assuming that the pairing operation *PO* costs more expensive than a point multiplication *M* of $E(F_w)$. Note that the infeasible security of the ID based signature scheme relies upon on the scale of ω^β as long as ϕ has a small cofactor. Since, the pairing operation *PO* is comparable to an exponential operation E_p in F_{ω^β}, so the signing value remains constant on changing the curve. Apart from this, the size of signature also remains small as the signing operation doesn't execute any pairing operation. Table 1 shows the comparison metrics in terms of performance of the proposed model with other existing models.

CONCLUSION AND FUTURE SCOPE

This chapter introduces a smart model which is a general framework used for managing data information in smart grids. The proposed framework is based on cloud computing technology and is formulated at three levels of hierarchy, i.e. *top, regional and end-user* levels. The top cloud manages the regional cloud whereas every regional cloud handles data received from various front-end intelligent devices. Additionally, we applied acknowledgement scheme so that the sender receives the feedback from the destined receiver to ensure that the data are not lost and has been delivered successfully.

We have also described the architecture showing that how entities in regional cloud, top cloud and end-user interact and transfer confidential data, signature and acknowledgement within the system. Furthermore, we utilize Identity-based Proxy Signature scheme in the standard model based on Compu-

Figure 7(e). Acknowledgment received by the sender

```
Decrypted Message :
Acknowlegment:
TC: Message Received.
Accepted: Signature Verified.
```

Table 1. Performance metrics

Scheme	Total computation overhead	Integrity Validation Adaptability
Wang (2013)	$6 \cdot PO + (2C + 1) \cdot M + 3 \cdot E_p + C \cdot H$	No
Zhang (2014)	$5 \cdot PO + (4 \cdot C + 1) \cdot M + 3 \cdot E_p + (C-1) \cdot H$	No
Proposed model	$4 \cdot PO + 4 \cdot M + 1 \cdot E_p + 6 \cdot H$	yes

(PO= pairing operation, M= point multiplication, E_p = exponential operation and H = hash function)

tational Diffie-Hellman Problem. This provides tight security reduction and complete security, including resisting the delegator attack. It has more efficient performance and less computational cost than other similar existing schemes. As a future work, the efficiency of this framework can be further extended by using Identity-based Conditional Proxy Re-encryption. This scheme is secure against the chosen cipher text and identity attack in the random oracle model. Furthermore, in place of the standard model, random oracle model can be used to secure our IDBPS scheme from various attacks.

REFERENCES

Ateniese, G., Fu, K., Green, M., & Hohenberger, S. (2006). Improved proxy re-encryption schemes with applications to secure distributed storage. *ACM Transactions on Information and System Security*, *9*(1), 1–30. doi:10.1145/1127345.1127346

Baek, J., Vu, Q. H., Liu, J. K., Huang, X., & Xiang, Y. (2015). A Secure Cloud Computing Based Framework for Big Data Information Management of Smart Grid. IEEE Transactions on Cloud Computing, 3(2).

Bojkovic, Z., & Bakmaz, B. (2012). Smart grid communications architecture: A survey and challenges. *Proc. 11th Int. Conf. Appl. Comput. Appl. Comput. Sci.*, 83–89.

Boldyreva, A., Palacio, A., & Warinschi, B. (2012). Secure proxy signature schemes for delegation of signing rights. *Journal of Cryptology*, *25*(1), 57–115. doi:10.100700145-010-9082-x

Boneh, D., & Franklin, M. K. (2001). Identity-based encryption from the weil pairing. *Proc. 21st Annu. Int. Cryptol. Conf. Adv. Cryptol.*, 2139, 213–229.

Boneh, D., & Hamburg, M. (2008). Generalized identity based and broadcast encryption schemes. *International Conference on the Theory and Application of Cryptology and Information Security*, 455-470. 10.1007/978-3-540-89255-7_28

Boneh, D., Lynn, B., & Shacham, H. (2001). Short signatures from the weil pairing. Advances in Cryptology, 2248, 514-532. doi:10.1007/3-540-45682-1_30

Cao, F., & Cao, Z. F. (2010). An identity based proxy signature scheme secure in the standard model. In *Proceeding of GRC 10*, (pp. 67–72). IEEE Computer Society. 10.1109/GrC.2010.174

Cao, H., Zhang, J., Liu, J., & Li, Z.-Y. (2016). A new quantum proxy multisignature scheme using maximally entangled seven-qubit states. *International Journal of Theoretical Physics*, *55*(2), 774–780. doi:10.100710773-015-2715-y

Cha, J. C., & Cheon, J. H. (2003). An identity-based signature from gap Diffie-Hellman groups. In *PKC 2003*. Lecture Notes in Computer Science. Springer Verlag.

Chu, C.-K., Liu, J. K., Wong, J. W., Zhao, Y., & Zhou, J. (2013). Privacy preserving smart metering with regional statistics and personal enquiry services. *Proc. 8th ACM SIGSAC Symp. Inf., Comput. Commun. Soc.*, 369–380. 10.1145/2484313.2484362

Dharavath, Mishra, & Edla. (n.d.). Secure Data Storage in Cloud: An e-Stream Cipher-Based Secure and Dynamic Updation Policy. *Arabian Journal for Science and Engineering*, 1-11.

Duff, J. (2009). Smart grid challenges. *Proc. Workshop High Perform. Trans. Syst.* Available: http://www.hpts.ws/papers/2009/session4/duff.pdf

Efthymiou, C., & Kalogridis, G. (2010). Smart grid privacy via anonymization of smart metering data. *Proc. 1st Int. Conf. Smart Grid Commun.*, 238–243. 10.1109/SMARTGRID.2010.5622050

Fan, Z., Kulkarni, P., Gormus, S., Efthymiou, C., Kalogridis, G., Sooriyabandara, M., ... Chin, W. (2012, January). Smart grid communications: Overview of research challenges, solutions, and standardization activities. *IEEE Communications Surveys and Tutorials*, *15*(1), 21–38. doi:10.1109/SURV.2011.122211.00021

Fang, L., Susilo, W., & Wang, J. (2009). Anonymous conditional proxy re-encryption without random oracle. In *International Conference on Provable Security*, (pp. 47-60). Springer Berlin Heidelberg. 10.1007/978-3-642-04642-1_6

Farhangi, H. (2010, January/February). The path of the smart grid. *IEEE Power & Energy Magazine*, *8*(1), 18–28. doi:10.1109/MPE.2009.934876

Gentry, C., & Silverberg, A. (2002). Hierarchical id-based cryptography. *Proceedings of ASiACRYPT '02*, 548-566.

Gou, Z., Yamaguchi, S., & Gupta, B. B. (2017). Analysis of various security issues and challenges in cloud computing environment: a survey. In Identity Theft: Breakthroughs in Research and Practice (pp. 221-247). IGI Global. doi:10.4018/978-1-5225-0808-3.ch011

Green, M., & Ateniese, G. (2007). Identity-based proxy re-encryption. *Proc. 5th Int. Conf. Appl. Cryptograph. Netw. Security*, 4521, 288–306. 10.1007/978-3-540-72738-5_19

Green, M., & Ateniese, G. (2007). Identity-based proxy re-encryption. *Proc. 5th Int. Conf. Appl. Cryptograph. Netw. Security*, 4521, 288–306. 10.1007/978-3-540-72738-5_19

Gu, C. X., & Zhu, Y. F. (2006). *An efficient id-based proxy signature scheme from pairings*. Retrieved from IACR ePrint Archive: http://eprint.iacr.org/2006/158

Gu, K., Jia, W., Chen, R., & Liu, X. (2013). Secure and efficient proxy signature scheme in the standard model. *Chinese Journal of Electronics*, *22*(4), 666–670.

Gu, K., Jia, W., & Jiang, C. (2015). Efficient identity-based proxy signature in the standard model. *The Computer Journal*, *58*(4), 792–807. doi:10.1093/comjnl/bxt132

Gupta, B., Agrawal, D. P., & Yamaguchi, S. (Eds.). (2016). *Handbook of research on modern cryptographic solutions for computer and cyber security*. IGI Global. doi:10.4018/978-1-5225-0105-3

Gupta, B. B. (Ed.). (2018). *Computer and cyber security: principles, algorithm, applications, and perspectives*. CRC Press.

Hai, H., Qing, X. D., & Ke, Q. (2018). A watermarking-based authentication and image restoration in multimedia sensor networks. *International Journal of High Performance Computing and Networking*, *12*(1), 65–73. doi:10.1504/IJHPCN.2018.093846

Hayes, B. (2008). Cloud computing. *Communications of the ACM*, *51*(7), 9–11. doi:10.1145/1364782.1364786

Hu, X., Lu, H., & Xu, H. (2015). An efficient identity-based proxy signature scheme in the standard model with tight reduction. In *Proceedings of International Joint Conference, Advances in Intelligent Systems and Computing*, (pp. 309–319). Springer International Publishing. 10.1007/978-3-319-19713-5_27

Hu, X., Wang, J., & Xu, H. (2015). An improved efficient identity based proxy signature in the standard model. *International Journal of Computer Mathematics*, 58(4), 1–18.

Hu, X., Zhang, X., Wang, J., Xu, H., Tan, W., & Yang, Y. (2016). Secure and Efficient Identity-Based Proxy Signature Scheme in the Standard Model Based on Computational Diffie–Hellman Problem. *Arabian Journal for Science and Engineering*, 1–11.

Ibtihal, M., & Hassan, N. (2017). Homomorphic encryption as a service for outsourced images in mobile cloud computing environment. *International Journal of Cloud Applications and Computing*, 7(2), 27–40. doi:10.4018/IJCAC.2017040103

IEEE. (2011). *P2030/D7.0 draft guide for smart grid interoperability of energy technology and information technology operation with the electric power system (EPS), and end-user applications and loads.* P2030/D670.

Kalogridis, G., Efthymiou, C., Denic, S., Lewis, T., & Cepeda, R. (2010). Privacy for smart meters: Towards undetectable appliance load signatures. *Proc. 1st Int. Conf. Smart Grid Commun.*, 232–237. 10.1109/SMARTGRID.2010.5622047

Katz, J., & Wang, N. (2003). Efficiency improvements for signature schemes with tight security reductions. In *Proceedings of CCS'03*, (pp. 1–10). ACM Press. 10.1145/948109.948132

Khurana, H., Hadley, M., Lu, N., & Frincke, D. (2010). Smart-grid security issues. *Security Privacy*, 8(1), 81–85. doi:10.1109/MSP.2010.49

Li, H., Dai, Y., Tian, L., & Yang, H. (2009). Identity-based authentication for cloud computing. *Proc. 1st Int. Conf. Cloud Comput.*, 5931, 157–166. 10.1007/978-3-642-10665-1_14

Li, H., Mao, R., Lai, L., & Qiu, R. (2010). Compressed meter reading for delay-sensitive and secure load report in smart grid. *Proc. 1st Int. Conf. Smart Grid Commun.*, 114–119. 10.1109/SMARTGRID.2010.5622027

Lim, H., & Paterson, K. G. (2011). Identity-based cryptography for grid security. *International Journal of Information Security*, 10(1), 15–32. doi:10.100710207-010-0116-z

Pointcheval, D., & Stern, J. (2000). Security arguments for digital signatures and blind signatures. *Cryptology*, 13(3), 361–396. doi:10.1007001450010003

Rogers, K., Klump, R., Khurana, H., Aquino-Lugo, A., & Overbye, T. (2010, June). An authenticated control framework for distributed voltage support on the smart grid. *IEEE Transactions on Smart Grid*, 1(1), 40–47. doi:10.1109/TSG.2010.2044816

Rusitschka, S., Eger, K., & Gerdes, C. (2010). Smart grid data cloud: A model for utilizing cloud computing in the smart grid domain. *Proc. 1st Int. Conf. Smart Grid Commun.*, 483–488. 10.1109/SMARTGRID.2010.5622089

Schuldt, J. C. N., Matsuura, K., & Paterson, K. G. (2008). Proxy signatures secure against proxy key exposure. In *Proc. PKC2008*, (pp. 141–161). Springer. 10.1007/978-3-540-78440-1_9

Shamir, A. (1984). Identity-based cryptosystems and signature schemes. *Proc. CRYPTO Adv. Cryptol.*, *196*, 47–53.

Shao, J., Wei, G., Ling, Y., & Xie, M. (2011). Identity-based conditional proxy re-encryption. In *Communications (ICC), 2011 IEEE International Conference on*, (pp. 1-5). IEEE. 10.1109/icc.2011.5962419

Sun, Y., Yu, Y., Zhang, X., & Chai, J. (2013). On the security of an identity based proxy signature scheme in the standard model. *IEICE Transactions on Fundamentals of Electronics, Communications and Computer Science*, *E96–A*(3), 721–723. doi:10.1587/transfun.E96.A.721

Tewari, A., & Gupta, B. B. (2017). Cryptanalysis of a novel ultra-lightweight mutual authentication protocol for IoT devices using RFID tags. *The Journal of Supercomputing*, *73*(3), 1085–1102. doi:10.100711227-016-1849-x

Verma, S., & Sharma, B. (2013). An efficient proxy signature scheme based on RSA cryptosystem. *Int. J. Adv. Sci.Technol.*, *51*, 121–126.

Wang, H. (2013). Proxy provable data possession in public clouds. *IEEE Transactions on Services Computing*, *6*(4), 551–559. doi:10.1109/TSC.2012.35

Wang, J., Guo, Q., & Wang, Y. (2015). Security analysisi of a designated verifier proxy signature scheme. *Xibei Shifan Daxue Xuebao. Ziran Kexue Ban*, *51*(5), 55–58.

Wang, T., & Wei, Z. (2016). Analysis of forgery attack on one-time proxy signature and the improvement. *International Journal of Theoretical Physics*, *55*(2), 743–745. doi:10.100710773-015-2711-2

Wang, W., Xu, Y., & Khanna, M. (2011). A survey on the communication architectures in smart grid. *Computer Networks*, *55*(15), 3604–3629. doi:10.1016/j.comnet.2011.07.010

Wei, D., Lu, Y., Jafari, M., Skare, P., & Rohde, K. (2010). An integrated security system of protecting smart grid against cyber attacks. *Proc. Eur. Conf. Innovative Smart Grid Technol.*, 1–7.

Wei, J., Yang, G., & Mu, Y. (2014). Anonymous proxy signature with restricted traceability. In *Proceedings of 2014 IEEE 13th International Conference on Trust, Security and Privacy in Computing and Communications*, (pp. 575–581). IEEE Press. 10.1109/TrustCom.2014.73

Wu, W., Mu, Y., Susilo, W., Seberry, J., & Huang, X. Y. (2007). Identity based proxy signature from pairings. In *Proceeding of ATC 2007*, (pp. 22–31). Springer.

Zhang, F., & Kim, K. (2003). Efficient id-based blind signature and proxy signature from bilinear pairings. In *Proceedings of ACISP 2003*, (pp. 312–323). Springer. 10.1007/3-540-45067-X_27

Zhang, J., & Mao, J. (2011). Another efficient proxy signature scheme in the standard model. *Journal of Information Science and Engineering, 27*, 1249–1264.

Zhang, J., Tang, W., & Mao, J. (2014). Efficient public verification proof of retrievability scheme in cloud. *Cluster Computing, 17*(4), 1401–1411. doi:10.100710586-014-0394-8

Zhang, T., Lin, W., Wang, Y., Deng, S., Shi, C., & Chen, L. (2010). The design of information security protection framework to support smart grid. *Proc. Int. Conf. Power Syst. Technol.*, 1–5. 10.1109/POWERCON.2010.5666681

Zkik, K., Orhanou, G., & El Hajji, S. (2017). Secure mobile multi cloud architecture for authentication and data storage. *International Journal of Cloud Applications and Computing, 7*(2), 62–76. doi:10.4018/IJCAC.2017040105

Chapter 5
Cloud Computing Adoption:
A Scale Development Approach

Pragati Priyadarshinee
https://orcid.org/0000-0003-1408-0577
CBIT, India

ABSTRACT

The purpose of this chapter is to develop a cloud computing adoption scale for Indian manufacturing, service, and process industries. The scale development procedure has been followed from the previous studies and is refined further for clear understanding to adopt easily. In the first step, the authors have conducted a qualitative study for item selection. The second step includes pilot testing of 110 responses for measurement scale purification, and finally, they are validating the scale with 660 sample respondents through convergent validity and discriminant validity. The initial result showed very poor threshold values for the items "top management support" and "marketplace establishment," which have strong literature support. This measurement scale will help managers to evaluate the level of cloud adoption to increase the business performance. The study is a first attempt to develop a validated scale for cloud adoption that can be used in Indian industries.

DOI: 10.4018/978-1-7998-1082-7.ch005

Copyright © 2020, IGI Global. Copying or distributing in print or electronic forms without written permission of IGI Global is prohibited.

INTRODUCTION

Cloud computing is a paradigm shift that needs to understand how to adopt a new technology.

It is important to understand companies' perceptions of cloud computing and technology adoption because it can be used to determine the factors those are likely to influence the business performance (Budriene & Zalieckaite, 2012). To be competitive in the current business world, many companies need to use cloud technologies to increase their performance. Many micro businesses and SMBs are still sitting on the fence and are contemplating whether to move to or not to move to the cloud computing trend (Gupta et al., 2013). Industries normally follow developments in the technology market place to define how well associated the developments are with their own budding business strategies. The business-led adoption of cloud computing forms a further key area of which the most persistent business welfares attributed to cloud relate to the perceived occasion to extremely reduced cost and difficulty for firms(Venter & Whitley,2012).Cloud computing adoption for the organization is just like a smooth innovation process. New businesses are increasingly looking into to start with cloud computing. Cloud adoption is equally being driven from the top level organizations as well as bubbling up from the bottom level organizations. Business becomes faster, cheaper, and better when they go in for cloud adoption (Trivedi, 2013). The low costs, minimum technical expertise requirements, flexible and dynamic applications of cloud computing makes it easier for technology adopters to make the switch to cloud computing. Business operations also become more agile and effective when they can scale their IT infrastructure which makes entering markets faster as well as meet customers' demands (Nkhoma& Dang, 2013).

Ziebell et al. (2019) researched on e-HRM (Electronic Human Resource Management) that includes Information technology and human resource management. Zheng et al. (2018) stated that with the rapid development cloud technology, there is a need for security to avoid unauthorized access to cloud. Huge volume of data is generated by different organizations through the usage of cloud computing and internet of things. An efficient storage is required with minimum cost. Data sharing and collaboration is the current area of research (Sambrekar et al., 2019). Jeba et al. (2019) identified there is a rigorous need of an energy efficient cloud technology which is known as green cloud computing. The computing technologies can be arranged with a rare impact on the environment.

The virtualization is the technology, which all providers employ in cloud computing, and provides abilities for resources through the network infrastructure. Moreover, instead of having only one system on a physical server, several systems with different OS (Operating System) can be run on that hardware. This is a special advantage of using cloud computing allowing sharing hardware and software, which it leads to reducing cost. The Customers only pay for what they have to use not for all other resources (Azarnik et al., 2012). The references of whether to adopt cloud services depend on the technological expertise, company's size, and corporate culture but not on the kind of process or data to be transferred (Brender & Markov, 2013).We will empirically examine the determinants of cloud adoption through the conceptual framework, which has been extensively used to explain enterprise IT adoption, and ask whether it can appropriately explain not only adoption decisions but also the modalities of adoption offered by cloud platforms. Thus, we could understand what factors can influence companies' business performance when choosing/considering cloud services from adopters' point of view and what factors will influence companies choice of cloud deployment models (Hsu et al., 2014).

We did not find any existing scale for SMEs sectors from the cloud computing literature which can measure adoption rate in the developing Countries like India. Hence, the present study is a first attempt for developing Countries to generate, purify, and validate a measurement scale for cloud computing adoption in the context of the Indian manufacturing, service and process sector to complete this major research gap. The paper is organized into five major sections. Theoretical background of cloud computing adoption is presented in the first section, the problem description is in second section, scale development methodology is explained in third section, the results and discussion in fourth section and the paper concludes with directions for the future research and managerial implications.

LITERATURE REVIEW

The main purpose of the literature review is to know the salient work was done previously in the area of cloud computing adoption and its usability challenges at present. It also projects the intention to adopt cloud computing and its various advantages for Industry. Opportunities and challenges are emerging for cloud providers, technology adopters, and industries from the increasing availability of low-cost cloud computing solutions. In order to determine the current state of knowledge and research, an extensive review and synthesis of the literature in cloud computing adoption had been undertaken. The literature covers various definitions of cloud computing, existing models, research gaps and factors to be considered for the Study.

Basic Concepts and Definitions

The term 'cloud' is metaphorical and usually points to a huge pool of working resources such as hardware and software that are simply available by the Internet. Features of cloud computing are somewhat well-defined by the existing computing concepts such as network computing, utility computing, grid computing, and service computing(Lin and Chen,2012). According to Buyya et al. (2008), traditional system-centric resource management architecture is measured by the supply and demand of cloud resources at market equilibrium. Market-oriented cloud computing is linked to the vision, hype, and reality for supplying its services as computing utilities.

Different types of descriptions of cloud computing are available in the literature. Usually, we use the definition given by NIST which talks about different types of computing resources, characteristics of cloud computing, associated service modes and deployment models. Gartner's definition of cloud discusses scalability, elasticity, and delivery as a service. IDC has discussed cloud computing as an evolving IT model. Forrester defines cloud as an abstraction, scalability, hosting and billing mechanism. **IBM** definition of cloud computing states that it is a platform for dynamic provisions and reconfigurations of servers as required. According to **AMR Research**, "cloud computing is the next generation of software as a service, in which a complete software environment is licensed as a subscription from a software vendor and low-cost, secure and dependable IT hardware infrastructure is 'rented' from a utility computing provider on demand". **Burton Group** says cloud computing as "The set of disciplines, technologies, and business models used to render IT capabilities as on demand services" (Madhavaiah et al., 2012).

Horrigan and John (2008) observed "cloud computing as an evolving computing paradigm where data and applications exist in the cyberspace, permitting users to access their data and information through any web-connected device be it fixed or dynamic". Buyya et al. (2008) explained cloud computing as "a type of equivalent and dispersed system consisting of a group of inter-connected and virtualized computers that are provisioned dynamically and accessible as one or more unified computing resources based on service-level agreements established through cooperation between the service provider and customers". Kim (2009) defined cloud computing as "a Web browser via the Internet that is hosted by a third party provider and paying only for the computing resources and services recycled". Marks and Lozano (2010) states, "cloud computing is on-demand access to the virtualized IT resources, shared by others, paid for via subscription, accessed over the Web, and simple to use".

There are 3 Service models (SAAS, IAAS, and PAAS) and 4 Deployment models (Private, Community, Public, and Hybrid) for cloud computing adoption according to the NIST definition of cloud computing.

Recent Studies on Cloud Computing

Marston et al. (2011) stated Cloud computing adoption needs attention from the Government organizations. A SWOT analysis could be recommended, when studying the mix of internal and external factors concerning the adoption of Cloud computing by SMEs (Neves et al., 2011). Priyadarshinee et al. (2017) proposed a new paradigm by extending the Technology Organization Environment (TOE) framework with external factors, 'perceived IT security risk' and 'risk analysis' for the first time along with 'trust'. Al-Somali and Baghabra (2017) tested a model of Cloud computing adoption that is influenced by individual characteristics, organisational context, technological context and social context. Ouf and Nasr (2015) stated that cloud computing is the best solution for managing Big-Data. Hence, there is no doubt that the future belongs to the cloud computing. Bhushan and Gupta (2017) discussed the taxonomy of security issues in cloud, taxonomy of DDoS (Distributed denial of service) attacks, and taxonomy of DDoS defence mechanisms in cloud computing. Yaokumah and Amponsah (2017) found that facilitating conditions, habit, performance expectancy, and price value had positive and significant effect on behavioural intention to adopt cloud computing with a sample from five Industries. Arpaci (2017) investigated the antecedents' and consequences of cloud computing adoption in education to achieve knowledge management.

Related Studies

Gupta and Badve (2017) presented an overview of distributed DoS attack that can be applied on Cloud computing and required tool were also explained. Stergiou et el. (2018) integrated IoT and Cloud computing focussing on the security issues to derive the benefits. Negi et al. (2013) proposed a modification to the confidence based filtering (CBF) method that is investigated for cloud environment. Gupta (2018) emphasized on emerging issues in computer security for which different techniques can be combined. Gupta et al. (2016) featured the theoretical perspectives of cryptography and cyber threats in a handbook. A cloud server can be used for data collection to manage and control from distance by a remote (Plageras et al., 2018).

Research Limitations and Gaps

Brender and Markov (2013) defined the restricted nature of the study whose drive was to assist as a preliminary survey of the risk analysis with respect to cloud adoption. Khanagha et al. (2013) stated it is vital to recognize which variables affect the time between the generation of an administrative problem and the real acknowledgment of such a problem by the executives. Gaurangkumar and Minubhai (2012) defined the lack of confidence in entrusting the sensitive information in Cloud computing service provider is one of the obstacles to cloud adoption. Nkhoma and Dang (2013) explained that their data quality (secondary data) could be the most challenging limitation of the study. Alshamaila et al. (2013) examined cloud computing adoption in dissimilar sectors and industries in various Countries in both a qualitative and quantitative way. Based on this research gaps the factors were identified and instrument was developed for the survey.

Factors Identified for the Study

The items selected necessarily represent the concept about which generalization has to be made to ensure the content validity of the scales. The best way to ensure content validity is to identify and adapt items from earlier validated instruments. To the extent possible, we attempted to borrow items from prior research. The items and questions in the proposed questionnaire for the study have been adopted from the previous research; as mentioned earlier, Questionnaire was sent to three experts from Academic and three experts from Industry in a related area. Their comments were asked and incorporated so that respondents will understand the statements and its context. The scales administered to collect the primary data with regard to various constructs used for the study are presented in table 1 below.

Lee et al. (2013) used a two-factor theory based on the Cloud adopters and barriers to analysing the newly recognised SAAS market in Korea. Total 32 factors are analysed using AHP-Matrix. The data was collected from 35 IT Consultants for the Survey. PEST Analysis is used for this study in which economic factor is the most important factor for cloud adoption and social, political and financial factors are the most important barriers for SAAS adoption.

Low et al. (2011) examined eight factors for a questionnaire-based survey for collecting data from 111 high-tech industries in Taiwan. The hypotheses were tested using logistic regression analysis. The result signifies cloud computing service providers a better understanding of what influences cloud adoption more.

Sobragi et al. (2014) applied a SMEs Case-Study method for a large retail corporation, a medium sized mobile marketing company, and a small IT Services businesses in Brazil to verify the factors influencing cloud computing adoption. The findings show cost, reliability and scalability affect cloud adoption. The factors sustainability, interoperability, and network access are irrelevant for cloud adoption.

Alshamaila et al. (2013) studied 15 different SMEs in North-east of England through a Survey with a semi-structured questionnaire to develop a cloud adoption model for SMEs which is based on TOE-framework. The result shows that apart from competitive pressure all other factors influence cloud adoption.

Gaurangkumar and Minubhai (2012) tried to give a preventive (Security & Privacy), detective (Accountability & Auditability) and corrective (Fault Recovery) measure to achieve trust on Cloud computing adoption. Khanagha et al. (2013) examined the effect of Management innovation on a large telecommunication firm through grounded theory approach. The findings show the innovation in administrative aspect can favour Cloud computing adoption.

Table 1. Factors with number of items

Factors	Operational Definitions	Items	Sources
Perceived IT Security Risk	PITSR captures an organization's perception or attitude related to risks that are affecting the safety and security of a company's IT when Cloud Computing is used as a sourcing model.	6	Ackermann(2012)
Risk Analysis	It refers to possible damages or potential losses of an investment-without taking potential profits into account. Therefore, they can be categorized as shortfall-oriented views of risk.	6	Dutta et al.(2013)
Management Style	It is an idea that relates to introduce new management practices, procedures, or structures planned to future organizational goals.	3	Khanagha et al.(2013)
Trust	In Cloud Computing, it will be defined as a unit of consumer confidence to adopt the cloud computing strategy.	3	Gaurangkumar and Minubhai(2012)
Technology Innovation	An invention should be an original solution which should have benefit in economic aspects.	6	Utterback(1971);Wu (2011); Alshamaila et al.(2012)
Usage of Technology	It is important to know how customers buy and sell a new technology that is an important aspect of business tactics.	5	Lee et al.(2013); Low et al.(2011) ; Nkhoma et al.(2013)
Industry Usage	It is to facilitate the intra-firm cloud computing adoption to maximise the rate of return in the business environment.	6	Lee et al.(2013);Low et al.(2011); Alshamaila et al.(2012) ; Godse and Mulik (2009)
Cloud Computing Adoption	It is the combined effect of Perceived IT Security Risk, Risk Analysis, Industry Usage and Trust.	9	Low et al.(2011); Guptaa et al.(2013); Alshamaila et al.(2012); Morgan and Conboy (2013)
Business Performance	It is the outcome of Cloud Computing Adoption technology.	10	Low et al. (2011);Lee et al.(2013); Venters and Whitley (2012); Sobragiet al.(2014);Godse and Mulik (2009)

Ackermann (2012) proposed a comprehensive conceptualization of Perceived IT Security Risks (PITSR) in the context of cloud computing adoption which is based on six distinct risk factors. The data collected from 356 organizations is found to support the study through a second-order Structural Equation Modelling analysis. The findings contribute to IT security and ITO research, help adopters to assess risks, and enable cloud providers to develop targeted strategies to mitigate risks.

Gupta et al. (2013) did a questionnaire survey on Singapore SMEs using Partial Least Squire technique. The findings of the five-factor model show SMEs do not rely on Cloud computing and SMEs do not want to use Cloud for Sharing and collaboration. Ease of Use and Convenience is the biggest favourable factor for SMEs to adopt Cloud computing. There is a need to study the research problem carefully before adopting any methodology. Hence, this section constitutes the problem statement, instrument development and survey administration and the need of measurement scale development to check the reliability and validity.

Relating to the problem statement, this study will focus on Industries who want to adopt or already adopted cloud computing. Understanding the relationships between the different factors will help us identify which ones influence more the business performance. This study will build on tested theories in technology acceptance to determine which factors play an important role in determining cloud computing adoption. In view of how different factors relate to business performance through cloud computing adoption, this study has the following objectives: Identify variables to measure business performance through cloud computing adoption; Examine the variables impacting the business performance through cloud computing adoption; Validate the scale developed to measure business performance through cloud computing adoption; Calculate the reliability of the scale.

Instrument Development and Survey Administration

Survey based method is used to measure business performance through cloud computing adoption. A survey instrument which questionnaire is designed to operationalize the measures of 9 constructs of cloud computing adoption. Both qualitative and quantitative questionnaire is prepared. To measure each of the constructs, items are prepared for each construct.

The survey instrument was planned for contributors to indicate agreement on selected statements on a 7-point scale. The questionnaire also had sections for demographic facts such as: Name, E-mail Id, Organizational Position, Years of Experience, Annual Turnover and Type of Industry. In the first stage, the descriptions of the factors, as well as the dimension items for each factor, were established. In this stage, a tentative indication of reliability and validity was also provided. This stage comprised item generation, pre-pilot study, and pilot study. The second phase will be the final survey and model validation. Based on the validated scales the questionnaire for the final survey will be modified. The measurement items are listed in table 2 below.

Need for the Study

The need of this study is to check the validity and reliability of the constructs used in the instrument. Validity is the measure of the accuracy of an instrument used in a study. Construct validity refers to "the vertical correspondence between a construct which is at an unobservable, conceptual level and a purported measure of it which is at an operational level" (Peter, 1981). It seeks agreement between a theoretical concept and a specific measuring procedure. It establishes relationships between latent (unobserved) variables and SMEs observable items. One way to check construct validity is to determine the convergent validity and discriminant validity. Convergent validity means an indicator of a defined construct should share a high percentage of variance. Convergent validity was checked by ensuring all average variance extracted values greater than 0.5 and factor loading (Hair et al. 1998, Fornell & Larcker, 1981). Discriminant validity was achieved by linking the shared variance between factors with the average variance extracted from the individual factors (Fornell & Larcker, 1981).

Cronbach's coefficient alpha is the maximum used estimator of the reliability of tests and scales. However, it has been criticized as being a lower bound and hence understanding true reliability. A popular alternative to coefficient alpha is composite reliability, which is usually calculated in conjunction with structural equation modelling (Peterson & Kim, 2013). The average composite reliability value is always higher than the average corresponding coefficient alpha.

Table 2. Measurement items

Variable	Description
Cloud Computing Adoption(CCA)	The assurance of privacy increases the Cloud computing adoption rate.
	A secured cloud service is more convenient for Industries.
	Simpler Cloud is easy for sharing.
	Social media helps in improved collaboration within their companies.
	Cloud is a quite familiar term for your organization.
	Top management support/Internal Business Process makes a supportive climate by providing adequate resources for the adoption of new technology.
	Your firm takes into consideration the advantages that stem from adopting innovations.
	The level of pressure from competitors is reduced by adopting a new technology.
	Market place establishment helps to establish an online marketplace for Cloud adoption.
	The complexity of an innovation is a barrier to evaluating a new technology.
Business Performance(BP)	Technology compatibility helps in Cloud computing adoption.
	Reduced cost helps in superior performance.
	Social media is an option for enhanced marketing for your cloud business.
	Economies of scale help the organization to gain profits in the long term.
	Adopting a new technology should help users to be more efficient economically.
	A new technology should provide a variety by increasing customer value.
	Interoperability helps in coordination between organizations.
	Sustainability helps the Cloud's ability to be energy efficient.
	Your manager has a strong understanding of how technology can be used to increase business performance (Managerial Capability).
	The availability of your internal systems is decreased.
Perceived IT Security Risk(PITR)	Your organization can detect unauthorized data on your internal systems.
	Your data is manipulated during transfer.
	Data transfer to a provider lessens the speed of your internal systems.
	It is difficult to import existing data.
	Personal detail is accessed without individual authorization on the system.
	User companies lack disaster recovery to deal with unpredicted technical problems in the cloud.
Risk Analysis(RA)	Challenging for user companies to transfer data across different cloud providers.
	User companies have limited control on testing applications in Cloud.
	Technology innovation will lead to Uncertainty.
	Legal disputes between enterprises are possible if they overlap.
	Fault recovery finds solution for any dispute in the system (Fault Recovery).
	Global distribution network helps the suppliers to widen the range of targets.
Industry Usage(IU)	Partnerships help the suppliers to work together to develop their services.
	Trading partner pressure helps with the adoption of new technology.
	Large firms are efficient enough to adopt new technology.
	Market scope is the horizontal extent of a company's operations which helps in Cloud adoption.
	Vender reputation/Supplier Reputation depends on the number of clients.
	Access to the latest software helps the clients to access the latest versions.
Usage of Technology(UT)	Rapid deployment helps customers to install any software packages.
	Easy maintenance helps customers to own any IT resources to maintain the system.
	Technology readiness helps with the adoption of Cloud computing.
	Lack of IT standards has a lesser effect on Cloud computing adoption.
	Mass media affects the firm for using a new technology.

continued on the following page

Table 2. Continued

Variable	Description
Technological Innovation(TI)	Your firm experiments on new technologies and services.
	Innovativeness helps a client to adopt innovations of the same social context.
	Prior experience with similar technology helps the user.
	Firms taking innovation strategy are more likely to adopt cloud computing.
	Your organization has the ability to quickly integrate new innovation into your existing infrastructure.
	Guarantee for privacy of data increases cloud adoption rate.
Trust(T)	Accountability gives the details about unexpected error during cloud application.
	Auditability helps to find any unexpected behaviour of the system.
	Learning routines help to assign resources.
Management Style(MS)	Resource allocation mechanisms help in coordination.
	Your organization Incentive system encourages you to reach organization goals.

$$\text{Composite Reliability}\left(\text{CR}\right) = \frac{\left(Standard\,Regression\,Weight\right)^2}{\left(Standard\,Regression\,Weight\right)^2 + Error}$$

$$\text{Convergent Validity}\left(\text{AVE}\right) = \frac{Square\,Multiple\,Correlation}{Squared\,Multiple\,Correlation + Error}$$

Discriminant Validity = $\sqrt{AVE}$

The thresholds for Composite reliability, convergent, and discriminant validity are as follows:

Reliability: CR>0.7

Convergent Validity: AVE>0.5

Discriminant Validity: $\sqrt{AVE}$ > Inter-construct correlations

RESEARCH METHODOLOGY

Exploratory study approach is used for this scale development. Qualitative and quantitative research approaches will be used to enhance the validity of findings. Constructs and variables are identified from the literature. Expert opinions are invited to confirm whether the identified constructs are best suited to measure business performance through cloud computing adoption. A two-step research methodology was used for this study. An authentic instrument should cover the content domain of every construct.

The items that measure a factor should agree with each other, and the items of one factor should disagree with measures of the other factors. Each factor should be reliable and short and easy to use. Scale development and improvement is a three-phase approach.

In the first step, the definitions of the factors, as well as the measurement items for each factor, were recognised. In this step, a tentative indication of reliability and validity was also provided. This step comprised item generation through qualitative enquiry.

The second phase is the scale purification based on the findings of the reliability and validity of 110 respondents. Based on the validated scales the questionnaire for the final survey will be modified. The third phase will be the final survey of 660 sample data through EFA (Exploratory Factor Analysis) and CFA (Confirmatory Factor Analysis) to validate the questionnaire/scale.

Validation of survey questionnaire is necessary before applying any statistical test in the research. (Straub, 1989; Straub et al., 2004) provides excellent guidelines for conducting survey questionnaire validation in the area of Cloud computing adoption. In their guidelines, these authors consider reliability and construct validity as mandatory for survey questionnaire validation. Reliability and construct validity of the questionnaire instrument were checked by calculation of Cronbach's alpha and exploratory factor analysis. In order to test the reliability and construct validity of the questionnaire and to further reduce the number of items to a manageable size, a pilot study had been conducted before the main survey was implemented. The pilot study allowed for evaluating the planned data collecting methods, alternative measures, statistical and analytical procedures for this study. The pilot test was conducted within a group of managers. Pilot participants did not participate in the subsequent study. Based on the pilot test results, the survey items were minimally revised. A reliability and validity test using SPSS was performed and successfully achieved.

Sample Characteristics

The demographic profile of the 660 respondents by title, industry and cloud structure are shown in table 3. It provides descriptive statistics on the demographic profile of the present study. It is clear from this table that highest qualified respondents are from PG and lowest are from Ph.D. The organizations having 500-1000 employee size and more than 1000 are the highest targets for data collection. The organizations having employee size of 100-250 and less than 100 are the lowest targets for data collection. It is clear from the table that the highest number of respondents is having 7 years of experience which is more than our minimum criteria of 5 years of experience. The lowest number of respondents is having 11 years of experience. Out of three targeted sectors, 296(45%) sample data is collected from manufacturing sector, 261(40%) sample data is collected from the service sector and 103(15%) sample data is collected from process industry.

Data Analysis

After collecting the data from the interviews, transcripts were prepared from the extensive notes were taken from the researchers. The reliability was improved by sending the transcripts to the respondents for verification and feedback. The transcripts were modified in case of interpretation.

The second round of interviews is a deeper question for Cloud Computing adoption. Based on the final 660 refined responses, we performed data screening for purification of the data. The data collected was analysed using EFA and CFA to examine structure, reliability and validity of the factors. The data was tabulated in Microsoft Excel sheet and then imported in SPSS (Statistical Package for the Social Sciences version 20) for analysis.

Table 3. Demographic Characteristics of the Respondents

Demographic Categories		Frequency	Percentage (%)
Qualification	B.E./B.Tech.	226	34.24
	M.Tech./P.G.	295	45
	Ph. D.	139	21.06
Experience(In term of No. of Years)	5	196	29.69
	6	95	14.39
	7	105	16
	8	73	11.06
	9	83	13
	11	108	16.3
Size of the Organization(In terms of no. of Employees)	100-250	206	31.2
	250-500	85	13
	500-1000	76	11.51
	Less than 100	227	34.39
	More than 1000	66	10
Turnover(Revenue in Crore)	100-500	226	34.24
	50-100	103	16
	500-1000	134	20.3
	More than 1000	197	30
Type of Industry	Manufacturing	296	45
	Process	103	15
	Service	261	40

Data Screening

Data screening (sometimes referred to as data screaming) is the process of ensuring your data is clean and ready to go before conducting further statistical analyses. Data must be screened in order to confirm the data is suitable, reliable, and valid for testing the causal theory. In table 4, six specific issues are discussed that need to be addressed when cleaning the data.

Exploratory Factor Analysis (EFA)

EFA is a statistical method for defining the correlation among the factors in a dataset. This type of study delivers a factor structure. Overall, an EFA organizes the factors to be recycled for cleaner structural equation modelling. Table 5 gives the steps of EFA. An EFA performs three functions:

1. Explores data for patterns
2. Determines relationship among patterns
3. Data reduction

Table 4. Steps followed for data screening

1. Missing Data	It was ensured that the all the 3 parts were collected from all the respondents, thus, no data was missed.
2. Outliers	To detect outliers on each variable, we produced boxplots in SPSS.
3. Normality	Normality was assessed in two different ways: skewness and kurtosis (flat/peaked) following the rules as: If your skewness value is greater than 1 then you are positive (right) skewed, if it is less than -1 you are negative (left) skewed, if it is in between, then you are fine. If the absolute value of the skewness is less than three times the standard error, then you are fine; otherwise, you are skewed. The data was found to be normal.
4. Linearity	Linearity was assessed by examining the relationship between the independent variables and dependent variables by forming composites. The significance value for *deviation from linearity* for each combination of independent variables and dependent variables was found to be greater than .05, thus indicating that all relationships were linear.
5. Homoscedasticity	Homoscedasticity means that the variable's residual (error) exhibits consistent variance across different levels of the variable. Our data showed homoscedasticity.
6. Multicollinearity	Multicollinearity is not desirable. It means that the variances our independent variables explain in our dependent variable are overlapping with each other and thus not each explaining unique variance in the dependent variable. The way to check this is to calculate a Variable Inflation Factor (VIF) for each independent variable after running a multivariate regression. The rules of thumb for the VIF are as follows: ■ VIF < 3: not a problem ■ VIF > 3; potential problem ■ VIF > 5; very likely problem ■ VIF > 10; definitely problem The VIF value in case of our data was found to be less than 3, thus indicating no multicollinearity.

Source: Encyclopaedia of Research Design, Volume 1 (2010), Sage Publications

Table 5. Steps of EFA

Appropriateness of Data	The appropriateness of data is measured through KMO Statistics and Bartlett's test of sphericity. Usually the KMO value >= 0.7 is always acceptable.
Factoring Methods	There are three types of factor extraction methods. 1. Principal Component Analysis (PCA): Considers all available variances. 2. Principal Axis Factoring (PAF): It considers only common variances. 3. Maximum Likelihood (ML): It provides the model fit estimates.
Rotation types	The rotation type is of two types; Orthogonal and Oblique. Usually, we use Varimax which comes in Orthogonal rotation type which is most commonly used for verifying a new scale.
Communalities	Communality is the degree to which an item correlates with all other items. Higher communalities are better. Low communalities value (<0.4) indicates items to be removed after the examination of pattern matrix.
Factor Structure	Factor structure/Pattern Matrix refers to inter-correlation among the variables being tested in EFA. Variables group into factors, more precisely load onto factors.
Correlation Matrix	It measures the linear relationship between variables.

Confirmatory Factor Analysis (CFA)

CFA is an integral part of structural equation modelling. It requires developing an understanding of presumed constructs in using structural equation modelling for confirmatory factor analysis (Chan et al., 2007). It is useful to depict the pattern of observed variables for which latent construct hypothesized model and validates their measurement. It assesses the reliability and validity of the measurements through the careful specification of constructs and their indicators prior to their actual testing with data. For the present study, we have multiple goodness-of-fit indices and validity and reliability as present in the above table.

Goodness of Fit Indices

The main advantage of structural equation modelling for validating the factors is multiple goodness-of-fit indices. Chan et al. (2007) explained several goodness-of-fit indices to evaluate how well the structural model fits the data. The chi-square goodness-of-fit test is popularly used in confirmatory factor analysis. A non-significant chi-square value indicates a good fit of the hypothesized model with the data though the test results are highly sensitive to sample size. Also, for well-fitted hypothesized models, the chi-square value should approximate the degree of freedom. Anotherimportant index is relative chi-square value that is determined by dividing the chi-square value by the degrees of freedom. This ratio should be 2:1 or 3:1 for an adequate fit between the hypothetical model and the sample data. The other prevalent measures of fit in structural equation modelling are the goodness-of-fit index (GFI), the comparative fit index (CFI), and the root means square error of approximation (RMSEA). For a good fit, GFI should be equal to or more than 0.90 and CFI should be equal to or more than 0.95. For RMSEA, the value should range from 0.04 to 0.07 where a value less than .05 predict close fit, values between .05 and .08 predict a fair fit, values between .08 and .10 predict a mediocre fit, and values more than .10 predict a poor fit.

Model Fit

There are specific measures that can be calculated to determine goodness of fit along with their threshold values as mentioned below:

Chi-square test/DF = <3 good; <5 sometimes permissible
GFI= Goodness-of-fit index =>.95
AGFI=Adjusted Goodness of Fit index=>.80
NFI=Normed Fit Index=>.80
CFI=Goodness-of-fit index=>.95 great; >.90 traditional; >.80 sometimes permissible
RMSEA=Root Mean Squared Error of Approximation <.05 good; .05-.10 moderate; >.10 bad

Combined Approach of EFA and CFA

The combined steps of EFA and CFA are presented in the following section. The nine variables are tested individually through EFA-CFA. Here, we have explained one variable, Cloud computing adoption (CCA) for clear understanding out of all nine variables.

For Cloud Computing Adoption (CCA)

The KMO value is given in table 6 as above.

1.   Total Variance Explained: 67.396
2.   Factor Extraction: Only one component is extracted in rotated component matrix
3.   Model Fit (Path Diagram):

The CFA model for CCA factor is given in figure 1. Confirmatory factor analysis was performed where all the items of each model such as nine items of Cloud computing adoption (CCA), ten items of Business performance(BP),six items of Perceived IT security risk(PITR), six items of Risk analysis(RA), three items of Management style(MS), three items of Trust(T), six items of Technology innovation(TI),five items of Usage of Technology(UT) and six items of Industry usage(IU) were checked individually. There are total nine path diagrams drawn individually for nine variables in AMOS 20 to check the model fit of each variable. Figure 1 shows the Cloud computing adoption (CCA) model in Confirmatory Factor Analysis (CFA) which initially having nine items. But two items 'Top management support' and 'Market place establishment' are removed in the second phase of pilot testing as it showed the threshold value below 0.5. As these two items are having strong literature support, it again verified with large sample of 660 in the third phase of scale validation and included in the validated final questionnaire. The model fit values of CCA are given in table 7.

The result shows KMO above 0.7 which is satisfactory. Similarly Bartlett's test of sphericity significance value is 0.000 which is below 0.05 that is significant at 95%age confidence level. All the values of total variance explained are above 60%age and so satisfactory for further analysis. For a good fit, GFI should be equal to or more than 0.90 and CFI should be equal to or more than 0.95. For RMSEA, the value should range from 0.04 to 0.07 where a value less than 0.05 predict close fit, values between 0.05 and 0.08 predict a fair fit, values between 0.08 and 0.10 predict a mediocre fit, and values more than 0.10 predict a poor fit.

The entire CFA (Confirmatory Factor Analysis) model with 9 factors and 54-items is shown which is drawn in AMOS (Analysis of Moment Structures) 20.0 version. The model shows the residual errors, measurement errors along with the Squired multiple correlations.

Table 6. Determining the appropriateness of data: KMO

KMO and Bartlett's Test		
Kaiser-Meyer-Olkin Measure of Sampling Adequacy.		.850
Bartlett's Test of Sphericity	Approx. Chi-Square	572.691
	Df	21
	Sig.	.000

Figure 1. CFA model for cloud computing adoption (CCA)

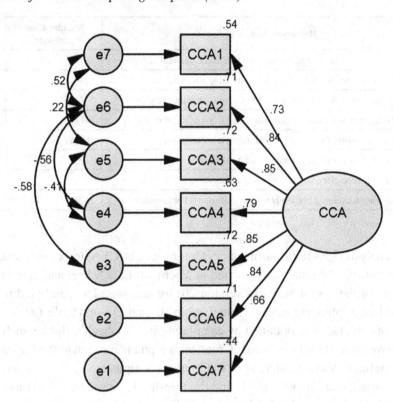

Table 7. Model fit values for CCA

CMIN/df	GFI	AGFI	CFI	RMSEA
2.573	.941	.817	.975	.120

RESULT AND DISCUSSION

Table 8 identifies the significance of each hypotheses in the study. Trust negatively influences perceived risk in e-commerce transactions (Kim et al., 2009). In the context of cloud computing, where uncertainty and interdependence are present, it is believed that trust helps users to overcome these concerns and encourages adopting cloud computing (Dimoka, 2010).So, out of remaining five factors Trust (T: 0.493) is having highest significant effect on Cloud computing adoption to measure the business performance.

Cloud computing and business performances are given equal value in organizations (Saha & Theingi, 2009). So, cloud computing adoption (CCA: 0.138) supports business performance in organizations.

The reliability was improved by sending the transcripts to the respondents for verification and feedback. The transcripts were modified in case of interpretation. The second round of interviews is a deeper question for Cloud Computing adoption. Based on the final 660 refined responses, we performed

Table 8. Significant hypotheses

Serial No.	Regression Relation	Standardized Estimate	Supported(Yes/No)
1	Perceived IT Security risk is negatively related to Cloud Computing adoption.	-0.062	Yes
2	Risk Analysis is positively related to Cloud Computing adoption.	0.084	Yes
3	Technology Innovation is positively related to Cloud Computing adoption.	0.125	Yes
4	Usage of Technology is positively related to Cloud Computing adoption.	-0.139	No
5	Industry Usage is positively related to Cloud Computing adoption.	-0.085	No
6	Management Style is positively related to Cloud Computing adoption.	0.085	Yes
7	Trust is positively related to Cloud Computing adoption.	0.493	Yes
8	Cloud Computing adoption is positively related to Business Performance.	0.138	Yes

exploratory factor analysis (EFA) and confirmatory factor analysis (CFA) to examine structure, reliability and validity of the factors. The data was tabulated in Microsoft Excel sheet and then imported in SPSS (Statistical Package for the Social Sciences version 20) for analysis. The combined result of EFA and CFA are presented in the following tables (table 9, table 10, table 11 and table 12).

The reliability of each factor is obtained by calculating its Cronbach's alpha which should be more than 0.7. In the above table 10, all the factors Cronbach's alpha is more than the threshold value.

The composite reliability is the alternative to Cronbach's alpha which is obtained by the standard formula given by Fornell and Larcker (1981) and the threshold values should be more than 0.7. In the above table 11, all the factors threshold values are satisfying the limit.

Convergent validity and discriminant validity are evaluated as per the formula is given by Fornell and Larcker (1981) in table 9 and table 10. The study revealed adequate convergent validity (AVE>0.5) and discriminant validity ($\sqrt{\text{AVE}}$) of all the measurement tools. From table 10, it can be referred that the square root of the AVE values of each factor is greater than the inter-construct correlations which support the discriminant validity of the study.

CONCLUSION, FUTURESCOPE AND IMPLICATION

The purpose of this study is to develop and validate the scale for Cloud computing adoption in Indian Industries. Analysing data from 660 respondents yielded important findings for the scale generation, purification, and validation. Li and Xie (2012) stated that firms taking innovation strategy are more likely to adopt cloud computing as a corporate strategy. Organizations have the capability to rapidly integrate new innovation into the current infrastructure. Managers have a strong understanding of how technology can be recycled to raise business performance (Garrison et al., 2015). Thus, from the extensive literature review three more significant items; corporate strategy, technical capability and managerial capability were identified and added to the study.

During the second phase of pilot data analysis with 110 responses two items; 'top management support' and 'marketplace establishment' in the construct Cloud computing adoption (CCA) showed the very poor result. So, to get significant output, these two items were dropped in the second phase. According

Table 9. Reliability (Cronbach's Alpha) calculation

Variables	Cronbach's Alpha(>0.7)
Business Performance(BP)	0.927
Cloud Computing Adoption(CCA)	0.916
Trust(T)	0.854
Industry Usage(IU)	0.874
Technology Innovation(TI)	0.938
Perceived IT Security Risk(PITR)	0.915
Management Style(MS)	0.911
Risk Analysis(RA)	0.889
Usage of Technology(UT)	0.892

Table 10. Composite reliability (CR) calculation

Variables	CR(Composite Reliability)>0.7
PITR(Perceived IT Security Risk)	0.9765
T(Trust)	0.9716
CCA(Cloud computing adoption)	0.98658
BP(Business Performance)	0.9858
UT(Usage of Technology)	0.983
RA(Risk Analysis)	0.9829
TI(Technology Innovation)	0.99
IU(Industry Usage)	0.966
MS(Management Style)	0.9759

Table 11. Convergent validity (AVE) calculation

Variables	AVE(Convergent Validity)>0.5
PITR(Perceived IT Security Risk)	0.874
T(Trust)	0.8969
CCA(Cloud computing adoption)	0.9098
BP(Business Performance)	0.8864
UT(Usage of Technology)	0.924
RA(Risk Analysis)	0.9218
TI(Technology Innovation)	0.9449
IU(Industry Usage)	0.836
MS(Management Style)	0.91

Table 12. Discriminant validity (√AVE) calculation

Variables	MS	IU	T	CCA	RA	BP	UT	PITR	TI
MS	**(0.953)**								
IU	0.911**	**(0.947)**							
T	0.243*	0.348**	**(0.914)**						
CCA	0.658**	0.851**	0.385**	**(0.9538)**					
RA	0.566**	**0.660****	0.183	0.628**	**(0.96)**				
BP	0.848**	0.932**	0.348**	0.951**	0.647**	**(0.941)**			
UT	0.470**	0.547**	0.198*	0.520**	0.620**	0.539**	**(0.961)**		
PITR	0.0313	0.0355	0.038	0.0126	0.0245	0.0135	0.0509	**(0.934)**	
TI	0.377**	0.469**	0.246**	0.446**	0.457**	0.455**	0.841**	.0384	**(0.972)**

**. Correlation is significant at the 0.01 level (2-tailed).
*. Correlation is significant at the 0.05 level (2-tailed).

to Low et al. (2011), 'Top management support' creates a supportive environment by providing suitable resources for the adoption of new technology. Lee et al. (2013) state that 'Market place establishment' helps to establish an online market for Cloud Computing Adoption. Hence, we verified these two items in the third phase with the final sample size of 660 and found a valid result for the measurement scale.

In future, the academicians should examine the consistency of their theoretical models and relationships with those that have been previously validated in traditional sampling frames before accepting the results at face value. We examined only the use of a pilot survey questionnaire through EFA and CFA analysis. Our results thus are specific to questionnaire studies, although researchers can run with more sample size as well as in another part of the region and may conclude similar findings from the study.

Managerial Implications

The results of this study have vital implications for managers. Firstly, the large-scale industries in the developing Countries can easily rely on this measurement scale for measuring the business performance through Cloud computing adoption. Secondly, this scale suggests that large-scale industries can evaluate the statistical link between Cloud computing adoption and business performance. Thirdly, this scale will be very important from a strategic point of view. The managers can find out the relative importance of all 9-factors for predicting the performance. Fourthly, this scale can be used to evaluate the strengths and weaknesses of the large-scale industries. Accordingly, sufficient resources need to be provided to the industries in order to achieve the success rate of cloud computing adoption.

Survey and online experimental designs developed by researchers could lead to improved tool integration to allow for easier development of such scale in future research. Further studies may comprise other measurement tools like ANN, Fuzzy-TOPSIS, and others in the measurement model to get more concrete results. In future, the researcher should measure the real influence of cloud adoption on firm performance (e.g., sales, profit and process efficiency). The researchers should examine inter-firm associated factors as well as other firm-specific competencies and how they impact technology success.

REFERENCES

Ackermann, T. (2012). *IT security risks management: perceived IT security risks in the context of Cloud Computing*. Springer Science & Business Media.

Al-Somali, S., & Baghabra, H. (2017). Investigating the Determinants of IT Professionals' Intention to Use Cloud-Based Applications and Solutions: An Extension of the Technology Acceptance. *International Journal of Cloud Applications and Computing*, *6*(3), 45–62. doi:10.4018/IJCAC.2016070104

Alshamaila, Y., Papagiannidis, S., & Li, F. (2013). Cloud computing adoption by SMEs in the north east of England: A multi-perspective framework. *Journal of Enterprise Information Management*, *26*(3), 250–275. doi:10.1108/17410391311325225

Arpaci, I. (2017). Antecedents and consequences of cloud computing adoption in education to achieve knowledge management. *Computers in Human Behavior*, *70*(1). 382-390.doi.org/10.1016/j.chb.2017.01.024

Azarnik, A., Shayan, J., Alizadeh, M., & Karamizadeh, S. (2013). Associated Risks of Cloud Computing for SMEs. *Open International Journal Informatics*, *1*(1), 37–45.

Bhushan, K., & Gupta, B. B. (2017). Security challenges in cloud computing: State-of-art. *International Journal of Big Data Intelligence*, *4*(2), 81–107. doi:10.1504/IJBDI.2017.083116

Brender, N., & Markov, I. (2013). Risk perception and risk management in cloud computing: Results from a case study of Swiss companies. *International Journal of Information Management*, *33*(5), 726–733. doi:10.1016/j.ijinfomgt.2013.05.004

Budrienė, D., & Zalieckaitė, L. (2012). Cloud computing application in small and medium-sized enterprises. *Issues of Business and Law*, *4*(1), 119–130. doi:10.5200/ibl.2012.11

Buyya, R., Yeo, C. S., & Venugopal, S. (2008). Market-oriented cloud computing: Vision, hype, and reality for delivering it services as computing utilities. *Proceeding of 10th IEEE international conference on high performance computing and communications*, 5–13. doi: 10.1109/hpcc.2008.172

Chan, F., Lee, G. K., Lee, E. J., Kubota, C., & Allen, C. A. (2007). Structural equation modeling in rehabilitation counseling research. *Rehabilitation Counseling Bulletin*, *51*(1), 44–57. doi:10.1177/003 43552070510010701

Dutta, A., Peng, G. C., & Choudhary, A. (2013). Risks in enterprise cloud computing: The perspective of IT experts. *Journal of Computer Information Systems*, *53*(4), 39–48. doi:10.1080/08874417.2013.1 1645649

Fornell, C., & Larcker, D. F. (1981). Structural equation models with unobservable variables and measurement error: Algebra and statistics. *JMR, Journal of Marketing Research*, *18*(3), 382–388. doi:10.1177/002224378101800313

Garrison, G., Wakefield, R. L., & Kim, S. (2015). The effects of IT capabilities and delivery model on cloud computing success and firm performance for cloud supported processes and operations. *International Journal of Information Management, 35*(4), 377–393. doi:10.1016/j.ijinfomgt.2015.03.001

Gaurangkumar, K., & Minubhai, C. (2012, January). To Achieve Trust in the Cloud. *Advanced Computing & Communication Technologies (ACCT), 2012 Second International Conference on*, 16-19. 10.1109/ACCT.2012.115

Godse, M., & Mulik, S. (2009, September). An approach for selecting software-as-a-service (SaaS) product. *Cloud Computing, 2009, CLOUD'09. IEEE International Conference on*, 155-158.doi: 10.1109/cloud.2009.74

Gupta, B., Agrawal, D. P., & Yamaguchi, S. (Eds.). (2016). *Handbook of research on modern cryptographic solutions for computer and cyber security*. IGI Global. doi:10.4018/978-1-5225-0105-3

Gupta, B. B. (Ed.). (2018). *Computer and cyber security: principles, algorithm, applications, and perspectives*. CRC Press.

Gupta, B. B., & Badve, O. P. (2017). Taxonomy of DoS and DDoS attacks and desirable defense mechanism in a cloud computing environment. *Neural Computing & Applications, 28*(12), 3655–3682. doi:10.100700521-016-2317-5

Gupta, P., Seetharaman, A., & Raj, J. R. (2013). The usage and adoption of cloud computing by small and medium businesses. *International Journal of Information Management, 33*(5), 861–874. doi:10.1016/j.ijinfomgt.2013.07.001

Hair, J. F., Anderson, R. E., Tatham, R. L., & Black, W. C. (1998). Multivariate data analysis. Academic Press.

Horrigan, J. B. (2008). *Use of cloud computing applications and services*. PEW Internet & American Life Project.

Hsu, P. F., Ray, S., & Li-Hsieh, Y. Y. (2014). Examining cloud computing adoption intention, pricing mechanism, and deployment model. *International Journal of Information Management, 34*(4), 474–488. doi:10.1016/j.ijinfomgt.2014.04.006

Jeba, J. A., Roy, S., Rashid, M. O., Atik, S. T., & Whaiduzzaman, M. (2019). Towards Green Cloud Computing an Algorithmic Approach for Energy Minimization in Cloud Data Centers. *International Journal of Cloud Applications and Computing, 9*(1), 59–81. doi:10.4018/IJCAC.2019010105

Keil, M. (1995). Pulling the plug: Software project management and the problem of project escalation. *Management Information Systems Quarterly, 19*(4), 421–447. doi:10.2307/249627

Khanagha, S., Volberda, H., Sidhu, J., & Oshri, I. (2013). Management innovation and adoption of emerging technologies: The case of cloud computing. *European Management Review, 10*(1), 51–67. doi:10.1111/emre.12004

Kim, W. (2009). Cloud computing: Today and tomorrow. *Journal of Object Technology*, *8*(1), 65–72. doi:10.5381/jot.2009.8.1.c4

Lee, S. G., Chae, S. H., & Cho, K. M. (2013). Drivers and inhibitors of SaaS adoption in Korea. *International Journal of Information Management*, *33*(3), 429–440. doi:10.1016/j.ijinfomgt.2013.01.006

Li, P., & Xie, W. (2012). A strategic framework for determining e-commerce adoption. *Journal of Technology Management in China*, *7*(1), 22–35. doi:10.1108/17468771211207321

Lin, A., & Chen, N. C. (2012). Cloud computing as an innovation: Percepetion, attitude, and adoption. *International Journal of Information Management*, *32*(6), 533–540. doi:10.1016/j.ijinfomgt.2012.04.001

Low, C., Chen, Y., & Wu, M. (2011). Understanding the determinants of cloud computing adoption. *Industrial Management & Data Systems*, *111*(7), 1006–1023. doi:10.1108/02635571111161262

Madhavaiah, C., Bashir, I., & Shafi, S. I. (2012). Defining cloud computing in business perspective: A review of Research. *Vision: The Journal of Business Perspective*, *16*(3), 163–173. doi:10.1177/0972262912460153

Marks, A. E., & Lozano, B. (2010). *Executive's guide to cloud computing*. John Wiley & Sons.

Marston, S., Li, Z., Bandyopadhyay, S., Zhang, J., & Ghalsasi, A. (2011). Cloud computing— The business perspective. *Decision Support Systems*, *51*(1), 176–189. doi:10.1016/j.dss.2010.12.006

Morgan, L., & Conboy, K. (2013). Factors Affecting The Adoption Of Cloud Computing: An Exploratory Study. *Proceedings of the 21st European Conference on Information Systems*, *34*(1), 28-36.

Negi, P., Mishra, A., & Gupta, B. B. (2013). *Enhanced CBF packet filtering method to detect DDoS attack in cloud computing environment*. arXiv preprint arXiv:1304.7073

Neves, F. T., Marta, F. C., Correia, A. M. R., & Neto, M. D. C. (2011). The adoption of cloud computing by SMEs: identifying and coping with external factors. *Conference Proceedings*.

Nkhoma, M., & Dang, D. (2013). Contributing factors of cloud computing adoption: A technology-organisation-environment framework approach. *International Journal of Information Systems and Engineering*, *1*(1), 38–49.

Ouf, S., & Nasr, M. (2015). Cloud Computing: The Future of Big Data Management. *International Journal of Cloud Applications and Computing*, *5*(2), 53–61. doi:10.4018/IJCAC.2015040104

Peter, J. P. (1981). Construct validity: A review of basic issues and marketing practices. *JMR, Journal of Marketing Research*, *18*(2), 133–145. doi:10.1177/002224378101800201

Peterson, R. A., & Kim, Y. (2013). On the relationship between coefficient alpha and composite reliability. *The Journal of Applied Psychology*, *98*(1), 194–198. doi:10.1037/a0030767 PMID:23127213

Plageras, A. P., Psannis, K. E., Stergiou, C., Wang, H., & Gupta, B. B. (2018). Efficient IoT-based sensor BIG Data collection–processing and analysis in smart buildings. *Future Generation Computer Systems*, *82*, 349–357. doi:10.1016/j.future.2017.09.082

Priyadarshinee, P., Raut, R. D., Jha, M. K., & Gardas, B. B. (2017). Understanding and predicting the determinants of cloud computing adoption: A two staged hybrid SEM-Neural Networks Approach. *Computers in Human Behavior*, *76*(1), 341–362. doi:10.1016/j.chb.2017.07.027

Sambrekar, K., & Rajpurohit, V. S. (2019). Fast and Efficient Multiview Access Control Mechanism for Cloud Based Agriculture Storage Management System. *International Journal of Cloud Applications and Computing*, *9*(1), 33–49. doi:10.4018/IJCAC.2019010103

Sobragi, C. G., Maçada, A. C. G., & Oliveira, M. (2014). Cloud computing adoption: A multiple case study. *BASE-Revista de Administração e Contabilidade da Unisinos*, *11*(1), 75–91.

Stergiou, C., Psannis, K. E., Kim, B. G., & Gupta, B. (2018). Secure integration of IoT and cloud computing. *Future Generation Computer Systems*, *78*, 964–975. doi:10.1016/j.future.2016.11.031

Straub, D., Boudreau, M. C., & Gefen, D. (2004). Validation guidelines for IS positivist research. *Communications of the Association for Information Systems*, *13*(1), 380–427.

Straub, D. W. (1989). Validating instruments in MIS research. *Management Information Systems Quarterly*, *13*(2), 147–169. doi:10.2307/248922

Trivedi, H. (2013). *Cloud Computing Adoption Model for Governments and Large Enterprises (Master of Science in Management)*. MIT School of Engineering.

Utterback, J. M. (1971). The process of technological innovation within the firm. *Academy of Management Journal*, *14*(1), 75–88. doi:10.2307/254712

Venters, W., & Whitley, E. A. (2012). A critical review of cloud computing: Researching desires and realities. *Journal of Information Technology*, *27*(3), 179–197. doi:10.1057/jit.2012.17

Wu, W. W. (2011). Mining significant factors affecting the adoption of SaaS using the rough set approach. *Journal of Systems and Software*, *84*(3), 435–441. doi:10.1016/j.jss.2010.11.890

Yaokumah, W., & Amponsah, R. A. (2017). Examining the Contributing Factors for Cloud Computing Adoption in a Developing Country. *International Journal of Enterprise Information Systems*, *13*(1), 17–37. doi:10.4018/IJEIS.2017010102

Zheng, Q., Wang, X., Khan, M. K., Zhang, W., Gupta, B. B., & Guo, W. (2018). A lightweight authenticated encryption scheme based on chaotic scml for railway cloud service. *IEEE Access: Practical Innovations, Open Solutions*, *6*, 711–722. doi:10.1109/ACCESS.2017.2775038

Ziebell, R. C., Albors-Garrigos, J., Schoeneberg, K. P., & Marin, M. R. P. (2019). Adoption and Success of e-HRM in a Cloud Computing Environment: A Field Study. *International Journal of Cloud Applications and Computing*, *9*(2), 1–27. doi:10.4018/IJCAC.2019040101

Chapter 6
A Computational Approach for Secure Cloud Computing Environments

Mouna Jouini

(iD) https://orcid.org/0000-0002-9623-7226

SMART Laboratory, Higher Institute of Management, Tunis University, Tunisia

Latifa Ben Arfa Rabai

SMART Laboratory, Higher Institute of Management, Tunis University, Tunisia & College of Business, University of Buraimi, Oman

ABSTRACT

The recent emergence of cloud computing has drastically altered everyone's perception of infrastructure architectures, software delivery, and development models. Projecting as an evolutionary step, cloud computing encompasses elements from grid computing, utility computing, and autonomic computing into an innovative deployment architecture. Cloud computing systems offer a lot of advantages like pay per use and rapid service provisioned on demand, while it suffers for some concerns specially security. In fact, a number of unchartered risks and challenges have been introduced from this new environment. This chapter explores the security issues in cloud computing systems and shows how to solve these problems using a quantitative security risk assessment model.

INTRODUCTION

Cloud computing is an emerging technology which recently has shown significant attention lately in the word. It provides services over the internet: users can utilize the online services of different software instead of purchasing or installing them on their own computers. The National Institute of Standard and Technology (NIST) definition defines cloud computing as a paradigm for enabling useful, on-demand network access to a shared pool of configurable computing resources (Mell, & Grance, 2010).

DOI: 10.4018/978-1-7998-1082-7.ch006

Copyright © 2020, IGI Global. Copying or distributing in print or electronic forms without written permission of IGI Global is prohibited.

Cloud computing is the delivery of computing services, servers, storage, databases, networking, software, analytics using the Internet to offer faster innovation, flexible resources, and economies of scale. It reduces your operating costs by paying just the services used, runs your infrastructure more efficiently, and scales as your business needs change. It presents a new model for IT service delivery. Cloud computing has, as well, the potential to improve the way businesses and IT operate by offering fast start-up, flexibility, scalability and cost efficiency. As well in n last decades, cloud services adoption haw increased and which has, also, followed consumer confidence with the security of cloud providers. As providers invest in the security of their platforms, a McAfee survey (Intel Security, 2017) showed complete trust in public cloud offerings increased 76 percent in 2017.

Moreover, Intel Security reports that in 15 months, 80% of all IT budgets will be committed to cloud apps and solutions. In fact, Cloud Computing being a global urgency for organizations that choose deploying applications in the cloud. The study found that the percentage of IT professionals who stated they don't think their IT budget will ever be 80% cloud dropped by 50% from 12% in 2015 to 6% in 2016 (Intel Security, 2017).

It offers several services presented in three models: Software as Service (SaaS), Platform as Service (PaaS), and Infrastructure as Service (IaaS). Software as Service (SaaS) provides services existing in the cloud or applications to end users, Platform as Service (PaaS) provides access to platforms and Infrastructure as Service (IaaS) offers processing storage and other computing resources. Thus, CC provides compelling benefits and cost-effective options for IT hosting and expansion, new risks and opportunities for security exploits are introduced. So, many are moving to the cloud to take advantage of the on-demand nature of documents, applications and services.

An area of cloud computing that is starting to garner more attention is security risks, as well as it presents a serious problem for this environment. In fact, these security threats are increasing in last few years like cyber thieves, data and confidential information loss, data privacy, data mobility, quality of service and service levels, bandwidth costs, data protection, and support.

Moreover, data users' externalization makes hard to maintain data integrity and privacy, and availability which causes serious consequences. Security is the big challenge in cloud computing systems. In fact, Intel security survey shows that the biggest security cloud concerns in 2018 are data loss and leakage (67%), threats to data privacy (61%), and breaches of confidentiality (53%) as compared to the previous year. Moreover, cloud computing accidental exposure issues are jumped from 26% in 2017 to 47% in 2018 (Intel Security, 2017).

This environment is threatened to several threats and the survey shows that there are three main serious threats types public cloud in 2018 which are: Misconfiguration of the cloud platform by a rate of 62%, unauthorized access through misuse of employee credentials and improper access controls by a rate of 55%, and insecure interfaces/APIs by a rate of 50%. In addition, Intel Security shows that there are three main barriers for cloud computing adoptions which are due to people and process and to technologies. These three aspects are: Staff expertise and training by 56%, data privacy concerns by 41% and lack of integration with on premises technology by 37% (Intel Security, 2017).

Additionally, McAfee reports that security is a major obstacle. In fact, 1 in 4 of Cloud users have experienced data theft from the public cloud and 1 in 5 of them have experienced an advanced attack against their public cloud infrastructure (McAfee, 2018).

In addition, organizations recognize several key advantages of deploying cloud-based security solutions. In fact, 47% of respondents cloud time to deployment is so fast and 47% of them estimate that the cost is very lower when using a cloud solution (McAfee, 2018).

However, many cloud providers offer a broad set of policies, technologies, and controls that strengthen the cloud security and helping protect your data, and infrastructure from potential threats. Indeed, security risk managements models exist to understand and analyse cloud computing risks in order to protect systems and data from security exploits. The focus of this chapter is on mitigation for cloud computing security risks as a fundamental step towards ensuring secure cloud computing environments.

In this chapter, we will show how to solve security problems in cloud computing systems using a quantitative security risk assessment model. We aim to present a generic framework that evaluate firstly cloud security by identifying unique security requirements, secondly to identify architectural components affected by this risk, thirdly to make out security threats that damage these components and finally to attempt to present viable solutions that eliminates these potential threats.

The remainder of this chapter is organized as follows. Section 2 presents related work. Section 3 presents related technologies. Section 4 presents security issues in cloud computing environments. Section 5 illustrates a quantitative security risk model that we will use in our new approach. Section 6 presents our security framework that solves security problems in Cloud Computing environments in a quantitative way. Finally, conclusions and a direction for future work are given in section 7.

RELATED WORK

Literature review was shown that there are many works that studied cloud security issues. All works provide a qualitative discussion of security related issues in CC environments submitting a quick analysis and survey of security issues. In fact, they develop and deploy a qualitative security management framework on cloud computing environment by proposing some security strategies (countermeasures).

Arijit Ukil et al, have analyzed in (Ukil, Jana & De Sarkar, 2013) security problem in cloud computing. They proposed a framework for satisfying cloud security ensuring the confidentiality, integrity and authentication of data. In fact, they provide security architecture and necessary support techniques for securing cloud computing infrastructure. The presented architecture incorporates different security schemes, techniques and protocols for cloud computing, particularly in Infrastructure-as-a-Service (IaaS) and Platform-as-a-Service (PaaS) systems. This would facilitate to manage the cloud system more effectively and provide the administrator to include the specific solution these security problems. Hu et al (Hu, Wu & Cheng, 2012) presented Law-as-a-Service (LaaS) model for automatic enforcing of legal policies in the super-peer to handle queries for consumers and clients. The law-aware super-peer acts as a guardian providing data integration as well as protection. They (Kantarcioglu, Khan & Thuraisingham, 2010) presented a dynamic multidimensional trust model with time-variant comprehensive evaluation multi-dimensional method. With this backdrop, we present our proposed architecture and security model towards better protection of confidentiality, privacy in a public domain cloud infrastructural backbone.

Velumadhava et al., highlight in (Velumadhava Raoa, & Selvamanib, 2015) data related security challenges in cloud-based environment and solutions to overcome. Gururaj et al., present an overview of security threats in cloud computing and the preventive methods (Gururaj, Mohsin & Farrukh, 2017). It presents security issues in CC and gives as well emerging solutions that may potentially mitigate the vulnerabilities in this environment. Avram analyses the positive and negative aspects or factors of cloud computing adoption. The article presents an informative analyse that need to be considered by an enterprise when making the decision of using cloud computing. These factors include the integration with existing IT infrastructure and existing software, cloud adoptions costs, return on investment, cloud service performances, and cloud security issues (Avram, 2014)

Zissis et al., identify in (Zissis & Lekkas, 2012), firstly security requirements that can be damage when a security problem rises. Then, they present a security strategy based on encryption technique to eliminate security threats in cloud systems. The proposed solution ensures the authentication, integrity and confidentiality of involved data and communications. The solution presents a horizontal level of service available to all implicated entities and maintains a trust between customers and cloud providers. In (Malik & Nazir, 2012), Malik et al., list the most common security threats that damages cloud computing environments and develop a methodology for cloud providers that will protect users' data and information. They provide countermeasures to protects users' data, messages, information against various attacks that are the major issue for anyone when they want to adopt cloud services for their work. They study the major threats arising in cloud environments, then propose countermeasures to them. The work in (Wang, Wang, Ren, & Li, 2011) studied the integrity problem of data storage in Cloud Computing. In particular, the authors considered the task of allowing a third-party auditor (TPA), to cloud client, in order to verify the integrity of the dynamic data stored in the cloud. The TPA allows eliminating the involvement of the client through the auditing of whether his data stored in the cloud are indeed intact. The work aims to ensure remote data integrity that supports public auditability and dynamic data operations. The authors constructed a verification scheme for the integration of these two salient features in their protocol design. In particular, to achieve efficient data dynamics, they improved the existing proof of storage models by manipulating the classic Merkle Hash Tree construction for block tag authentication. To support efficient handling of multiple auditing tasks, they explored the technique of bilinear aggregate signature to extend their main result into a multiuser setting, where TPA can perform multiple auditing tasks simultaneously. In (Băsescu, Carpen-Amarie, Leordeanu, Costan & Antoniu, 2011), the authors proposed a generic security management framework allowing providers of cloud data management systems to define and enforce complex security policies. They designed a framework to detect and stop a large number of attacks defined through an expressive policy description language and to be easily interfaced with various data management systems. They showed that they can efficiently protect a data storage system by evaluating their security framework on top of the BlobSeer data management platform.

Several frameworks have been carried out relating to security issues in cloud computing in a quantitative way. In fact, they do not propose a quantitative approach to analyze and evaluate privacy, and security in cloud computing environment. This chapter primarily aims to analyze and evaluate the most known cloud computing security issues using a quantitative security risk analysis model called as the Multi-dimension Mean Failure Cost (M^{2}FC).

RELATED TECHNOLOGIES

Cloud computing appears after to the emergence of information technologies (IT) like distributed system, and virtualisation and after the emergence of several related aspects with cloud computing which is discussed in this section (Liang, Sherif, Anna & Athman, 2014).

Grid Computing: Grid computing is a distributed computing concept that coordinates networked resources to achieve a common computational objective. Cloud computing is similar to Grid computing in that it also employs distributed resources to achieve application-level objectives. However, cloud

Table 1. Features similarities and differences between cloud computing and related technologies

	Differences	Similarities
Virtualization	Cloud computing allows allocating computing resources to manage concurrent resources demands of the customers.	Both isolate and abstract the low-level resources for high-level applications.
Autonomic computing	Cloud Computing aims is to focus on reducing resource cost rather than falling system complexity as it is in autonomic computing.	Both interconnect and integrate distributed computing systems.
Grid computing	Cloud computing use virtualization to achieve on-demand resource sharing.	Both employ distributed resources.
Utility computing	Cloud computing is a use of utility computing.	Both offer better economic profits.

computing takes one step further by leveraging virtualization technologies at multiple levels (hardware and application platform) to realize resource sharing and dynamic resource provisioning.

Utility Computing: Utility computing represents the model of providing resources on-demand and charging customers based on usage rather than a flat rate. Cloud computing can be perceived as a realization of utility computing. It adopts a utility-based pricing scheme entirely for economic reasons. With on-demand resource provisioning and utility-based pricing, service providers can truly maximize resource utilization and minimize their operating costs.

Virtualization: Virtualization is a technology that abstracts away the details of physical hardware and provides virtualized resources for high-level applications. A virtualized server is commonly called a virtual machine (VM). Virtualization forms the basis of cloud computing, as it provides the capability of pooling computing resources from clusters of servers and dynamically assigning or reassigning virtual resources to applications on-demand.

Autonomic Computing: Originally coined by IBM in 2001, autonomic computing aims at building computing systems capable of self-management, i.e. reacting to internal and external observations without human intervention. The goal of autonomic computing is to overcome the management complexity of today's computer systems. Although cloud computing exhibits certain autonomic features such as automatic resource provisioning, its objective is to lower the resource cost rather than to reduce system complexity.

To summarize, cloud computing leverages virtualization technology to achieve the goal of providing computing resources as a utility. It shares certain aspects with grid computing and autonomic computing but differs from them in other aspects. Therefore, it offers unique benefits and imposes distinctive challenges to meet its requirements.

SECURITY ISSUES IN CLOUD COMPUTING SYSTEM

Security is a major problem for cloud computing system and providers also falls into their ability to quickly detect, contain, and mitigate an attack (Cloud Security Alliance, 2018). Additionally, cyber-attacks are making headlines every day and organizations are expected to stay up to date and protect against the latest threats, and vulnerabilities. For example, Ransomware attacks like WannaCry affected over 250,000 computers in 2017. Additionally, Bad Rabbit, Petya, and Not Petya also stormed the industry in 2017. Distributed-Denial-of-Service (DDOS) attacks like the one on Dyn DNS affected over 70 major online services. Other malware like the Mirai botnet in 2016 was responsible for multiple DDOS attacks on credible sites due to unsanitary security practices. Misconfigured cloud services such as the S3 bucket leaks by Alteryx that exposed information on 123 million Americans and one at Verizon impacting 6 million individuals. Meltdown and Spectre vulnerabilities exploited almost every modern processor to leaky data and passwords (Cloud Security Alliance, 2018).

There are numerous security issues and challenges in cloud computing because it encompasses many new information technologies like networks, databases, operating system, virtualization, resource scheduling, transaction management, concurrent control and memory management (Sarddar, Sen & Sanya, 2016). In fact, cloud users resit in the cloud data centers which cause serious security concerns for example a malicious user may pretend to be the legitimate users and infecting the data cloud.

Literature review was shown that there are many works that studied cloud security issues (Ukil, Jana & De Sarkar, 2013; Hu, Wu & Cheng, 2012; Liang, Sherif, Anna & Athman, 2014; Hamlen, Kantarcioglu, Khan & Thuraisingham, 2010; Jouini & Ben Arfa Rabai, 2013, Jouini, & Ben Arfa Rabai, 2016; Kadhim, Yusof, Mahdi, Ali Al-shami & Selamat, 2018; An, Zaaba, & Samsudin, 2016). For example, in our previous work (Jouini, Ben Arfa Rabai, Ben Aissa & Mili, 2013; Jouini, Ben Arfa Rabai & Ben Aissa 2014; Jouini & Ben Arfa Rabai, 2013; Jouini, & Ben Arfa Rabai, 2016), we survey the major security issues in present existing cloud computing environments and help users and cloud service provider recognize security threats that cause these problems and security requirements associated with them. We presented a detailed survey of cloud security problems and identified nine security problems: network security issues, data security issues, privacy issues and applications issues.

Network Security Issues

Cloud Computing allows convenient, on-demand network access to a shared pool of configurable networks that can be quickly provisioned and free with negligible management effort or service provider communication (Soofi & Khan, 2014). Due to the fact that the Cloud Computing embodies a comparatively new computing model, there is an important deal of vagueness about how security at network can be attained and how applications security is progressed to Cloud Computing (Rajesh & Sharma, 2015).

Data Security Issues

Users may store all their private, or even sensitive data in the cloud which can be accessed by anyone anywhere which let to many problems like data theft. Moreover, some cloud service providers even don't provide their own server because of the cost effectiveness and flexibility. Data loss which might be also a grave concern for the cloud subscribers. For example, the server may swiftly shut down and causes data loss of the users. Additionally, natural disaster might also cause data corruption. Besides, the cloud data storage is a model of data storage in which the integrity data is stored in logical pools. It allows cloud users to store their data in a remote server to get rid of expensive local storage and managing brand cost and then flexibility access data of interest anytime and anywhere (Dinh, Lee, Niyato, & Wang, 2013).

Privacy Issues

Many security issues let to privacy problems in the cloud. In fact, cloud providers must impose efficient policies in the cloud system to ensure the security of subscribers' data. They must know who is actually accessing the cloud stored data. They must ensure that these data are used only by authorized users. Cloud service provider should provide a good layer of security protection for the users while the users should not tampered with the other user's data. The cloud computing is a good way to reduce the cost and provide more storage if and only if the security is done by both provider and user (An, Zaaba, & Samsudin, 2016).

Application Issues

Malicious code can be uploaded by hackers to the cloud to steal private and sensitive information and damage cloud user's data and applications. Cloud providers must, so, protect the cloud services (applications) by monitoring and maintenance of their cloud programs.

THE M²FC MODEL

In (Jouini, Ben Arfa Rabai & Khedri, 2015), Jouini et al., introduced a quantitative security risk assessment measure that quantifies this risk in terms of financial loss per unit of operation time (for example dollars per hour ($/h)) due to security threats considering several dimensions within the threat world. The measure is called as the Multidimension Mean Failure Cost (M²FC). The M²FC is a stakeholder-based security threats assessment model. It estimates the security of a system in terms of the loss that each stakeholder incurs due to security breaches considering several dimensions within the threat world. In fact, the world of security threats is a segmentation of this world according to each of its dimensions where a dimension can be defined as an elementary aspect or extent of the threat word. The domain or world of threats can be perceived as having several dimensions like architectural components, environmental elements, time, deployment site...For example, when considering the deployment dimension, we give the mean failure cost per deployment site where a security breach occurs. The basic idea is to consider threat perspectives to estimate security failure. To better explain the usage of the proposed M²FC model, we apply on a case study to estimate the security of a system in terms of loss incurred by each stakeholder.

The M²FC model takes into account the stakeholders' assessment of the cost related to their requirements with regard to the elements of two security threats dimensions. That is why, in the following model, the set H of stakeholders and the set R of their requirements are distinguished from the set of the leading dimension (where we called a leading dimension a dimension that is used to guide our decomposition of the multidimensional threat world into several slides of two dimensions each) and the set of the other considered dimension.

Model: Let S be the set of elements in the leading dimension, D be the set of elements of the other considered dimension, H be the set of stakeholders, R is a set of requirements, and T be a set of threats. For every element s ∈ S, we define the Multidimension Mean Failure Costs M(s;D) of elements as follows (Jouini, Ben Arfa Rabai & Khedri, 2015):

$$M(s;D) = V_s \circ PFR_s \circ C_s \circ P_s$$

Where:

Figure 1. A framework for secure cloud computing environments

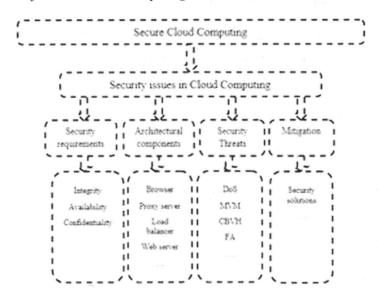

- We denote ∘ by the matrix multiplication operation
- V_s is a matrix of size $|H| \times |R|$ that each entry $(i; j)$ represents the value of the stake that stakeholder H_i has in meeting requirement R_j. We denote by $|H|$ (resp. $|R|$) the size of the set H (resp. R).
- PFR_s is a matrix of size $(|H|; |R|)$ that each entry $(i; j)$ represents the probability of failing requirement R_i due to a failure originating from element $d_j \in D$.
- C_s is a matrix of size $(|D|; |T|)$ that each entry $(i; j)$ represents the probability that an element $d_i \in D$ fails once the threat t_j has materialized.
- P_s is a column vector of size $(|T|)$ that each entry i represents the probability that threats materialize during unitary period of operation.

The M²FC model is a formula in the form of a hierarchical linear system composed of stakeholders, security requirements (such as confidentiality, integrity, and availability), and two perspectives (architectural components, and environmental entities). In fact, an information system has its stakeholders which have its own issues in the proper functioning of the system. The proper functioning requires certain attributes of dependability which called as security requirements. If we consider the architecture of the system that has several components, a failure exhibiting a security requirement essentially is relative to a particular component. These components fail because of vulnerability due to a security threat. Finally, a threat has several dimensions like source, users and location that affect information systems.

We applied the Multi-dimension Mean Failure Cost model (M²FC) is a practical application namely a Cloud Computing environment (Jouini, Ben Arfa Rabai & Khedri, 2015). We computed the M2FC model for three kinds of stakeholders (bronze, silver and gold stakeholders) considering the following threats dimensions: partner application, time, components and connectors.

A NEW APPROACH FOR SECURE CLOUD COMPUTING SYSTEMS

We show in this section how to use a quantitative security risk analysis model to suggest our framework for secure Cloud Computing environment. We used the Multi-dimensional Mean Failure Cost model (M²FC) presented in previous section to propose an approach for secure CC systems.

After introducing security issues in cloud computing system, we need to make approach that allows analyzing and making relation between security problems and their solutions. We notice that some investigators proposed solutions to threats but, they didn't relate solutions to security issues. We propose, in this section, an approach that uses quantitative analysis in order to ensure that our results are more logical and efficient. We will present framework that identifies security and privacy challenges in cloud computing. It highlights cloud-specific attacks and risks and clearly illustrates their mitigations and countermeasures. Our proposed architecture is modular because we consider the threats individually and seek solution for that. This helps to manage the cloud system more effectively and provide the security analysts to include the specific solution to counter the threat. For example, in some cases or for some users, confidentiality is the only requirement whereas for some users other security requirements are also required. Based on the requirement like security strength, latency, bandwidth, the administrator can choose the appropriate primitives.

Figure 1 shows our framework for secure cloud computing. It consists of four main security steps which are (Jouini, & Ben Arfa Rabai, 2016):

- **Associate Security Requirements to Security Problems:** For each issue, we will choose the security requirement affected by this problem.
- **Associate Security Problems to System Components:** For each security requirement, we analyze the probabilities of failure requirements matrix (PFR_s) in order to select architectural components with the higher probabilities where system fails to meet this requirement if a C component fails.
- **Associate Threats to the Components:** For each component C, we analyze the probabilities of failure requirements matrix (C_s) to choose security threats that materialized where the probability when C is compromised is high.
- **Mitigation:** Propose countermeasures per security threat.

Using Methodology to Solve Security Problems in Cloud Computing Environment

We applied in this section our framework to an illustrative example of cloud computing system. We applied the M²FC model to quantify cloud systems and estimate the financial cost for each stakeholder regarding the architectural component and deployment site dimensions. In fact, we take into account the architectural perspective in which we consider the deployment sites dimension and the components dimension. Our assessment varies according to the stakes that each stakeholder has in meeting each security requirement per system site. We opt, as well, for using the deployment dimension (i.e., sites dimension) as the leading dimension. For each site of the considered system, we have the lists of stakeholders, security requirements, components, and threats as we mentioned above (Jouini, & Ben Arfa Rabai, 2016)

Security Requirements

This step identifies security requirements related to each cloud computing security problem cited above. Based on our quantitative assessment security model, we identified in previous work the following security requirement:

- Availability
- Integrity
- Confidentiality

Next, we will present security requirements associated to security problems in CC environments.

Network Security Issues

Services availability problem poses a devastating impact on the brand and the reputation of organizations by causing unavailability of cloud services. Moreover, VM-based malware affects the confidentiality, the integrity and the availability security requirements of cloud computing systems (Băsescu, Carpen-Amarie, Leordeanu, Costan & Antoniu, 2011; Ben Arfa Rabai, Ben Aissa & Mili, 2012). In fact, confidentiality is at risk because the customers' data could be intercepted by malware. Integrity is at risk because the operation of the VM can be changed by malware which could lead to loss of integrity of the customers' data. Availability is at risk because by malware can potentially erase, or obfuscate the customers' data.

Therefore, the security requirements related to this issue and can be affect in case of attack are integrity, confidentiality, availability

Application Security Risks

Reliance on a weak set of interfaces and APIs in cloud computing system exposes organizations to a variety of security issues related to confidentiality, integrity, availability, authentification and authorization and accountability (Băsescu, Carpen-Amarie, Leordeanu, Costan & Antoniu, 2011; Ben Arfa Rabai, Ben Aissa & Mili, 2012)

The security requirements related to this issue and can be affect in case of attack are integrity, confidentiality and availability.

Data Breaches

Many security threats can compromise data and provide losses and corruption and it provoke a serious problem related to integrity, confidentiality and availability of data.

The security requirements related to this issue and can be affect in case of attack are integrity, confidentiality and availability.

Privacy Issues

Privacy breaches allow confidentiality problems and data leakage which leads to serious financial implications to organization. Therefore, the security requirement related to this issue and can be affect in case of attack is confidentiality.

Table 2. Probabilities of failure requirements for sites (Jouini, Ben Arfa Rabai & Khedri, 2015)

	Components							
	Site 1				Site 2			
	Browser	Web_server	Proxy_server	No_failure	Browser	Web_server	Proxy_server	No_failure
Security Requirements								
Availability	0,2	0,1	0,3	0,4	0,2	0,3	0,3	0.5
Confidentiality	0,1	0,1	0,2	0,6	0,3	0,3	0,3	0.7
Integrity	0,1	0,2	0,4	0,3	0,2	0,2	0,2	0.6

Table 3. Probabilities of failure components matrix for sites (Jouini, Ben Arfa Rabai & Khedri, 2015)

	Threats						
	Site 1			Site 2			
	Virus	Data_Bases_Attacks	No_Threat (NoT)	Virus	Data_Bases_Attacks	Denial_of_Servive (DoS)	No_Threat (NoT)
Components							
Browser	0 .2	0 .5	0 .3	0 .2	0 .2	0 .1	0 .5
Web_Server	0 .5	0 .4	0 .1	0 .2	0 .35	0 .1	0 .35
Proxy_Server	0 .3	0 .6	0 .1	-	-	-	-
No_Failure (NoF)	0 .1	0 .3	0 .6	0 .11	0 .2	0 .09	0 .6

- In **confidentiality** cases, we find that the higher probabilities of impact of attack with the following components: Browser, Proxy server and Web server.

Architectural Components

Since the failure of security requirement depends on which component of the system architecture is operational, we will identify in this step using probabilities of failure requirements matrix (PFR$_s$) for each security requirement components causing this failure. We take for each security requirement the higher probability of failing this requirement R$_i$ once component C$_k$ has failed as show in table 2:

- In **integrity** case, we find that the higher probabilities of impact of attack with the following components: Browser, Proxy server and Web server.
- In **availability** case, we find that the higher probabilities of impact of attack with the following components: Browser, Proxy server and Web server.

Security Threats

Components of the architecture may fail to operate properly as a result of security break sdowns brought about by malicious activity. Therefore, we specify, in this step, the catalog of threats that causes components failure. We select for each component, the higher probabilities that in which a component C$_k$

fails once threat T_q has materialized. We will present threats that affected components above, through an analysis of probabilities of failure components matrix (table 3):

- **Denial of service (DoS):** Browser, Proxy server, Web server.
- **Account, service and traffic hijacking:** Web server, Proxy server.
- **Malicious insiders (MI):** Browser, Web server, Proxy server.

We will make synthesis of our analysis in the three steps. For example, we take "Regulatory compliance" has seven security requirements: Integrity, Confidentiality, and Availability. Each security requirement related to some components. The components are: Browser, Web Server, Proxy server.

Each component affected by some threats. The threats are: Denial of service (DoS), Malicious insiders, and Account, service and traffic hijacking.

According to the analysis, we can conclude that all threats presented by MFC are the cause of security issues, because of the threats' distribution which is uniform for cloud computing system. We propose to focus on each threat and suggest solutions. These threats are: Denial of service (DoS), Malicious insiders, and Account, service and traffic hijacking.

Mitigation

In this part, we will describe threats related to security issues and we will give countermeasures to prevent against them. The aim of this step is to propose solutions to security problems.

Denial of Service

The denial of service attack (DoS) (Ben Arfa Rabai, Jouini, Ben Aissa & Mili, 2012) is a critical problem for virtual machines (VMs) used on cloud components. In fact, it indicates that the hypervisor software is allowing a single VM to consume all the system resources and thus starving the remaining VMs and impairing their function. Because the VMs and the host share CPU, memory, disk, and network resources, virtual machines may be able to cause some form of denial of service attack against another VM (Qaisar, & Khawaja, 2012; Priyadharshini, 2013).

As a countermeasure for this attack, you can reduce the privileges of the user that connected to a server. This will help to reduce the DOS attack. Furthermore, the best approach to prevent a guest consuming all the resources is to limit the resources allocated to the guests. Current virtualization technologies offer a mechanism to limit the resources allocated to each guest machines in the environment. Therefore, the underlying virtualization technology should be properly configured, which can then prevent one guest consuming all the available resources, thereby preventing the denial of service attack (Qaisar, & Khawaja, 2012; Priyadharshini, 2013).

Malicious Insiders

The malicious insider threat (Ben Arfa Rabai, Jouini, Ben Aissa & Mili, 2012; Jouini, Ben Arfa Rabai, Ben Aissa & Mili, 2012) is one that gains in importance as many providers still don't reveal how they hire people, how they grant them access to assets or how they monitor them. Transparency is, in this case, vital to a secure cloud offering, along with compliance reporting and breach notification.

To confront this threat, one should enforce strict supply chain management and conduct a comprehensive supplier assessment. Another effective measure is to specify human resource requirements as part of legal contracts, and require transparency into overall information security and management practices, as well as compliance reporting. Another useful step to take is to determine security breach notification processes (Qaisar, & Khawaja, 2012).

Account, Service and Traffic Hijacking

Account service and traffic hijacking (Ben Arfa Rabai, Jouini, Ben Aissa & Mili, 2012; Jouini, Ben Arfa Rabai, Ben Aissa & Mili, 2012) is another issue that cloud users need to be aware of. These threats range from man-in-the-middle attacks, to phishing and spam campaigns, to denial-of service attacks. Account hijacking (Barron, Yu & Zhan, 2013) is usually carried out with stolen credentials. Using the stolen credentials, attackers can access sensitive information and compromise the confidentiality, integrity, and availability of the services offered.

As solution, (Qaisar, & Khawaja, 2012) one should prohibit the sharing of account credentials between users and services. Another effective measure is to leverage strong two-factor authentication techniques where possible, and employ proactive monitoring to detect unauthorized activity. Another useful step to take is to understand cloud provider security policies and SLAs (Qaisar, & Khawaja, 2012; Priyadharshini, 2013).

In (Hashizume & Rosado, 2013), we find a presentation of two approaches to confront this threat. The first is identity and access management guidance. However, the second is dynamic credentials (Hashizume & Rosado, 2013). It presents an algorithm to create dynamic credentials for mobile cloud computing systems. The dynamic credential changes its value once a user changes its location or when he has exchanged a certain number of data packets.

CONCLUSION

Cloud Computing trend is rapidly increasing that has a technology connection with Grid Computing, Utility Computing, and Distributed Computing. Security problems present a major issue in information systems adopting and especially in cloud computing environments in which sensitive applications and data are moved into the cloud data centers. Cloud computing poses many novel vulnerabilities like virtualization vulnerabilities, data vulnerabilities and software vulnerabilities.

Furthermore, with advancement of cloud computing technologies and increasing number of cloud users, security dimensions will continuously increase. In this chapter, we primarily classify and highlight the major security problems in cloud computing systems and help users recognize threats associated with their uses. We propose a framework that analyzes and evaluates security issues in cloud computing environment by a quantifiable approach. Our proposed framework is modular in nature that is we consider the threats individually and seek solution for that. This helps to manage the cloud system more effectively and provide the administrator to include the specific solution to counter the threat.

We envision develop a complete security evaluation and management framework as a part of cloud computing services to satisfy the security demands and then deploy this framework on really cloud computing environments.

REFERENCES

An, Y. Z., Zaaba, Z. F., & Samsudin, N. F. (2016). Reviews on Security Issues and Challenges in Cloud Computing. *International Engineering Research and Innovation Symposium (IRIS)*, 160. 10.1088/1757-899X/160/1/012106

Avram, M. G. (2014). Advantages and Challenges of Adopting Cloud Computing from an Enterprise Perspective. *The 7th International Conference Interdisciplinarity in Engineering, 12*, 529-534.

Barron, C., Yu, H., & Zhan, J. (2013). Cloud Computing Security Case Studies and Research. *The 2013 International Conference of Parallel and Distributed Computing*.

Băsescu, C. A., Carpen-Amarie, C., Leordeanu, A., & Antoniu, G. (2011). Managing Data Access on Clouds: A Generic Framework for Enforcing Security Policies. *International Conference on Advanced Information Networking and Applications (AINA)*. 10.1109/AINA.2011.61

Ben Arfa Rabai, L., Jouini, M., Ben Aissa, A., & Mili, A. (2012). An economic model of security threats for cloud computing systems. *International Conference on Cyber Security, Cyber Warfare and Digital Forensic (CyberSec)*, 100–105. 10.1109/CyberSec.2012.6246112

Cloud Security Alliance. (2018). *State of Cloud Security 2018*. Author.

Dinh, H. T., Lee, C., Niyato, D., & Wang, P. (2013). A Survey of Mobile Cloud Computing: Architecture, Applications, and Approaches. *Wirel. Commun. Mob. Comput*, 1–38.

Gururaj, R., Mohsin, I., & Farrukh, A. (2017). A Comprehensive Survey on Security in Cloud Computing. *FNC/ MobiSPC 2017, 110*, 465-472.

Hamlen, K., Kantarcioglu, M., Khan, L., & Thuraisingham, B. (2010). Security issues for Cloud Computing. *International Journal of Information Security and Privacy, 4*(2), 39–51. doi:10.4018/jisp.2010040103

Hashizume, K., Rosado, D. G., Fernández-Medina, E., & Fernandez, E. B. (2013). Fernández-Medina E, & Fernandez E. B, An analysis of security issues for cloud computing. *Journal of Internet Services and Applications, 4*(1), 1–13. doi:10.1186/1869-0238-4-5

Hu, Y., Wu, W., & Cheng, D. (2012). Towards law-aware semantic cloud policies with exceptions for data integration and protection. *2nd International Conference on Web Intelligence, Mining and Semantics*. 10.1145/2254129.2254162

Intel Security. (2017). *Building Trust in a Cloudy Sky: The State of Cloud Adoption and Security*. Retrieved from http://usdatavault.com/library/Building-Trust-in-a-Cloudy-Sky.pdf

Jouini, M., & Ben Arfa Rabai, L. (2014). Surveying and Analyzing Security Problems in Cloud Computing Environments. *The 10th International Conference on Computational Intelligence and Security (CIS 2014)*, 689–493.

Jouini, M., & Ben Arfa Rabai, L. (2016). Security Framework for Secure Cloud Computing Environments. *International Journal of Cloud Applications and Computing, 6*(3), 32–44. doi:10.4018/IJCAC.2016070103

Jouini, M., Ben Arfa Rabai, L., & Ben Aissa, A. (2014). Classification of security threats in information systems. *ANT/SEIT 2014*.

Jouini, M., Ben Arfa Rabai, L., Ben Aissa, A., & Mili, A. (2012). Towards quantitative measures of information security: A cloud computing case study. *International Journal of Cyber-Security and Digital Forensics*, *1*(3), 265–279.

Jouini, M., Ben Arfa Rabai, L., Ben Aissa, A., & Mili, A. (2013). A cyber security model in cloud computing environments. *Journal of King Saud University-Computer and Information Sciences*, *25*(1), 63–75. doi:10.1016/j.jksuci.2012.06.002

Jouini, M., Ben Arfa Rabai, L., & Khedri, R. (2015). A Multidimensional Approach Towards a Quantitative Assessment of Security Threats. *ANT/SEIT 2015*, 507-514.

Kadhim, Q. K., Yusof, R., Mahdi, H. S., Ali Al-shami, S.S., & Selamat, S. R. (2018). A Review Study on Cloud Computing Issues. *1st International Conference on Big Data and Cloud Computing (ICoBiC 2017)*. 10.1088/1742-6596/1018/1/012006

Liang, Z. (2014). *Cloud Data Management*. doi:10.1007/978-3-319-04765-2__2

Malik, A., & Nazir, M. M. (2012). Security Framework for Cloud Computing Environment: A Review. *Journal of Emerging Trends in Computing and Information Sciences*, *3*(3).

McAfee. (2018). *Navigating a Cloudy Sky: Practical Guidance and the State of Cloud Security*. Retrieved from https://www.mcafee.com/enterprise/en-us/assets/executive-summaries/es-navigating-cloudy-sky.pdf

Mell, P., & Grance, T. (2010). The NIST definition of cloud computing. *Communications of the ACM*, *53*(6).

Priyadharshini, A. (2013). A survey on security issues and countermeasures in cloud computing storage and a tour towards multi-clouds. *International Journal of Research in Engineering & Technology*, *1*(2), 1–10.

Qaisar, S., & Khawaja, K. F. (2012). Cloud computing: Network/ security threats and countermeasures. *Interdisciplinary Journal of Contemporary Research in Business*, *3*(9).

Rajesh, K., & Sharma, S. (2015). Security Challenges and Issues in Cloud Computing – The Way Ahead. *Int. J. Innov. Res. Adv. Eng.*, *2*(9), 32–35.

Sarddar, D., Sen, P., & Sanyal, M. K. (2016). Central Controller Framework for Mobile Cloud Computing. *International Journal of Grid and Distributed Computing*, *9*(4), 233–240. doi:10.14257/ijgdc.2016.9.4.21

Soofi, A. A., Khan, M. I., & Amin, F. (2014). Encryption Techniques for Cloud Data Confidentiality. *International Journal of Grid and Distributed Computing*, *7*(4), 11–20. doi:10.14257/ijgdc.2014.7.4.02

Ukil, A., Jana, D., & De Sarkar, A. (2013). A security framework in cloud computing infrastructure. *International Journal of Network Security & Its Applications*, *5*(5), 11–24. doi:10.5121/ijnsa.2013.5502

Velumadhava Raoa, R., & Selvamanib, K. (2015). Data Security Challenges and Its Solutions in Cloud Computing. *International Conference on Computer, Communication and Convergence (ICCC 2015)*, *48*, 204-209.

Wang, Q., Wang, C., Ren, K., Lou, W., & Li, J. (2011). Enabling Public Auditability and Data Dynamics for Storage Security in Cloud Computing. *IEEE Transactions on Parallel and Distributed Systems*, *22*(5), 847–859. doi:10.1109/TPDS.2010.183

Zissis, D., & Lekkas, D. (2012). Addressing cloud computing security issues. *Future Generation Computer Systems*, *28*(3), 583–592. doi:10.1016/j.future.2010.12.006

Chapter 7
Security Threats and Recent Countermeasures in Cloud Computing

Anupama Mishra
Gurukul Kangri Viswavidyalaya, India

Neena Gupta
Gurukul Kangri Viswavidyalaya, India

Brij B. Gupta
National Institute of Technology, Kurukshetra, India

ABSTRACT

The cloud is an appealing innovation that has driven, in record time, an extraordinary interest. It is right now one of the busiest regions of research in IT, due to its adaptability, vigor, and capacity to altogether lessen the expenses of administrations to clients on the web. Additionally, cloud stores all client information in server farms dispersed the world over. In this manner, security has turned into a foremost worry that anticipates numerous organizations to receive its administrations. Clients should store their information, a few of which are ordinarily secret or individual; in this way, the authors are exceptionally mindful to information honesty and classification amid exchange to a cloud server. This exploration chapter plans to build up an investigation on the different security threats engaged with distributed computing along with their recent countermeasures.

INTRODUCTION

Cloud computing basically referred to applications and service that are offered over the internet from the data centers all over the world. So it is the delivery of computing as a service rather than a product, whereby shared resources, software, and information are provided to computers and other devices as a utility over a network.

DOI: 10.4018/978-1-7998-1082-7.ch007

Copyright © 2020, IGI Global. Copying or distributing in print or electronic forms without written permission of IGI Global is prohibited.

As per NIST (Mell et al, 2010), the cloud model is composed of five essential characteristics, three service models, and four deployment models. As shown in figure 1, the Essential Characteristics are On-demand self-service, broad network access, Resource pooling, rapid elasticity, Measured Service. Services of cloud computing is offered on the basis of three models i.e Infrastructure as a service (IaaS), Platform as a service (PaaS) and Software as a service (SaaS). Cloud computing is a model for enabling convenient, on-demand network access to a shared pool of configurable computing resources (e.g., networks, servers, storage, applications, and services) that can be rapidly provisioned and released with minimal management effort or service provider interaction (Rittinghouse et al, 2016).

The Cloud Services Models

1. **SaaS:** Software as a Service (SaaS) constitutes all applications running on a cloud infrastructure, and made available to consumers as a service, accessible from various devices through either the web or a program. Maintenance, updating and security of SaaS are managed by the suppliers.

Example: Google Doc, Mobileme, Zoho

2. **PaaS:** Platform as a Service(PaaS) is a service category for companies. It consists in providing the environment and a favorable platform for developers and administrators. This allows them to develop, configure and even set up their various services and tools on the internet in a few clicks, without any programming knowledge.

Example: Microsoft Azure
Google App Engine
Force.com

3. **IaaS:** Infrastructure as a Service (IaaS) represents all of on demand delivered software and hardware resources such as (operating systems, server, storage and network) in a virtualized environment.

Example: Amazon EC2, S3

Figure 1. Definition of cloud computing provided by NIST

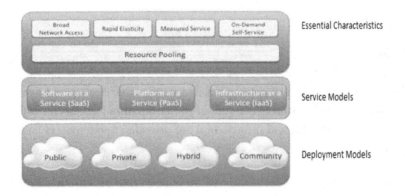

Rack space Moss Offering
Sun's Cloud Services
Terre mark cloud Offering

The Cloud Deployment Models

1. **Private cloud** is a cloud platform dedicated to a single organization.
2. **Public cloud** is a cloud platform accessible by public users.
3. **Hybrid** cloud is a combination of two or more deployment models interconnected (public, private).
4. **Community cloud** is a platform shared between different organizations forming a community with the same concerns.

The Cloud Characteristics

1. **On Demand Self-Services:** The user can book the services without any human interaction with the supplier, processing and storage capabilities as needed.
2. **Broad Network Access:** User resources are available and accessible through a wide range of devices connected to the network.
3. **Resources Pooling:** The supplier provides a pool of common computing resources (storage, memory, bandwidth, virtual machine) to satisfy multiple users through physical and virtual resources that can be assigned and reassigned according to users demands.**4) Rapid Elasticity:** Resources can be quickly sized up or down according to demand of the user.
4. **Measured Service:** Cloud Computing automatically measures resource usage (CPU, storage, bandwidth, etc.) made by a user to enable him to calculate the invoices automatically.

SECURITY OBJECTIVES

Security means prevent our information or hardware or software from the unauthorized access and fabrication of the data by providing security mechanism such as Authorization, Digital Signature, Access Control, Non-Repudiation, Authorization, Data Integrity and Data Confidentiality. The objective of security (Chang et al, 2016; Sethi et al, 2016) is to maintain confidentiality, Integrity and Availability of the data. Figure 2; show that by the help of these three objectives, the secure information can be achieved.

1. **Confidentiality:** Our aim to protect our information from unauthorized access. In the confidentiality, the transmission media is important where the information is floating. For example, In the era of e-business, hiding some company information from competitors is crucial to the operation of the company.

    Threat to Confidentiality: Data Breach, snooping, traffic analysis, phishing and Social Engineering.

2. **Integrity:** Information keeps changing and to maintain the integrity only the authorized entity can modify the information via some authorized mechanism.For example: Modification of any employee details can be done through the authorized members such as HR of the company.

Figure 2. Security objectives

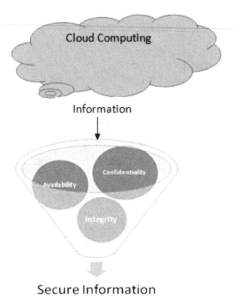

Threat to Integrity: Data Loss, Modification, Replaying, Repudiation, data-diddling, Man-in-the-middle and Salami Attack.

3. **Availability:** As per the need of the information, it must be available to the authorized members; it is just garbage if it is unavailable when the information is required by the authenticated entity.

Threat to Availability: DDoS (Distributed Denial of Services), Electric Power attack, Server Room Environment attack, SYN flood attack and ICMP flood attack.

SECURITY ISSUES IN CLOUD SERVICE MODELS

Although the cloud fulfills all the resource requirement of the client on the optimum cost whenever the requirement occurs but as it provides large amount of sharable resources online and that in turn leads to many security issues related to data, identity and access. There are many issues (Sehti et al, 2016; Fernandes et al, 2014) in cloud service models IaaS, PaaS and SaaS but in this chapter we focuses on Data Breach, Shared Technology Vulnerability, Distributed Denial of Service, Outdated Versions & Patching, Abuse &Nefarious Use of Cloud as shown in Table1.

Data Breaches

Data breaches (Bradford et al, 2017) can disclose the confidential information to competitors, criminals, terrorists, rogue nation states and other malevolent users. It occurs on all the three service models(IaaS,PaaS and SaaS) of cloud. It is an event when private, protected and sensitive information is stolen or leaked by

Table 1. Security issues in cloud service models

Security Issues	Infrastructure as a Service (IaaS)	Platform as a Service (PaaS)	Software as a Service (SaaS)
Data Breaches	✓	✓	✓
Insecure Interface API	✓	✓	✓
Shard Technology Vulnerability	✓	✗	✗
Distibuted Denial of Service	✓	✓	✓
Outdted Versions & Patching	✗	✓	✓
Abus & Nefarious Use of Cloud	✓	✓	✗

a third party who is not authorized to access it. This kind of attacks can be targeted or could be a result of human mistake or vulnerabilities of system. These issues mainly impact data which is not intended to be made public, intellectual property, financial information or personal information. An incidence of data breach had occurred in 2010, Microsoft faced a breach issue with Business Productivity Online Suite, where unauthorized cloud access was detected in their offline employee address books. These issues mainly impact data which is not intended to be made public, intellectual property, financial information or personal information. As per Cloud Security Alliance, There was a potential violation of confidentiality regarding company intellectual property; furthermore, (Bradford et al, 2017) a swing of brute force attacks was identified after this incident. In 2012, LinkedIn revealed that six million passwords were stolen, yet changed the number to 167 million in 2016. This break prompted account commandeering episodes in different administrations because of secret key reuse. In such cases attacker(who has performed the attack), threat (an attack) and vulnerability(loopholes through which the attack can happen) are identified as below:

Threat actor (Attacker): An internal, disgruntled employee/team leader (a malicious insider) in research and development.

Threat: The malicious insider downloaded highly confidential business documents—in accord with his designated access rights and the need-to-know-principle—and removed them from a company laptop (and premises) before "defecting" to a competitor.

Vulnerability: No document-level data loss prevention controls were applied; no security controls alerted a distributed bulk folder/file download from the company cloud storage; and no physical data loss prevention controls were practiced.

From figure 3, it can be seen that every year data breaches are increasing like anything which are needed to be taken care by some strong security mechanisms.

Insecure Interface API

Cloud computing service providers uses a set of software user interfaces (Gunjan et al, 2013) (UIs), application interfaces and virtual infrastructure that is build up on some hardware. Thus, unsecure or compromised hardware or interfaces can cause accidental and malicious breaches to the security of overall system. An example of this threat was noted in Home Depot in 2014, when an attack had self-checkout lanes for several days before detection, affecting around 56 million credit card numbers. As per Cloud Security alliance report (Fernandes et al, 2014), an attack occurs on MangoDB database in 2016 and the attacker has compromised the insecure interfaces. The details of the attack are:

Figure 3. Cyber crime: number of breaches and records exposed 2005-2018

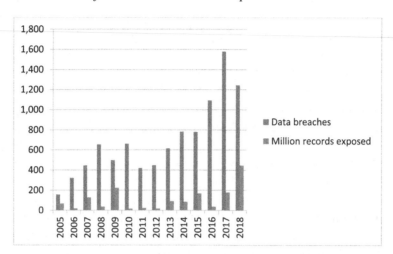

Threat Actor: A threat actor could be any malicious actor who discovers an unprotected default installation of a MongoDB database.

Threat: A default installation the MongoDB database could be accessed without any authentication or access control when browsing the open MongoDB 27017 port issue. Cyber security expert Chris Vickery found data stored in an Amazon Web Services (AWS) MongoDB database—including personally identifiable information (PII) and voting records of 93 million Mexican voters—to be at-risk.

Vulnerability: An unsecured MongoDB port 27017 allowed an outside network attack, and no authentication or access control was

enforced for the backend database MongoDB. All data could be manipulated (added, removed, modified and queried) by anyone.

Shared Technology Vulnerability

Many of the security issues on cloud are result of lax authentication, poor key management and weak passwords (Radhan et al, 2012). It is essential for a consumer to know about the secure identification measure used by their cloud service provider. In addition to this, centralization of identities on a solitary repository is also a potentially high risks factor, as it can become an easy target for attackers. In 2012 such an issue occurred at LinkedIn when 6 million user passwords were published online by attackers. In 2015 Attacker compromised the vulnerable Cloudflare site and the details are:

Threat actor: An external malicious actor could send HyperText Transfer Protocol (HTTP) requests to Cloudflare's vulnerable services. The vulnerability was dubbed "Cloudbleed."

Threat: To trigger the vulnerability, the following requirements had to be met: (1) the final buffer had to finish with a malformed script or .img tag; (2) the buffer had to be less than 4KB in length; (3) the customer had to have either e-mail obfuscation enabled or

automatic HTTPS rewrites/server-side excludes in combination with another feature that utilized the old parser; and (4) the client IP must have a poor reputation.

Vulnerability: In a buffer over-read vulnerability, more memory was returned to the requester than was desired, resulting in memory leakage. Furthermore, Cloudflare is a shared technology, so the vulnerability affects more than just one tenant in a cloud service.

Distributed Denial of Service

This is not a new threat, the methods of attack include fraud, exploitation of software bugs and phishing. With cloud platform, by compromising your credential information attacker can intrude on your every web activity and transaction. It can result into distribution of falsified information, redirecting to illegitimate sites, manipulation of data and consumes inordinate amounts of finite system resources such as processor power, memory, disk space or network bandwidth . Such incident had occurred in 2012, when hackers hacked into 68 million accounts of Dropbox and sold stolen credentials on dark web. In 2016, On the Dyn website has reported about DNS DDoS attack and the details are (Bradford et al, 2017)

Threat actor: Malicious externals targeted attacks through connected IoT devices, causing a Distributed Denial of Service (DDoS) in October 2016.

Threat: The mastermind behind the attack utilized Mirai malware to infect IoT devices to create a botnet. The botnet was then used to launch the DDoS attack.

Vulnerability: IoT devices were compromised due to the use of default credentials. These compromised devices were then incorporated into a botnet. This botnet was later configured to launch the DDoS attack on Dyn, a domain name system (DNS) provider.

Customers of Dyn who did not have a backup DNS provider were impacted, as DNS queries to their sites couldn't be resolved.

Outdated Versions and Patching

This threat includes exploitation of bugs in the program, poorly configured database, illegal software use. It enables attackers to infiltrate into cloud system for stealing data or controlling system or disrupting operations. In addition to this, multi-tenancy in cloud computing and shared pool of resources adds to this issue (Gunjan et al, 2013). An example of this threat was noted in 2016, when confidential data of voters from National Electoral Institute of Mexico was compromised, due to poorly configured database by illegally hosting Amazon cloud server (Bradford et al, 2017). Also, in 2017 Equifix, an organization failed to get the alert and apply the available patch, which later compromises the system vulnerability. The attack details are:

Threat actor: Malicious externals targeted attacks through default patches which are available publicly

Threat: Poorly configured database, Patches flaws are in the knowledge of public domain.

Vulnerability: If the alerts are not pop up or may be ignored then the automated update will install all the flaws available in the default patch.

Abuse and Nefarious Use of Cloud

This threat arises due to relatively weak registration systems present in the cloud computing environment. (Ashraf et al, 2018) In cloud computing registration process (Hamza et al, 2013), anyone having a valid credit card can register and use the service. This facilitates anonymity, due to which spammer, malicious code authors and criminals can attack the system. In 2016 (Bradford et al, 2017), The company Zepto faced this attack, the details of attacks are given below:

Threat actor: An ignorant employee opened a spam message with a ".wsf" or ".docm" file attachment.

Threat: The .wsf file included detection evasion scripts combining multiple programming languages, allowing it to pass through emulation engines that rely on a single language. The malicious file also used sharing and collaboration in Software as a Service (SaaS) cloud services—including Microsoft OneDrive, Google Drive, Box and Dropbox—to infect other systems.

Vulnerability: Windows changes a .wsf file icon to look like a valid spreadsheet file. Furthermore, collaboration software made the .wsf file look like a local file to employees with inadequate training.

LITERATURE SURVEY

Summary of Proposed Security Solutions

In the paper (El-Yahyaoui et al, 2018) Authors presented a new fully homomorphic encryption scheme from integers. Which uses a large integer ring as cleartext space and only one sharable key for encryption and decryption for symmetric encryption. Due to Fully homomorphic the scheme was able to compute on any type of data. In this scheme they have almost achieved data security but unable to control the noise which was introduces at the time of encryption.

The paper (Ashraf et al, 2018) focused on the protection of client data. In this author have presented a Transparency Service Model which provides a mechanism where cloud provider configures the service on the cloud by giving the service information about the cloud storage devices that would exist the data. It is then responsibility of the TSM to store data on those devices and cloud providers no longer direct access to data storage on those devices. Also they have used access control policies along with the authentication mechanism towards having a secure cloud API.

In the paper (Hamza et al, 2013) authors explored and investigated the scope and magnitude of one of the top cloud computing security threats "abuse and nefarious use of cloud computing" and present some of the attacks specific to this top threat as it represents a major barrier for decision makers to adopting cloud computing model.

Insecure interface API is an violation against integrity and confidentiality, in paper (Jabir et al, 2016), author discussed a strong authentication mechanisms along with access control to protect the information.

Cloud is all about sharing the resources but what about the security when sharing is itself became a vulnerability, therefore the authors in paper (Musa et al, 2016) presented access control mechanism along with the strong service level agreements between the users and vendors to provide and maintain the security.

In the paper (Mondal et al, 2017)Author presented a Fuzzy based mechanism, which is helpful for the detection of Distributed Denial of Service (DDoS) attack in cloud computing environment. In the system they have taken three inputs and calculated one output. In the input section, entropy of source IP, port address and packet arrival rate are considered. Using these parameters they have shown attack status based on Fuzzy IF-THEN rules.

In the paper (Bhushan et al, 2018) proposed an approach to detect DDoS attacks in SDN-based cloud by utilizing the features of SDN. The proposed approach can detect the DDoS attacks with very low communicational and computational overhead.

All the safety measures against the security issues in cloud computing having some limitations also, therefore along with their research context, used technique in the paper, advantages and limitations are mentioned in a summarized form in the below table 1.

Table 2. Summary of most popular attacks and their recent countermeasures

References	Research Context	Technique Used	Advantages	Limitations
(El-Yahyaoui et al, 2018)	Data Breach	Fully Homomorphism Encryption from Integers	Work on any type of computation over encrypted data	Control of noise
(Ashraf et al, 2018)		Transparency Service Model	The mechanisms is responsible to store data on The devices via TSM and the access of those devices are not given to the cloud provides	Not implemented yet
(Jabir et al, 2016)	Insecure Interface API	Through Authentication & Access Control	Provides security to data and grant access to authorized person	Auto & default options are still there for some API.
(Musa et al, 2016)	Shared Technology Vulnerability	Access control to the authenticated administrator or users as per their need. Remove all the user data after use. Evaluating the unauthorized environment A strong service level agreement for vulnerability remediation	Providing authentication and integrity	SLA are not being updated as per the technology updated
[(Mondal et al, 2017)	Distributed Denial of Service	-Used openFlow from SDN	Information distance was created between attack and non attack flow	-Quality of Service, Cost and Performance are not being considered as a parameter at the time of testing. -False Alarm generate d very frequently
		A Fuzzy based mechanism	Better Results in case of only three inputs	Less no of inputs for calculating Entropy
(Hamza et al, 2013)	Outdated Versions & Patching	Heterogeneous platform support -Perform Application patching -Patch every week -Be agaentless in the data center -Mitigate after exceptions	Platform Independent patches	Even for a small requirement, the entire patch will be downloaded instead of that single resource file requirement
(Hamza et al, 2013)	Abusive & Nefarious Use of Cloud	Tto check the reputation of the CSP along with the SLAs that they offer. The CSP can implement various compensatory controls, for example limiting per instance bandwidth, or implementing reputation based IP filtering, and choose a subscription model that makes it harder for a criminal to abuse the services on offer.	SLA, Filtering and checks at many levels	Processing so many checks for security increases the overhead.

Critical Evaluation

There are a series of research on various security Issues such as data breaches, Insecure Interface API, DDoS, Outdated Patches & versions, Abuse & Nefarious use of cloud and shared technology over the cloud computing. Many tools, Models and approaches have been proposed to address and handle those issues. Table I presents the summary of the proposed mechanisms along with their advantages and limitations against those issues.

Also from figure 4, it can be concluded easily that there are lots of other reasons which make the system vulnerable such as traditional security mechanisms are still exists but they are not capable enough to fight against the vulnerability. Businesses have good visibility of all critical data but this factor has very less number. Even in this era, databases are not encrypted and people are using it. Many organization are still keeping the user inforamation such as name, password and profile information in plain text which can be captured by the attacker any time. Figure 4 shows commonly used factors for cloud ecurity.

THREAT MODELING

In the definition of information security, a threat is a potential violation of the security of system (Verburg et al, 2016; Hassan et al, 2019) but on the other hand, the vulnerability can be defined as a defect that makes a system vulnerable to attack. An attack is the exploitation of vulnerability. The countermeasures are defensive mechanisms used to combat against the vulnerabilities. Threat modeling for cloud computing platforms can help to identify the events of the threat, its attack surface and access points on the assets of the Cloud. Modeling is used to analyze threats and associated risks in order to developing defensive strategies for them.

Figure 4. Cloud security statistics

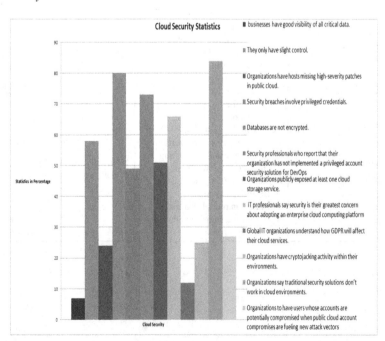

The Classification of Security Issues

The classification of security issues in cloud computing can be done into six classes, which are summarized in Table 2. In paper (Chitchyan et al, 2015) which has a similar approach, the authors addressed a small set of issues in cloud computing but all those issues are covered partially in four category.

The Data Breaches (C1) represents the violation of data integrity and data privacy issues in all three service models. The Insecure Interface API (C2) covers all the operations with poor authentication mechanisms by which users interact with the resources, it is also break the integrity. The (C3) class which is shared technology works on the basic infrastructure resources. The DDoS (C4), can also be categorized in network category is all the means by which users connect to the cloud infrastructure to perform the desired calculations. It includes browsers, network connections and information exchange but this class make the service unavailable for the user. The Outdated Versions and patching (C5) is a user-oriented class and includes issues of installation of a new patch or having the older version only. The Abuse & Nefarious use of cloud category (C6) includes cloud security issues in SaaS, PaaS and IaaS and it is particularly related to unwanted use of a cloud in a improper manner. These six categories are illustrated in Table 2. In fact, (C1) is considered as the greatest security challenge in the cloud as well as big data. Cloud computing is more prone to attacks linked to networks over traditional computing paradigms. In addition, cloud operations are closely coupled and highly dependent on the network implementation.

Table 3. The classification of security issues

Name	Classification	Explanation
C1	Data Breaches	This issue is a violation of the Security goal-confidentiality. The confidential information is disclosed to attackers. In the data breach, the information can be either stolen or leaked by an un authorized person who is not authorized to access it.
C2	Insecure Interface API	Users on the cloud computing are managing their resources through API only and insecure interface API means there is a trap in which user give their useful and confidential information to the attacker or a third party. Also, these insecure API has a weaker authentication methods or static methods which in turn grant access of the resources to an unauthorized person.
C3	Shared Technology Vulnerability	Describes sharing of the cloud infrastructure. It makes the system vulnerable based on weak key management and poor authentication systems.
C4	DDoS	Distributed denial of service attacks means exploitation of the resources such as Network Bandwidth, Power and other resources so that the authorized user can not access the resources for which he/she is authorized.
C5	Outdated Versions & Patching	Outdated versions can be compromised by the attacker by compromising the loopholes available in that older versions so users are advised to always have the updated software and also install the patches through the authentic sources.
C6	Abuse & Nefarious Use of Cloud	The common and multi-occupancy nature of distributed computing makes a rich ground for insider danger and advances danger of "benefit misuse" to private client Facilitating delicate data from various customers on the equivalent physical machine absolutely lures clients with high benefit jobs, for example, framework directors and data security chiefs to misuse their special access to customers' touchy information and the likelihood of spilling or selling that data to contenders or different gatherings of intrigue. The likelihood, and subsequently sway, of this hazard can be further intensified if cloud supplier does not uphold severe meaning of jobs and obligations or does not apply the "need to know" guideline

Analysis of Security Issues

Table 3 represents the factors of classification in security issues in Cloud Computing. Factors are marked with questions with "Q1, Q2, ..., Qn" where Qx is the number of security problem x. In the classification of Data Breaches, there are many questions raised such as Data redundancy (Q1), Data loss and leakage (Q2), Data Privacy (Q3), Data Protection (Q4) and Data availability (Q5). All these issues are talking about breaching against data integrity. While in the another classification Insecure Interface API, there are Browser Security (Q6) which led the attacker inside the system, it is the first step where security measures have to be taken into account because its vulnerabilities open the window to many attacks. Here the question is about vulnerabilities in the set of APIs in the cloud, customers view that use these APIs to connect to platforms which can expose an organization to several threats such as unauthorized access, transmission of content, and data logging. A client can access data and compose services of multiple cloud providers, using a mobile application or a browser. This kind of access brings a level of inherent risk and this risk has been called the access of privileged users (Q7). The conventional Authentication Mechanisms (Q8) are not sufficient now a days to deal with security. Malicious insiders (Q9), like administrators, can seriously damage the security organizations, due to their high level of access, and cause considerable losses to both the organization finance and production. Therefore, it is essential for cloud customers to clearly identify the policies that their cloud providers use to detect and defend against internal threats.

A simple error in the configuration of a cloud component may lead to serious consequences because the cloud configurations could be shared by many services. Technical defects of the shares (Q10), also known as sharing the fate, in which errors are transferred from a corrupted server to each virtual machine created on the server. So, it is extremely important to identify and correct problems of sharing also implementing best practices to prevent them from reproducing.

The reliability of suppliers (Q11) is an important factor that requires verification of personal history to control data and access to the material. It is strongly recommended that companies assess its staff in order to protect its assets, data and gain customer trust. The servers in the cloud are the backbone of its infrastructure that provides many services such as directory services, data storage. Attackers can access the system if the servers of security attributes are not configured correctly, security miconfiguration (Q12). This misconfiguration could occur in the web server and platform. The Cloud is used to serve multiple concurrent users through virtualization, which allows sharing the same hardware and software resources by different users. This multi tenancy capability (Q13) could result in a leak of information from a tenant to other companion servers.

In terms of server location (Q14), it is important to keep in mind that the room should have an anti-seismic protection and should have no window for safety reasons.

The rate of network attacks increases dramatically especially when the migrating data to the cloud. The possible lack of suitable network firewall facilities (Q15) and poor network security configurations (Q16) make it easier for attackers to impersonate a legitimate system user to gain access to the cloud. They can make cloud resources unavailable by generating false data, or injecting and execute malicious code on the server in question. A Dos attack can be launched by exploiting vulnerabilities in the identification of internet protocols (Q17), which would highlight the insecurity of the internet. Cloud adoption will increase dependence to internet (Q18), since it is the primary means to access the cloud. Consequently, if internet is deactivated, because of some attacks, it means that cloud services become unavailable and the cloud severely paralyzed. This implies all network reliability issues.

The hijacking of accounts and services (Q20) is a frequent security risk due to phishing, which is a technique used by hackers to steal identifying information in order to gain unauthorized access to servers. This unauthorized access is a threat to data integrity, confidentiality and availability. Unauthorized access can be launched from inside or outside the organization.

Cloud computing lacks of proper security controls (Q21). Even if the safety measures are set correctly, many safety problems are still associated with compliance risk (Q22) mainly because of the location of data and identification of corresponding law. One of the most important aspects of the security in cloud is auditability (Q23) to ensure traceability of access and the preservation of these traces in case of need.

However, we do not have verification tool of standards for cloud services providers. If a supplier subcontracts a service to a third party where the feature is not transparent, users should be able to inspect the entire process. Security Controls(Q21) and the governing bodies are defined in SLA (Q24), but the legal aspects are not taken in the practices of cloud computing.

The service level agreement (Mahmood et al, 2011; Abghour et al, 2018; Ahuja et al, 2018; Kashif et al, 2019; Li et al, 2018; Yin et al, 2018) is a contract that defines the relationship between the parties clients and suppliers, which is extremely important for both of them. It includes the definition of customer needs, simplifies complex problems, encourages dialogue in the event of disputes, provides a framework for understanding, reduces and eliminates conflict area.

In Table 4 we categorized the most popular attacks in the cloud and their recent countermeasure . Table 4 presents the cause of attack and also the classified class as per Table 1 and Table 3 along with their references.

Table 4. Factors for classification of security issues in cloud computing

Classification	Label	Issues
Data Breaches	Q1	Data redundancy
	Q2	Data loss and leakage
	Q3	Data privacy
	Q4	Data protection
	Q5	Data availability
Insecure Interface API	Q6	Browser Security
	Q7	Privileged User Access
	Q8	Authentication Mechanisms
	Q9	Malicious Insider
Shared Technology Vulnerability	Q10	Sharing technical flaws
	Q11	Reliability of suppliers
	Q12	Security misconfiguration
	Q13	Multi tenancy
	Q14	Server Location and Backup Data
DDoS	Q15	Improper installation of network firewalls
	Q16	Poor Network security configurations
	Q17	Internet protocol vulnerabilities
	Q18	Dependence of Cloud on Internet Access
Outdated Versions & Patching	Q19	Cloud infrastructure
	Q20	Account and service hijacking
Abuse & Nefarious Use of Cloud	Q21	Lack of security standards
	Q22	Compliance risks
	Q23	Lack of auditing
	Q24	Lack of legal aspects (service level agreement)

Table 5. The most common attacks and proposed countermeasures in the cloud

References	Attack	Countermeasures	Vulnerability	Class of Attack
(El-Yahyaoui et al,2018)	Malicious Insider	Fully Homomorphism Encryption from Integers	Q2,Q3,Q4,Q5,Q9	C1
(Ashraf et al, 2018)	Malware Injection	Transparency Service Model	Q1,Q2,Q3	C1
(Jabir etal, 2016)	Insecure Interface API	Through Authentication & Access Control	Q6,Q7,Q8	C1,C2,C4
(Musa et l, 2016)	Shared Technology Vulnerability	Access control to the authenticated administrator or users as per their need. Remove all the user data after use. Evaluating the unauthorized environment A strong service level agreement for vulnerability remediation	Q11,Q12,Q13,Q14,Q15, Q20, Q21,Q23	C3,C4
(Moundal et al, 2017)	Distributed Denial of Service	-Used openFlow from SDN	Q6,Q7,Q8,Q9,Q10	C1,C4
(Bushan et al, 2018)		A Fuzzy based mechanism	Q20,Q21,Q23	C1,C4
(Radhan et al, 2012)	Outdated Versions & Patching	Heterogeneous platform support -Perform Application patching -Patch every week -Be agaentless in the data center -Mitigate after exceptions	Q6,Q16,Q17,Q19,Q20	C2,C4,C5
[(Hamza et al, 2013)	Abusive & Nefarious Use of Cloud	There is not much a cloud consumer can do, other than to check the reputation of the CSP along with the SLAs that they offer. The CSP can implement various compensatory controls, for example limiting per instance bandwidth, or implementing reputation based IP filtering, and choose a subscription model that makes it harder for a criminal to abuse the services on offer.	Q18,Q21,Q22,Q23,Q24	C4,C5,C6

CONCLUSION AND PERSPECTIVE

Cloud computing is a relatively new concept that offers many benefits such as storage capacity, cost reduction, processing power, scalability and more. In fact, the cloud encompasses several technologies like traditional web applications, data hosting as well as virtualization. It also inherits their security problems, the reason that prevent most organizations from adopting it. The cloud security is the main concern, a lot of security solutions in this area have been proposed but most of these are immature while some risks remain unresolved.

This chapter performs an analysis on current cloud security challenges, so we have specified security issues such as data breach, insecure interface API, shared technology vulnerability, Distributed Denial of service attacks, outdated versions & patching and abuse & nefarious use of cloud. Then we classify these problems into six security categories. We also summarized the most popular attacks against the cloud, for each type of attack we specify the security category to which it belongs, the vulnerabilities and issues it can lead, as well we discussed some recent countermeasures against the security issues along with their advantages and limitations. It can be seen from the critical evaluation that alone the security scheme is not enough to maintain the security goals therefore there is a need of an integrated approach which will take care of the information by preserving its confidentiality, integrity and availability.

REFERENCES

Abghour, N., & Ouzzif, M. (2018). A novel security framework for managing Android permissions using blockchain technology. *International Journal of Cloud Applications and Computing, 8*(1), 55-79.

Ahuja, S. P., & Deval, N. (2018). On the Performance Evaluation of IaaS Cloud Services With System-Level Benchmarks. *International Journal of Cloud Applications and Computing, 8*(1), 80–96. doi:10.4018/IJCAC.2018010104

Ashraf, Kehkashan, Gull, & Moin u Din. (2018). Transparency service model for data security in cloud computing. *2018 International Conference on Computing, Mathematics and Engineering Technologies (iCoMET)*, 1-6. doi: 10.1109/ICOMET.2018.8346365

Bhushan, K., & Gupta, B. B. (2018). Detecting DDoS Attack using Software Defined Network (SDN) in Cloud Computing Environment. In *2018 5th International Conference on Signal Processing and Integrated Networks (SPIN)*. IEEE. 10.1109/SPIN.2018.8474062

Bradford, C. (2017). *7 Most Infamous Cloud Security Breaches*. Retrieved from https://blog.storagecraft.com/7-infamous-cloudsecurity-breaches/

Chang, V., & Ramachandran, M. (2016). Towards achieving data security with the cloud computing adoption framework. IEEE Transactions on Services Computing, 9(1), 138–151. doi:10.1109/TSC.2015.2491281

El-Yahyaoui & Ech-Chrif El Kettani. (2018). Data privacy in cloud computing. *2018 4th International Conference on Computer and Technology Applications (ICCTA)*, 25-28.

Fernandes, D. A., Soares, L. F., Gomes, J. V., Freire, M. M., & Inácio, P. R. (2014). Security issues in cloud environments: A survey. *International Journal of Information Security, 13*(2), 113–170. doi:10.100710207-013-0208-7

Gunjan, Tiwari, & Sahoo. (2013). *Towards Securing APIs in Cloud Computing*. arXiv preprint arXiv:1307.6649

Hamza, Y. A., & Omar, M. D. (2013). Cloud computing security: Abuse and nefarious use of cloud computing. *Int. J. Comput. Eng. Res, 3*(6), 22–27.

Hassan, H. A., Kashkoush, M. S., Azab, M., & Sheta, W. M. (2019). Impact of using multi-levels of parallelism on HPC applications performance hosted on Azure cloud computing. *International Journal of High Performance Computing and Networking, 13*(3), 251–260. doi:10.1504/IJHPCN.2019.098579

Islam, Manivannan, & Zeadally. (2016). A classification and characterization of security threats in cloud computing. *Int. J. Next-Gener.Comput, 7*(1).

Jabir, R. M. (2016). Analysis of cloud computing attacks and countermeasures. In *2016 18th International Conference on Advanced Communication Technology (ICACT)*. IEEE.

Kashif, U. A. (2019). *Architectural design of trusted platform for IaaS cloud computing. In Cloud Security: Concepts, Methodologies, Tools, and Applications* (pp. 393–411). IGI Global.

Li, C., Zhang, Z., & Zhang, L. (2018). A Novel Authorization Scheme for Multimedia Social Networks Under Cloud Storage Method by Using MA-CP-ABE. *International Journal of Cloud Applications and Computing*, *8*(3), 32–47. doi:10.4018/IJCAC.2018070103

Mahmood, Z. (2011). Data location and security issues in cloud computing. In *Emerging Intelligent Data and Web Technologies (EIDWT), 2011 International Conference on*. IEEE. 10.1109/EIDWT.2011.16

Mathisen, E. (2011). Security challenges and solutions in cloud computing. *5th IEEE International Conference on Digital Ecosystems and Technologies (IEEE DEST 2011)*. 10.1109/DEST.2011.5936627

Mell, P., & Grance, T. (2010). The nist definition of cloud computing. *Communications of the ACM*, *53*(6), 50.

Miki, N., Ino, F., & Hagihara, K. (2019). PACC: A directive-based programming framework for out-of-core stencil computation on accelerators. *International Journal of High Performance Computing and Networking*, *13*(1), 19–34. doi:10.1504/IJHPCN.2019.097046

Mondal, H. S. (2017). Enhancing secure cloud computing environment by Detecting DDoS attack using fuzzy logic. In *2017 3rd International Conference on Electrical Information and Communication Technology (EICT)*. IEEE. 10.1109/EICT.2017.8275211

Musa, F. A., & Sani, S. M. (2016). Security Threats and Countermeasures In Cloud Computing. *International Research Journal of Electronics and Computer Engineering*, *2*(4), 22–27.

Radhan, T., Patidar, M., Reddy, K., & Asha, A. (2012). *Understanding Shared Technology in Cloud Computing and Data Recovery Vulnerability*. Retrieved from www.ijcst.com

Rittinghouse, J. W., & Ransome, J. F. (2016). *Cloud computing: implementation, management, and security*. CRC Press.

Sengupta, S., Kaulgud, V., & Sharma, V. S. (2011). Cloud computing security–trends and research directions. *2011 IEEE World Congress on Services*, 524–531. 10.1109/SERVICES.2011.20

Sethi, S., & Sruti, S. (2016). *Cloud security issues and challenges*. Resource Management and Efficiency in Cloud Computing Environments.

Sethi, S., & Sruti, S. (2016). *Cloud security issues and challenges*. Resource Management and Efficiency in Cloud Computing Environments.

Verburg, P. H., Dearing, J. A., Dyke, J. G., van der Leeuw, S., Seitzinger, S., Steffen, W., & Syvitski, J. (2016). Methods and approaches to modelling the anthropocene. *Global Environmental Change*, *39*, 328–340. doi:10.1016/j.gloenvcha.2015.08.007

Wang, H., Han, H., Wang, X., Fang, R., & Mei, W. (2019). A high efficient map-matching algorithm for the GPS data processing intended for the highways. *IJHPCN, 13*(2), 132–140. doi:10.1504/IJH-PCN.2019.097504

Yin, H., Zhao, Q., Xu, D., Chen, X., Chang, Y., Yue, H., & Zhao, N. (2019). 1.25 Gbits/s-message experimental transmission utilising chaos-based fibre-optic secure communications over 143 km. *International Journal of High Performance Computing and Networking, 14*(1), 42–51. doi:10.1504/IJHPCN.2019.099738

Zhou, F., Goel, M., Desnoyers, P., & Sundaram, R. (2013). Scheduler vulnerabilities and coordinated attacks in cloud computing. *Journal of Computer Security, 21*(4), 533–559. doi:10.3233/JCS-130474

Chapter 8

A Framework Strategy to Overcome Trust Issues on Cloud Computing Adoption in Higher Education

Mohammed Banu Ali

(iD) https://orcid.org/0000-0001-5854-8245

Alliance Manchester Business School, The University of Manchester, UK

Trevor Wood-Harper

Alliance Manchester Business School, The University of Manchester, UK

Ronald Ramlogan

Alliance Manchester Business School, The University of Manchester, UK

ABSTRACT

Cloud computing has the potential of adding strategic value to the higher education domain owing to exemplary growth in ubiquitous data and communication services ranging from student access to educational materials to developing teaching and research practices. Despite the wide adoption of CC in HEIs, there is a paucity of research that specifically addresses the issue of trust in cloud adoption in the UK HEI context, as well as identifying smarter and more efficient strategies to overcome the existing CC trust issue in this domain. The authors propose a five-stage strategic roadmap to address the trust issues impacting the uptake of cloud services in UK universities. They conclude that IT and management participation and support are the keys to the success of the strategic framework.

INTRODUCTION

Given the exemplary growth in ubiquitous data and communication services ranging from student access to educational materials to developing teaching and research practices, cloud computing (CC) is a potential game changer in the higher education sector (Ali, 2019a; Jawad et al., 2017; Tariq et al., 2017;

DOI: 10.4018/978-1-7998-1082-7.ch008

Copyright © 2020, IGI Global. Copying or distributing in print or electronic forms without written permission of IGI Global is prohibited.

Wasilah et al., 2017). This affirms the enormity of IT support needs for innovative teaching and research activities. However, stakeholders such as IT staff and administrators in higher education institutions (HEIs) are expected to address various challenges in the form trust and security (Rao & Selvamani, 2015), which the cloud can potentially manage effectively. Therefore, there is a need to find more innovative ways to manage the increasing demand for data and communication services while controlling costs and keeping stakeholders happy.

A 2014 Compuware study suggests that over 70% of companies do not trust their cloud vendor and that IT professionals perceive service contracts that are designed by the cloud vendors regarding availability fail to mitigate the potential risks pertaining to the management of cloud applications (Compuware, 2014). Despite the abundance of cloud adoption studies in the wider HEI context (Ali, 2019b; Muriithi et al., 2016; Odeh et al., 2017; Tariq et al., 2017; Yuvaraj, 2016), research on smarter strategies to overcome the existing CC trust issue to increase the uptake of cloud in HEIs have been ignored (Ali, 2019c; Mohammed Banu et al., 2019; Chiregi & Jafari Navimipour, 2017; Kouatli, 2016). Therefore, the motivation of this paper stems from the lack of key stakeholders' trust in making their adoptive decision of CC. In order to tackle this problem, this paper develops a strategic framework Universities can use to work collaboratively with cloud vendors, maximise the use of cloud services to enhance institutional practices and more importantly, build stakeholders' trust in cloud services.

LITERATURE REVIEW

In this section, the key literature pertaining to cloud computing (CC) issues are reviewed. Here, a logical connection between various secondary sources are drawn, including journals, books, white papers and other scholarly resources. In particular, our review also focuses on the trust issues of CC adoption in the higher education domain.

Cloud Computing (CC)

There are number of CC definitions cited in the existing body of literature. A well-known definition cited by Sultan (2010) refers to CC as a cluster of data centers that offers a range of on-demand resources and services over the internet. CC also refers to the scalable IT resources that are offered to users over a network as an alternative to hosting these resources in-house. Therefore, there is a much wider concept of unified and centralised technology and shared services (Metheny, 2017).

Supporters of CC claim that organisations do not have to face burden of upfront infrastructure costs and allows them to focus their attention towards their core business practices if they adopt the technology (Armbrust et al., 2010; CSA, 2011; Hesarlo, 2014; Thilakarathne & Wijayanayake, 2014). CC is also a good method to rapidly deploy applications with minimal management and maintenance. This allows organisational information communication technologies (ICT) to be rapidly adapted to meet an organisation's changing and unanticipated business needs and demands (Willcocks et al., 2014). For higher education, it can exploit this opportunity to enhance IT agility and ultimately facilitate a number of institutional practices such as teaching, research and innovation activities via the cloud (Encalada & Sequera, 2017).

Table 1. CC components (Mell & Grance, 2011)

Cloud Components		
Characteristics	**Service Models**	**Deployment Models**
On-demand self-service: A consumer is able to provide themselves computing capabilities like network storage and server time without the need for other human interaction, anytime anywhere.	**SaaS** grants consumers the ability to utilise software applications running on the vendor's cloud infrastructure and can be accessed via any client device with internet access and a web browser (e.g. SalesForce, CRM).	**Private cloud** deployment model is the location in which the cloud infrastructure operates on or off the organisation's premises.
Broad Network Access: network capabilities which are access via standard mechanisms that promote heterogeneous client platforms such as workstations, mobile devices, tablets and laptops.	**PaaS** offers a development environment that grants users the freedom to create and run their own custom applications using programming languages and vendor provided tools such as Google App Engine and MS Azure.	**Community cloud** is a cloud which is shared by a number of organisations that have a shared goal. The community cloud is run by the cloud vendor.
Resources pooling: resources are centralised or pooled on the cloud to serve multiple consumers according to their level of demand (e.g. storage, processing, memory and network bandwidth).	**Iaas** enables users to manage processing power, networks, storage and other computing resources on demand (e.g. cloud EC2, Amazon Elastic Compute and Rackspace).	**Public cloud** model is the most common and cost-effective model which is available to the general public, which is owned and managed by the cloud vendor.
Rapid elasticity: capacities can be elastically released and provided. In other words, cloud features can be scaled up and down to meet user/organisational demand.		**Hybrid cloud** combines the best of private, public and community clouds, which are all bound by standardised technologies that allow for communication between these models.

Cloud Service/Deployment Models

Mell and Grance (2011) identified five vital CC characteristics, as well as several key service and deployment models. On-demand self-service, broad network access, resource pooling, rapid elasticity, and measured (pay-per-use) service make up the five essential CC characteristics, whereas Software as a Service (SaaS), Platform as a Service (PaaS), and Infrastructure as a Service (IaaS) make up the service models and finally private, community, public, and hybrid models make up the deployment models (Mell & Grance, 2011). Table 1 summarises the aforementioned CC components, while Table 2 summarises the application of a trust model to the CC components mentioned in Table 1.

Trust Issues in CC Adoption in Organisational and HEI Contexts

Trust can be seen as a sign of recommendation and service selection in the CC domain, and is still an emerging phenomenon in information systems research (Alhanahnah et al., 2017; Matthew & Md, 2017). According to Muchahari and Sinha (2012), trust is closely attached to the CC phenomenon, and plays a significant role in its growth and adoption. Although the trust phenomenon has been widely studied in different research domains, there is no universal definition of the term in the existing literature (Filali & Yagoubi, 2015), with most definitions considering the impact of security on trust in facilitating the decision making process (Moyano et al., 2013). Walterbusch et al. (2013) identified that trust occurs between individuals and other parties. For the cloud, Fan et al. (2012) established that trust is gradually attracting the attention of stakeholders, particularly in the community cloud given its very open environment to external users.

Table 2. Application of trust in cloud service/deployment models (Zargari & Smith, 2014; Kshetri, 2013; Weis & Alves-Foss, 2011; Mell & Grance, 2009)

Service Models	Deployment Models
SaaS is a software distribution model, where users or institutional stakeholders (e.g. academic staff, students and admins) are offered specific pieces of software to support their teaching, learning and research practices. However, trust in SaaS will depend on the user's experience of using the software or whether they can trust that the software is not malicious. Another trust issue rests on the cloud provider who runs the software and enables the user to access it, and thus SaaS users are burdened with less responsibility.	The **private cloud**, this is a cloud infrastructure for exclusive use by the HEI, hosted either internally or externally and managed by a third-party, internally or a combination of them. Although the private cloud may sound more trustworthy as the name suggests, the fact that it can still be controlled by the cloud vendor is a cause for concern, and thus defeats the purpose of a private cloud.
IaaS is an on-demand service of computing power and storage space, and the main trust issue rests on the users' inability to manage the underlying cloud infrastructure.	The **community cloud** is a cloud infrastructure that is shared between several communities or customers that can be hosted and managed internally or externally by a third party or even a combination of the two. However, the community cloud can pose several common trust concerns for HEIs, such as security requirements, mission, compliance considerations and jurisdiction.
PaaS offers users an application environment. The applications are developed and executed by cloud vendors and the platforms. This presents a further trust issue as users cannot control and are unaware of the cloud vendor's activities of the applications that are being installed on the platform, and thus in many cases, users take the risk to trust the cloud vendor.	The **public cloud** is a cloud infrastructure that is made for open use by the general public and can be owned by HEIs. However, the greatest trust concern is that the public cloud is that it is hosted on the cloud provider's premises and is open to the general public. For HEIs, public clouds run the risk of exposing sensitive institutional data to potential hackers and attackers, not to mention the vendor's full control of the public cloud.
	The **hybrid cloud** combines at least two of the aforementioned deployment models, and thus has the greatest trust issue as it can adopt a combination of the aforementioned trust issues.

Trust can be defined as an entity that relies on someone or something to execute a given action e.g. leaving confidential information in the hands of a reliable individual who is expected not to view this information or disclose it to another party. Similarly, Ko et al. (2011) defines trust as "the confidence levels in something or someone" e.g. a user trusting a cloud vendor with their private data (Rathi et al., 2015). Trust also considers security in terms of communication, data storing and resource distribution among other CC determinants (Ding et al., 2015). Khan and Malluhi (2010) explains that establishing trust in CC calls for security measures such as encryption, which helps to maintain data integrity, identity, and data privacy (Stergiou et al., 2018). Therefore, trust provides a good means to enhance system security.

Despite the benefits of the cloud being associated with scalable, flexible and agile services offered by the cloud vendor, high exposure on data privacy and security persists thereby impacting stakeholders' trust in these cloud vendors (Pearson & Benameur, 2010). This lack of trust presents an even greater challenge for institutions of higher learning (e.g. Universities) since these institutions handle large batches of sensitive information or data. Failing to efficiently control data would leave institutions powerless to secure their data from unauthorised parties (Chiregi & Jafari Navimipour, 2017).

CC is also impacted by users' perceptions of trust in the cloud. There are two key determinants that can impact users' trust in cloud services, and these are lack of control and transparency, which in turn impacts the adoption of cloud services (Khan & Malluhi, 2010). According to Sun et al. (2011), trust in distributed computing environments involves soft security elements, which are responsible for handling security in the cloud, and helps to combat malicious entities, thus helping to keep the CC environment safe and secure. However, without a proper security mechanism can lead to data loss and exposure to unauthorised third parties (Abbadi & Martin, 2011; Chiregi & Jafari Navimipour, 2017; Mohammed Banu et al., 2018). Another problem with trust in the cloud is that the contractor can decide to subcontract leading to business exposure since the sub-contractor may have no existing data protection standards in place (Pearson & Benameur, 2010).

The user's perceptions of the cloud are highly significant in cloud adoption. This aligns with the idea that the cloud provider has the ability to safely manage and host cloud data without being involved in the business side. Khan and Malluhi (2010) identified a number of elements that directly affect users' degree of trust, including security, control, ownership and prevention. In addition, lack of trust and transparency are also identified as contributing determinants of limited uptake of the cloud (Khan & Malluhi, 2010). As a means to improve users' trust in cloud services, service providers have to be transparent about their actions and their role in protecting users' data (Ismail et al., 2016).

Measuring Trust in Cloud

When measuring trust relations, there are two significant parties: the trustor and trustee. In the CC context, a trustee refers to the cloud vendor who offers the required services to the trustor. In other words, the trustor utilises the services that the trustee provides. Huang and Nicol (2013) argue that the trustee's expected behaviour is out of the control of the trustor, but a core set of values should be defined as a means to guide them and thus establish a trustee and trustor relationship. As a result, the trustor will depend on the goodwill, capacity and integrity of the trustee to ensure that secure and reliable services are offered to the trustor. Huang and Nicol (2013) identified a number of trust mechanisms that enable cloud users to rate cloud provider's services:

It can be deduced that measuring cloud trust covers a number of specific areas, including evidence, policy, service quality, vendor reputation, service level agreement and transparency. These areas are considered on the cloud trust model presented in section three. In short, it can be deduced that cloud

Table 3. Trust mechanisms of cloud

Trust Mechanism	Description
Cloud Transparency Tool	This can help cloud users to assess a given provider's performance and operations. The criticism of this tool is that it is provided by the cloud service provider which creates an element of bias as they can easily manipulate the data in their favour.
Evidence based trust	This is based on sources of trust, including competence, goodwill and integrity, as well as the trustor's envisaged goals in a specific domain (e.g. quality of service for higher education learning systems).
Policy based trust	This revolves around Public Key Infrastructure (PKI) authentication, which allows two parties to share data over networks via authentication enablers such as digital signatures and public key certificates.
Reputation based trust	This reflects the perceptions of an entire community towards cloud service providers, as well as gathering large groups of peer users rating as means to establish the trustworthiness of the cloud provider. Higher response rates are essential for accurate and meaningful feedback.
SLA Verification and QoS Monitoring	Quality of service (QoS) monitoring helps to verify trust by tracking the provider's performance whereas the service level agreement (SLA) helps to adjust trust based on the agreed service metrics, where it tracks and penalizes vendors in the event of breaching these service metrics. However, the SLA and QoS cannot observe invisible issues such as security and privacy.

Table 4. Summary of key trust concepts

Concept(s)	Author	Trust Element
Trust in Service/Deployment Model Concepts		
Users' experience Malicious software Lack of trust in cloud provider Lack of transparency	Zargari and Smith (2014) Weis and Alves-Foss (2011)	SaaS Service Model
Lack of management of cloud infrastructure Lack of transparency	Zargari and Smith (2014) Weis and Alves-Foss (2011)	IaaS Service Model
Lack of control Lack of transparency Unsafe platform	Zargari and Smith (2014) Weis and Alves-Foss (2011)	PaaS Service Model
Cloud vendor control	Kshetri (2010) Mell and Grance (2009)	Private Deployment Model
Cloud vendor control Open to anyone Disclosure of sensitive institutional data	Kshetri (2010) Mell and Grance (2009)	Public Deployment Model
Security requirements Compliance issues Lack of transparency	Kshetri (2010) Mell and Grance (2009)	Community Deployment Model
A combination of other service model concepts	Kshetri (2010) Mell and Grance (2009)	Hybrid Deployment Model
Trust in Cloud Uptake Concepts		
Data management	Chiregi and Jafari Navimipour (2017) Ding et al. (2015) Chiregi and Jafari Navimipour (2017)	Availability/integrity
Evidence trust	Huang and Nicol (2013)	Confidentiality
Policy trust	Huang and Nicol (2013) Okai et al. (2014)	Integrity
Scalable, agile and flexible services	Pearson and Benameur (2010)	Availability
Security	Khan and Malluhi (2010) Sultan (2010) Krauss and Van der Schyff (2014)	Availability
Service Level Agreement (SLA) & Quality of Service (QoS)	Huang and Nicol (2013) Almajalid (2017)	Confidentiality
Transparency	Huang and Nicol (2013) Khan and Malluhi (2010) Ismail et al. (2016)	Confidentiality
Vendor reputation	Huang and Nicol (2013) Sultan (2010)	Integrity

trust covers a number of areas including confidentiality, availability, integrity and resources. Table 4 summarises the key concepts derived from the literature review.

Conceptual Model

The trust model developed by Mayer et al. (1995) inspires the conceptual model. This trust model helps to determine organisational trust by the trustee, trustor and perceived risks. Availability, integrity and confidentiality are the main elements of trust that make up the trust model and some of these elements have emerged from the existing literature. In particular, these elements affect users' acceptance of cloud services. A fourth element was also added, which is resources as this is an influencing factor in cloud adoption, which reflects the human and technical resources needed to fully benefit from cloud services.

Model Description

This section describes each element included in the conceptual model. Mayer et al. (1995) stated that *ability* reflects the trustee's competence in a given context; *benevolence* reflects the trustee's intention to look out for the trustor's best interests; and *integrity* reflects the core set of values that influence the actions of the trustee. In the context of CC, trust is split into three security elements that reflect trustees' characteristics. *Ability* was changed to *availability* (discretion), since the trustee has to ensure that access to information is granted to only authorised parties and *benevolence* was changed to *confidentiality* (convenience), since the trustee has to ensure that access to information is prohibited to unauthorized users or is not disclosed to the public.

Some risks will be perceived by the trustor based on their own degree of trust of the cloud and the cloud vendor. Therefore, the *risk outcome* (based on *individual behaviour*, *perceived risk* and *willingness to take risk*) determines the uptake of cloud services, since there will be varying degrees of trust among the trustors, thereby influencing cloud service adoption (Mayer et al., 1995).

The trustor's propensity to trust exhibits degrees of comfort to collaborate with trustees. This means that some trustors will require some assurance to gain their trust, whereas others will not require it. A number of key barriers of CC adoption were identified and categorised based on key security elements, such as availability, integrity and confidentiality they affect. Another element known as resources or assets was added to help understand and capture the trustors' capabilities and experiences. This also helped to give insight of the different stakeholder views that affect the uptake of cloud services in HEI settings.

Based on the main themes derived from the literature review, which are incorporated in our conceptual model, this paper proposes the following research questions:

RQ1: To what extent can a trust framework improve the uptake of cloud services in UK higher education?

SRQ1: What are the barriers of trust in existing CC models in HEIs?

SRQ2: What are the barriers of trust affecting the uptake of CC in HEIs?

METHOD

Design

For the research design, a descriptive research design was employed. Here, a descriptive design is valuable, since it enables the researcher to gather data from relevant secondary research sources in order to develop a trust model that reflects a potential adoption strategy to improve the uptake of CC in HEIs, and the identification of key barriers pertaining to CC adoption by the key stakeholders in HEIs. For the empirical study, variables in the form of barriers or trust elements of CC were assessed to determine the existing state of the uptake of cloud services from the perspective of key HEI stakeholders. Both dependent and independent variables were used (Cater-Steel, 2008; Willcocks et al., 2016). The depen-

Figure 1. Conceptual model of cloud trust issues

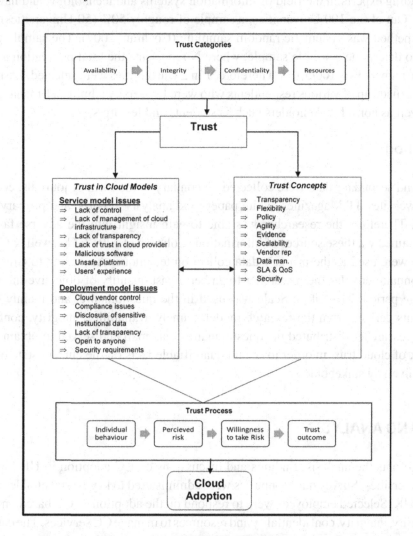

dent variable reflects the current state of CC adoption in HEIs from the perspective of key stakeholders, namely IT security personnel, administrators and IT managers, whereas the independent variable reflects the three security elements that influence trust that were identified in the research model, namely data confidentiality, integrity and availability. Moreover, a quantitative approach was used to obtain data reflecting users' feedback of cloud trust via a questionnaire (Hai-Jew, 2014). Several Universities with key stakeholders were asked to complete a questionnaire.

Population/Sample

The research population was drawn from a list of the top 100 ranked Universities situated in the UK. This included 24 known Russell Group Universities in the UK, all of which are ranked in the top 25 of UK Universities (The Guardian, 2018). The rationale for choosing top raking and Russell Group Universities in the UK was on basis that these Universities have some of the country's top innovation schools and leading experts in the field of information systems and technology, and having varying IT infrastructures. Out of the 100 Universities, a sample of roughly 50% (50 Universities) were selected. The sampling method was systematic random sampling (Cochran, 2007). The sampling constant K = N/n was used to determine a sizable sample, where N represents the total population and n represents the sample size, namely K = 100/50=2. Therefore, 1 in 2 Universities were selected. Lastly, the sampled population were made up of various respondents who were University admins, IT managers and security managers, as well as non-IT stakeholders such as students and lecturers.

Data Collection

Both primary and secondary data were collected. Secondary in the form of journals, company reports, news articles, websites, IT Magazines, white papers and analysts' reports, and primary in the form of empirical data. Therefore, the researcher was able to gain insight into the adverse factors of the research topic obtained via these sources of information (Cohen et al., 2017; Creswell & Creswell, 2018). Questionnaires were used as the primary data collection technique. According to Creswell and Clark (2011), questionnaire enables the researcher to gather a vast quantity of objective information within a restricted time period. The Likert Scale was used in the questionnaire, and mainly focused on the security elements derived from the research model, namely availability, integrity, confidentiality and resources. The researcher distributed the questionnaires via email and served to obtain data reflecting users' feedback of cloud trust in order to obtain quantifiable facts on the current state of cloud service trust among University stakeholders.

FINDINGS AND ANALYSIS

This section presents the analysis, findings and discussions on CC adoption in UK higher education, namely UK universities. Survey questionnaires were administered to key IT stakeholders of the selected universities in UK. Selected employees were to respond on the adoption of CC based on trust elements, such as availability, integrity, confidentiality and resources to manage CC services. The data was analysed with the help of Microsoft Excel Spreadsheet and presented using tables, charts, frequencies, percentages and some statistical summaries.

BACKGROUND INFORMATION

Response Rate

The current study issued 375 questionnaires. The respondents responded to questions on availability and reliability of infrastructures and productivity levels, and resource skills capability, whether there are plans to adopt CC and their current adoption level. They also responded on confidentiality and integrity of the policies for purchasing CC resources by the universities in UK. The employees also ranked the CC services and their efficiency for service delivery.

Table 5. Respondents summary

Position									
Institution	Admin	ITM	SM	Total	Institution	Admin	ITM	SM	Total
1	2	3	3	8	26	2	3	3	8
2	1	3	3	7	27	4	1	1	6
3	2	4	2	8	28	3	3	1	7
4	3	5	1	9	29	1	2	3	6
5	3	4	2	9	30	3	2	1	6
6	2	2	3	7	31	2	5	1	8
7	3	2	4	9	32	1	3	4	8
8	2	4	2	8	33	1	4	2	7
9	2	3	4	9	34	2	2	3	7
10	3	3	2	8	35	1	2	4	7
11	1	3	2	6	36	4	2	1	7
12	2	3	4	9	37	2	4	2	8
13	2	3	2	7	38	1	3	5	9
14	2	2	3	7	39	5	3	1	9
15	3	4	2	9	40	1	2	2	5
16	1	4	2	7	41	2	3	2	7
17	2	3	3	8	42	3	3	2	8
18	5	2	2	9	43	2	3	3	8
19	2	4	2	8	44	3	3	2	8
20	3	2	4	9	45	3	3	3	9
21	1	3	3	7	46	4	2	1	7
22	3	2	2	7	47	2	2	2	6
23	1	2	1	4	48	3	3	2	8
24	4	2	1	7	49	2	1	4	7
25	4	1	1	6	50	2	3	2	7
								Total	375

From Table 5 and figures 2 and 3, IT managers made up the majority of the population, standing at 140 of the 375 respondents surveyed (37%) with admins (118/375) and security managers (117/375) slightly lagging behind.

Availability

Availability was measured based on three fundamental aspects: cloud services, features or functionality hosted on the cloud and the impact of cloud services on productivity. Therefore, availability reflects the trustee's tendencies to check whether information is always available or accessible to permitted users. This is consistent with the security and reliability aspects of cloud systems, and the results are presented below.

Figure 2. Percentage of sampled participants

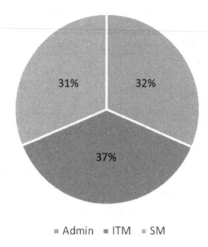

Figure 3. Percentage of sampled universities

System security and infrastructure in terms of reliability were highly ineffective. IT managers and security managers ranked these areas ineffective in terms of security, whilst admins were unaware of the system's security. Most respondents reported infrastructure availability in terms of reliability as effective (244/375) and in terms of security, 232 deemed it effective. Respondents who reported highly effective systems held a similar view concerning the availability of infrastructure in terms of reliability and security. Therefore, infrastructure reliability and system security are effective, thereby affirming the ubiquitous and efficient nature of the University cloud.

With regards to identifying any cloud service(s) that could potentially be hosted on their network, majority strongly agreed that some services are hosted on the cloud (211/375). However, very few respondents (44/375) were aware of the type of cloud service model the University had adopted. Regarding the presence of cloud service functions, functions such as mail or file based storage, faculty, student and information management systems, Google apps and virtualized services were highlighted.

Concerning whether cloud services can increase institutional productivity, the majority disagreed (22/375), whilst others were unsure about cloud services increasing institutional productivity (34/375). However, the majority strongly agreed (201/375) that cloud services can increase institutional productivity.

Integrity

This helped to determine whether the trustee held any core values that encourage behaviour in order to formulate a strategy to resolve any trust issues concerning the uptake of cloud services in UK Universities. This included a set of sub variables, such as strategic integrity, barriers to the uptake of cloud service adoption and emphasis on cloud service providers.

Cloud services were rated, comments about the relationship between cloud service adoption and operational efficiency and views on security in terms of hosting sensitive information on the cloud were deliberated. The results were measured using the Likert scale.

The rating of cloud services to UK Universities yielded a mean of 3.75, indicating its effectiveness. The small deviation of .25 indicates that cloud services are effective in University settings. Regarding cloud services offering operational efficiency, this yielded a mean of 1.82, indicating a moderate agreement. The small deviation of 1.049 indicated that the acceptance of cloud services can improve operation efficiency. With respect to the security of sensitive data stored on the cloud, this yielded a mean of 2.29, indicating a moderate agreement. The small deviation of 1.098 indicated a wide acceptance of the data stored on the cloud is secure.

Concerning the loss of control of data, data privacy, data loss and other general security issues, this yielded a mean of 4.295, 4.041, 3.714 and 3.998 respectively, indicating that these particular factors are a barrier to cloud service adoption. In terms of migration issues, data portability, performance, availability and contractual issues, all these factors yielded a mean score of 3.5 and over, indicating further barriers to cloud service adoption in University settings. For the legal issues affecting the cloud, this yielded a mean score of 3.5 and under, indicating that this particular factor is somewhat of a barrier to cloud service adoption. Moreover, all of the factors under investigation yielded a significant value at $p<.05$, indicating that they had a significant impact on cloud service adoption. Other results indicated that cost (33/375) and trust (54/375) were the least significant barriers to cloud service adoption.

Views on cloud service providers' capability and skills to effectively manage institutional data. The results indicate that 87 out of 375 respondents strongly agree with cloud vendors being fully capable of managing intuitional data, whereas 233 out of the 375 respondents felt unsure.

Confidentiality

This particular variable helped to determine the issues concerning cloud service confidentiality in UK Universities, including factors such as cloud adoption process, service level agreement (SLA), responding to security threats and the cloud vendor's privacy policy.

Views on how the privacy policy impacts the University's purchasing decision were given. The results indicate that majority of respondents (288/375) agreed that the privacy policy has a high or significant impact on cloud purchasing decision, indicating that the privacy policy can be a dissuading factor in the University's cloud purchasing decision.

Next, the respondents gave their perception on security threats concerning cloud services.

Data loss, unavailability of cloud services and data, privacy and vulnerability of shared technology, yielded a mean of 3.795, 4.088, 3.634, 3.701 respectively, indicating that these factors pose a serious security threat. In terms of vendor lock-in and application security and controls, these yielded a mean of 3.5 and over, also indicating that these factors pose a serious security threat. Other factors, such as legal issues and other cloud vulnerabilities e.g. hypervisor, yielded a mean of 3.5 and under, indicating that these factors pose a moderate security threat. Moreover, all of the respondent's perceptions on cloud security threats yielded a significant value at $p < .05$, thereby suggesting that this particular variable has significant influence on the uptake of cloud services.

Thereafter, respondents gave their perception on how cloud security threats are remedied or how they respond to such threats at their respected University.

In terms of reporting security instances, managing threats and vulnerabilities and managing identity and system access, these yielded a mode of 5 (very frequently), indicating that such incidences are a very common means to how these Universities lever security threats. For managing incidence response, this yielded a mode of 4 (frequently), indicating that such incidences are a common means to how these Universities lever security threats.

The respondents then gave their perceptions on the visibility and transparency of cloud vendors.

The results indicate some visibility over cloud services provided by the cloud vendor, yielding a mean of 2.07, indicating that the majority of respondents somewhat agreed. Regarding the cloud vendor's responsibility of signing the SLA, this yielded a mean of 1.06, indicating that the majority of respondents strongly agreed that cloud vendors should be accountable for signing the SLA. However, concerning the impact of the transparency of cloud service operations on the uptake of cloud service adoption, this yielded a mean of 1.47, indicating that the majority of respondents strongly agreed that cloud vendors' provision of transparency over the cloud services has a significant impact on the rate of uptake of cloud services in their respected Universities.

Resources

This particular variable deals with the resources used to manage systems within UK HEIs.

In terms of having sufficient resources and skills to effectively manage internal systems, this yielded a mode of 1, indicating that the majority of respondents agreed. Regarding the average working experience, this yielded a mode of 2, indicating that the majority of respondents somewhat agreed that UK Universities have average working experience in terms of handling system resources.

For suggesting the significance of cloud service adoption, this yielded a mode of 1, indicating that the majority of respondents strongly agreed that CC adds value to their respected Universities. In terms of plan to fully implement cloud services as a cost cutting solution to enhance operational efficiency, this yielded a mode of 2, indicating that the majority of respondents somewhat agreed that UK Universities are planning to fully adopt cloud services as a cost cutting and performance enhancing venture. Finally, concerning the current state of cloud service adoption in UK Universities, this yielded a mode of 1, indicating that UK Universities are already using or have implemented some cloud services, thereby suggesting that they place some degree of trust in cloud services.

DISCUSSION

Our analysis covered four significant areas of cloud adoption trust, namely availability, integrity, confidentiality and resources. Trust characteristics concerning cloud service and development models were also measured, such as vendor control, compliance issues, disclosure of sensitive information, lack of control, lack of management, lack of transparency, lack of trust in cloud provider, malicious software, open to anyone, security requirements, unsafe platform and users' experience. These trust characteristics were found to be consistent with the trust concepts which are discussed below.

Availability was measured in terms of cloud services, features/characteristics or functionality hosted on the cloud and the impact of cloud services on productivity. Integrity was measured in terms of strategic integrity, barriers to the uptake of cloud service adoption and emphasis on cloud service providers. Confidentiality was measured in terms of cloud adoption process, service level agreement (SLA), responding to security threats and the cloud vendor's privacy policy. Resources was measured in terms of the skills and manpower to manage cloud services.

For availability, the respondents came to a consensus about the effectiveness of infrastructure reliability and system security, which affirms the ubiquitous and efficient nature of the cloud that supports internal services within UK Universities. The findings also indicated that technical staffs in HEIs must be effectively trained in order to become versed in cloud service and deployment models in order to boost operational efficiency and draw practical solutions to achieve this (Chiregi and Jafari Navimipour, 2017; Ding et al., 2015; Krauss and Van der Schyff, 2014; Sultan, 2010). Owing to the high availability of cloud systems, it will improve work performances from University staff resulting in high productivity.

For integrity, the respondents agreed that CC is worthy of potential adoption owing to factors, such as the provision of operational efficiency and data security. However, the loss of control of data, data privacy, data loss and other general security issues, were considered barriers to cloud service adoption. This findings was consistent with the trust characteristics derived from the cloud service and deployment models in terms of lack of transparency, disclosure of sensitive information and lack of control from the vendor's side. Migration issues, data portability, performance, availability and contractual issues, were identified as additional barriers to cloud service adoption in University settings. Interestingly, general cost and trust issues were the least significant barriers to cloud service adoption, meaning that they have very little influence on non-adoption of cloud services (Okai et al., 2014; Huang and Nicol, 2013; Sultan, 2010). However, it was also deduced that respondents may be unsure about the role of the cloud vendor and how they handle institutional data, thereby suggesting that Universities place very little faith or trust in the skills and capabilities of cloud vendors to effectively manage institutional data.

For confidentiality, the privacy policy was found to be a dissuading factor in the University's cloud purchasing decision, thus indicating a further barrier to the uptake of cloud service adoption in UK HEIs. Data loss, unavailability of cloud services and data, privacy and vulnerability of shared technology, vendor lock-in and application security and controls were found be key factors that pose a serious security threat that would significantly impact the uptake of cloud service adoption. This is also consistent with the trust characteristics derived from the cloud service and deployment models in terms of a lack of transparency from the vendor's side. Concerning the reporting of security instances, managing threats and vulnerabilities and managing identity and system access, these were found to be common incidences to lever security threats in UK Universities. In terms of the cloud vendor's visibility and their responsibility of signing the SLA, found that they should be held accountable for this. However, in terms of the transparency of cloud service operations, cloud vendors' provision of transparency over the cloud services plays a significant role in cloud service uptake (Almajalid, 2017; Ismail et al., 2016; Huang and Nicol, 2013).

For resources, having sufficient resources and skills to effectively manage internal systems was deemed a significant area to the respondents since this would help to place trust in competent system managers. In terms of the role of resources influencing the uptake of cloud service adoption, it was found that CC would add value to their respected Universities granted they had the sufficient internal resources. The respondents also mentioned that they would adopt the cloud as a cost efficient and production development innovation and that they are currently employing some cloud services to test out this perception. This indicates that some UK Universities do place some degree of trust in the cloud, but will differ across

Table 6. Summary of key trust concepts from empirical study

Trust Element	Concepts
Cloud Models	Cloud vendor control Compliance issues Disclosure of sensitive institutional data Lack of transparency Security requirements
Availability	Effectiveness of infrastructure reliability IT training Performance Productivity System security
Integrity	Availability Contractual issues Cost Data loss Data portability Data privacy Data security Lack of cloud awareness Loss of control of data Migration issues Performance Provision of operational efficiency Trust
Confidentiality	Application security and controls Cloud vendors' visibility and accountability Data loss Privacy Privacy policy Reporting of security instances SLA Transparency Unavailability of cloud services and data Vendor lock-in Vulnerability of shared technology
Resources	Added value Efficacy Skills Systems knowledge

Figure 4. Proposed strategic roadmap to overcome cloud trust issues

these institutions depending on their institutional needs, and how far the aforesaid barriers would impact their trust in the cloud in order to consider its potential uptake. Table 6 summarises the key concepts derived from the findings and discussion.

Interestingly, there were some overlapping and recurring themes from the literature review in comparison to the empirical findings with security, data issues, vendor issues and transparency being the most common. Therefore, it can be deduced that the four aforesaid factors play the most significant role in the trust issues associated with the uptake of cloud services in UK Universities. This deduction can be affirmed in several existing studies (Krauss and Van der Schyff, 2014; Khan and Malluhi, 2010; Sultan, 2010).

PROPOSED STRATEGIC FRAMEWORK

Our proposed strategic framework is developed based on the conceptual model derived from the existing literature and the themes derived from empirical findings to overcome the trust issues impacting the uptake of cloud adoption in UK University settings. This will ultimately support UK Universities to maximise the benefits of cloud services, whilst informing them of the barriers to cloud services and how to mitigate them. Our proposed strategy is a 5 stage roadmap or framework that can be applied to UK HEIs to address the existing cloud uptake problem in terms of trust (see Figure 4).

Our strategic roadmap covers the following stages (Table 7):

The above stages will ensure that UK Universities will trust their proposed cloud solution since they will be fully informed of the benefits and challenges, and acquiring the necessary skills to adopt, implement and eventually utilise the cloud service solution. Moreover, conceptual model has been modified to consider this strategic roadmap to address the trust issues associated with the uptake of cloud services in UK University settings (see Figure 5):

CONCLUSION AND REFLECTION

On reflection, this paper has developed a strategic framework to address the existing trust issues concerning the uptake of cloud services in UK HEIs. Based on our findings, the following conclusions can be drawn.

There is a growing interest of CC services in UK Universities, where the majority appear to be aware of the innovation and only a minority is aware of cloud models. Therefore, there is a need to raise awareness of cloud services to these institutions to ensure that IT staff are well versed with the rapid technological trends like CC. How this can be achieved is by training IT staff in-house and encouraging them to attend a series of CC workshops and seminars to equip them with the necessary knowledge on cloud deployments. This will help to determine a viable solution to fulfil on demand service require-

Figure 5. Adapted Conceptual model to address trust issues of cloud uptake

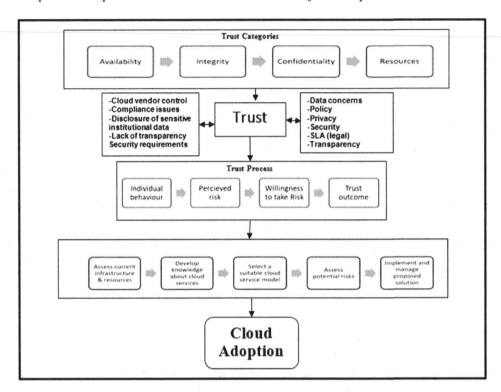

Table 7. Summary of strategic roadmap stages to overcome cloud trust issues

Roadmap Stage	Description
Assessing HEIs' existing resource and infrastructure capabilities	This helps to determine the suitability of the cloud solution by evaluating existing strengths and weaknesses
Building knowledge and competencies	Raising awareness about the cloud service models via conferencing and workshops that teach about cloud services and can encourage collaboration between cloud vendors and UK Universities by learning about different cloud solutions in a practical environment. Engagement can help to capture both theoretical and practical experience of potential cloud solutions
Choosing a suitable cloud model	This involves several key activities, such as cost benefit analysis, identifying the key benefits of cloud services, specific to the University, involving key University stakeholders and decision makers to keep them informed about the proposed cloud solution and a mitigation plan to minimise potential barriers or risks to the cloud deployment
Conducting a risk assessment	This enables the University to measure the potential of the proposed solution and cloud vendor capability in order to determine its feasibility. All important legal issues regarding the proposed cloud solution are also considered, such as legal, contractual and compliance issues, the service level agreement (SLA) between the University and the cloud vendor. This ensures that the availability, integrity and confidentiality concerns regarding the proposed cloud solution are clearly emphasised
Actual adoption and eventual implementation	Adoption and deployment of the proposed cloud solution. IT staff would require internal training to inform them of the nature of the cloud solution and how to use it. After training, preparation for unforeseen issues are carefully planned and all resources are ready to be deployed, the flexible and agile cloud solution can then be implemented in order to reduce costs and bolster operating efficiency and productivity

ments for UK Universities to ultimately reduce costs and increase operational efficiency. Therefore, it can be concluded that UK Universities highly regard CC as an innovative solution to enhance operational efficiency and cut cost.

Statistical analysis indicates a number of key barriers to cloud service adoption in relation to trust, including: compliance issues, contractual issues, data loss, data portability/migration issues, lack of standards, legal issues, limited availability, loss of control of data, performance issues, privacy issues and security issues. The cloud vendor should also be responsible for the cloud service provided to Universities, clearly emphasising the operations on cloud services and adhering to privacy policy, all of which will significantly influence cloud purchasing decisions and ultimately increase the uptake of cloud services.

Formulation of our 5 stage strategic roadmap can help to address the trust issues impacting the uptake of cloud services in UK Universities, and encourage the implementation of cloud services. Our strategic roadmap (see Figure 4) was developed based on a combination of the barriers identified in our findings and existing concepts derived from the literature and proposed conceptual framework. This helped to build our final strategic framework of the trust issues impacting the uptake of cloud service adoption in the UK HEI context (see Figure 5). We conclude that IT and management participation and support is the key to the success of our strategic framework.

LIMITATIONS

The limitations of this paper are threefold:

1. Some questionnaires were incomplete and were omitted from the analysis. However, this did not impact the reliability of the findings as there was an 86.4% response rate, which was a strong representation of the total sampled population;
2. Since email was used to distribute the questionnaire to the respondents, this delayed the data analysis process as it took longer to collect all the data.
3. As this is quantitative study, it failed to fully capture the respondents' wider perceptions of trust in cloud services and had to rely on mean and mode scores to capture this information which had limited detail. Therefore, a qualitative study would help to better capture these trust perceptions.

FUTURE STUDIES

Future studies should consider the following recommendations:

1. Conduct a study on implementation challenges during the adoption phase of cloud services in UK HEIs;
2. To focus on the cost and trust issues as potential barriers and how they impact the uptake of cloud services in UK HEIs;
3. Similar to our strategic framework regarding cloud trust affecting cloud adoption, another study could develop an effective implementation roadmap to raise further awareness of practical CC cases in the UK HEI context.

REFERENCES

Abbadi, I. M. & Martin, A. (2011). Trust in the Cloud. *Information Security Technical Report, 16*(3-4), 108-114.

Alhanahnah, M., Bertok, P., & Tari, Z. (2017). Trusting cloud service providers: Trust phases and a taxonomy of trust factors. *IEEE Cloud Computing, 4*(1), 44–54. doi:10.1109/MCC.2017.20

Ali, M. (2019a). Multiple Perspective of Cloud Computing Adoption Determinants in Higher Education a Systematic Review. *International Journal of Cloud Applications and Computing, 9*(3), 89–109. doi:10.4018/IJCAC.2019070106

Ali, M. (2019b). Cloud Computing at a Cross Road: Quality and Risks in Higher Education. *Advances in Internet of Things, 9*(3), 33–49. doi:10.4236/ait.2019.93003

Ali, M. (2019c). The Barriers and Enablers of the Educational Cloud: A Doctoral Student Perspective. *Open Journal of Business and Management, 7*(1), 24. doi:10.4236/ojbm.2019.71001

Ali, M., Wood-Harper, T., & Al-Gahtani, A. S. (2019). Contextual Analysis of Educational Monitoring and Progression as a Service (EMPaaS) System in Higher Education. *Open Journal of Business and Management, 7*(3), 1525–1542. doi:10.4236/ojbm.2019.73105

Armbrust, M., Fox, A., Griffith, R., Joseph, A. D., Katz, R., Konwinski, A., ... Stoica, I. (2010). A View of Cloud Computing. *Communications of the ACM, 53*(4), 50–58. doi:10.1145/1721654.1721672

Cater-Steel, A. (2008). *Information Systems Research Methods, Epistemology, and Applications.* Information Science Reference.

Chiregi, M. & Jafari Navimipour, N. (2017). Cloud computing and trust evaluation: A systematic literature review of the state-of-the-art mechanisms. *Journal of Electrical Systems and Information Technology.*

Cochran, W. G. (2007). *Sampling techniques.* John Wiley & Sons.

Cohen, L., Manion, L., & Morrison, K. (2017). *Research Methods in Education.* Taylor & Francis. doi:10.4324/9781315456539

Compuware. (2014). *73% of Companies Fear Cloud Providers Hide Performance Problems.* Available: https://www.cnbc.com/2014/04/30/globe-newswire-73-of-companies-fear-cloud-providers-hide-performance-problems.html

Creswell, J. W., & Clark, V. L. P. (2011). *Designing and Conducting Mixed Methods Research.* SAGE Publications.

Creswell, J. W., & Creswell, J. D. (2018). *Research Design: Qualitative, Quantitative, and Mixed Methods Approaches.* SAGE Publications.

CSA. (2011). *Security Guidance for Critical Areas of Focus in Cloud Computing V3.0.* Cloud Security Alliance (CSA).

Ding, H., Li, X., & Gong, C. (2015). Trust model research in cloud computing environment. *2015 International Symposium on Computers & Informatics.* 10.2991/isci-15.2015.143

Encalada, W. L., & Sequera, J. L. C. (2017). Model to Implement Virtual Computing Labs via Cloud Computing Services. *Symmetry*, *9*(7), 117. doi:10.3390ym9070117

Fan, W., Yang, S., Pei, J., & Luo, H. (2012). Building trust into cloud. *International Journal of Cloud Computing and Services Science*, *1*(3), 115–122.

Filali, F. Z., & Yagoubi, B. (2015). Global trust: A trust model for cloud service selection. *International Journal of Computer Network and Information Security*, *7*(5), 41–50. doi:10.5815/ijcnis.2015.05.06

Hai-Jew, S. (2014). *Enhancing Qualitative and Mixed Methods Research with Technology*. IGI Global.

Hesarlo, P. S. (2014). Security, Privacy and Trust Challenges in Cloud Computing and Solutions. *International Journal of Computer Network and Information Security*, *6*(8), 34–40. doi:10.5815/ijcnis.2014.08.05

Huang, J., & Nicol, D. M. (2013). Trust mechanisms for cloud computing. *Journal of Cloud Computing: Advances. Systems and Applications*, *2*(1), 9.

Ismail, U. M., Islam, S., Ouedraogo, M., & Weippl, E. (2016). A framework for security transparency in cloud computing. *Future Internet*, *8*(1), 5. doi:10.3390/fi8010005

Jawad, Z. M., Ajlan, I. K., & Abdulameer, Z. D. (2017). Cloud Computing Adoption by Higher Education Institutions of Iraq: An Empirical Study. *Journal of Education College Wasit University*, *1*(28), 591–608. doi:10.31185/eduj.Vol1.Iss28.24

Khan, K. M., & Malluhi, Q. (2010). Establishing trust in cloud computing. *IT Professional*, *12*(5), 20–27. doi:10.1109/MITP.2010.128

Ko, R. K., Jagadpramana, P., Mowbray, M., Pearson, S., Kirchberg, M., Liang, Q., & Lee, B. S. (2011). TrustCloud: A framework for accountability and trust in cloud computing. In *Services (SERVICES), 2011 IEEE World Congress on, 2011*. IEEE.

Kouatli, I. (2016). Managing Cloud Computing Environment: Gaining Customer Trust with Security and Ethical Management. *Procedia Computer Science*, 91412–91421.

Matthew, K., & Md, A. (2017). An Effective Way of Evaluating Trust in Inter-cloud Computing. *International Journal of Computer Network and Information Security*, *9*(2), 36–42. doi:10.5815/ijcnis.2017.02.05

Mayer, R. C., Davis, J. H., & Schoorman, F. D. (1995). An integrative model of organizational trust. *Academy of Management Review*, *20*(3), 709–734. doi:10.5465/amr.1995.9508080335

Mell, P., & Grance, T. (2009). The NIST definition of cloud computing. *National Institute of Standards and Technology*, *53*(6), 50.

Mell, P., & Grance, T. (2011). *The NIST definition of cloud computing*. Available: https://www.nist.gov/sites/default/files/documents/itl/cloud/cloud-def-v15.pdf

Metheny, M. (2017). *Federal Cloud Computing: The Definitive Guide for Cloud Service Providers*. Elsevier Science.

Mohammed Banu, A., Trevor, W.-H., & Mostafa, M. (2018). Benefits and Challenges of Cloud Computing Adoption and Usage in Higher Education: A Systematic Literature Review. *International Journal of Enterprise Information Systems*, *14*(4), 64–77. doi:10.4018/IJEIS.2018100105

Moyano, F., Fernandez-Gago, C., & Lopez, J. (2013). A framework for enabling trust requirements in social cloud applications. *Requirements Engineering*, *18*(4), 321–341. doi:10.100700766-013-0171-x

Muchahari, M. K., & Sinha, S. K. (2012). A new trust management architecture for cloud computing environment. In *Cloud and Services Computing (ISCOS), 2012 International Symposium on, 2012*. IEEE.

Muriithi, P., Horner, D. & Pemberton, L. (2016). Factors contributing to adoption and use of information and communication technologies within research collaborations in Kenya. *Information Technology for Development, 22*(sup1), 84-100.

Odeh, M., Garcia-Perez, A., & Warwick, K. (2017). Cloud Computing Adoption at Higher Education Institutions in Developing Countries: A Qualitative Investigation of Main Enablers and Barriers. *International Journal of Information and Education Technology (IJIET)*, *7*(12), 921–927. doi:10.18178/ijiet.2017.7.12.996

Pearson, S., & Benameur, A. (2010). Privacy, security and trust issues arising from cloud computing. In *Cloud Computing Technology and Science (CloudCom), 2010 IEEE Second International Conference on, 2010*. IEEE.

Rao, R. V., & Selvamani, K. (2015). Data Security Challenges and Its Solutions in Cloud Computing. *Procedia Computer Science*, 48204–48209.

Rathi, K., Kumari, S., & Student, M. (2015). A Survey on Trust in Cloud Computing. *International Journal of Engineering Technology. Management and Applied Sciences*, *3*(1), 175–181.

Stergiou, C., Psannis, K. E., Gupta, B. B., & Ishibashi, Y. (2018). Security, privacy & efficiency of sustainable cloud computing for big data & IoT. *Sustainable Computing: Informatics and Systems*, *19*, 174–184.

Sultan, N. (2010). Cloud computing for education: A new dawn? *International Journal of Information Management*, *30*(2), 109–116. doi:10.1016/j.ijinfomgt.2009.09.004

Sun, D., Chang, G., Sun, L., & Wang, X. (2011). Surveying and analyzing security, privacy and trust issues in cloud computing environments. *Procedia Engineering*, 152852–152856.

Tariq, M. I., Tayyaba, S., Rasheed, H., & Ashraf, M. W. (2017). Factors influencing the Cloud Computing adoption in Higher Education Institutions of Punjab, Pakistan. In *Communication, Computing and Digital Systems (C-CODE), International Conference on, 2017*. IEEE.

The Guardian. (2018). *University Research Excellence Framework 2014 – the full rankings*. Available: https://www.theguardian.com/news/datablog/ng-interactive/2014/dec/18/university-research-excellence-framework-2014-full-rankings

Thilakarathne, A., & Wijayanayake, J. I. (2014). Security Challenges Of Cloud Computing. *International Journal of Scientific & Technology Research*, *3*(11), 200–203.

Walterbusch, M., Martens, B., & Teuteberg, F. (2013). Exploring Trust. In *Cloud Computing: A Multi-Method Approach* (p. 145). ECIS.

Wasilah, N. L. E., Santosa, P. I., & Ferdiana, R. (2017). Recommendation of cloud computing use for the academic data storage in University in Lampung Province, Indonesia. *2017 7th International Annual Engineering Seminar (InAES)*, 1-5.

Weis, J., & Alves-Foss, J. (2011). Securing database as a service: Issues and compromises. *IEEE Security and Privacy*, *9*(6), 49–55. doi:10.1109/MSP.2011.127

Willcocks, L., Venters, W., & Whitley, E. (2014). *Moving to the Cloud Corporation*. Palgrave Macmillan. doi:10.1057/9781137347473

Willcocks, L. P., Sauer, C., & Lacity, M. C. (2016). *Enacting Research Methods in Information Systems* (Vol. 2). Palgrave Macmillan.

Yuvaraj, M. (2016). Determining factors for the adoption of cloud computing in developing countries: A case study of Indian academic libraries. *The Bottom Line (New York, N.Y.)*, *29*(4), 259–272. doi:10.1108/BL-02-2016-0009

Zargari, S. A. & Smith, A. (2014). Policing as a service in the cloud. *Information Security Journal: A Global Perspective, 23*(4-6), 148-158.

Chapter 9

A Proposal of Improvement for Transmission Channels in Cloud Environments Using the CBEDE Methodology

Reinaldo Padilha França

State University of Campinas (UNICAMP), Brazil

Yuzo Iano

State University of Campinas (UNICAMP), Brazil

Ana Carolina Borges Monteiro

State University of Campinas (UNICAMP), Brazil

Rangel Arthur

State University of Campinas (UNICAMP), Brazil

ABSTRACT

Sharing, transmitting, and storing data has been one of the great needs of today. In the last years, concepts and developed methodologies of cloud computing systems have been improved. This concept created in the 1960s today is present in daily life from ordinary users to even large companies. The present study aims to develop a method of data transmission based on discrete event concepts. This methodology was named CBEDE (by the acronym). The experiments were matched in the MATLAB software simulation environment, where the memory consumption of the proposed methodology was evaluated. Therefore, the CBEDE methodology presents great potential to intermediate users and computer systems, ensuring speed, low memory consumption, and reliability. Being the differential of this research, the use of discrete events applied in the physical layer of a transmission medium, the bit itself, being this to low-level of abstraction, the results show better computational performance related to memory utilization related to the compression of the information, showing an improvement reaching up to 69.93%

DOI: 10.4018/978-1-7998-1082-7.ch009

Copyright © 2020, IGI Global. Copying or distributing in print or electronic forms without written permission of IGI Global is prohibited.

INTRODUCTION

The roots of the Internet are in the 1960s, but their relevance to business was only first noticed in the early 1990s. The World Wide Web was born in 1991, and in 1993 a browser called Mosaic was released, allowing users to view text pages with graphics. This fostered the creation of the first corporate websites and, not surprisingly, most of them were from computer and technology companies. As Internet connections became faster and more reliable, a new type of enterprise, called the Application Service Provider (ASP), began to emerge. ASPs managed existing business applications for their customers. These companies acquired computing power and administered the applications to their customers who then paid a monthly fee to access the applications over the Internet (Comer, 2018). But it was not until the late 1990s that cloud computing as we know it today began to emerge. Cloud computing is the on-demand delivery of computing power, database storage, applications, and other IT resources through an Internet-based cloud service platform with a price-by-use setting (Jain, Deshpande, Raghu, & Khanaa, 2017).

In 1997, during an academic lecture given by Ramnath Chellap came to the term Cloud Computing. However, many consider this concept to be associated with John Mccarthy, he is considered the pioneer in Artificial Intelligence technology and also the creator of the LISP programming language. This association of the term cloud computing to Mccarthy is due to the fact that in 1960 he stated that "computing may someday be considered as a public utility." In addition, since that time he had been discussing the term time-shared computing sharing. For him could computing allow a computer to be used simultaneously by two or more users in order to perform tasks, taking advantage of the amount of time available between each process. In this way, using the computer together could generate better use and decrease of expenses, since the user would pay only for the time of use of the equipment or, in this case, the technology of the Cloud (Jain, Deshpande, Raghu, & Khanaa, 2017; Rittinghouse & Ransome,2016).

At that time along with Mccarthy, the physicist and scientist of ARPA (Advanced Research Projects Agency) Joseph Carl Licklider, was also creating another concept that would revolutionize the world. Licklider was looking for other useful utilities for the computer and ended up discovering a powerful way to connect people, allowing the communication and sharing of data on a global scale. He is currently considered the pioneer in creating the Internet in the form we know today. From this, it was possible to create a global network of sharing and communication, the ARPANET that evolved to the Internet and enabled the Cloud Computing to begin to take shape. The origin of its name, the cloud, comes from the diagrams of the old ISDN (Digital Services Network) and Frame Relay data networks designed by telephony operators. The interconnection between the two was shown by cloud drawings, to signal something that was out of the reach of the companies. Therefore, we do not always know which computers are the applications in Cloud Computing (Jain, Deshpande, Raghu, & Khanaa, 2017; Rittinghouse & Ransome,2016).

Nowadays, more than 50 years after John Mccarthy's phrase about computing as a public utility, Cloud Computing technology already has a strong breadth. This technology began to be offered commercially in 2008, when small, medium and large companies gradually adopted the technology. In the year 2013 already had an immense acceptance by the corporate universe. This great acceptance has been transforming the service, so that the processing and storage of data began to be treated in the same way as a service of electricity supply, where it is only paid for consumption (de Bruin & Floridi, 2017; Chang, 2015).

Substituting capital expenditures for variable expenses, ie investing substantially in data centers and servers, in cloud computing, establishes the philosophy of paying only when consuming computing resources, and paying only for the quantity consumed. Since then the cloud has grown steadily. It is estimated that by 2013, global investment in cloud-based services has reached $ 47 billion. And this number is projected to double and exceed $ 100 billion over the next few years as companies increase their investment in cloud services as the foundation of their new, more competitive products. In the cloud computing environment, additional IT resources are within reach in just one click, meaning the time it takes to make these resources available to developers is reduced, "what used to be weeks to weeks. This results in a dramatic increase in the agility of the organization, as the cost and time required to experiment and develop are significantly lower (Jain, Deshpande, Raghu, & Khanaa, 2017; Rittinghouse & Ransome,2016).

In this context, many companies have adhered to this new business model, implementing outsourced services by a cloud computing vendor, or building servers and data centers within the company to meet customer and process demands. Meanwhile, other companies are gearing up to serve users and corporations who want to get into the Cloud, be it public, private, or hybrid. With this, Cloud Computing proves to be a bold technology that has come about to change the way we do business and communicate. This is because one of the biggest needs of companies around the world is to have constant access to the company's strategic information to facilitate and qualify the decision-making process (Jain, Deshpande, Raghu, & Khanaa, 2017; Rani,Rani & Babu, 2015).

Cloud computing services are changing how businesses and public institutions use information technology, because the cloud services are available to meet most any existing IT (Information Technology) needs. Although there is a great variety among cloud computing services, all these services have certain basic features and benefits in common, and all can be categorized into a few basic cloud service types. Cloud Computing Services provides Information Technology that can offer a service over the Internet or dedicated network, with delivery on demand, ranging from full applications and development platforms, to servers, storage, and virtual desktops among other applications. Cloud services may vary in their particulars, corporate and government entities. It is may be used as well as colleges and universities to address a variety of application and infrastructure needs such as a database, computing, and data storage (Jain, Deshpande, Raghu, & Khanaa, 2017; Rittinghouse & Ransome,2016).

Unlike a traditional IT environment, where software and hardware are physically funded, which in contrast cloud computing services deliver IT resources in minutes to hours and align costs to current usage. As a result, these organizations have greater agility and can manage their data - information - and expenses more efficiently. Similarly, consumers who use cloud computing services to simplify application utilization like a store, share, and protect content, and enable access from any web-connected device. In this digitally globalized world, we deal with a huge set of data all the time. Data refers to facts, events, actions, activities, and transactions which have been and can be recorded, i.e., the raw material from which information is produced, nurturing the infrastructure and components that enable modern computing (Jain, Deshpande, Raghu, & Khanaa, 2017; Rani,Rani & Babu, 2015).

Cloud Computing Services associated with information technology (IT) encompasses both the internet-enabled sphere as well as the mobile one powered by wireless networks, being able to reach technologies of the type telephones, cellphone, radio, and television broadcast, all of which are still widely used today. In this ample scope, data are a description of the world, being the Information making meaning from the data, and based on the data, one can conclude diverse aspects and relative issues in the world. This conclusion is the information, putting in other words, the information itself is the processed data. Most of the decisions taken in and around the world by and large scale are based on the data and information. In short, Information is the key guiding force of the world today (Schneider & Sunyaev, 2016; Botta, De Donato, Persico & Pescapé, 2016).

In a few words, cloud computing is the delivery of computing services – servers, storage, databases, networking, software, analytics, intelligence and more – over the Internet. "The cloud", popularly called this technology, to offer faster innovation, flexible resources, and economies of scale. Creating a business environment of the type: you pay only for cloud services you use, helping lower your operating costs, run your infrastructure more efficiently, and scale your business needs change (Rittinghouse & Ransome,2016).

Cloud computing is a big shift from traditional business to an increasingly digital and modern world. There are six common reasons organizations and universities are turning to cloud computing services: cost, speed, global scale, productivity, performance, and security. No matter the type of cloud computing service is in use, one thing is certain: large amounts of data will move back and forth between your end users and the cloud provider's data centers, over the internet (Mosco, 2015).

The recent innovations and increasing popularity of smart cities, video analytics are by social media, entertainment, surveillance, smart health monitoring, or even crowd management are used in a range of application domains highly interconnected devices, sensors, and other smart city stakeholders, and as this technology grows with the help of the internet, intranet, extranet, there is a need for the creation of environments that allow the performance of this technology. And with cloud computing this is possible by creating systems where the resources of the data center are shared using virtualization technology, such that it provides an elastic technology, as regards demand and instant services to their customers and charges them based on the resources they use, and its users have developed an innovative era of great global content sharing, without loss of quality, or low effectiveness, being able to environments with cloud computing a large storage of information than conventional often still practiced (Hossain,Muhammad, Abdul,Song & Gupta, 2018; Gou, Z., Yamaguchi, S., & Gupta, 2017; Gupta,2018; Stergiou, Psannis, Kim & Gupta, 2018).

The market in this area grew 47.4% in 2016, according to a study by ABES (Brazilian Association of Software Companies) in partnership with IDC (International Data Corporation). This is because the platforms in the service model are great allies of industry startups to accelerate business and meet the strong demand generated by emerging technologies. Currently, developers can now shorten the time to create, test, and distribute creative, quality apps, especially for smartphones. These entrepreneurs can quickly hire IaaS (infrastructure as a service), SaaS (software as a service), PaaS (Platform as a service), security and other advanced Technologies (Rittinghouse & Ransome,2016; Assunção,Calheiros, Bianchi, Netto & Buyya, 2015).

Cloud Computing debuted by offering SaaS, then added to its portfolio solutions such as IaaS and PaaS, delivered by the Private, Public and Hybrid Cloud. Since Cloud has infinite capacity to provide services, various solutions are emerging in the service model such as DRaaS (Disaster Recovery as a Service), focused on information security; CaaS (Communication as a Service); EaaS (Everything as a Service or DBaas) and DBaas (DataBase as a Service or Database as a Service); among others. Due to its potential for service dissemination, Cloud Computing adoption grows at rates of 20% per year, according to market consultants. These results are associated with the popularization of broadband and mobility (Rittinghouse & Ransome,2016; Schneider & Sunyaev, 2016; Assunção, Calheiros, Bianchi, Netto & Buyya, 2015).

The advantage of IaaS is being able to meet punctual demands, such as sporadic peaks in the use of IT resources, or eliminate expenses with maintenance and allocation of physical devices, without losing control over the installation, management, and configuration of enterprise applications. The advantage of PaaS is that it includes operating systems, development tools, database management systems, business intelligence services, and more, as well as all the infrastructure required to run or refine an application. Another advantage is the need not to worry about capacity planning, acquisition, and maintenance of licenses and software or the management of secondary applications for the success of your projects and developments (Rittinghouse & Ransome, 2016; Assunção, Calheiros, Bianchi, Netto & Buyya, 2015).

Service (SaaS) is the most common type of cloud service, which the company hires the application itself and is only responsible for the use of the resources. The solution provider is responsible for maintaining the infrastructure, ensuring security and supporting the contracted application. The most common examples of SaaS are corporate email services and customer relationship management (CRM) software. Various systems can be found, such as inventory control, cash flow, among other purposes, totally in the cloud, facilitating the routines of the managers of establishments, companies or institutions of the most diverse branches of activity (Rittinghouse & Ransome,2016; Assunção, Calheiros, Bianchi, Netto & Buyya, 2015).

The idea is not just to put files on the internet and access them from any location and any device, for example. Being in the cloud means turning something that would be restricted to a server and/or physical space into something that can be built collaboratively through the knowledge and actions of various people. Centralizing the system of your company in this system has, as a direct consequence, the integration of the different areas of the company and the increase of the effectiveness of the projects, consequences of the digital transformation. One of its main advantages is the best use of hardware investments. Because the heaviest part of the processing is in the "cloud", the user only needs a browser and a good internet connection to use the service. Another huge advantage is the elasticity. If more or less space is needed for storage, simply request an upgrade, without having to change equipment (Stergiou & Psannis, 2017; Marinescu, 2017).

Some researchers believe that by 2020, not having Cloud will be like not owning the Internet these days, something that is essential for survival in such a competitive market. In addition, by using this type of service, it is possible to reduce the space spent on servers and cooling systems, reducing the consumption of electricity and the emission of carbon dioxide. These actions can generate a positive image of the company that employs cloud computing in its business, demonstrating that it is engaged in environmentally friendly policies, making the market and consumers have a positive impression of the business (Stergiou & Psannis, 2017; Marinescu, 2017; Etro, 2015)

Based on this, the present study aims to develop a model of information transmission based on discrete event concepts. This methodology aims to increase the speed in sending and receiving data between cloud computing systems and computers, in addition to consuming less computational memory during this process. Next, we will discuss the concepts of methodologies that contribute to the development of the CBEDE methodology (Coding of Bits for Entities by means of Discrete Events).

Cloud Services

A cloud service is any service created on the Internet from a cloud computing provider's servers as opposed to being provided from a company's own on-premises servers or institutions. Cloud services are designed to provide easy, scalable access to applications, resources and services, and are fully managed by the cloud services provider, generating greater flexibility. This service can dynamically scale to meet the needs of its users, and because the service provider supplies the hardware and software necessary for the service, there's no need for a company to provision or deploy its own resources or allocate IT staff to manage the service (de Bruin & Floridi, 2017).

Once at work, you can use the cloud whether you write code using Github as a code repository, share a document with a colleague using Box, be it Microsoft or Google. When we go home, we may open up photos to a friend sent to us on Dropbox without giving it a second thought that we are consuming the cloud service built on top of another cloud service (Dropbox for example). From relatively new companies (such as Box, Mega, and DropBox) to even the giants (like Google, Apple, and Microsoft), many vendors use free offers as a way to attract customers to their clouds. The strategy brings with it the hope that consumers will pay for larger volumes and also additional services. Examples of cloud services include online data storage and backup solutions, web-based e-mail services, hosted office suites and document collaboration services, database processing, managed technical support services and more (de Bruin & Floridi, 2017; Garg, Versteeg & Buyya, 2013)

Private cloud services, in contrast, are not generally available to the public, or individual or corporate users, or even subscribers. Private cloud-based services use technologies and approaches associated with public clouds, such as virtualization and self-service services. But private cloud services run on an organization's own infrastructure and are dedicated to internal users, usually specialists or technical personnel, able to use them with greater vigor and experience rather than multiple, external customers (Doelitzscher, Sulistio, Reich,Kuijs & Wolf,2011).

Discrete Events

Discrete Events, usually called by the abbreviation DES, is an effective tool to approach a wide variety of communication issues. The discrete events are used mainly to relates a model that represented a system as a sequence of operations performed on entities (transactions) of certain types such as data packets, bits, among others. The discrete events are derived from the results of actions taken in a system, and can be classified as an occurrence responsible for the change in the state of the system in which they act, and may be of all kinds, where they are generally capable of producing state changes at random intervals of time, generating data and consequently the information (Brito, Trevisan & Booter, 2011).

The universe of actions that provide events is subjective and depends on the ability of the modeler/ designer to abstract the events of this universe in which the system is being modeled. These entities are discrete in a discrete event simulation. This technique has been used to model concepts with a high-level of abstraction, as patients, nurses, doctors, ranging from the exchange of emails on a server to transmission of data packets between devices connected in a network, also uses the queuing concept and can be used to manage people data and so forth, i.e., the entire extent of a communication system (Chahal & Eldabi, 2010).

This logic can be observed in Figure 1, where from e1 to e4 represent the states of a system. From X1 to X5 the events themselves are presented, and from t1 to t4 the times in which these events occurred. In this way, it is possible to understand the interaction between events and the state of the system over time. The events (e1, e2, e3, e4) depend on the actions that cause the state changes (X1, X2, X3, X4, X5) resulting in the evolution of the states in a certain period of time (t1, t2, t3, t4). Thus, the relationship between the sequence of events with the components used in the modeling must respect the principle of operation of each component and its applicability in the modeling system (Chahal & Eldabi, 2010).

In this way, the diversity of applications that the technique of the discrete event provides, showing its importance in several areas of knowledge, as well as in engineering (area of the proposal of this research), was remarkable, being able to apply it in a telecommunication system, more specifically in the transmission of data in a channel.

Figure 1. Events chart

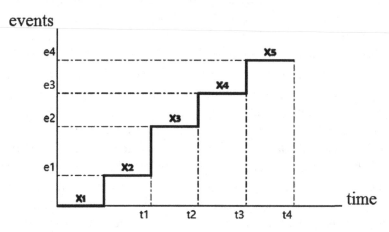

Entities

Entities are defined as discrete items of interest in a discrete event simulation. However, the meaning of an entity depends on what is being modeled and the type of system used. This occurs because the presence of certain attributes may be able to affect the way events are treated or cause changes as the entity flows through the process. In this context is important to emphasize that the concepts entities and events are different. Events are instantaneous discrete incidents that can change a state variable, an output, and/ or an occurrence from another event. In turn, an entity is somewhat dependent on what is being modeled and the type of system. Thus, the characteristic of a discrete event signal indicates that something (eg, an accident, an earthquake, a fault, a control, a person, a heartbeat, or any other desirable concept within a system) occurred. In turn, an event is a conceptual notation that denotes a state change in a system. Discrete event modeling allows performing discrete changes within a system (Padilha, 2018; Lane, 2000)

AWGN Channel

A telecommunication system follows a logic that can be applied to any communication system. This logic includes the presence of three basic components: (1) a transmitter responsible for sending information and subsequent conversion into a signal, (2) a transmission medium to carry this signal, and (3) a receiver receiving the same signal, and then convert it into useful information. The communication channel is the medium responsible for providing the physical connection between transmitters and receivers in a communication system, either as a wire or for a logical connection in a multiplexed medium, for example, a radio channel in telecommunications networks and computers. Data transport typically uses two types of media: physical (twisted pair and fiber optic cable) and electromagnetic (microwave, satellite, radio, and infrared) (Tozer, 2012).

A widely used model applicable to a large set of physical channels is the Additive White Gaussian Noise (AWGN) channel model. This model has the characteristic of introducing a statistically modeled noise, such as a white Gaussian additive process, into the transmitted signals. The existence of disturbances/noise in the channel (free space/atmosphere) has multiple causes. One of them is the thermal noise by the virtue of the movement of the electrons in the electronic circuit used for transmission and reception of the signal. The AWGN channel models such as existing imperfections, naturally, in a communication channel (Rama Krishna, Chakravarthy & Sastry,2016).

DPSK and PSK

Differential Phase Shift Keying (DPSK) is a modulation scheme responsible for facilitating non-coherent demodulation. However, PSK (Phase Shift Keying) modulation generally requires only coherent demodulation. This coherent demodulation is related to the carrier, which is modulated to obtain the signal in the passband. In turn, this signal is reproduced at the receiver and subsequently used for demodulation in the passband to obtain the message. When the same carrier frequency as the transmitted signal is used, a noisy demodulated signal is generated, which results in a laborious process for the receiver to generate the received carrier (Couch II, 2013).

In the DPSK modulation, in turn, there is the modification of the transmissions so that each transmitted signal also depends on the previous one. Thus, the demodulation of the current signal is dependent on the signal received in the previous time period, and can be used as the local carrier. This equality leads to the cancellation of the signals, allowing their demodulation. Accordingly, the phase of that modulated signal is shifted relative to the phase element of the previous signal (Tozer, 2012; Couch II, 2013).

In this modulation, its modulation format can be differentiated by encoding the data by similarity or by the difference of the symbols in relation to the previous signal, determined by the presence of bit 1 and bit 0. The DBPSK modulation eliminates phase ambiguity and the need for phase acquisition and tracking, resulting in reduced energy consumption. In this modulation, a non-coherent way is used to solve the need for a coherent reference signal at the receiver. Thus, the input binary sequence is first differentially encoded and then modulated using a Binary Phase Shift Keying (BPSK) modulator. In demodulation, there is no need to know the initial state of the bit, simplifying synchronization (Tozer, 2012; Couch II, 2013).

DBPSK and BPSK modulation are widely used in wireless LAN, RFID and Bluetooth communication applications, are also used for long distance wireless communication, is also a modulation technique in most of the adaptive modulation technique adopted in cellular communication. This is the case with the CDMA, WiMAX (16d, 16e), WLAN 11a, 11b, 11g, 11n, Satellite, DVB, Cable modem among others, due to the difference of 180 degree between two constellation points, withstand the severe amount of channel conditions or channel fading. It is used in OFDM and OFDMA to modulate the pilot subcarriers used for channel estimation and equalization, which applied in different channels are used for specific data transmission in cellular systems. These modulations are used by most of the cellular towers for long distance communication or transmission of the data. Its demodulator requires to make only two decisions in order to recover original binary information, being very simple compared to other modulation types. The power-efficient modulation technique the less power is needed to transmit the carrier with less number of bits (Tozer, 2012).

Methodology

The development of this methodology was performed in a computer with hardware configuration being an Intel Core i3 processor, containing two processing cores, Intel Hyper-Threading Technology, and 4GB RAM. To provide enhancements in cloud environments, the present study implements a model CBEDE applied to a communication system, and advanced modulation format DBPSK (Differential

Figure 2. Traditional model of a telecommunication system

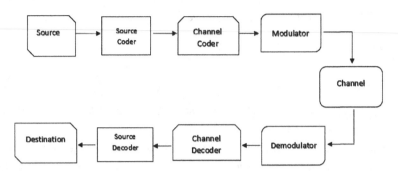

Binary Phase Shift Keying) in a simulation environment, the Simulink simulation environment of the MATLAB software, improving the transmission of data, through a pre-coding process of bits applying discrete events in the signal before of the modulation process.

The experiments were conducted through the Simulink tool, from Matlab (2014 a). This simulation environment was chosen because it is already consolidated in the scientific medium, having a development and simulation environment already tested and validated. DBPSK and BPSK modulation were chosen in this study, because are considered the most robust of modulation schemes in terms of noise immunity, is less immune to the interference, allowing the highest level of distortion in the signal being still successfully demodulated.

Four libraries were used: (1) Communications System ™, which is designed to design, simulate and analyze systems, being able to model dynamic communication systems; (2) the DSP System ™ that is capable of designing and simulating systems with signal processing; (3) Simulink®, which is a block diagram environment for multi-domain simulation, capable of supporting system-level projects for the modeling and simulation of telecommunication systems, and (4) the library SimEvents®, which is classified as a discrete event simulation mechanism and components to develop systems models oriented to specific events

Previous work (Padilha, 2018; Couch II, 2013; Padilha, Iano, Moschim & Loschi,2017; Padilha, Iano, Moschim, Monteiro & Loschi, 2017; Padilha, Iano, Moschim, Monteiro & Loschi, 2017) demonstrated that bit 0 treatment is viable, presenting significant results in the compression of the transmitted information, as well as in the reduction of processing time. In this way, the proposed methodology is based on the development of an AWGN hybrid channel, characterized by the introduction of the discrete event technique in the bit generation process, focusing on bit 1.

In the proposed model, Figure 2, the signals corresponding to bits 0 and 1 will be generated and modulated with the advanced modulation format DBPSK, which will use the phase shift, coming from the modulation format itself. It will then proceed to an AWGN channel according to the parameters shown in Table 01. The signal will then be demodulated to perform the Bit Error Rate (BER) calculation of the channel. The values obtained for BER will be sent to the Matlab workspace, in the name variables "yout" for equality verification and generation of the signal BER graph.

The modeling according to the proposal implemented with discrete events is similar to the one presented previously, differentiating that in this model by the addition of discrete events in the pre-coding phase. The proposed bit precoding was implemented through the discrete event methodology. Bit processing is

Figure 3. Proposed bit precoding

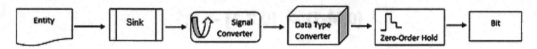

understood as the discrete event methodology in the step of generating signal bits (information) to make it more appropriate for a specific application.

The complexity of the proposed methodology can be explained through the logic presented in Figure 3, which consists of an event-based signal is a signal susceptible to treatment by the SimEvents® library, and posteriorly passed by conversion to the specific format required for manipulation by the Simulink® library. Both time-based signals and event-based signals were in the time domain. This treatment had an emphasis on bits 1 and 0, which were generated as a discrete entity and followed the parameters as presented in Table 1. Then, Entity Sink® represents the end of the modeling of discrete events by SimEvents library.

This tool is responsible for marking the specific point in which Entity Sink will be located, where later the event-based signal conversion will be performed for a time-based signal. This time-based signal was converted to a specific type that followed the desired output data parameter, an integer, the bit. By means of the Real-World Value (RWV) function, the actual value of the input signal was preserved. Then a rounding was performed with the floor function. This function is responsible for rounding the values to the nearest smallest integer.

Also used to a Zero-Order Hold (ZOH) which is responsible for defining sampling in a practical sense, being used for discrete samples at regular intervals (Dragotti, Vetterli, Blu, 2007). The ZOH describe the effect of converting a signal to the time domain, causing its reconstruction and maintaining each sample value for a specific time interval. The treatment logic on bits 1 and 0 is shown in Figure 3.

Subsequently, the signal is modulated with the advanced modulation format DBPSK and is inserted into the AWGN channel, and then demodulated for the purposes of calculating the BER of the signal. The relative values of the BER are sent to the Matlab workspace in the name variable "yout1" to verify equality and generate the BER graph of the signal, as shown in Figure 4.

Figure 4. Model of a telecommunication system with the proposal

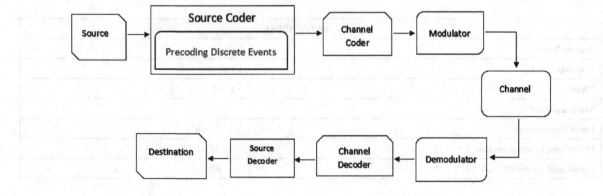

Figure 5. Generation M-ary numbers for bits 0 and 1

$$[0,M-1] \rightarrow [0,2-1] \rightarrow 0,1$$

Figure 6. Traditional Model of a Telecommunication System

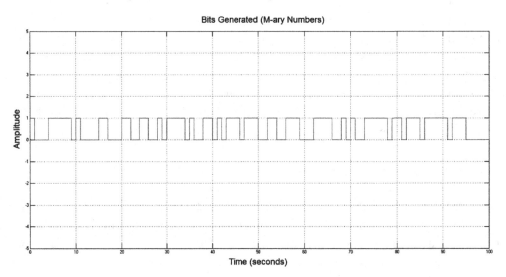

In the proposed model, Figure 2 and 4, the signals corresponding to bits 0 and 1 will be generated, respecting the rule and mathematical logic shown in Figure 5 below.

This rule and mathematical logic with respect to PSK M-ary numbers generate randomly distributed integers in the interval [0, M-1], where M is the definition for bit representation, following the nomenclature of the MATLAB software. Figure 6 shows the respective generation of the bits by means of this logic.

The models are shown in Figures 2 and 4 run with 10000 seconds of simulation and will respect the configuration defined according to Table 1.

Table 1. Parameters channel models DBPSK

AWGN DBPSK	
Sample Time	1 sec
Simulation time	10000 sec
Eb/N0	0 a 7 dB
Symbol period	1 sec
Input signal power	1 watt
Initial seed in the generator	37
Initial seed on the channel	67

Figure 7. Theoretical DBPSK constellation

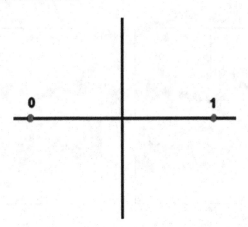

The verification of equality of the signals is performed through the "size" and "isequal" functions of the Matlab software, as well as through the bit error rate (BER). These functions are responsible for the mathematical comparison proving that the signals have the same size and the same size. Together with the BER check, it will state that the same amount of information will be transmitted (bits) in both the proposed methodology (hybrid AWGN channel) and the conventional methodology (AWGN channel). Thus, if the signals are of the same size and size, the logical value 1 (true) is returned and the same volume of data is transmitted, indicating that the equality of the signals is true. Otherwise, the value will be 0 (false). This check will show that the submitted proposal does not add or remove information to the originally transmitted signal.

The constellation has a function to analyze both signals transmitted by the models. In the case of the DBPSK constellation, a phase represents the binary 1 and the other phase represents the binary 0. As the digital input signal changes its state, the output signal phase will be changed between two angles separated by 180° (Tozer, 2012; Couch II, 2013). This validation methodology has as function to affirm that the proposal will not modify the amount of bits transmitted by the signal, since both signals transmitted in the conventional channel and in the channel containing the proposal of this study, will be of the same size. In Figure 7 the DBPSK constellation diagram.

RESULTS AND DISCUSS

The research presented in this section shows an AWGN transmission channel with DBPSK modulation, being used the Simulink simulation environment of the MATLAB. The model from Figure 8 incorporates the traditional method (left) and the proposed innovation of this chapter (right) is presented, showing the signal transmission flow (corresponding to bits 0 and 1), is generated and then modulated in DBPSK, passing through the channel AWGN. The Figures 9 display the constellations for 9 dB for the proposed (left) and the traditional methods (right)

The models developed were investigated from the perspective of memory consumption evaluation. The first simulation of both models in each command is analyzed, since it is in the first simulation that the construction of the model in a virtual environment is performed from scratch, it is in it where all

Figure 8. Transmission Flow for DBPSK

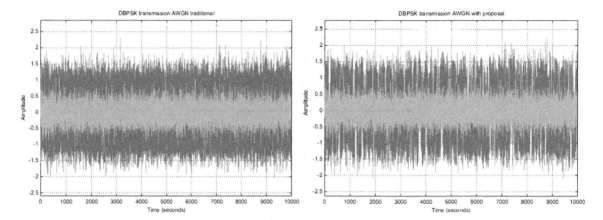

Figure 9. Simulated DBPSK Constellations

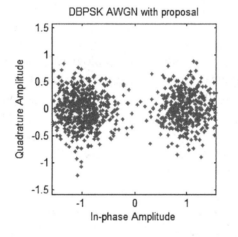
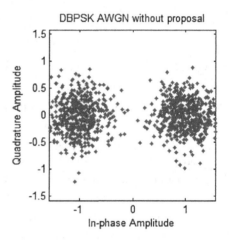

the variables of the model are allocated, the memory of the operating system in which the MATLAB is running is reserved for the execution of the model and the results of this model, according to the evaluation parameters are, in fact, real.

Thus, the experiments considered the memory consumption. For memory calculation, the "sldiagnostics" function will be used, where the "TotalMemory" variable will receive the sum of all the memory consumption processes used in the model, by the "ProcessMemUsage" parameter. This parameter counting the amount of memory used in each process, throughout the simulation, returning the total in MB (megabyte). For this was used a computer with hardware configuration being an Intel Core i3 processor, containing two processing cores, Intel Hyper-Threading Technology, and 4GB RAM. This machine relates the proposal to the dynamics of the real world and will affirm its efficiency and applicability. A physical machines with hardware configuration were used, consisting of an Intel Core i3 processor and 4GB RAM, as previously discussed. The experiments were carried out through 10 simulations of each model developed in order to develop the analysis of this chapter, as shown in Figure 10.

The results obtained by the "size" and "isequal" functions, the DBPSK modulation were analyzed through its constellation, by means of the "compass" function, which will display a compass graph with

Figure 10. First simulations (memory) model DBPSK

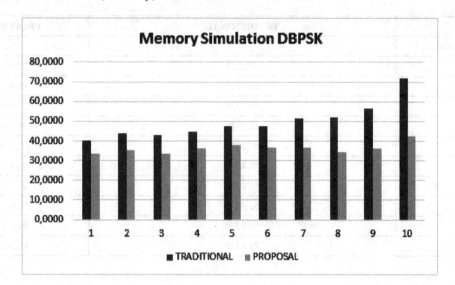

n arrows, and how the constellations will be PSKs, their representations of points will be radial. This feature, the graph format has a compass shape, where n is the number of elements in Z. The location of the base of each arrow will be its origin. In turn, the location of the tip of each arrow will be determined by the real and imaginary components of Z, relative to the constellation of the signal. In the same way and with the same intention will be used the diagram of the constellation.

In the Figure 11 is shown the comparison between a traditional methodology and the CBEDE methodology. In this context, the traditional methodology corresponds to a channel without discrete events

Figure 11. simulated DBPSK constellation

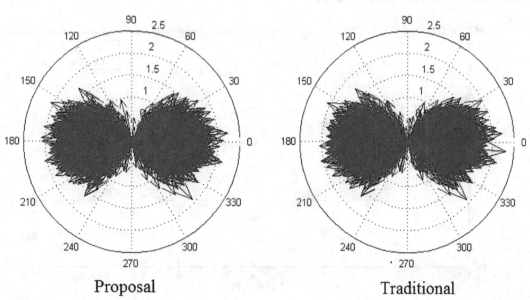

Table 2. Amounts of Memory Consumption

	TRADITIONAL	PROPOSAL
Simulation		
1	40,0117	33,2734
2	43,7305	35,3828
3	42,7930	33,6328
4	44,7070	36,2305
5	47,2891	37,8164
6	47,4609	36,5039
7	51,4258	36,8125
8	51,8320	34,1406
9	56,3320	36,1211
10	71,8477	42,2813

As important as developing the methodology is an improvement of the transmission of a signal that shows better performance, is to make the know-how available to the academic community, as well as to contribute to the area of study of the proposal as well as the theme that this chapter deals with.

The respective amounts of memory consumption shown in Figure 10 are found previously are in Table 2:

To analyze the relationship between the simulation methodology (proposed x traditional method), and the impact on the physical layer of the channel, scripts were made in the MATLAB for processing of the graph BER. Figure 12 display the performance of the models during transmission with noise ranging from 0 to 7 dB.

Figure12. BER between the models DBPSK

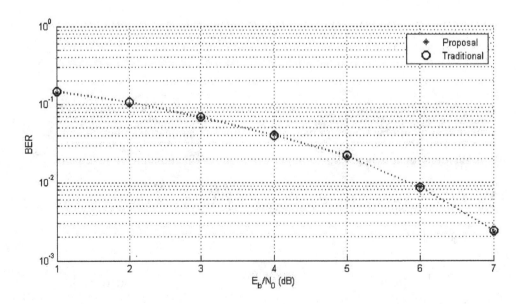

This proposal brings a new approach to signal transmission. In this case, the transmission is performed in the discrete domain with the implementation of discrete entities in the bit generation process. In this way is possible to increase the capacity of information transmission for communication systems. Given the above, the technique of discrete events can be applied in the treatment of bits in its generation stage, being responsible for their conversion into discrete entities. This process is the result of a methodology used in a lower level of application, which acts on the physical layer, than the already used, usually in the transport layer. Able to reduce the consumption of computational resources, such as memory, which is an important parameter to meet the needs of an increasingly technological world.

The use of the methodology under study is based on the technique of discrete events, which by its nature has several application scenarios in a wide variety of real-world systems ranging from manufacturing systems and business processes, computers in computer systems, networks, service delivery systems such as banks, transaction systems for databases, communication protocols, additional services for digital exchanges such as call centers, intelligent transport systems, processes in control engineering, defense systems and military equipment, however the application of this technique in these contexts occurs through concepts of high level of abstraction, such as clients in a queue, emails on a server, flow of vehicles, transmission of data packets, thus the complexity of the application of the use of this technique in the modeling of bits in a system is the innovative point where, through an approach different from the usual technique in a telecommunication system, transmission in the channel is performed in the discrete domain with the implementation of discrete entities in the bit generation process. Reaching the consideration that when it comes to data transmission, its agility, better response time, the better response of communication between users in the system, is obtainable by a better efficiency in the data transmission, being the own bits, making it more fluid and Light. In the same way that the memory consumption of the device used by the organization is of extreme importance, because currently ordinary users tend to generate data every second, worldwide, so the slowness is often related to the speed of communication and the technology implemented in the system structure used by these users, can often generate device crashes, and inconvenience sometimes due to loss of data, even if these are in real time, send such points, briefly touched and weighted, as well as all its technological extensions can be avoided with the application of the proposal, CBEDE, favoring an improvement in the transmission of data.

Considering also that speed is a key issue when choosing a methodology, whether it is used by a user, companies or universities, the CBEDE methodology can be seen as a great allied to cloud computing systems. Even if the cloud has large storage capacity and provides security in data storage, the user always cares about the time it takes to upload or download your data. For this, it is important to invest in systems that intermediate the cloud computing systems and users. With the result reaching up to 69,93% in the improvement of memory consumption of the CBEDE methodology can be employed in this process, since the amount of data of the user greater is the concern with the speed of the transmission.

Another important factor when it comes to data transmission is the memory consumption of the device. Currently, the cloud computing system is linked to computers and mobile phones. As is well known, the use of cell phones today is much larger than that of a computer due to its mobility. Ordinary users tend to upload documents, images, and videos for the purpose of sharing their common social network, or even save their personal files (docx, pdf, avi, jpg, among others) in their "personal cloud".

The slowness related to the speed of communication and the cloud technology implemented in the system structure used by these users, can often generate device crashes, inconvenience to the user and sometimes even loss of data, if these are in real time. When this happens, often the reliability of Cloud computing can be put to the test by the user who can from that moment prefer to store their data on physical platforms. This bad impression can be intensified when this situation occurs with companies and universities. Thus, in order to break this bad impression and generate greater reliability, the CBEDE methodology can also be seen as a great ally. This is because the experiments demonstrate a lower reaching up to 69,93% memory consumption in data transmission, being better than the traditional methodologies, which do not require the use of discrete events.

FUTURE RESEARCH DIRECTIONS

Future work on the CBEDE methodology includes simulations on a wider variety of hardware, including Intel Dual Core Processor, Intel i3 Processor, and Intel i5 Processor. These physical platforms will be targeted for research as they are the most common on the market today. In addition, testing of data transmission via mobile devices is expected due to its greater popularization in recent years. It is also intended to conduct data transmission tests with Cloud Computing platforms.

CONCLUSION

Being the differential of this research, the use of discrete events applied in the physical layer of a transmission medium, the bit itself, being this a low-level of abstraction, the results show better computational performance related to memory utilization related to the compression of the information, showing an improvement reaching up to 69,93%. This demonstrates that the CBEDE has great potential in the improvement of the communication services potential, as well as improving Cloud Computing services, improving of already existing processes can increase the performance of communication response between all the devices in the system and in the cloud environment, because the flow of data will consume fewer resources and, therefore, can improve the interactions between the users.

The objective of this research is in the use of discrete events being applied at the lowest level of abstraction possible within a communication system, as is done in bit generation, and as a result make the cloud environment more productive, faster and with better performance.

Thus, information compression is a byproduct, since the proposal acts on the bits, having a substantial impact on the compression methods performed in higher layers (for example, format types such as HEVC, MPEG-4 AVC / H.264, JPG, PNG, among others) in a communication system, for example, affecting all the media information (data of examinations of the most varied types) that can be transmitted, resulting in a higher quality of both sending and receiving.

REFERENCES

Assunção, M. D., Calheiros, R. N., Bianchi, S., Netto, M. A., & Buyya, R. (2015). Big Data computing and clouds: Trends and future directions. *Journal of Parallel and Distributed Computing*, *79*, 3–15. doi:10.1016/j.jpdc.2014.08.003

Botta, A., De Donato, W., Persico, V., & Pescapé, A. (2016). Integration of cloud computing and internet of things: A survey. *Future Generation Computer Systems*, *56*, 684–700. doi:10.1016/j.future.2015.09.021

Brito, T. B., Trevisan, E. F., & Booter, R. C. (2011). A Conceptual Comparison Between Discrete and Continuous Simulation to Motivate the Hybrid Simulation Technology. *Proceedings of the 2011 Winter Simulation Conference*, 3915-3927.

Chahal, K., & Eldabi, T. (2010). A multi-perspective comparison between system dynamics and discrete event simulation. *Journal of Business Information Systems*, 4-17.

Chang, V. (2015). *A proposed cloud computing business framework*. Nova Science Publisher.

Comer, D. E. (2018). *The Internet book: everything you need to know about computer networking and how the Internet works*. Chapman and Hall/CRC. doi:10.1201/9780429447358

Couch, L. W. II. (2013). *Digital and Analog Communication Systems* (8th ed.). Prentice Hall.

de Bruin, B., & Floridi, L. (2017). The ethics of cloud computing. *Science and Engineering Ethics*, *23*(1), 21–39. doi:10.100711948-016-9759-0 PMID:26886482

Doelitzscher, F., Sulistio, A., Reich, C., Kuijs, H., & Wolf, D. (2011). Private cloud for collaboration and e-Learning services: From IaaS to SaaS. *Computing*, *91*(1), 23–42. doi:10.100700607-010-0106-z

Dragotti, P. L., Vetterli, M., & Blu, T. (2007). Sampling Moments and Reconstructing Signals of Finite Rate of Innovation: Shannon Meets Strang-Fix. *IEEE Transactions on Signal Processing*, *55*(5), 1741–1757. doi:10.1109/TSP.2006.890907

Etro, F. (2015). The economics of cloud computing. In Cloud Technology: Concepts, Methodologies, Tools, and Applications (pp. 2135-2148). IGI Global. doi:10.4018/978-1-4666-6539-2.ch101

Garg, S. K., Versteeg, S., & Buyya, R. (2013). A framework for ranking of cloud computing services. *Future Generation Computer Systems*, *29*(4), 1012–1023. doi:10.1016/j.future.2012.06.006

Gou, Z., Yamaguchi, S., & Gupta, B. B. (2017). Analysis of various security issues and challenges in cloud computing environment: a survey. In Identity Theft: Breakthroughs in Research and Practice (pp. 221-247). IGI Global. doi:10.4018/978-1-5225-0808-3.ch011

Gupta, B. B. (Ed.). (2018). *Computer and cyber security: principles, algorithm, applications, and perspectives*. CRC Press.

Hossain, M. S., Muhammad, G., Abdul, W., Song, B., & Gupta, B. B. (2018). Cloud-assisted secure video transmission and sharing framework for smart cities. *Future Generation Computer Systems*, *83*, 596–606. doi:10.1016/j.future.2017.03.029

Jain, N., Deshpande, A. V., Raghu, B., & Khanaa, V. (2017). *A eficácia dos bancos de dados em nuvem. In 2017 Conferência Internacional sobre Algoritmos, Metodologia, Modelos e Aplicações em Tecnologias Emergentes (ICAMMAET)* (pp. 1–3). IEEE.

Lane, D. C. (2000). *You Just Don't Understand Me*. Working Paper, London School of Economics, Operational Research Group.

Marinescu, D. C. (2017). *Cloud computing: theory and practice*. Morgan Kaufmann.

MATLAB and Simulink® Release. (2014a). The MathWorks, Inc.

Mosco, V. (2015). *To the cloud: Big data in a turbulent world*. Routledge.

Padilha, R. (2018). Proposta de Um Método Complementar de Compressão de Dados Por Meio da Metodologia de Eventos Discretos Aplicada. In *Um Baixo Nível de Abstração. Dissertação (Mestrado em Engenharia Elétrica)*. Campinas, SP, Brasil: Faculdade de Engenharia Elétrica e de Computação, Universidade Estadual de Campinas.

Padilha, R., Iano, Y., Moschim, E., & Loschi, H. J. (2017). Computational Simulation Performance Based In Hybrid Model For Broadcasting Systems, in Set. *International Journal Of Broadcast Engineering, 3*.

Padilha, R., Iano, Y., Moschim, E., Monteiro, A. C. B., & Loschi, H. J. (2017a). Computational Simulation Performance based in Hybrid Model for Telecommunication Systems. *BTSym'17, 3*.

Padilha, R., Iano, Y., Moschim, E., Monteiro, A. C. B., & Loschi, H. J. (2017b). Computational Performance of An Hybrid Model for Wireless Telecommunication Systems with Multipath Rayleigh. *BTSym'17, 3*.

Padilha, R., Martins, I. B., & Moschim, E. (2016). Discrete Event Simulation and Dynamical Systems: A study of art. BTSym'16, Campinas, SP, Brazil.

Rama Krishna, A., Chakravarthy, A. S. N. & Sastry, A. S. C. S. (2016). Variable Modulation Schemes for AWGN Channel based Device to Device Communication. *Indian Journal of Science and Technology, 9*(20).

Rani, B. K., Rani, B. P., & Babu, A. V. (2015). Cloud computing and inter-clouds–types, topologies and research issues. *Procedia Computer Science, 50*, 24–29. doi:10.1016/j.procs.2015.04.006

Rittinghouse, J. W., & Ransome, J. F. (2016). *Cloud computing: implementation, management, and security*. CRC Press.

Schneider, S., & Sunyaev, A. (2016). Determinant factors of cloud-sourcing decisions: Reflecting on the IT outsourcing literature in the era of cloud computing. *Journal of Information Technology, 31*(1), 1–31. doi:10.1057/jit.2014.25

Stergiou, C., & Psannis, K. E. (2017). Recent advances delivered by Mobile Cloud Computing and Internet of Things for Big Data applications: A survey. *International Journal of Network Management, 27*(3), e1930. doi:10.1002/nem.1930

Stergiou, C., Psannis, K. E., Kim, B. G., & Gupta, B. (2018). Secure integration of IoT and cloud computing. *Future Generation Computer Systems, 78*, 964–975. doi:10.1016/j.future.2016.11.031

Tozer, E. P. (2012). *Broadcast Engineer's Reference Book* (1st ed.). Focal Press.

Chapter 10
Meta–Heuristic and Non–Meta–Heuristic Energy–Efficient Load Balancing Algorithms in Cloud Computing

Rojalina Priyadarshini
C. V. Raman College of Engineering, India

Rabindra Kumar Barik
https://orcid.org/0000-0003-3086-3782
KIIT Deemed to be University, India

Brojo Kishore Mishra
https://orcid.org/0000-0002-7836-052X
GIET University, India

ABSTRACT

The number of users of cloud computing services is drastically increasing, thereby increasing the size of data centers across the globe. In virtue of it, the consumption of power and energy is a major concern for system designers and developers. Their goal is now to develop power and energy-efficient products at the same time maintaining the quality and cost of products and services. For managing the power and efficiency, several aspects are taken into consideration in cloud computing paradigm. Load balancing, task scheduling, task migration, resource allocation are some of the techniques, which need to be efficiently employed to minimize the energy consumption. This chapter represents the detailed survey of the existing solutions and approaches for energy-efficient load balancing algorithms used in cloud environments. The research challenges as well as future research directions are also discussed in this chapter.

DOI: 10.4018/978-1-7998-1082-7.ch010

Copyright © 2020, IGI Global. Copying or distributing in print or electronic forms without written permission of IGI Global is prohibited.

INTRODUCTION

In IT industry, the demand of energy is constantly rising. Recent study shows that in US, 10% of the total commercial electricity is consumed by ICT and that is 20% in Germany (Koomey et al, 2010). The study also projects that the power requirement of data centres in US will be increased drastically from 60TWh/y in 2005 to 250TWh/y by 2017 (Aebischer et al, 2015).These projections and predictions are generating a requirement towards use of sustainable and energy efficient mechanisms and approaches in ICT sector (Procaccianti et al, 2015). Cloud computing (CC) is a most recent computing paradigm (Buyya et al, 2009) which is widely used in IT services based on pay-as-you-go model (Kord et al, 2013). Some of the major challenges lie in the underlying domain is: data privacy, legal regulations, utility and risk management, on demand provisioning and security (Zapata et al, 2015).However, energy efficiency has turned out to be a main apprehension especially in cloud data centers (Liu et al, 2011). In US, data centres put away a fraction of 1/15 of the whole commercial electricity use in 2006, whose monetary value is approximately of 4.5 billion per year (Dabbagh et al, 2015). As a consequence the proprietors of data centre are very much serious to adopt naive ways for energy saving strategies which can minimize their operational costs. Along with this, it is reported in (Pettey et al, 2007). that the ICT sector contributes 2% of total carbon emission which is environmental concern and is an alarming issue and a great concern for everyone (Borah et al, 2015). It has been investigated that the top 500 High performance computers consume 20 MW of energy which is equivalent to a small thermal power plant's power consumption (Filiposka et al, 2016). The energy charges and carbon footprints are surely going to increase in coming days as data centres are expected to raise radically in terms of volume and count in order to meet the current service needs. As an outcome the prime objective of the entire fraternity of industry, academia, and government agencies in present days are towards searching solutions and methods which can lessen energy consumption in all aspects of computing by using standard energy conservation techniques.

A broad classification of energy management schemes in CC environment is shown in Fig. 1. The energy management schemes can be largely classified into two groups as 1) Static Energy Management (SEM) and 2) Dynamic Energy Management (DEM) (Beloglazov et al, 2011). The SEM schemes are based on methods which use optimization of design time at different levels. In circuit level the optimized methods try to lessen power consumption caused due to switch flipping in logic gates and transistors by using optimized number and size of transistors. In logic level, the techniques are aimed to be employed to minimize the power consumption due to switching activity of logic gates and transistors by using appropriate complex gate design and minimizing the number of transistors (Dasgupta et al, 2013). But, only by optimal hardware design and use is not sufficient to achieve better performance in terms of energy consumption. The overall performance can be enhanced only if at both hardware and software level, optimized design techniques will be used.

The DEM schemes include the methodologies and techniques which support run time adjustment of system's properties and characteristic as per current system needs. DEM techniques applied at software level include load allocation, load management, scheduling, load balancing, and task consolidation etc. As a consequence, the current research presents a detail insight of various ways by which energy efficiency is achieved in CC in terms of fair distribution of work load among various nodes across the cloud system.

The paper is structured as follows. In Section 2, we provide the details about the load balancing in CC and the matrices used to evaluate the load balancing schemes in CC. The existing load balancing algorithms are described briefly in Section 3. The observations made from the survey are highlighted in Section 4. Section 5 contains the conclusion along with the future scope of research.

LOAD BALANCING IN CC

Load balancing (LB) task in cloud environment can be formulated as assigning N number of tasks requested by cloud users which are kept in a job pool to M number of processing units available in the Cloud (Dasgupta et al, 2013). It can become a NP hard problem if both the present number of resources and tasks to be executed is huge in a system. It is used to maximize resource utilization by distributing the workload among different servers, data centres or any other computing resource. As a result the cloud service providers can satisfy more number of service requests coming from different user groups. On the basis of implementation level, LB algorithms can be grouped into hardware level and software level (He et al, 2015). Hardware LB techniques include extra hardware component attached to the system which will take care of LB task and software techniques take the help of software which are associated with operating system software whereas some techniques use a hybrid model using both simultaneously. On the basis of decision making time, these schemes can be static or dynamic. If the distribution of load is decided at compile time, it falls into the category of static type. These types of algorithms are very simple to implement, but are not mostly applicable to cloud environment. At the other hand if the decision of load distribution happens at run time, then they belong to the category of dynamic LB techniques which are actually used in cloud environment. These types of algorithm make use of current knowledge regarding the load to take decisions about load distribution (Malarvizhi et al, 2009). Some of the algorithms are satisfying user requirements and considered the SLA constraints (Gencay et al, 2008; Fillin et al, 2008) and some are focussing on evenly distribution of load among different nodes. The LB problem in cloud has been investigated and addressed by using different aspect, some algorithm focus is to design energy aware schemes and some focus on minimizing network traffic (Lang et al, 2010; Buyya et al, 2010; Patel et al, 2013).

Performance Matrices Used for LB

In this section, the parameters which are required to be optimized during the process of LB is described in details and are as follows:

1. **Makespan:** It is defined as the finish time of the last task queued on a particular resource (Kalra et al, 2015). In LB, this parameter is needed to be minimized, so that the jobs can have a faster execution.
2. **Response Time:** It is the duration of waiting time for the user after submission of the request till the first response comes and the repose time should be possibly least.
3. **Migration cost:** This is the overhead incurred by any system while its current load is partially or fully transferred from one machine to the other, which needs to be minimized.
4. **Resource Utilization:** This property tries to keep all the nodes always busy in doing something. It should be maximized
5. **Power Consumption:** It refers to the total CPU clock rates consumed during the solution process which is required to be less.

6. Waiting time: It refers to the duration of time a task waits to get its own turn after submission. A good LB algorithm tries to decrease this value as much as possible.

7. **Throughput:** It defines the amount of task completed in unit time. Throughput of a system must be maximized 8) Economic cost: This refers to the total amount of cost a user has to pay. This value also needs to be optimized.

8. **Tardiness:** It signifies the delay in task implementation which is the difference between deadline of task finish and actual task finish time (Nuaimi et al, 2012). This value must approaches towards zero.

9. **Workload Distribution:** It represents the fairness in distribute the task to all the nodes present in the system so that no node can be overloaded or under loaded.

Existing LB Strategies

In this section, we describe the existing LB strategies proposed in the literature for cloud computing environment. The solution strategies used for LB can be broadly classified into two groups. The LB algorithms used can either (1) Non-heuristic or (2) Heuristic and Meta-heuristic type. The detail classification of these algorithms is shown in Fig. 2.

Non-Heuristic Based LB Algorithms

The traditional LB algorithms like round robin allocation, random allocation or weighted round robin allocation only use network parameters to make a decision for assigning a task to a system (Nuaimi et al, 2012; Elzeki eta l, 2012). These approaches do not consider other parameters such as current status of load exhibiting on a system, availability of database servers etc. They do not consider other parameters like current status of load exhibiting on a system, availability of database servers etc.

In Max-Min algorithm (Mao et al, 2014), the job having the largest completion time is assigned to a processing unit. In terms of make span it performs equally well as min-min. But, it falls into starvation if a job having longer finish time encounters first. It makes the smaller tasks to wait for an unexpectedly longer time. Max–Min task scheduling algorithm for the elastic cloud (ECMM) has been conceptualized in (Mao et al, 2014). It constitutes a table consisting of running jobs and one more table containing the status information of VM. Both are kept in load balancer module. When a group of task reach at a time, a task with maximum execution time is chosen then an approximated completion time from each VM is computed from the VM status table, and then the job is assigned to the appropriate VM. The authors in (Patel et al, 2015) proposed a mechanism called as Enhanced LB Min-Min algorithm (ELBMM). This algorithm is an advanced version of Min-Min algorithm (Etminani et al, 2007). In this algorithm, the Minimum Completion Time (MCT) is calculated first for all the requested jobs in the queue for each of the available machines, then the task with the least completion time is chosen and been allocated to the corresponding machine. It decreases the overall make-span but the problem lies with this algorithm is that, it gives priority to jobs having smaller completion time which thereby increases the response time of bigger jobs. In ELBMM, after the expected time completion matrix for each task is created, the task having the minimum earliest completion time with respect to a resource is allocated to the same resource. Then makespan for remaining tasks is also computed and the resulting resource Rj is also identified. After that makespan of task Ti is compared with its MCT, if it is found that the makespan is less than the MCT, then that is assigned to the exhibited resource having the least completion time is assigned to the machine Rj otherwise the task with next minimum completion time is selected.

The Opportunistic LB (OLB) algorithm (Wang et al, 2010) does not take into consideration the approximated Task Execution Time and allocates the task randomly as a result yielding poor makespan. The Minimum Completion Time (MCT(Kokilvani et al, 2011) approach applies statistical means to select the VM having the least completion time, but jobs with shorter execution time will not get a chance to execute. Allocating tasks to VM, the Minimum Execution Time (MET) algorithm would not distribute tasks evenly so it is not suitable in heterogeneous environment. On the other hand, Load balance Min-Min (LBMM) scheduling algorithm proposed by T. Kokilavani et al considers both the MCT and the MET, and chooses nodes for executing a task after considering remaining CPU space and memory and also the transmission rate, which overcomes the shortcomings of min-min scheduling algorithms and improvised a better version called as LB Min-Min (LBMM).

In OLB (Wang et al, 2010) jobs are assigned to the task for keeping all the nodes busy but execution time of node during assignment, which may put some of the tasks to wait for a longer time if any of the nodes could not make it free due to larger execution time. A variation of LBMM overcomes it by following a three layered architecture. In the top level, there exist a request manager whose job is to receive task and in second level it allocates tasks to a service manager. Upon receiving the request, it breaks the entire task into smaller divisions and assigns the sub tasks to a service node for execution thereby speeding up the processing time. But, the decision about the task assignments are based on the node / memory availability and transmission rate.

Radojevicn et al. proposed an improvised version of round robin algorithm for LB and named that as Central LB Decision Model (CLBDM) (Radojevic et al, 2011). It first checks the availability of application servers for doing the work, and then runs the weighted round robin algorithm (Ni et al, 2011) to select a node for assigning the incoming task. It uses the concept of session switching in between the application servers where after getting the information about the available servers, if any of the server is busy or active in doing a work then task is forwarded to the next freely available application servers.

Junjie et al. (2011) suggested a LB algorithm in cloud which is grounded on a mapping policy in between virtual machine and real machines. This method posses a central scheduling controller which finds the appropriate resource to accomplish the work and allocate the same to the identified resource and a resource monitor which is responsible for keeping the detail information about the available resource. The objective of (Wu et al, 2012) is to fetch an algorithm which can decrease duplication and redundancy in data and was known as Index Name Server (INS). This algorithm tries to use optimization technique to choose the access point. The parameters which are taken into account for choosing the access point are the hash code of the data block needed to be downloaded, the server location carrying the target block, quality of transition, and bandwidth of the located server containing the intended block. A computation is done to check if a current connection is able to carry additional nodes. Ren et al. (2011) proposed an improved algorithm for LB in cloud environment, inspired by a pre-existing algorithm "weighted least connection (WLC)" (Lee et al, 2011) and is named as ESWLC (Exponential Smooth Forecast based on Weighted Least Connection) . In WLC algorithm, task allocation is done to the node which has the least number of connections after counting the number of connections made on that particular node. But, the problem lies with WLC is that it is ignorant about the abilities of every node's processing speed, storage limitations and bandwidth. ESWLC overcomes this by considering the longevity or task duration and also use the information of each nodes capacity in terms of processing power, memory, current allocation of disk space size, server load occupation along with number of connections. ESWLC forecast to select the node by using exponential smoothing forecasting algorithm.

A Map- Reduce (MR) based approach was suggested by Lars Kolb et al. to handle data intensive task (Kolb et al, 2012). They have taken the work of solving entity resolution problem in data analytics. Two approaches are used for dividing the data intensive tasks into several partitions, which are to be distributed to the reducer, which are i) Blocksplit: which divides large blocks in order of their input partition; resulting varying sized sub-blocks which may make the reducers load in an unfair manner. ii) Pair-Range: It divides the blocks into equal sized sub blocks, which can do the allocation of sub-blocks to the reducer in a fair way. Again an MR based algorithm was proposed in (Gunarathne et al, 2010) for the same purpose. In any MR algorithm there exist two phases. One is mapping of tasks and the other is reducing of results. Along with this the three methods used in this representation are part, comp and group. Part method is called first to start the Mapping of tasks. Each of the requested tasks is assigned to a part and a key is generated and saved in a hash table for every part. The comp method compares the parts to do grouping of similar parts. Grouping is established by group method. All the Map tasks are carried out and processed parallel, as a result this may lead an overloading on the Reduce tasks. So, the authors in this paper introduced one additional level between the Map task and the Reduce task which may lessen the overloading issue.

Few of LB algorithms use the data migration to achieve a uniform load distribution across the system. Some try to transfer the running instances from VM to other host simply by pausing the source VM and then copying the system image to any other destined physical machine. During this process the migrating applications do not work (Sapuntzakis et al, 2002; Whitaker et al, 2004; Nelson et al, 2005; Clark et al, 2005) causing unavailability of services and support to customers. Some do live migration of task from one machine to the other by using pre-copy method. In the later approach the run time state of the migrated task are copied to the source machine in beforehand. But if the content is heavier, it generates a huge dirty memory in original host machine Maximum of these algorithms try to transfer tasks from overburdened VMs. (Ramezani et al, 2014; Kozuch et al, 2002)This type of migration policies are very simple to execute but contain severe drawbacks such as (1)leave dirty memory which mount up still after copy in live VM migration, (2) uses a huge chunk of memory in both source and destination machines (3) requires the source machine to stop for a while causing an increase in downtime (4) containing risk of losing online customers at that point of time (5) not time and cost effective. Ramezani et al. (2014) attempt to conquer the said limitations by not selecting a blind underloaded node rather they chose a homogeneous machine to transfer partial load from the overwhelmed machine. In (Gutierrez-Garcia et al, 2013), J. Octavio Gutierrez-Garcia and Adrian Ramirez-Nafarrate proposed an algorithm which is named as Multi-agent protocol for LB (MapLoad) where they targeted to find out an appropriate VM which could be selected, so that the data could be migrated from this to the other for live migration. They considered both server heterogeneity and VM usage heterogeneity. But they have not calculated the migration overhead in their work. The same author have done a work in (Banerjee et al, 2009) and extended the work by considering the heuristics to chose the victim node for migration, to decide the time of migration and got a better result from the previous one.

Heuristic or Meta-Heuristic Based LB Algorithms

Many researchers applied Ant Colony Optimization (ACO) technique to design solutions for the problem of LB in cloud environment. In (Banerjee et al, 2009), authors have created an input space consisting of ants representing all the possible solutions consisting of the nodes present in the cloud system. The ants are used to collect the information about the cloud nodes. This input space of the solutions was constantly revised by the ants pheromone trails. In this piece of research, the ants employs basic formula for pheromone updation and node selection which shares out the work load among the nodes in a fair way without overburdening any single node. The algorithm presented by Zhang and Zhang in (Zhang et al, 2010) used ACO approach for addressing the LB algorithm and called that as Open Cloud Computing Federation (OCCF). The working of this algorithm is as follows: when any request comes, the ants are initiated with their pheromone and the head node is selected randomly. Then the ants start their forward path from the head nodes. An ant follows a forward path if it encounters an overloaded node and next proceeds to search for any of the neighbouring under-loaded node. If no under-loaded is found, the ant takes a backward path to reach to the previously searched under-loaded node. But the problem arises when the previously found under loaded node was no longer Under-loaded when visited for the second time.

The ACO algorithm is further used in a different way by Kumar et al. (2012) to overcome the above cited problem and they added the foraging and trailing phenomena of pheromones which are used for searching the nodes with more than and less than required load. They have added a suicide mechanism to the ant if it searches the target end thereby eliminating the overhead incurred by unnecessary backtracks. They also proposed an ACO based algorithm to provide a solution for performing the task of LB. In their algorithm, at the outset a head node called as a Regional LB node is selected by the cloud computing service provider randomly. Then this node is updated to a new one if it does not work appropriately at any situation. Basing on the highest number of neighbouring node, the head node is selected in a way that it has the highest number of neighbouring nodes, which can help the ants to pass through in all probable directions of the network and they would not get any dead end. In the original ACO approach, ants develop the whole solution gradually after building an individual solution. The global solution was created by updating the set of individual solutions. But, in Kumar et al. work (Nishant et al, 2012), ants keeps on updating a single developed solution rather than changing all individual solutions which will avoid the local optimum and premature convergence problem of ACO (Guo et al, 2012). This has been further extended in (Khan et al, 2014) which not only considers the LB but also emphasized on power utilization and infringement in Service level agreement (SLA).

ACO is used in several works Lu and Gu (2011) also applied ACO for LB work. They observed and tried to fetch certain VMs which consume more CPU Power, memory and network bandwidth than the prefixed threshold while executing and named them as hotspot. They have used ACO to find the idle node which is residing at minimum distance from these hotspots. In (Dam et al, 2014), the authors proposed an approach where, the loads are given in order of their arrival time. But, when the number of free VM is becoming less than a prefixed threshold value, ants are produced in cloud which continuously searches the VM with minimum load to give away the next coming tasks. They claimed an improvement in response time which was decreased by 4.2%, 2.4%, 27.6% and 27.7% than ACO (Banerjee et al, 2009), SHC and FCFS respectively, and the authors experimented on one data center containing 75 VM and were simulated on Cloud-Analyst. In (Singh et al, 2015), authors applied an ant based system to design an algorithm and named as Autonomous agent based LB (A2LB). It considers three components: A couple of static agents which are Load and Channel and the third one is a dynamic one which is Migration Agent. The migration agents are set up as ants due to the reason that they can find out a minimal path from the source and target same as the biological ants. These ants are used for finding the under loaded nodes. Pacini et al. (2014) proposed a solution for LB and focused on total throughput and response time management in the situation where multiple clients executing their experiments in parallel in an online private cloud platform.

Dasgupta et al. (2013) presented a LB scheme which used Genetic Algorithm (GA) . In their work, authors created two vectors which are Processing Unit Vector (PUV) and Job Unit Vector (JUV). PUV is a direct function of three parameters which are MIPS (Million instructions per second), the delay cost 'α' and instruction execution cost 'L'. JUV is dependent on three parameters, which are count of instructions contained in a task (NIC), job arrival time (AT) and the least time to accomplish the job (wc) and 't' represents the type of cloud service. The fitness function they have taken as a cost function which depends on these two parameters: PUV and JUV, which was needed to be minimized. They simulate the model in cloud analyst and compare the performance with FCFS and Round Robin algorithm and got a significant improvement over the existing algorithms. However, the inherent disadvantages like local minima problem, slow convergence issue of GA is still lying with the model and the priority of the tasks are not taken into consideration while doing the job assignments. In (Hu et al, 2010), authors used a GA based LB approach to address the problem of LB. They had mainly focused on task migration cost which is incurred during dynamic transfer of partially completed high granular processes. GA has been used to select the victim VM, which can cause less harm to the system in case of data transmission. They have used real cloud environment through an open source cloud interface - Open Nebula. Spanning tree has been used for generating the initial population, where the leaf node represents the VM and root represents the managers and the fitness function considers the load constraints. The algorithm is at par performance wise and stable even in load variance situation. Wang et al. (2014) proposed a GA based approach and called it as Job-spanning and LB Genetic Algorithm (JLGA). This work used two fitness functions taking care of minimizing job completion time and load variance. For generating the initial population, a greedy approach has been used which selects the best current solution to build up the solution space. Main focus of this work was to minimize the makespan along with minimizing the load variance.

Ramezani et al. (Ramezani et al, 2014) applied a particle swarm optimization based LB scheme known as "Balancing in Cloud Computing Using Particle Swarm Optimization (TBSLB-PSO)", where they undertake to obtain optimal node selection done by PSO. They tried to reduce the migration overhead which is incurred during transferring jobs from one machine to the next. This approach transfers the task from a node when it is overloaded, but inspite of transferring all tasks, it selects the task which caused overloading. Further, they used PSO for finding the next node to assign the transferred task. They tried to minimize the total task execution time as well as the maximum execution time. In 2015, Pan et al. came up with a advanced PSO for balancing the load in cloud environment- (LB-IPSO) (Pan et al, 2015). They used two objective functions which were optimized using PSO. Those are standard deviation of load balancing (BL) and overall task completion time (RT). These two parameters are tried to be kept as minimum as possible. They used CloudSim (Calheiros et al, 2011) simulator to test their model and got a better result than existing max-min algorithm.

Liu and Wang proposed a PSO approach to do the LB among VMs in cloud environment (Liu et al, 2012) which aims to lessen the overall makespan (Mishra et al, 2018) and increase the resource utilization. They have improvised the classical PSO by adding a self adaptable inertia weight.

Sidhu et al. (2013) developed a LB scheme (PSO-LR) which was meant for cloud environment. it selects the most little task from the most overloaded node to any other system which is having least amount of load. The same is repeated for the remaining machines and eventually making the whole system equally-balanced. But this may cause an overhead due to extensive searching.

In Yassa et al. (2013) came out with an idea which was basing on PSO and targeted to lessen the makespan, user cost and energy consumption of computing machines present in the data centres by applying a concept of Dynamic Voltage and Frequency scaling or DVFS. The used technique worked by reducing the supplying voltage, thereby reducing the clock frequency and overall power consumption of CPU. It takes the CPU in sleep mode when not in use. To satisfy multiple optimization criteria, a pareto optimization is used.

In (Tang et al, 2015), for balancing the load in cloud environment, a nature inspired algorithm was used which was based on honey bee behaviour and named as honey bee behaviour inspired LB (HBB-LB). This algorithm tries to optimize the load as well as takes the priority of each task. Here, the tasks taken out of the virtual machines are assumed as honey bees. When the jobs are assigned to the under loaded node, the information about the priority value for each of the task and load assigned to that particular VM is updated. So that when a new task comes with a greater priority value, it will be assigned to the VM containing least number of high priority jobs.

In (Pan et al, 2015), authors proposed a load overloading avoidance algorithm by applying meta-heuristic search method Artificial Bee Colony (ABC) optimization named it as Interactive ABC (IABC). They first select a smaller group of virtual machines and distribute the available task to them as a result, a VM does not overwhelm. When a new task arrives the search is again done to check whether it can overload a VM. If so, the algorithm reschedules the task. The results are compared with simple ABC algorithm by taking number of cloud lets and are found to be outperformed with IABC. However the complexity of the algorithm is high due to extensive search work. Linlin Tang and et al. presented a naive approach for LB which uses a member of swarm intelligence group i.e. artificial bee colony optimization (Tang et al, 2015). They have used ABC to schedule the task among various nodes. They simulated their proposed model with CloudSim package and found claimed from the outputs, it distributes the load among different cloudlets in a fair way.

The authors in (Tang et al, 2015) used an approach which was motivated by a soft computing methodology known as Stochastic Hill Climbing (SHC) algorithm for addressing the problem of LB. They assigned a probability to each of the VM according to their present load. Then they choose random virtual machines for allocating a task which can do the task effectively, but later on the performance of that particular VM is analysed according to its cost function. If it is found to be less, than the probability value for the assignment in the next iteration is reduced.

Table 1 presents the work done in LB in CC, their working environment, the performance matrices to test them along with some findings on the limitations of the same set. Table 2 represents the classification of LB algorithms according to the satisfying performance criteria. The environment used for testing LB algorithms can be either performed either in a (i) original cloud setup or (ii) by using a simulation software. Fig. 2 shows the details about the environment used to implement LB algorithms in CC which are found during the survey.

OBSERVATIONS

Based on the literature survey done in LB in CC, the following observations can be made.

1. **Use of Heuristic Approach:** The non-heuristic methods are used for doing LB task initially. But, later on the heuristic algorithms are also used for the same purpose. The reason behind is that the problem of LB is a NP complete problem, so there is always a hope to get a better and more closer to the original solution in comparable less time.

Table 1. Summary of LB algorithms with their descriptions and limitations

Authors & References	Schemes &, Enhancement	Description	Limitations
Radojevic *et al.* (2011)	CLDBM	Mitigate the concerns of Round Robin algorithm. Automated tasks forwarding minimizes the need for a human administrator	1) Individual node capacity is not considered 2) Single point of failure 3) The threshold might not be applied to all cases.
Banerjee *et al.* (2009)	Basic ACO	At the beginning all the under-loaded nodes are fetched by using basic ACO algorithm	1) The algorithm is concerned about a single parameter- Node availability 2) Network overhead due to large solution space 3) Random selection of initial ants
Zhang *et al.*(2010)	OCCF	Upon request, the ants with pheromone selected randomly. chooses a forward path, if overloaded node found, finds neighbouring under-loaded node	1) Unnecessary backtracks if the ant does not find any underloaded node in the forwarding path
Nishant *et al.*(2012)	ACO with pheromone foraging & trailing	Ants update a single result rather updating a set of individual results.	1) Slower than other algorithms because Work must pass through three layers to be processed.
Khan *et al.* (2014)	SALB with ACO	It follows a multi criteria optimization by ACO for multiple objectives like LB, CPU power consumption, SLA infringement	1) Implementation complexity
Lu *et al.* (2011)	Enhanced ACO	Initially nodes are allocated in a FCFS fashion, when number of available VMs decreases then ACO is used to find a VM with minimal load	1) Inherits the problem of FCFS in initial phase. 2) If longer task arrive first, the waiting time for remaining task may increase
Dam *et al.* (2014)	Basic ACO	Load are initially given as per FCFS principle, when no. Of VMs is downed ACO is used to find underloaded node	1) High processing time 2) Waiting time slightly increases if larger jobs execute first
Kolb *et al.* (2012)	Map Reduce	Block split and pairwise are the two approaches are used to divide the task to create one or more match to be given to the reducer	1) In block split approach, all reducers will not get nearly equal amount of load
Gunarathne *et al.* (2010)	Enhanced Map-Reduce	Less overhead for the reduce tasks High processing time Reduce tasks capabilities are not taken into consideration	1) Less overhead for the reduce tasks 2) High processing time 3) Reduce tasks capabilities are not taken into consideration
T-Y. *et al.* (2012)	INS	The goal is to find an approach which has minimum data redundancy when distributing the task across different nodes by utilizing optimized backup management	1) Prediction algorithm is absent to guess future traffic. 2) Complicated in terms of implementation in heavily loaded cloud atmosphere
Ren, X., R. *et al.* (2011)	ESWLC	Uses information of individual node's capacity while allocating.	1)use of forecasting algorithm may increase processing time
LEE *et al.* (2011)	WLC	Allocation is done with the node having minimum number of connections	1) Algorithm is ignorant about individual capacity of each node.
Dasgupta *et al.* (2015)	GA based load balancing	It uses a fitness function as a coast function which minimizes response time and overall completion time	1) Priority of the tasks is not considered.
Gu *et al.* (2010)	Basic GA	GA has been used to select a victim VM, from which task is transferred causing less harm to entire system.	1) Inherent disadvantages of GA like slow convergence problem

continued on following page

Table 1. Continued

Authors & References	Schemes &, Enhancement	Description	Limitations
Wang *et al.* (2014)	GA with two objective functions	Used a greedy method for initial population, then used GA with two fitness functions to reduce overall makespan & task imbalance	1) Priority of the tasks is not considered. 2) Population scale parameter, number of iteration is static
Babu *et al.* (2013)	HBB-LB	Assigns high priority jobs to the under loaded VMs. Waiting time of the task is less	1)Extra overhead due to continues scanning the priority values
Pal *et al.* [2012]	SHC	Uses soft computing approach – hill climbing algorithm to find out the VM to be allocated with the task	1) The performance is tasted with limited and non-soft computing algorithms like FCFS and Round Robin
Fahimeh *et al.*(2014)	TBSLBPSO	Tries to transfer extra load from an overloaded machine Reduces the VM migration overhead	1)Takes more time to execute 2) Not Cost-effective 3) Space complexity is more
Pan *et al.* (2015)	LB-IPSO	PSO is used to minimize overall task completion time and load variation among nodes.	1)Not tested on varying population size
Sidhu *et al* (2013)	PSO-SLR	Classical PSO is improvised by adding a self adaptable inertia weight meant to search the overloaded node	1) Extra overhead due to extensive searching
Yassa *et al.* (2013)	PSO-DVFS	It uses a pareto optimization to satisfy multiple constraints like reducing power consumption, cost and makespan	1)idle time CPU power consumption is not considered.
Pan *et al.* (2015)	IABC	First evenly distribute load among small group of VMs, when new jobs arrives it again searches during overloading condition	1) Heavy searching work increase complexity of algorithm.
Tang *et al.* (2015)	ABC optimization 2016	It uses ABC algorithm to schedule the task so that load can be distributed fairly.	1)Searching of tasks are computationally intensive
Patel *et al.* (2015)	ELBMM	Maximum completion time of each task is calculated and task having the minimum is chosen.	1) Priority is given to task with least completion time which can make the bigger task to starve
Singh *et al.* (2010)	A2LB	Taken care of CPU utilization, response time and overall throughput	1) Does not consider the priority of the jobs

2. **LB as a Multi-Objective Optimization Problem:** The problem of LB can be stated as a multi-objective optimization problem. This is because the parameters that affect the performance of LB algorithms are needed to be minimized or maximized to produce competent results. Most of the algorithms proposed tried to optimize either makespan or workload distribution. Later on new improvised version of hybridized meta-heuristic algorithms such as PSO, ACO and ABC are used which could satisfy multiple constraints at a single point of time.

3. **Improving Quality of Solution Using Heuristic Algorithm**: Most of the solutions which use population based tools like GA and PSO, there is a scope for improving the quality of solutions by optimizing some of the local parameters such as population scale parameter, number of iterations; initial population generation in case of GA and PSO and can be improvised by using some heuristic. Wang et al. in (2014) used a greedy method which chooses the initial population from the best of current available solutions, which thereby improvises the result. In ACO, the pheromone updation could be improvised because new ants are generated for next generation by updating the pheromones. If this process improvises, the standard of solution can also be improved.

Table 2. Schemes for LB along with performance parameters and simulation environment used

References	Schemes	Performance Parameters Used	Simulation Environment
(Radojevic ET al, 2011)	CLDBM	Response time, Resource utilization	Not mentioned
[(Banerjee et al, 2009)	Basic ACO	Response time, Workload distribution	Cloud-Analyst
[(Mondal et al, 2012)	SHC	Response time	Cloud-analyst
(Ren et al, 2011)	LB-IPSO	Response time, Workload distribution, Makespan	CloudSim
(Dabbagh et al, 2015)	GA based LB	Response time, Makespan,	Cloud- Analytics
(He et al, 2015)	Basic ACO	Workload distribution	Not mentioned
(Zahng et al, 2010	OCCF	Workload distribution	JAVA
(Nishant et al, 2012)	ACO with pheromone foraging & trailing	Workload distribution	CloudSim
(Kolb et al, 2012)	Map Reduce	Workload distribution	Amazon EC2 cloud with Hadoop
(abu et al, 2013)	HBB-LB	Workload distribution	CloudSim
(Tang et al, 2015)	ABC optimization	Workload distribution	CloudSim
[Liu et al, 2011]	Enhanced ACO	Workload distribution	Cloud Environment
(Lee ta l, 2011)	WLC	Workload distribution	Cloud setup
(Sidhu et al, 2013)	PSO-SLR	Workload distribution	
(Khan et al, 2014)	SALB with ACO	Workload distribution, Power consumption, SLA infringement	CloudSim
(Ren et al, 2011)	ESWLC	Work Load distribution, Power and memory consumption	Cloud setup
(Wang et al, 2010)	A2LB	Workload distribution, Transfer time	JAVA
(Wu et al, 2012)	INS	Transfer time, Migration cost, Remote Backup efficiency	Cloud setup
(Hu et al, 2010)	Basic GA	Resource utilization, Migration cost, Workload distribution	Open Nebula
(Ramezani et al, 2014)	TBSLBPSO	Migration cost, Transfer time, Makespan, Throughput	Cloudsim, Jswarm
(Gumarathne et al, 2010)	Enhanced Map-Reduce	Throughput	Microsoft Azure cloud infrastructure
Wang et al, 2014)	GA with two objective functions	Makespan, Workload distribution	Hadoop, Matlab
(Pan et al, 2015)	IABC	Makespan, Workload distribution	Cloud setup
(Yassa et al, 2013)	PSO with DVFS	Makespan, power consumption, CPU utilization.	
(Patel et al, 2015)	ELBMM	Makespan,	Not mentioned

Figure 1. Broad classification of energy management scheme in cloud computing paradigm

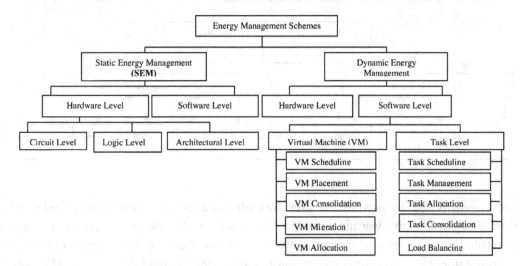

Figure 2. Broad Division of Solution Approaches for LB

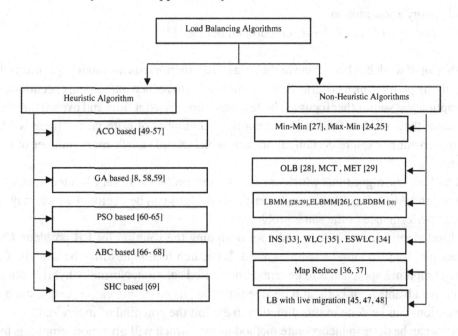

CONCLUDING REMARKS AND FUTURE RESEARCH DIRECTIONS

This survey includes the recent study of both heuristic and non-heuristic algorithms applied in LB in CC environment. The deterministic algorithms are always faster than heuristic algorithms. But, as LB is a NP hard problem, no polynomial time algorithm exists for the solution and heuristic algorithms are used to produce some nearly optimal solutions. A lot of research is going on to get even more im-provised solutions by exploring and exploiting new techniques in this domain. For LB problem, there exist diverse optimization criteria. All the algorithms try to optimize few of them. But, SLA constraint

Figure 3. Division of performance evaluation environment

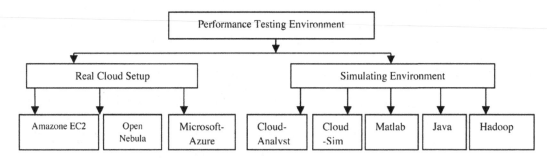

satisfaction, security, and privacy are the grey area which needs to be lime lighted. Today the entire world is suffering from global warming problem, due to more CO_2 emission. So, priority of the time is to develop solution strategies in a direction towards minimizing energy consumption in terms of CPU power consumption, CPU utilization etc. and at the same time without degrading performance. The challenge is still lying with the heating effect and carbon footprints occurring in due course of these solutions. An extensive research should be done in this regard to develop solutions with minimum heat emission and energy consumption.

The future scope for LB in CC has been outlined below.

1. Though a lot of work has been done in the area of LB, there exists no single algorithm which would satisfy all the performance criteria. Some authors tried to reduce makespan, execution cost, energy consumption and some other focussed on response time, transfer time and overall throughput. Most of the algorithms used so far, are satisfying limited number of criteria. So, there is a large scope and requirement to explore certain algorithms which could satisfy more number of performance attributes.

2. The meta-heuristic algorithms which are used for this problem are very limited in numbers such as GA, ABC and ACO. So, other meta-heuristic algorithms can be explored which may put forward enhanced performance of the same problem.

3. Hybridised algorithms are not yet used for designing the solution for LB problem. Classical approaches like backtracking techniques and local search techniques may be exploited along with the soft-computing approaches to generate improvised solution. Normally hybridization is used to take out the advantage of both, at the same time the lacuna of one can be overcome by the other. So, inventions can be done in this direction to exploit the potential of individual.

4. Inventions can be done to incorporate methodologies which will give more emphasis to SLA constraints in CC environment. Ultimately the sole objective of every management system and software is to design and develop quality product and services for the end users. Security and privacy aspect is not been addressed by any of the proposed methods. There is a big gap between these and the designed solutions. This could be taken as an open challenge in this area.

5. There is a lot of scope where Software defined network (SDN) could be used and LB algorithms could be seamlessly used with better performance. The centralized control behavior of SDN could greatly help in executing the LB algorithms in a hassle free way.

REFERENCES

Aebischer, B., & Hilty, L. M. (2015). The energy demand of ICT: A historical perspective and current methodological challenges. In *ICT Innovations for Sustainability* (pp. 71–103). Springer International Publishing. doi:10.1007/978-3-319-09228-7_4

Al Nuaimi, K., Mohamed, N., Al Nuaimi, M., & Al-Jaroodi, J. (2012, December). A survey of load balancing in cloud computing: Challenges and algorithms. In *Network Cloud Computing and Applications (NCCA), 2012 Second Symposium on* (pp. 137-142). IEEE.

Babu, D. (2013). Honey bee behavior inspired load balancing of tasks in cloud computing environments. *Applied Soft Computing*, *13*(5), 2292–2303. doi:10.1016/j.asoc.2013.01.025

Banerjee, S., Mukherjee, I., & Mahanti, P. K. (2009). Cloud computing initiative using modified ant colony framework. *World Academy of Science, Engineering and Technology*, *56*, 221–224.

Beloglazov, A., Buyya, R., Lee, Y. C., & Zomaya, A. (2011). A taxonomy and survey of energy-efficient data centers and cloud computing systems. *Advances in Computers*, *82*(2), 47–111. doi:10.1016/B978-0-12-385512-1.00003-7

Borah, A. D., Muchahary, D., Singh, S. K., & Borah, J. (2015). Power Saving Strategies in Green Cloud Computing Systems. *International Journal of Grid and Distributed Computing*, *8*(1), 299–306. doi:10.14257/ijgdc.2015.8.1.28

Buyya, R., Beloglazov, A., & Abawajy, J. (2010). *Energy-efficient management of data center resources for cloud computing: A vision, architectural elements, and open challenges.* arXiv preprint arXiv:1006.0308

Buyya, R., Yeo, C. S., Venugopal, S., Broberg, J., & Brandic, I. (2009). Cloud computing and emerging IT platforms: Vision, hype, and reality for delivering computing as the 5th utility. *Future Generation Computer Systems*, *25*(6), 599–616. doi:10.1016/j.future.2008.12.001

Calheiros, R. N., Ranjan, R., Beloglazov, A., De Rose, C. A., & Buyya, R. (2011). CloudSim: A toolkit for modeling and simulation of cloud computing environments and evaluation of resource provisioning algorithms. *Software, Practice & Experience*, *41*(1), 23–50. doi:10.1002pe.995

Clark, C., Fraser, K., Hand, S., Hansen, J. G., Jul, E., Limpach, C., . . . Warfield, A. (2005, May). Live migration of virtual machines. In *Proceedings of the 2nd conference on Symposium on Networked Systems Design & Implementation-Volume 2* (pp. 273-286). USENIX Association.

Dabbagh, M., Hamdaoui, B., Guizani, M., & Rayes, A. (2015). Toward energy-efficient cloud computing: Prediction, consolidation, and overcommitment. *IEEE Network*, *29*(2), 56–61. doi:10.1109/MNET.2015.7064904

Dam, S., Mandal, G., Dasgupta, K., & Dutta, P. (2014). An ant colony based load balancing strategy in cloud computing. In Advanced Computing, Networking and Informatics-Volume 2 (pp. 403-413). Springer International Publishing. doi:10.1007/978-3-319-07350-7_45

Dasgupta, K., Mandal, B., Dutta, P., Mandal, J. K., & Dam, S. (2013). A genetic algorithm (ga) based load balancing strategy for cloud computing. *Procedia Technology*, *10*, 340–347. doi:10.1016/j.protcy.2013.12.369

Devadas, S., & Malik, S. (1995, January). A survey of optimization techniques targeting low power VLSI circuits. In *Proceedings of the 32nd annual ACM/IEEE Design Automation Conference* (pp. 242-247). ACM. 10.1145/217474.217536

Elzeki, O. M., Reshad, M. Z., & Elsoud, M. A. (2012). Improved max-min algorithm in Cloud computing. *International Journal of Computers and Applications*, *50*(12).

Etminani, K., & Naghibzadeh, M. (2007, September). A min-min max-min selective algorihtm for grid task scheduling. In *Internet, 2007. ICI 2007. 3rd IEEE/IFIP International Conference in Central Asia on* (pp. 1-7). IEEE. 10.1109/CANET.2007.4401694

Filin, S., Harada, H., Hasegawa, M., & Kato, S. (2008, September). QoS-guaranteed load-balancing dynamic spectrum access algorithm. In *2008 IEEE 19th International Symposium on Personal, Indoor and Mobile Radio Communications* (pp. 1-6). IEEE. 10.1109/PIMRC.2008.4699466

Filiposka, S., Mishev, A., & Juiz, C. (2016). Current Prospects Towards Energy-Efficient Top HPC Systems. *Computer Science and Information Systems*, *13*(1), 151–171. doi:10.2298/CSIS150228063F

Gençay, E., Sinz, C., & Kuchlin, W. (2008, April). Towards SLA-based optimal workload distribution in SANs. In *NOMS 2008-2008 IEEE Network Operations and Management Symposium* (pp. 755-758). IEEE.

Gunarathne, T., Wu, T. L., Qiu, J., & Fox, G. (2010, November). MapReduce in the Clouds for Science. In *Cloud Computing Technology and Science (CloudCom), 2010 IEEE Second International Conference on* (pp. 565-572). IEEE. 10.1109/CloudCom.2010.107

Guo, P., & Liu, Z. (2012). An Ant System based on Moderate Search for TSP. *Computer Science and Information Systems*, *9*(4), 1533–1552. doi:10.2298/CSIS120302057G

Gutierrez-Garcia, J. O., & Ramirez-Nafarrate, A. (2013, June). Policy-based agents for virtual machine migration in cloud data centers. In *Services Computing (SCC), 2013 IEEE International Conference on* (pp. 603-610). IEEE. 10.1109/SCC.2013.55

Gutierrez-Garcia, J. O., & Ramirez-Nafarrate, A. (2015). Agent-based load balancing in Cloud data centers. *Cluster Computing*, *18*(3), 1041–1062. doi:10.100710586-015-0460-x

He, H., Feng, Y., Li, Z., Zhu, Z., Zhang, W., & Cheng, A. (2015). Dynamic Load Balancing Technology for Cloud-oriented CDN. *Computer Science and Information Systems*, *12*(2), 765–786. doi:10.2298/CSIS141104025H

He, X., Ren, Z., Shi, C., & Fang, J. (2016). A novel load balancing strategy of software-defined cloud/fog networking in the Internet of Vehicles. *China Communications*, *13*(Supplement2), 140–149. doi:10.1109/CC.2016.7833468

Hu, J., Gu, J., Sun, G., & Zhao, T. (2010, December). A scheduling strategy on load balancing of virtual machine resources in cloud computing environment. In *2010 3rd International symposium on parallel architectures, algorithms and programming* (pp. 89-96). IEEE.

Jin, H., Gao, W., Wu, S., Shi, X., Wu, X., & Zhou, F. (2011). Optimizing the live migration of virtual machine by CPU scheduling. *Journal of Network and Computer Applications*, *34*(4), 1088–1096. doi:10.1016/j.jnca.2010.06.013

Jun, C. (2011). IPv6 virtual machine live migration framework for cloud computing. *Energy Procedia*, *13*, 5753–5757.

Kalra, M., & Singh, S. (2015). A review of metaheuristic scheduling techniques in cloud computing. *Egyptian Informatics Journal*, *16*(3), 275–295. doi:10.1016/j.eij.2015.07.001

Khan, S., & Sharma, N. (2014). Effective scheduling algorithm for load balancing (SALB) using ant colony optimization in cloud computing. *International Journal of Advanced Research in Computer Science and Software Engineering, 4*.

Kokilavani, T., & Amalarethinam, D. D. G. (2011). Load balanced min-min algorithm for static meta-task scheduling in grid computing. *International Journal of Computers and Applications*, *20*(2), 43–49.

Kolb, L., Thor, A., & Rahm, E. (2012, April). Load balancing for mapreduce-based entity resolution. In *2012 IEEE 28th international conference on data engineering* (pp. 618-629). IEEE. 10.1109/ICDE.2012.22

Koomey, J. (2011). *Growth in data center electricity use 2005 to 2010*. A report by Analytical Press.

Kord, N., & Haghighi, H. (2013, May). An energy-efficient approach for virtual machine placement in cloud based data centers. In *Information and Knowledge Technology (IKT), 2013 5th Conference on* (pp. 44-49). IEEE. 10.1109/IKT.2013.6620036

Kozuch, M., & Satyanarayanan, M. (2002). Internet suspend/resume. In *Mobile Computing Systems and Applications, 2002. Proceedings Fourth IEEE Workshop on* (pp. 40-46). IEEE.

Lang, W., Patel, J. M., & Naughton, J. F. (2010). On energy management, load balancing and replication. *SIGMOD Record*, *38*(4), 35–42. doi:10.1145/1815948.1815956

Lee, R., & Jeng, B. (2011, October). Load-balancing tactics in cloud. In *Cyber-Enabled Distributed Computing and Knowledge Discovery (CyberC), 2011 International Conference on* (pp. 447-454). IEEE. 10.1109/CyberC.2011.79

Liao, X., Jin, H., & Liu, H. (2012). Towards a green cluster through dynamic remapping of virtual machines. *Future Generation Computer Systems*, *28*(2), 469–477. doi:10.1016/j.future.2011.04.013

Liu, H., Xia, F., Yang, Z., & Cao, Y. (2011). An Energy-Efficient Localization Strategy for Smartphones. *Computer Science and Information Systems*, *8*(4), 1117–1128. doi:10.2298/CSIS110430065L

Liu, Z., & Wang, X. (2012, June). A PSO-based algorithm for load balancing in virtual machines of cloud computing environment. In *International Conference in Swarm Intelligence* (pp. 142-147). Springer Berlin Heidelberg. 10.1007/978-3-642-30976-2_17

Lu, X., & Gu, Z. (2011, September). A load-adapative cloud resource scheduling model based on ant colony algorithm. In *2011 IEEE International Conference on Cloud Computing and Intelligence Systems* (pp. 296-300). IEEE. 10.1109/CCIS.2011.6045078

Malarvizhi, N., & Uthariaraj, V. R. (2009, December). Hierarchical load balancing scheme for computational intensive jobs in Grid computing environment. In *2009 First International Conference on Advanced Computing* (pp. 97-104). IEEE. 10.1109/ICADVC.2009.5378268

Mao, Y., Chen, X., & Li, X. (2014). Max–min task scheduling algorithm for load balance in cloud computing. In *Proceedings of International Conference on Computer Science and Information Technology* (pp. 457-465). Springer India. 10.1007/978-81-322-1759-6_53

Mishra, S. K., Sahoo, B., & Parida, P. P. (2018). Load balancing in cloud computing: a big picture. *Journal of King Saud University-Computer and Information Sciences*.

Mondal, B., Dasgupta, K., & Dutta, P. (2012). Load balancing in cloud computing using stochastic hill climbing-a soft computing approach. *Procedia Technology, 4,* 783–789. doi:10.1016/j.protcy.2012.05.128

Naqvi, S. A. A., Javaid, N., Butt, H., Kamal, M. B., Hamza, A., & Kashif, M. (2018, September). Metaheuristic optimization technique for load balancing in cloud-fog environment integrated with smart grid. In *International Conference on Network-Based Information Systems* (pp. 700-711). Springer, Cham.

Nelson, M., Lim, B. H., & Hutchins, G. (2005). Fast transparent migration for virtual machines. *USENIX Annual Technical Conference*, 391–394.

Ni, J., Huang, Y., Luan, Z., Zhang, J., & Qian, D. (2011, December). Virtual machine mapping policy based on load balancing in private cloud environment. In *Cloud and Service Computing (CSC), 2011 International Conference on* (pp. 292-295). IEEE. 10.1109/CSC.2011.6138536

Nishant, K., Sharma, P., Krishna, V., Gupta, C., Singh, K. P., & Rastogi, R. (2012, March). Load balancing of nodes in cloud using ant colony optimization. In *Computer Modelling and Simulation (UKSim), 2012 UKSim 14th International Conference on* (pp. 3-8). IEEE. 10.1109/UKSim.2012.11

Pacinia, E., Mateosb, C., & Garinoa, C. G. (2014). Balancing Throughput and Response Time in Online Scientific Clouds via Ant Colony Optimization. *Advances in Engineering Software, 84,* 31-47.

Pan, J. S., Wang, H., Zhao, H., & Tang, L. (2015). Interaction artificial bee colony based load balance method in cloud computing. In *Genetic and Evolutionary Computing* (pp. 49–57). Springer International Publishing. doi:10.1007/978-3-319-12286-1_6

Pan, K., & Chen, J. (2015, September). Load balancing in cloud computing environment based on an improved particle swarm optimization. In *Software Engineering and Service Science (ICSESS), 2015 6th IEEE International Conference on* (pp. 595-598). IEEE. 10.1109/ICSESS.2015.7339128

Patel, G., Mehta, R., & Bhoi, U. (2015). Enhanced Load Balanced Min-min Algorithm for Static Meta Task Scheduling in Cloud Computing. *Procedia Computer Science, 57,* 545–553. doi:10.1016/j.procs.2015.07.385

Patel, P., Bansal, D., Yuan, L., Murthy, A., Greenberg, A., Maltz, D. A., ... Kim, C. (2013, August). Ananta: Cloud scale load balancing. *Computer Communication Review, 43*(4), 207–218. doi:10.1145/2534169.2486026

Pettey, C. (2007). *Gartner estimates ICT industry accounts for 2 percent of global CO2 emissions.* Dostupno na: https://www. gartner. com/newsroom/id/503867

Procaccianti, G., Lago, P., & Bevini, S. (2015). A systematic literature review on energy efficiency in cloud software architectures. *Sustainable Computing: Informatics and Systems, 7,* 2–10.

Puthal, D., Obaidat, M. S., Nanda, P., Prasad, M., Mohanty, S. P., & Zomaya, A. Y. (2018). Secure and sustainable load balancing of edge data centers in fog computing. *IEEE Communications Magazine*, *56*(5), 60–65. doi:10.1109/MCOM.2018.1700795

Radojević, B., & Žagar, M. (2011, May). Analysis of issues with load balancing algorithms in hosted (cloud) environments. In *MIPRO, 2011 Proceedings of the 34th International Convention* (pp. 416-420). IEEE.

Ragmani, A., El Omri, A., Abghour, N., Moussaid, K., & Rida, M. (2018). A performed load balancing algorithm for public Cloud computing using ant colony optimization. *Recent Patents on Computer Science*, *11*(3), 179–195. doi:10.2174/2213275911666180903124609

Ramezani, F., Lu, J., & Hussain, F. (2014). Task based system load balancing approach in cloud environments. In *Knowledge Engineering and Management* (pp. 31–42). Springer Berlin Heidelberg. doi:10.1007/978-3-642-37832-4_4

Ramezani, F., Lu, J., & Hussain, F. K. (2014). Task-based system load balancing in cloud computing using particle swarm optimization. *International Journal of Parallel Programming*, *42*(5), 739–754. doi:10.100710766-013-0275-4

Ren, X., Lin, R., & Zou, H. (2011, September). A dynamic load balancing strategy for cloud computing platform based on exponential smoothing forecast. In *2011 IEEE International Conference on Cloud Computing and Intelligence Systems* (pp. 220-224). IEEE. 10.1109/CCIS.2011.6045063

Sapuntzakis, C. P., Chandra, R., Pfaff, B., Chow, J., Lam, M. S., & Rosenblum, M. (2002). Optimizing the migration of virtual computers. *ACM SIGOPS Operating Systems Review, 36*(SI), 377-390.

Sidhu, M. S., Thulasiraman, P., & Thulasiram, R. K. (2013, April). A load-rebalance PSO heuristic for task matching in heterogeneous computing systems. In *Swarm Intelligence (SIS), 2013 IEEE Symposium on* (pp. 180-187). IEEE. 10.1109/SIS.2013.6615176

Singh, A., Juneja, D., & Malhotra, M. (2015). Autonomous agent based load balancing algorithm in cloud computing. *Procedia Computer Science*, *45*, 832–841. doi:10.1016/j.procs.2015.03.168

Sotomayor, B., Montero, R. S., Llorente, I. M., & Foster, I. (2009). Virtual infrastructure management in private and hybrid clouds. *IEEE Internet Computing, 13*(5), 14–22. doi:10.1109/MIC.2009.119

Tang, L., Pan, J. S., Hu, Y., Ren, P., Tian, Y., & Zhao, H. (2015, August). A Novel Load Balance Algorithm for Cloud Computing. In *International Conference on Genetic and Evolutionary Computing* (pp. 21-30). Springer International Publishing.

Wang, S. C., Yan, K. Q., Liao, W. P., & Wang, S. S. (2010, July). Towards a load balancing in a three-level cloud computing network. In *Computer Science and Information Technology (ICCSIT), 2010 3rd IEEE International Conference on* (Vol. 1, pp. 108-113). IEEE.

Wang, T., Liu, Z., Chen, Y., Xu, Y., & Dai, X. (2014, August). Load balancing task scheduling based on genetic algorithm in cloud computing. In *Dependable, Autonomic and Secure Computing (DASC), 2014 IEEE 12th International Conference on* (pp. 146-152). IEEE. 10.1109/DASC.2014.35

Whitaker, A., Cox, R. S., Shaw, M., & Gribble, S. D. (2004, March). Constructing Services with Interposable Virtual Hardware. In NSDI (pp. 169-182). Academic Press.

Wu, T. Y., Lee, W. T., Lin, Y. S., Lin, Y. S., Chan, H. L., & Huang, J. S. (2012, January). Dynamic load balancing mechanism based on cloud storage. In *Computing, Communications and Applications Conference (ComComAp)*, 2012 (pp. 102-106). IEEE. 10.1109/ComComAp.2012.6154011

Yassa, S., Chelouah, R., Kadima, H., & Granado, B. (2013). Multi-objective approach for energy-aware workflow scheduling in cloud computing environments. The Scientific World Journal. PubMed.

Zapata, B. C., Fernández-Alemán, J. L., & Toval, A. (2015). Security in Cloud Computing: A Mapping Study. *Computer Science and Information Systems*, *12*(1), 161–184. doi:10.2298/CSIS140205086C

Zhang, Z., & Zhang, X. (2010, May). A load balancing mechanism based on ant colony and complex network theory in open cloud computing federation. In *Industrial Mechatronics and Automation (ICIMA), 2010 2nd International Conference on* (Vol. 2, pp. 240-243). IEEE. 10.1109/ICINDMA.2010.5538385

Chapter 11
Distributed Algorithms for Finding Meta–Paths of a Large Heterogeneous Information Network on Cloud

Phuc Do

University of Information Technology, Vietnam National University, Ho Chi Minh City, Vietnam

ABSTRACT

Meta-path is an important concept of heterogeneous information networks (HINs). Meta-paths were used in many tasks such as information retrieval, decision making, and product recommendation. Normally meta-paths were proposed by human experts. Recently, works on meta-path discovery have proposed in-memory solutions that fit in one computer. With large HINs, the whole HIN cannot be loaded in the memory. In this chapter, the authors proposed distributed algorithms to discover meta-paths of large HINs on cloud. They develop the distributed algorithms to discover the significant meta-path, maximal significant meta-path, and top-k meta-paths between two vertices of HIN. Calculation of the support of meta-paths or performing breadth first search can be computational costly in very large HINs. Conveniently, the distributed algorithms utilize the GraphFrames library of Apache Spark on cloud computing environment to efficiently query large HINs. The authors conduct the experiments on large DBLP dataset to prove the performance of our algorithms on cloud.

INTRODUCTION

Heterogeneous Information Networks (HINs) is a graph model in which both arcs and vertices are associated with types. Real world data is often represented as a HIN, for example, DBLP bibliographic networks, FreeBase, YaGo. In DBLP bibliographic networks, vertices have several vertex types such as authors, papers, venues, topics, words. These vertex types are connected via various link types such as *write* relation (author–[writes]→paper), *cite* relation (paper–[cite]→paper), *publishedAt* relation (paper-[published_At] →venue), to name but a few. Let us consider an example from DBLP. There are

DOI: 10.4018/978-1-7998-1082-7.ch011

Copyright © 2020, IGI Global. Copying or distributing in print or electronic forms without written permission of IGI Global is prohibited.

three vertices in the graph, namely "Rakesh Agrawal", "Fast algorithms for mining association rules", "VLDB", with their corresponding vertex type "author", "paper" and "venue". The two links connecting between three vertices are labeled with *write* and *publishedAt* relation, which describe the fact "Rakesh Agrawal" published paper named "Fast algorithms for mining association rules" at the VLDB conference. With a vast number of interrelated facts study on HINs has gained traction recently.

One of the important concepts in HINs is meta-path, or sequences of vertex types and link types between two given nodes (Y. Sun, J. Han, X. Yan, P. Yu, and T. Wu, 2011). In the DBLP example, we have a meta-path of length one: author−[writes]→paper. We can also have a path length of more than one, such as author−[write]→ paper-[published_At]→venue, which explains an indirect relation between author and venue. Since a meta-path can express various kinds of relationships among nodes, ranging from one-hop relation (path length equal to one) to many-hop relation (path length larger than one), it has been extensively used in many HIN applications such as Similarity Measure PathSim (Y. Sun, 2011), HeteSim (Chuan Shi X. K., 2013), Clustering and Classification (Xiangnan Kong, 2012). In these applications, meta-paths are provided by domain experts, which can be challenging in some scenarios of large HINs. First, domain experts may not always be available. Secondly, when HINs becomes larger, manually selecting meta-paths can be labor-intensive. Hence, there is a need for a tool to query meta-paths efficiently in large HINs. While most of extant meta-path based studies focus on analytical applications of meta-paths (Chuan Shi Y. L., 2017), there are recent works proposing automatic solutions to mine meta-paths from HINs. However, those solutions assume the input HIN must fit into the memory of one computer. It is not clear how to extend these works in distributed environments with many worker computers on Cloud computing environment to process large HIN that cannot fit into memory of one computer. With Cloud computing environment, we can leverage the power of computing and data storage of many computers to solve the challenging problem (Christos Stergiou, Kostas E. Psannis, Brij B. Gupta, Yutaka Ishibashi, 2018).

A majority of meta-path based studies focus on its HIN applications. In (Y. Sun, J. Han, X. Yan, P. Yu, and T. Wu, 2011), the authors study similarity search defined among the same type of vertices in HINs. They propose the concept of meta-path and PathSim, a meta-path based similarity between two vertices of the same type. Through experiments, the authors show the effectiveness of using PathSim over random-walk based similarity measures. Subsequently, there are works focusing on analytic applications of meta-paths.

Besides PathSim, there are other measures such as Path-Constrained Random Walks (Ni Lao, 2010), HeteSim (Chuan Shi X. K., 2013). In (Phuc Do, Phu Pham., 2018), the authors proposed W-PathSim to focus on improving the topic-driven weighted similarity measurement between same-typed objects in HIN. Other than similarity measure, there are works on recommendation (Binbin Hu, 2018). There are also works focusing on automatically mining meta-paths from a HIN. In (Changping Meng, 2015), the authors proposed an algorithm to discover the meta-paths from large HINs. They proposed the Frequent Stage wise Path Generation algorithm (or FSPG) which seek meta-paths that best predict the similarity between a given list of node pairs. FSPG contains greedy strategies that generate the most relevant subset of meta-paths under a given regression model. Path Count and Path-Constraint Random Walk (PCWR) are new methods which was used to measure the similarity score between two objects (Ni Lao, 2010) . A GreedyTree was also used to improve the performance of execution. In (Lijun Chang, 2015), a method for finding the top-k shortest paths from one set of target nodes to another set of target nodes in a graph was proposed. This method is called top-k shortest path join (KPJ) between two sets of target nodes. In this method, the best-first search paradigm was used to recursively divide search subspaces into smaller subspaces, and two index structures to reduce the exploration area of a graph. With these combinations, the performance is improved significantly. In (H. Liu, 2018.), general framework was proposed to solve the k-shortest path problem. This framework was used to choose the potential path which is more similar to the current path with a user specified similarity threshold. In (Zichen Zhu, 2018), a top-k Path Queries on Large Heterogeneous Information Networks algorithm was proposed. They can be used to find the shortest meta-paths between two vertices based on the A* search framework.

In this chapter, we study how to leverage GraphFrames - a Large Graph Processing Library which runs on distributed computing environment with one master and many worker computers (Tomasz Drabas, 2017) (Yadav., Rishi, 2015) on Cloud Computing Environment to efficiently discover significant meta-paths and maximal significant meta-paths in a given large HIN. We develop distributed algorithms to calculate the support (path-instances) of a meta-path, and discover the shortest meta-paths between two vertices of large HINs. Our algorithms leverage a novel approach to construct the breadth-first tree by expanding the path and the motif search with joining operation with the participation of several workers of distributed computing framework on Cloud computing environment. Since the operation is executed in parallel with one master node and several worker nodes of Cloud computing environment, the performance of our meta-path finding is increased, and our proposed algorithms can process very large HINs.

In this chapter, we have the following contributions:

- Proposing algorithms for detecting all the significant meta-paths of HIN and maximal significant meta-paths of HIN based on GraphFrames of Apache Spark on Cloud computing environment
- Proposing algorithm for detecting all the shortest significant meta-paths between two vertices based on the conducting motif search of GraphFrames of Apache Spark on Cloud computing environment
- Conducting experiments of our proposed distributed algorithms with large HIN to prove the performance of our proposed solution.

The chapter is organized as follows 1) Introduction 2) Preliminaries 3) Using GraphFrames of Apache Spark on Cloud computing environment to calculate the support of a meta-path in large HIN 4) Translate Meta-path to Motif Search of GraphFrames 5) Discovering the significant meta-paths HIN 6) Discovering the maximal significant meta-path of large HIN 7) Discovering top-k meta-path queries of very large HIN 8) Experiment and discussion 9) Conclusion and future works

PRELIMINARIES

Definition 1: (Information Network): An information network is defined as a directed graph $G = (V, E)$ with an object type mapping function $\varphi: V \rightarrow A$ and a link type mapping function $\psi: E \rightarrow R$, where each object $v \in V$ belongs to one particular object type $\varphi(v) \in A$, and each link $e \in E$ belongs to a particular relation $\psi(e) \in R$ (Chuan Shi, Yitong Li, Jiawei Zhang, Yizhou Sun, and Philip S. Yu., 2017). if $|A| = 1$ and $|R|=1$, we have homogeneous information network. if $|A| > 1$ and $|R| > 1$, we have heterogeneous information network (Y. Sun, 2011).

Example 1: DBLP is a typical heterogeneous information network. DBLB is a large repository which contains a high volume of scientific papers. Each paper has an abstract. To enhance the content of DBLP, we used LDA topic modeling (David M. Blei, Andrew Y. Ng, Michael, I. Jordan., 2003) to discover

Figure 1. Typical network schema of DBLP

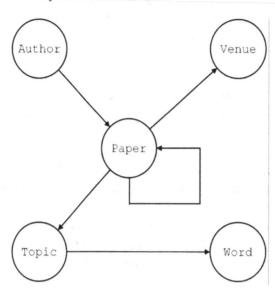

the topic of document abstract in DBLP. So, our DBLP HIN has vertex types and link or arc types. The vertex types are Author, Paper, Topic, Venue, Word. The link or arc types are: write, published_At, mention, contain, cite. We use LDA topic modeling to discover the topics of paper and words of each topic in paper (David M. Blei, Andrew Y. Ng, Michael, I. Jordan., 2003) (Thanh Ho, Phuc Do, 2018).

Definition 2: (Network Schema). The network schema is a meta template for a heterogeneous information network G= (V, E) with the object type mapping φ: V → A and the link mapping ψ: E→ R, which is a directed graph defined over object types A, with arc as relations from R, denoted as TG = (A, R). We can infer the structure of Heterogeneous Information Network by using the network schema.

Example 2: Bibliographic network schema. For a bibliographic network defined in Example 1, the network schema is shown in Figure 1. With network schema, we can infer the relations or arcs between vertices of DBLP. We have the following links/arcs such as links/arcs exist between authors and papers denoting the writing or written-by relations, between venues and papers denoting the publishing or published_At relations, between papers and topic denoting paper mentioning topic, and between papers, denoting citing or cited-by relations, between topic and words denoting topic containing word. Figure 1 shows the network schema of bibliographic network of DBLP (Phuc, 2019).

Definition 3: (Meta-Path). A meta-path P is a path defined on the graph of network schema TG = (A,R), and is denoted in the form of $A_1 \xrightarrow{R1} A_2 \xrightarrow{R2} .. \xrightarrow{Rl} A_{l+1}$, which defines a composite relation $R = R_1 \circ R_2 \circ ... \circ R_l$ between type A_1 and A_{l+1}, where ∘ denotes the composition operator on relations (Y. Sun, J. Han, X. Yan, P. Yu, and T. Wu, 2011). Some meta-paths of DBLP are listed in Table 1 (Do, 2019) (Phu Pham, Phuc Do, 2019).

Definition 4: (Sub Meta-Path of a Meta-Path)

Given a meta-path $P = A_1 \xrightarrow{Rp1} A_2 \xrightarrow{Rp2} .. \xrightarrow{Rpl} A_{l+1}$ and a meta-path $Q = B_1 \xrightarrow{Rq1} B_2 \xrightarrow{Rq2} .. \xrightarrow{Rql} B_{k+1,}$

Meta-path Q is called a sub meta-path of a meta-path P if ∃j∈[1,...,l-k] such than $B_1=A_j$, $B_2=A_{J+1}$,... $R_{q1}=R_{p1}, R_{q2}=R_{p2}$...

Example 3: Given a meta-path A→ P →T→W. This meta-path has the following sub meta-paths:

Table 1. List of the meta-paths of DBLP

A→P	Author-[Write]-Paper
P→V	Paper-[Published_At]-Venue
P→T	Paper-]Mention]-Topic
T→W	Topic-[Contain]-Word
P→P	Paper-[Cite]-Papers
A→P→V	Author-[Write]-Paper-[Published_At]-Venue
P→P→V	Paper-[Cite]-Paper-[Published_At]-Venue
P→T→W	Paper-[Mention]-Topic-[Contain]-Word
A→P→P	Author-[Write]-Paper-[Cite]-Paper
A→P→T→W	Author-[Write]-Paper-[Mention]-Topics-[Contain]-Word
A→P→P→T	Author-[Write]-Paper-[Cite]-Paper-[Mention]-Topic

A→ P, P →T, T→W, A→ P →T, P →T→W

Definition 5: (support of a meta-path): The support of a meta-path is the number of path instances of this meta-path. We denote support(P) as a support of meta-path P.

Definition 6: (Significant Meta-Path): A meta-path P is called a significant meta-path if support(P) > 0.

Example 4: Some significant meta-paths of DBLP and their support are shown in Table 2.

Property 1. if $P = A_1 \rightarrow A_2 \rightarrow ... \rightarrow A_1$ is a significant meta-path and $Q = B_1 \rightarrow B_2 \rightarrow ... \rightarrow B_k$ is a sub meta-path of P than the Q is a significant meta-path.

Proof: Since $P1 = A_1 \rightarrow A_2 \rightarrow ... \rightarrow A_k$ is a significant meta-path, then there is at least a path instance $p_i = pv_{i1} \rightarrow pv_{i2} ... \rightarrow pv_{ik}$ where vertextype(pv_{ij})=A_j. From this path instance, we can extract a path instance $q_i = qv_{i1} \rightarrow qv_{i2} ... \rightarrow qv_{ik}$ of meta-path $Q = B_1 \rightarrow B_2 \rightarrow ... \rightarrow B_k$ such that vertextype(qv_{i1})=B_1, vertextype(qv_{i2})=B_2,..... It means that meta-path Q is a significant meta-path.

Example 5: In DBLP, meta-path P=A→P→T→W is a significant meta-path. This meta-path expresses the relation Author→Paper→Topic →Word. From P, we extract sub meta-path Q = A→P→T which is the sub meta-path of P. Obviously, Q is a significant meta-path.

Definition 7: (Maximal Significant Meta-Path): Maximal significant meta-path p is a significant meta-path and there is no significant meta-path q such that p is a sub meta-path of q.

Example 6: In our DBLP HIN, the maximal significant meta-paths are as follows:

Table 2. Some significant meta-paths of length 1 and their support

Meta-Path	Support
T →W	494
P →T	34260
P →P	10234
P →V	126
A →P	7844

A→P→T→W, A→P→V. They are Author→Paper→Topic→Word and Author→Paper→Venue.

Property 2: Sub meta-path of a maximal significant meta-path is a significant meta-path

Proof: Property 2 is from property 1

Example 7: Let A→P→T→W be a maximal significant meta-path, then the sub meta-paths of this maximal significant meta-path are also the significant meta-paths. We have the following significant meta-paths of maximal significant meta-path A→P→T→W:

A→P→T→W, A→P→T, P→T→W, A→P, P→T, T→W

In this paper, we would like to develop algorithms to solve the following problems:

Problem Statement: Given a large HIN. We will develop the distributed algorithm for:

- Finding all significant meta-paths of a given large HIN.
- Finding all maximal significant meta-paths of given HIN.
- Finding top-k significant meta-paths between two given vertices of a large HIN.

Using GraphFrames of Apache Spark on Cloud Computing Environment to Calculate the Support of a Meta-Path in Large HIN

GraphFrames package is a library of large graph processing of Apache Spark. Apache Spark is a software system which can enable users to build a distributed computing framework for big data processing. In 2009, Apache Spark was created in AMPLab, University of Berkeley. Instead of using disk in Hadoop Map Reduce for transferring the temporary result, Apache Spark used memory to compute and stores objects in computing process, Apache Spark can work with Hadoop Distributed File System (HDFS) to read and write file (Tomasz Drabas, 2017) (Yadav., Rishi, 2015). Each file is divided into many blocks which are saved in the HDFS. There are four libraries of Apache Spark. They are Spark SQL, Spark Streaming, MLlib for machine learning and GraphX for large graph processing. These libraries contain a lot of API which can help us to process big data such as big table processing, large scale machine learning, motif search in large graph....

In 2016, DataBricks created GraphFrames based on dataframes for large graph processing (Michael S. Malak, 2016) (Yadav., Rishi, 2015) (Ankur Dave, 2016). GraphFrames contains several APIs such as Motif Search, label propagation, strong connected component, triangle count, shortest path, label propagation for cummunity detection…In this chapter, we use motif search of GraphFrames for structural pattern search in large Heterogeneous Information Network.

We run GraphFrames on Spark cluster of Cloud computing environment with one driver and many worker nodes. With the Cloud computing environment, we can use the disk storage and computing of the servicer. The Cloud computing framework provides high-capacity networks, low-cost computers and storage devices as well as the widespread adoption of hardware virtualization, service-oriented architecture and autonomic and utility computing for big data processing. We can leverage the utilities of the cloud computing environment to solve our problems (Christos Stergiou, Kostas E. Psannis, Brij B. Gupta, Yutaka Ishibashi, 2018).

In our research, we used Apache Spark in Azure HDInsight which is the implementation of Apache Spark in the Cloud computing environment. HDInsight provides the capability to create and configure Spark clusters in Azure. We know that the Spark clusters in HDInsight are compatible with Azure Stor-

Figure 2. HDInsight cluster configuration

age and Azure Data Lake Storage. Therefore, we can leverage the HDInsight Spark cluster to process large HIN data of graph in Azure. In Figure 2, we use the Azure portal to create HDInsight Spark cluster. The cluster uses Azure Storage Blobs as the cluster storage. We create Apache Spark cluster in Azure HDInsight using Azure portal (Nitin Mehrotra et al., 2019) .

The tasks for processing the Heterogeneous Information Network will be executed on the Worker nodes of Spark Cluster. They execute the join operation in order to find the path instances of a particular meta-path. We use a special partition strategy based on the source vertices of graph arcs. This partition strategy will keep the arcs with the same source vertices in the same memory of Worker node. The join of two tuples will be executed very fast without moving the arcs among parts of Worker nodes. In Figure 3, when all tasks of Worker nodes are completed, the result will send back to the Master nodes for summary.

In HDInsight, YARN cluster manager will manage and run Spark operations. After connection, Apache Spark activates the executors on the worker nodes of the Spark Cluster. These executors store data and run computation program. Next, Apache Spark sends code of our program (jar file or Python files to SparkContext) to the executors. Finally, the SparkContext will send tasks to the executors of worker nodes for running. The programs are executed in parallel on the worker nodes of Spark Cluster. In our proposed system, the programs focus on finding the meta-path of large Heterogeneous Information Network. The worker nodes will read and write data from HDFS. The SparkContext will collect the results from Worker nodes. Resilient Distributed Datasets (RDD) is a main element of Spark. RDD has function to distribute data and process to the Worker nodes and collect results after finishing the parallel process of Worker nodes (Phuc, 2019).

Let G=(V,E) be a large graph of HIN. We divide set E into n parts $E_1, E_2, ..., E_n$ such that

1. $E_i \cap E_j = \emptyset, \forall i, j \in [1,n]$
2. $\bigcup_{i=1...n} E_i = E$

Each E_i is called as a part and is moved to the memory of the Worker node W_i. Besides of part E_i, the function f for processing data is also moved to the worker. All of the workers will receive the same function f. Function f is processed in parallel with the data E_i at each Worker node Wi. Let R_i be the

Figure 3.The Distributed computing environment with one master and three workers

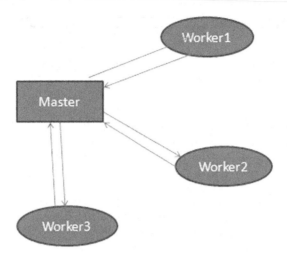

result of processing function f with data E_i at worker W_i. After finishing f at each Worker node W_i, all result R_i will be sent back to the Master node for summarizing. The final result will be generated at Master node. GraphFrame provides powerful tools for processing large scale graph. Motif search is a power tool to discover structural patterns in large scale graph. We use motif search to find all the path instances of a given meta-path. GraphFrames use Domain Specific Language (DSL) for expressing the structural queries. Motif pattern contains names of vertices and arcs. The basic pattern is an arc, for example (a)-[e]→(p) where a is an author, p is an paper. Each pattern can be joined together to generate a path (Yadav., Rishi, 2015).

Example 8: The pattern (a)—[e1]→ (p); (p) — [e2]→(v) specifies a path from vertex a to vertex p then from vertex p to vertex v.

Motif search can be executed by using Python and Spark GraphFrame. The columns of dataframe result can be specified by using the select phrase as follows:

```
motif = g.find("(a) — [e1] → (p) ; (p) — [e2] → (v)")
.filter("a.type="Author" and
p.type="Paper" and v.type="Venue")
.select("a.id","b.id","c.id")
```

We need the instances of the meta-path A→P and meta-path P→V which are Author→Paper and Paper→Venue. They are the arcs of HIN and they are stored in dataframe named ArcDataFrame. Then we use join operation to create path instance of meta-path A→ P→V. The motif search can be processed in distributed environment on Cloud as follows:

Suppose that the graph is divided into 3 parts of a partition. These parts are moved to three Worker nodes as shown in Table 3.

The motif search pattern is moved to the memory of the Worker nodes with the function f for querying the local motif search pattern. This function f will process the sub-graph in the memory of each Worker node. The results are shown in Table 4. The function f will be processed in parallel at each Worker node.

Table 3. Part of arc partition of the graph in worker nodes

Worker1	Worker2	Workers
<A1,P1>	<A5,P2>	<A8,P3>
<A2,P1>	<A6,P2>	<A8,P3>
<A3,P2>	<A7,P4>	<A9,P5>
<A4,P2>		

Table 4. The temporary result of motif search in each worker node

Worker1	Worker2	Worker 3
<A1,P1,A2>	<A5,P2,A6>	<A8,P3,A7>

Table 5. The final result of motif search on distributed computing framwork

Master
<A1,P1,A2>
<A5,P2,A6>
<A8,P3,A7>

Because the function f is processed in parallel at many Worker nodes, the efficiency of this process will be high compared with one computer based model (Zichen Zhu, 2018) (Changping Meng, 2015) . In the experiment session, we will discuss the details of this experiment. We will prove the performance of our distributed algorithms.

After finishing the process, the result is sent backto the master node for generating the final result of motif search as shown in Table 5.

The process of calculating the path instances of a given meta-paths by using GraphFrames motif search can be described in Algorithm 1.

Example 9. The support of meta-path A→P←A is calculated by using the following code:

```
MotifPattern = "(a1)-[e1]->(p);(a2)-[e2]->(p);
filterpattern= "a1.vertextype='Author'
and p.vertextype='Paper'
and a2.vertextype='Author'
FieldList="a1.id,p1.id,a2.id"
PathInstanceList= PathInstanceMetaPath(MotifPattern, FilterPattern,FieldList)
```

Translating Meta-path to Motif Search of GraphFrames

We propose a distributed algorithm to translate the meta-path to motif pattern of Motif Search as follows:

Given a meta-path P and the reverse meta-path P^{-1}. Meta-path $A_i \xrightarrow{R} A_j$ expresses a binary relation R(A_i, A_j) of x in A_i and y in A_j .

The reverse of meta-path $A_i \xrightarrow{R} A_j$ is meta-path $A_i \xrightarrow{R^{-1}} A_j$. This meta-path expresses a binary relation R^{-1} (A_j, A_i). We can use Motif Search to generate the relation for a reverse meta-path.

Table 6. Algorithm 1. Algorithm for finding all path instances of meta-path by using the motif search of GraphFrames

	Input: **Graph is the Large HIN of GraphFrames** **MotifPattern is the pattern of** **FilterPattern is the filtering pattern** **FieldList is the list of selected field** **Output: the path instances of meta-path**
1:	**Function PathInstanceMetaPath**(Graph, MotifPattern, FilterPattern, FieldList):
2:	motifs = Graph.find(MotifPattern)
3:	Results =Motifs.Filter(FilterPattern)
4:	ResultList = Results.Select(FieldList).Collect();
5:	Return ResultList;
6:	**End Function**

There are two cases for meta-path.

Case 1: Un-Symmetric Meta-Path

Given a meta path $A_1 \xrightarrow{R1} A_2 \dots \xrightarrow{R2} A_l$. If string $A_1 A_2 \dots A_l$ is not symmetric, we can translate this meta-path by using the following steps.

For each $A_i A_{i+1}$, we generate a motif pattern $(A_i)[E_i]A_{i+1}$, then we concatenate two consecutive patterns as follows:

$$(A_1)[E_1]A_2; (A_2)[E_2]A_3; \dots \dots : (A_{l-1})[E_l]A_l$$

Example 10: With meta-path A→P→V, we can translate this meta-path to the motif search as follows:

```
MotifPattern = "(a1)-[e1]->(p);(p)-[e2]->(v);
FilterPattern= "a1.vertextype='Author'
and p.vertextype='Paper'
and a2.vertextype="Venue'
FieldList="a1.id,p.id,a2.id"
```

Case 2: Symmetric Meta- Path

Given a meta-path $A_1 A_2 \dots A_l A_2' A_3' \dots A_l'$ or (PP^{-1})

Where P= $A_1 A_2 \dots A_l$ and $P^{-1} = A_l A_2' A_3' \dots A_l'$.

For a symmetric meta-path, we compute the Dataframe of meta-path P and Dataframe meta-path P^{-1}. then we join the two Dataframes.

Example 11: For meta path A→P←A, we decompose this meta-path into 2 smaller symmetric sub meta-paths. They are meta-path A→P and meta-path P←A

```
# For meta-path A→P
MotifPattern = "(a1) -[e1] → (b);
FilterPattern= "a.vertextype='Author' and b.vertextype='Paper' "
FieldList="a.id,b.id"
PathInstanceForwardList= PathInstanceMetaPath(MotifPattern,
FilterPattern,FieldList)
# For meta-path P←A
MotifPattern = "(c) - [e2] → (d);
FilterPattern= "c.vertextype='Paper' and c.vertextype='Author' "
FieldList="c.id,d.id"
PathInstanceReverseList= PathInstanceMetaPath(MotifPattern,
FilterPattern,FieldList)
# Join PathInstanceForwardList With PathInstanceReverseList
from pyspark.sql.functions import *
df1 = ResultForward.alias('df1')
df2 = ResultReverse.alias('df2')
df3= df1.join(df2, df1.b == df2.c)
df4= df3.filter(df3.a != df3.d)
df4.select("a","c","d").show(10)
```

Discovering the Significant Meta-Paths HIN

We propose a distributed algorithm to discover the meta-paths from HIN on Cloud computing environment. Our algorithm has two phases. In phase 1, we discover the significant meta-path of length 1. In phase 2, we discover the significant meta-paths of length k based on the significant meta-paths of length (k-1) and significant meta-paths of length 1. The algorithm stops if at step k, the number of discovered significant meta-paths of length k is equal 0.

Meta-path A→P→T→W is the join operation of the dataframe containing the path instances of meta-path p= A→P→T with dataframe containing the path instances of meta-path q= T→W with the condition that the tail vertex of meta-path p is equal to the head vertex of meta-path q.

With this idea, we create the meta-path of length 1 first. Then we join two meta-paths of length 1 to gather the meta-path of length 2. Next, we join meta-paths of length 2 with meta-paths of length 1 to collect meta-paths of length 2 and etc...We have the meta-paths of length k. The algorithm stops if the set of meta-path of length k+1 is empty.

Example 12: For k =1, we have significant meta-path of length 1 as follows:

$$MP_1=\{A{\rightarrow}P, P{\rightarrow}V, P{\rightarrow}T, T{\rightarrow}W, P{\rightarrow}P\}$$

For k=2, we join meta-path s of MP1 and meta-path t of MP2 such that the tail vertex of s is equal the head vertex of t. Let q be the join result of meat-path s and t, then we calculate the support(q), if support(q) ≥ 0 then q is a significant meta-path of length 2.

Table 7. Algorithm 2. Algorithm for discovering the meta-paths of length 1.

	Function DiscoverMetaPathLength_1 ():
	Input network schema $G_s = \left(V_s, E_s \right)$, HIN $G_H=(V_H,E_H)$
	Output: MP1: set of meta-path of length 1
1:	MP1=[]
2:	For each vertex s of Vs:
3:	source=s
4:	For each vertex t of Vs:
5:	target=t
6:	MotifPattern = **GenerateMotifPattern**(s,t)
7:	FilterPattern = **GenerateFilterPattern**(s,t)
8:	FieldList= **GenerateFieldList**(s,t)
6:	List= **PathInstancesMetaPath** (MotifPattern, FilterPattern,FieldList))
7:	If Len(List) > 0:
8:	Mp_1.append(<s,v>)
9:	Endif
10:	Endfor
11:	Endfor
12:	Return MP1
GenerateFilterPattern(s,t) is a function to generate filter pattern. **GenerateFieldList**(s,t) is a function to generate field list.	

Finally, we have

MP$_2$={ A→P→T, A→P→V, A→P→P, P→T→W, P→P→T}.

For k=3, we join meta-path s of MP2 and meta-path t of MP1 such that the tail vertex of s is equal the head vertex of t. Let q be the join result of s and t, then we calculate the support(q), if support(q) ≥ 0 then q is a significant meta-path of length 3.

Finally, we have

MP$_3$={ A→P→T→W, A→P→P→P, P→P→T→W}

The algorithm stops when MP$_k$=∅

Discovering the Maximal Significant Meta-Path of Large HIN

We propose a distributed algorithm to discover the maximal meta-path. According to property 1, we hold that a sub meta-path of a significant meta-path is a significant meta-path.

Example 13: With the set of significant meta-paths as follows:

Table 8. Algorithm 3. Algorithm for discovering the meta-path of length k

	Function GenerateMetaPathLength_k() **Input: Meta-path MP1 and MPkMinus1** **Output: Meta-path MPk**
1:	MPk=[]
2:	For each meta-path p of MPkMinus1:
3:	For each meta-path q of MP1
4:	If TailVertex(p)=HeadVertex(q)
5:	s=generate(p.q)
5:	MotifPattern = GenerateMotifPatternPath(s)
6:	FilterPattern = GenerateFilterPatternPath(s)
7:	FieldList= GenerateFieldListPath(s)
8:	List= PathInstancesMetaPath (MotifPattern, FilterPattern,FieldList))
9:	If len(List)> 0:
10:	MPk.append(s)
11:	Endif
12:	Endif
13:	Endfor
14:	Endfor
15:	Return MPk

$MP_1 = \{A \rightarrow P, P \rightarrow V, P \rightarrow T, T \rightarrow W, P \rightarrow P\}$

$MP_2 == \{A \rightarrow P \rightarrow T, A \rightarrow P \rightarrow V, A \rightarrow P \rightarrow P, P \rightarrow T \rightarrow W, P \rightarrow P \rightarrow T\}$

$MP_3 = \{A \rightarrow P \rightarrow T \rightarrow W, A \rightarrow P \rightarrow P \rightarrow P, P \rightarrow P \rightarrow T \rightarrow W\}$

We have the following maximal significant meta-paths as follows:

MaximalSignificantMetaPathsSet= $\{A \rightarrow P \rightarrow T \rightarrow W, A \rightarrow P \rightarrow P \rightarrow P, P \rightarrow P \rightarrow T \rightarrow W, A \rightarrow P \rightarrow V\}$

Figure 4. Lattice of the significant meta-paths

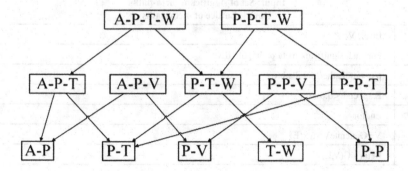

Table 9. Algorithm 4. Algorithm for discovering the maximal significant meta-paths

	Function CalculateMaximalMetaPath()
	Input: Set of significant meta-paths
	Output: Set of maximal meta-paths
1:	MaximalSignificantMetaPathSet=[]
2:	For each significant meta path p of HIN:
3:	Found= FALSE
4:	For each significant meta path q of HIN::
5:	If q.contain(p)
6:	Found = TRUE
7:	break
8:	Endif
9:	Endfor
10:	If not Found
11:	MaximalSignifiantMetaPathSet.append(p)
12:	Endif
13:	Endfor
14:	Endfor
15:	Return MaximalSignificantMetaPathSet

A lattice is used to express the maximal significant meta-paths by the order relation as shown in Figure 4 (Muangprathub, 2014).

The algorithm 5 is used to construct a lattice as follows:

Then we scan the lattice and find the vertices with in degree = 0. They are the maximal significant meta-paths. With the above lattice, we have the following maximal significant meta-paths:

A→P→T→W, P→P→T→W, A→P→V, P→P→V

Table 10. Algorithm 5. Constructing the lattice

	Function ConstructLattice() Input: Set of significant meta-paths Ouput: Lattice of meta-paths
1:	E=∅, V=∅
2:	For each significant meta path q of HIN:
3:	p = FindFatherMetaPath(q)
4:	E.append(<q,p>)
5:	Endfor
6:	V=GenerateVertex(E)
7:	Return G(V,E)

Figure 5. A typical HIN

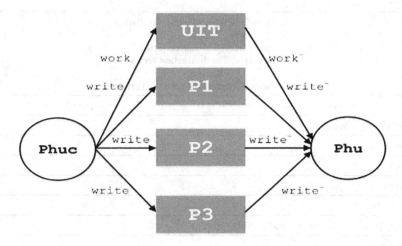

Property 3: Sub meta-path of a maximal significant meta-path is a significant meta-path

According to Property 1, if we know the maximal significant meta-paths, we can list all significant meta-paths of HIN. Therefore, maximal significant meta-paths are the compact representation of the significant meta-paths of a HIN.

Discovering Top-K Meta-Path Queries of Very Large HIN

We propose a distributed algorithm to find all the shortest meta-paths between two vertices of a very large HIN (Zichen Zhu, 2018) on Hadoop distributed environment with one Master and many workers by using the breadth-first search (bfs). The Apache GraphFrames Library runs on the top of Hadoop to process large graph on Hadoop distributed environment.

We use API breadth-first search of GraphFrames to find all the shortest paths between two vertices.

In Figure 5, between two Author vertices "Phuc" and "Phu", there are 4 shortest paths as follows:

```
p1:Phuc→UIT→Phu
p2:Phuc→P1→Phu
p3:Phuc→P2→Phu
p4:Phuc→P3→Phu
```

In Figure 5, Phuc and Phu are author vertices; UIT is an affiliation vertex; P1 and P2 and P3 are paper vertices. The meta-paths with support are listed as follows:

```
Path1: Author→Affiliation←Author with Support = 1
Path2: Author→Paper←Author with Support = 3
```

We develop algorithm 6 to discover the top-k shortest significant meta-paths between two vertices of HIN as follows:

Table 11. Algorithm 6. Algorithm for find the top-k shortest meta-path between vertices of HIN

Function FindTopKShortestMetaPath()   **Input:**   **SrcVertex: The source vertex**   **DstVertex: The destination vertex**   **Output:**   **The Shortest Meta-paths between Vertices**

1:	SrcPatt="id="+'"'+SrcVertex+'"'
2:	DstPatt="id="+'"'+DstVertex+'"'
3:	fillteredPaths=g.bfs(
4:	fromExpr=SrcPatt
5:	toExpr = DstPatt
6:	maxPathLength=3)
7:	ShortestMeta-paths= GenerateShortestMetaPath(fillteredPaths)
8:	Return ShortestMeta-paths

Table 12. Sort the arcs in each part of worker node

Worker1	Worker2	Workers3	Worker4
Set 1	Set 2	Set 3	Set 4
V2,V6	V2,V10	V4,V15	V4,V19
V2,V7	V2,V11	V4,V16	V5,V20
V2,V8	V3,V12	V4,V17	V6,V20
V2,V9	V3,V14	V4,V18	V7,V20

Table 13.

<V1,V2,V6>
<V1,V2,V7>
<V1,V2,V8>
<V1,V2,V9>
<V1,V2,V10>

The result contains the discovered paths. The **GenerateShortestMetaPath**(fillteredPaths) will convert the discovered path-instances to the shortest meta-paths. The breadth first search API of GraphFrames can be summarized as follows. The breadth-first tree is built based on the Distributed Computing environment on Cloud. In GraphFrames, we use two dataframes to represent graph of HIN. One dataframe contains vertices and the other dataframe contains arcs. In distributed computing environment, the arcs dataframes is divided into many parts and moved to Worker nodes. Before we move the parts to worker nodes, we sort the arcs of graph based on the source vertexid of arc. A typical sorted parts are shown in Table 12.

The breadth-first tree is created by joining the arcs of dataframes. Suppose that we are in arc <V1,V2>, we can extend the path by joining <V1,V2> with the arcs in part of the memory in Worker nodes. This

Figure 6. Breadth-first tree

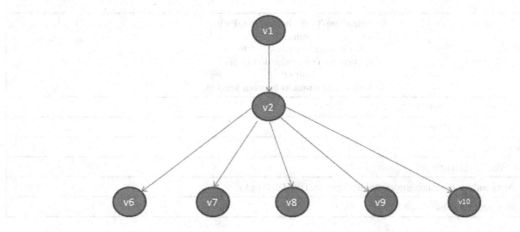

join operation can be processed in parallel. The arc <V1,V2> is sent to each worker node, then this arc will be joined in parallel with arc in each workers. Since the arcs are sorted based on the source vertices, the time for finding the matched arc that have the source vertex ID equal V2 will be reduced. After joining, the result path of each Worker node will be sent back to the Master node. The Master node will summarize the result paths from Worker nodes as follows:

These are the new branches of breadth- first tree as shown in Figure 6.

The execution of breadth- first tree on large HIN is time consumption. We propose another method to calculate the top-k meta-paths between two vertices of large HIN. According to the algorithms mentioned above, we propose algorithm 7 to find the shortest path between two vertices as follows:

The algorithm 7 receives 2 vertices, we use VertexType function to discover the type of source vertex and the type of destination vertex. Based on these type we select all the shortest meta-paths discovered

Figure 7. Breadth first tree with vertex type

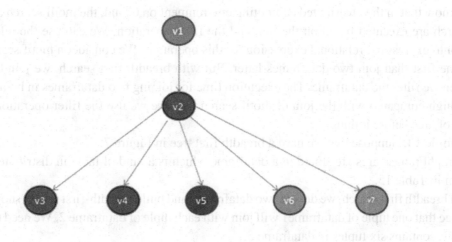

V1: Author; V2,V3,V4:Paper; V5:Venue ; V6,V7: Topic

Table 14. Algorithm 7. Find the top-k shortest meta-path between vertices of HIN

Function FindTopKShortestMetaPath() Input: SrcVertex: The source vertex DstVertex: The destination vertex Output: The Shortest Meta-paths between Vertices	
1	SrcPatt="id="+'"'+SrcVertex+'"'
2	DstPatt="id="+'"'+DstVertex+'"'
3	SrcType=VertexType(SrcPatt)
4	DstType=VertexType(DstType)
5	ShortestMeta-paths = FindShortestMetaPathBetween(SrcType,DstType,k)
6	Return ShortestMeta-paths

Table 15. Typical arc dataframe

Src	Dst
V1	V2
V2	V3
V2	V4
V2	V5
V2	V6
V2	V7

by algorithm 2, algorithm 3. Finally we check whether the path instances contain the source and destination vertex or not.

Property 4: The execution time for executing motif search of a motif pattern is faster than the execution time for executing bfs search.

We know that in the Distributed computing environment on Cloud, the motif search and the breadth first search are executed based on the join and the filter operation. We can use the relational algebra operationto express the relational expression for this operation. We consider a motif search as filter the dataframe first than join two dataframes latter. But with breadth first search, we join two dataframes first, then we filter the dataframe. The execution time for joining two dataframes in breadth first search is very high compared with the join of motif search because we use the filter operation to reduce the number of arcs before joining.

Example 14: Suppose that we have a breadth first tree in Figure 7.

In GraphFrames, arcs are stored in a dataframe which is a kind of table in distributed environment as shown in Table 15.

With breadth first search, we do join two dataframes and build breadth-first tree as shown in Table 16.

We see that one tuple of dataframe1 will join with each tuple of dataframe 2. We need to join 6 tuples. The result contains six tuples in dataframe 3.

Table 16. Join operation of breadth first search (bfs)

dataframe1		dataframe2		dataframe3		
Src	Dst	Src	Dst	Vertex1	Vertex2	Vertex3
V1	V2	V2	V3	V1	V2	V3
		V2	V4	V1	V2	V4
		V2	V5	V1	V2	V5
		V2	V6	V1	V2	V6
		V2	V7	V1	V2	V7

Table 17. Join operation of Motif search

dataframe1		dataframe2		dataframe3		
Src	Dst	Src	Dst	Vertex1	Vertex2	Vertex3
V1	V2	V2	V5	V1	V2	V5

With motif search, we focus on v5, because v5 is a venue vertex. We filter the dataframe to collect the tuples satisfying the filter condition. In this case, we have only one tuple as shown in Table 17. The result is in dataframe3.

We join dataframe 1 with dataframe2. One tuple of dataframe 1 will join with one tuple of dataframe 2. The result contains one tuple of dataframe 3 (execution time for joining 1 tuple). According to the property 4 the execution time of Motif Search is less than the time of executing bfs. We hold that if we know the motif, we can reduce the execution time by using motif motif search instead of using breadth first search.

EXPERIMENT AND DISCUSSION

Dataset

The Dataset for testing our distributed algorithms is a DBLP graph which contains 11,721 vertices and 105,916 arcs. This dataset is a subset of DBLP-Citation-network V3 and was downloaded from Aminer website (https://aminer.org/citation). After pre-processing, the downloaded dataset, we store the DBLP dataset in Neo4j graph database. During distributed processing the dataset on Cloud computing environment, we move the dataset to HDFS of Hadoop Spark Cluster on Cloud Computing environment.

Improving the Motif Search Operation by Repartition

We use two dataframes to represent the graph of Heterogeneous Information Network. One dataframe is used to store vertices and the other dataframe is used to store arcs. We choose a reparation strategy in order to divide the dataframes into several parts and move these parts to the memory of worker nodes.

Table 18. A portion of 3 parts after repartition

Part 1	Part 2	Part 3
63,50	86,97	112,134
63,53	86,60	112,135
63,54	86,98	112,136
62,55	86,99	112,137
62,56	86,100	112,138
62,57	86,101	112,139
62,58	86,102	112,103
62,59	86,103	112,105
62,48	88,50	102,42

There are several strategies for graph partitioning. The main operation of Motif search is the join operation of two dataframes. We would like to join dataframe D1(A,P) with the dataframe D2(P,V). Dataframe D1(A,P) and D2(P,V) are divided into many parts and move to memory of Worker nodes. Suppose that tuple (a1,p1) of DataFrame D1(p,v) and tuple (p1,v1) of DataFrame D2(p,v) are not in the same memory of Worker nodes, they must be moved to the same memory of Worker nodes. This movement takes time in join operation. Therefore, we need a repartition strategy in order to guarantee these tuples are moved to the same memory to reduce the time of join operation.

The dataframes are sorted based on the source vertex of arcs. After sorting, the dataframe containing arcs will be divided into 5 parts and moved to the memory of the worker nodes. Most of arcs of HIN with the same source vertex will be stored in the same parts of Worker node memory. With this partition strategy, we can reduce the time for joining two dataframes because the joined tuples are in the same memory of worker node. We conduct an experiment with two scenarios to prove the performance of our repartition strategy.

Case #1, we use the default partition with 4 parts of dataframes.

Case #2, we repartition the dataframes with 3 parts by sorting the source vertex of arc before creating GraphFrames. A portion of 3 parts are shown in Table 18.

We build a column chart of comparison between repartition and no-repartition as shown in Table 19 and Figure 8. From Table 19, we see the execution time for significant meta-path discovery is reduced significantly in repartition mode because of joining tuples are in the same memory of worker nodes.

Table 19. Comparison between repartition and no-repartition

Length	Without Repartion (In Minutes)	Repartition (in Minutes)
1	6.617	3.183
2	3.400	2.050
3	3.333	2.450
4	2.850	1.817

Figure 8.Comparison between repartition and no-repartition

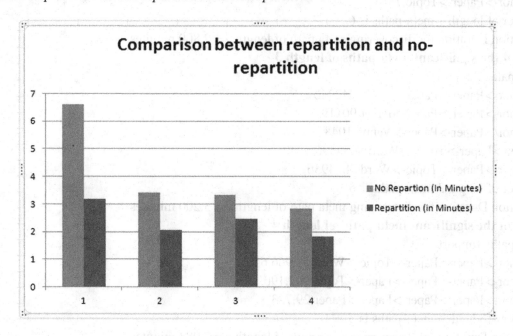

Discovering Significant Meta-Paths of DBLP

We run our proposed distributed algorithms to discover the significant meta-path with the tested HIN, we have the following results:

Number of vertices 11,721
Number of arcs 105,916
We have the following results:
*List of the significant meta-path of length 1
Meta-paths Support
1 Topic->Word 494
2 Paper->Topic 34260
3 Paper->Paper 10234
4 Paper->Venue 126
5 Author->Paper 7844
Number of length 1 meta-paths 5
Execution Duration for discovering meta path of length 1= 4.250 minutes
*List of the significant meta-paths of length 2
Meta-Paths Support
1 Paper>Topic>Word 1692444
2 Author->Paper->Paper 24224
3 Author->Paper->Venue 308
4 Paper->Paper->Topic 102340
5 Paper->Paper->Venue 444

6 Author->Paper->Topic 78440

Number of length 1 meta-paths is 6

Execution Duration for discovering meta path of length 2= 2.800 minutes

*List of the significant meta-paths of length 3

Meta-paths Support

1 Author->Paper->Paper->Topic 242240

2 Author->Paper->Paper->Paper 90119

3 Author->Paper->Paper->Venue 1048

4 Paper->Paper->Topic->Word 5055596

5 Author->Paper->Topic->Word 3874936

Number of length 3 meta-paths is 5

Execution Duration for discovering meta path of length 3= 3.200 minutes

* List of the significant meta-paths of length 4

Meta-paths support

1 Author->Paper->Paper->Topic->Word 11,966,656

2 Author->Paper->Paper->Paper->Topic 901,190

3 Author->Paper->Paper->Paper->Paper 29,783

Number of length 4 meta-paths is 3

Execution Duration for discovering meta path of length 4= 2.983 minutes

*List of the significant meta-paths of length 5

Meta-paths support

1 Author->Paper->Paper->Paper ->Topic->Word 44,518,786

2 Author->Paper->Paper->Paper ->Paper->Topic 3,297,830

3 Author->Paper->Paper->Paper->Paper->Venue 29,783

Number of length 5 meta-paths 3

Execution Duration for discovering meta path of length 4= 2.883 minutes

*List of the significant meta-paths of length 5

Meta-path Support

1 Author->Paper->Paper->Paper->Paper->Topic->Word 162,912,802

Number of length 6 meta-paths 1

Execution Duration for discovering meta path of length 6= 1.567 minutes

* List of maximal significant meta-paths

Maximal significant meta-path Support

1 Author->Paper->Venue 308

2 Author->Paper->Topic->Word 3,874,936

3 Author->Paper->Paper->Venue 1,048

4 Author->Paper->Paper->Topic->Word 11,966,656

5 Author->Paper->Paper->Paper->Topic->Word 44,518,786

6 Author->Paper->Paper->Paper->Paper->Venue 29,783

7 Author->Paper->Paper->Paper->Paper->Topic->Word 162,912,802

*List of symmetric meta paths

symmetric meta paths

1 Topic->Word<-Topic

2 Paper->Topic<-Paper

3 Paper->Paper<-Paper

4 Paper->Venue<-Paper

5 Author->Paper<-Author

6 Paper->Topic->Word<-Topic<-Paper

7 Paper->Paper->Topic<-Paper<-Paper

8 Paper->Paper->Venue<-Paper<-Paper

9 Author->Paper->Topic<-Paper<-Author

10 Author->Paper->Paper<-Paper<-Author

11 Author->Paper->Venue<-Paper<-Author

12 Paper->Paper->Topic->Word<-Topic<-Paper<-Paper

13 Author->Paper->Topic->Word<-Topic<-Paper<-Author

14 Author->Paper->Paper->Topic<-Paper<-Paper<-Author

15 Author->Paper->Paper->Paper<-Paper<-Paper<-Author

16 Author->Paper->Paper->Venue<-Paper<-Paper<-Author

17 Author->Paper->Paper->Topic->Word<-Topic<-Paper<-Paper<-Author

18 Author->Paper->Paper->Paper->Topic<-Paper<-Paper<-Paper<-Author

19 Author->Paper->Paper->Paper->Paper<-Paper<-Paper<-Paper<-Author

20 Author->Paper->Paper->Paper->Topic->Word<-Topic<-Paper<-Paper<-Paper<-Author

21 Author->Paper->Paper->Paper->Paper->Topic<-Paper<-Paper<-Paper<-Paper<-Author

22 Author->Paper->Paper->Paper->Paper->Venue<-Paper<-Paper<-Paper<-Paper<-Author

23 Author->Paper->Paper->Paper->Paper->Topic->Word<-Topic<-Paper<-Paper<-Paper<-Paper<-Author

Discovering the Top-K Shortest Meta- Paths Between Two Vertices of HIN

Given two same vertices s and t. Find the vertextype(s) and vertextype(t). Find all the symmetric meta-path with start element and end element are equal to vertextype(s). Then we find all the shortest symmetric meta-path with start element and end element are equal to vertextype(s) .

Example 15: Given two vertices a, b with a.id=9653 and c.id = 9650. We know that the vertex type of vertex a is Author and the vertex type of vertex b is Venue. We list the shortest meta-path between vertices with Author and Venue vertex type, we have one of this meta-path such as Author->Paper->Venue.

We compare the motif search Author->Paper->Venue and breadth first search with only one computer as follows:

Execution time of motif search is 0.167 minutes

Execution time of BFS is 1.083 minutes

We conduct the experiment for discovering the path instances of the following meta-path by using motif search and API bfs of GraphFrames. The following meta-paths are collected:

```
Author->Paper
Author ->Paper ->Venue
Author->Paper->Topic-Word
```

Table 20. Comparison of motif search and breadth-first-search

Length of meta-path	Motif Search (In Minutes)	Bfs (in Minutes)
1	0.025	0.567
2	0.167	1.083
3	0.425	2.719

Table 21. The comparison of execution times based on the number of workers in Spark Cluster.

Number of workers	Motif Search (In Minutes)	Bfs (in Minutes)
1	0.167	1.083
2	0.104	0.823
3	0.085	0.642
4	0.034	0.452

The comparison of execution time is shown in Figure 9.

We see that the execution time of Motif search is shorter than the execution time of breadth first search. Of course, we need execution time for discovering all significant meta-paths of large HIN, but this process run only one time and the result will be used many times during the similarity search of two objects.

We also compare the execution time of our algorithms based on the number of workers of Spark Cluster for discovering the path instances of the meta-path Author-Paper-Venue by using Motif Search and breadth-first-search of GraphFrames on Hadoop distributed computing on Spark. The result is shown in Table 21.

We observe that when the number of workers increases, the execution time will increase, too.

Table 21 and Figure 10 is the comparison of execution times based on the number of workers in Spark Cluster.

CONCLUSION AND FUTURE WORK

In this chapter, we proposed distributed algorithms to discover the significant meta-paths, maximal significant meta-paths, top-k shortest meta-paths between two vertices of large HIN on Cloud. Many algorithms for finding the meta-paths of HIN have been developed. However, these algorithms work in memory of a single computer and they cannot process large HIN which cannot fit in the memory of one computer. Recently, Apache Hadoop has been developed for distributed computing environment. We can use Cloud Computing environment to run Apache Spark. We leverage GraphFrames Library of Apache Spark processes the large HIN on Cloud computing environment. With the cloud computing environment, we can leverage the disk storage and computing power of the servicer without direct active management. We use the Cloud Computing Service from Azure HDInsight. Azure HDInsight provide the capability of Spark Cluster for disk storage and computing power. We use the Azure portal

Figure 9. Comparison of execution time between motif search and breadth-first-search of GraphFrames

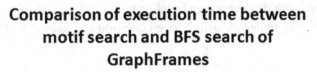

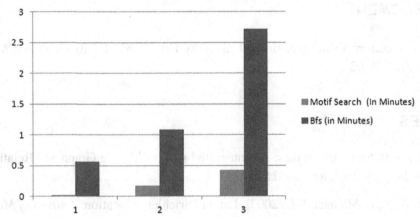

Figure 10. Comparison of execution times based on the number of workers of Spark Cluster on Cloud

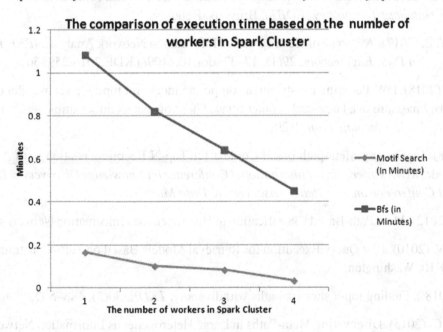

to create an HDInsight Spark cluster. The Spark cluster uses Azure Storage Blobs as the cluster storage. We create Apache Spark cluster in Azure HDInsight using Azure portal. A HIN graph is repartitioned based on sorting source vertices of arcs. We conduct the experiments of our algorithm with large HIN of DBLP and compare our distributed methods of Cloud computing environment with the one computer based traditional methods. The result proves the capability of our distributed algorithms to process large HINs in the Cloud computing environment. In the future, we will develop the distributed algorithms to discover the weighted meta-paths of weighted large Heterogeneous Information Network on Cloud. We also want to use the meta-path discovery as a baseline to generate question-answer dataset for training convolutional neural network in deep learning based question and answer system.

ACKNOWLEDGMENT

This research is funded by Vietnam National University Ho Chi Minh City (VNU-HCMC) under the grant number B2017-26-02.

REFERENCES

Ankur Dave, A. J. (2016). GraphFrames: An Integrated API for Mixing Graph and Relational Queries. GRADES 2016, June 24 2016, Redwood Shores, CA.

Blei, D. M., Ng, A. Y., & Michael, I. J. (2003). Latent Dirichlet Allocation. *Journal of Machine Learning Research*.

Chang, L. X. L. (2015). Efficiently Computing Top-K Shortest Path Join. *18th International Conference on Extending Database Technology (EDBT)*, Brussels, Belgium.

Chuan Shi, Y. L. (2017). A Survey of Heterogeneous Information Network Analysis. *IEEE Transactions on Knowledge and Data Engineering*, 29(1), 17–37. doi:10.1109/TKDE.2016.2598561

Do & Pham. (2018). DW-PathSim: a distributed computing model for topic-driven weighted meta-path-based similarity measure in a large-scale content-based heterogeneous information network. *Journal of Information and Telecommunication*, 1-20.

Hu, B. (2018). Leveraging Meta-path based Context for Top-N Recommendation with A Neural Co-Attention Mode. *KDD: Proceedings / International Conference on Knowledge Discovery & Data Mining. International Conference on Knowledge Discovery & Data Mining*.

Kong, P. S. (2012). Meta Path-Based Classification in Heterogeneous Information Networks. *CIKM'12*.

Lao, N. W. W. (2010). Fast Query Execution for Retrieval Models Based on Path-Constrained Random Walks. KDD'10, Washington, DC.

Liu, C. J. (2018.). Finding top-k shortest paths withdiversity. *TKDE, 30*(3), 488–502.

Meng, C. R. C. (2015). Discovering Meta-Paths in Large Heterogeneous Information Networks. WWW 2015, Florence, Italy.

Michael, S., & Malak, R. E. (2016). *GraphX in Action*. Manning.

Muangprathub, J. (2014). A Novel Algorithm for Building Concept Lattice. *Applied Mathematical Sciences*, 8(11), 507–515. doi:10.12988/ams.2014.312682

Nitin Mehrotra et al. (2019, August 10). *What is Apache Hadoop in Azure HDInsight?* Retrieved from Microsoft Azure: https://docs.microsoft.com/en-us/azure/hdinsight/hadoop/apache-hadoop-introduction

Pham, P., & Do, P. (2019). W-MetaPath2Vec: The topic-driven meta-path-based model for large-scaled content-based heterogeneous information network representation learning. *Expert Systems with Applications, 123*, 328–344. doi:10.1016/j.eswa.2019.01.015

Phuc, D. (2019). A System for Natural language Interaction With the heterogeneous information network. In B. B. Gupta (Ed.), *Handbook of Research on Cloud Computing and Big Data Applications in IoT*. IGI Global.

Shi, C. X. K. (2013). *HeteSim: A General Framework for Relevance Measure in Heterogeneous Networks*. Retrieved October 31, 2018, from https://arxiv.org/abs/1309.7393

Shi, C., Li, Y., Zhang, J., Sun, Y., & Philip, S. Yu. (2017). A Survey of Heterogeneous Information Network Analysis. *IEEE Transactions on Knowledge and Data Engineering, 29*(1), 17–37. doi:10.1109/TKDE.2016.2598561

Stergiou, C., Psannis, K. E., Gupta, B. B., & Ishibashi, Y. (2018, September). Security, privacy & efficiency of sustainable Cloud Computing for Big Data & IoT. *Sustainable Computing: Informatics and Systems, 19*, 174–184.

Sun, Y. J. H. (2011). Path-Sim: Meta path-based top-k similarity search in heterogeneous information networks. VLDB, 992–1003.

Sun, Y., Han, J., Yan, X., Yu, P., & Wu, T. (2011). *Path-Sim: Meta path-based top-k similarity search in heterogeneous information networks*. VLDB.

Thanh, Ho., & Phuc, Do. (2018). *Social Network Analysis Based on Topic Model with Temporal Factor. International Journal of Knowledge and Systems Science (IJKSS)*.

Tomasz Drabas, D. L. (2017). *Learning PySpark*. Packt.

Yadav, R. (2015). *Spark Cookbook*. Packt Publishing.

Zhu, Z. R. C. (2018). Evaluating Top-k Meta Path Queries on Large Heterogeneous Information Networks. IEEE ICDM 2018.

Chapter 12
A Tree Computing Block Chain Protocol Crypto–Signature Model

Cyrus Nourani

AFWMTS, Germany & TU Berlin AI, Germany

ABSTRACT

This author has for the past decade developed a mathematical basis for product languages, at times with colleagues, applying agent crypto-signatures to authenticate business process models. This chapter is the newest application for what is at recent times called block chain. A new algebraic tree based public key cryptography techniques and algorithm for crypto-signatured block chain processing is presented. The techniques apply agent crypto-signatured algebras and block product language signatures for an agenda-based block chain protocol. An algorithm with a new public key computable trust model for signature tree block parties accomplishes the block chain goals.

INTRODUCTION

The origins of blockchain are a bit nebulous. A person or group of people known by the pseudonym Satoshi Nakamura invented and released the tech in 2009 as a way to digitally and anonymously send payments between two parties without needing a third party to verify the transaction. It was initially designed to facilitate, authorize, and log the transfer of bitcoins and other cryptocurrencies. Crypto-currencies are essentially just digital money, digital tools of exchange that use cryptography and the aforementioned blockchain technology to facilitate secure and anonymous transactions. There had been several iterations of cryptocurrency over the years, but Bitcoin truly thrust cryptocurrencies forward in the late 2000s. There are thousands of cryptocurrencies floating out on the market now. One of the biggest challenges that most distributed systems face is coming to a consensus. This problem is usually called "Byzantine General's Problem (". This authors group publications on agent cryptsignatures date back to 1990´s, (e.g. Nourani et.al. 1996,1998).

DOI: 10.4018/978-1-7998-1082-7.ch012

Copyright © 2020, IGI Global. Copying or distributing in print or electronic forms without written permission of IGI Global is prohibited.

What is the Byzantine General's Problem? imagine that there is a group of Byzantine generals and they want to attack a city. They are facing two very distinct problems: The generals and their armies are very far apart so centralized authority is impossible, which makes coordinated attack very tough. The city has a huge army and the only way that they can win is if they all attack at once. In order to make successful coordination, the armies on the left of the castle send a messenger to the armies on the right of the castle with a message that says "Action Wednesday." However, suppose the armies on the right are not prepared for the attack and say, "NO. Action FRIDAY" and send back the messenger through the city back to the armies on the left. This is where we face a problem. A number of things can happen to the poor messenger. He could get captured, compromised, killed and replace with another messenger by the city. This would lead to the armies getting tampered information which may result in an uncoordinated attack and defeat. The chain is a huge network; how can you possibly trust them? If you were sending someone 4 Ether from your wallet, how would you know for sure that someone in the network isn't going to tamper with it and change 4 to 40 Ether?

A blockchain is a distributed database, meaning that the storage devices for the database are not all connected to a common processor. It maintains a growing list of ordered records, called blocks. Each block has a timestamp and a link to a previous block. Cryptography ensures that users can only edit the parts of the blockchain that they "own" by possessing the private keys necessary to write to the file. It also ensures that everyone's copy of the distributed blockchain is kept in synch. Imagine a digital medical record: each entry is a block. It has a timestamp, the date and time when the record was created. By design, the entry is not changeable retroactively, because the record of diagnosis, treatment, etc. has to be clear and unmodified. Only the doctor, who has one private key, and the patient, who has the other, can access the information, and then information is only shared when one of those users shares his or her private key with a third party — say, a hospital or specialist, on a blockchain for that medical database. Blockchains are secure databases by design. The concept was introduced in 2008, and then implemented for the first time in 2009 as part of the digital bitcoin currency, The blockchain serves as the public ledger for all bitcoin transactions. Satoshi Nakamoto, the creator of Bitcoin was able to bypass the Byzantine General's problem by inventing the proof of work protocol. In this paper we develop an agent agenda-based processor for consensus-based block chain protocol management. This author group publications on agent computing models for economics models range from (Nourani 1992) to (Nourani-Schulte 2014). Here we have crypto-economics applications. Agent computing applications to microeconomics examples are on CS curricula since 2017. A host or references are included on the new block chain areas. (Gupta 2018) and (IGI Global Handbook -31) are new overviews to the cybersecurity areas considered.

The chapters is structured as follows: chapter 2 presents the bases for cryptosigaure agent computing that is essential for block chain. This section includes agent state machines, signature tree algebras and a computational basis for processing cryptosignature computing. Agent intelligent languages are applied with cryptosignatured trees to authenticate, process or as a consensus game language. Block product agent sinagure trees are presented for characterzing block chain transactions. The mathematical basis on product models presenting a necessary and sufficient conditions for consensus on block chain transactions. Section 3 develops a specific block chain protocol based on crypto-signature trees. That process is applied to present block chain processes based on events and agendas, blocks board on actions and agendas are created to reach a new block chain protocol algorithm. These are the kind of algorithms that are usually on patents and are the recipe for crypto currency mines. So our algorithm here is also copy righted.

AGENT CRYPTO- SIGNATURES

A basis for agent computing with intelligent languages and crypto-signatures trees was presented in (Nourani 2002) with applications to WWW interfaces. We present intelligent syntax and put forth intelligent tree computing. Multiagent signatures are defined and applied to define the basis for tree information- theoretic computing and agent cyberspace applications. The project is applicable to design multiagent protocol and has been applied to put forth crypto signatures. The project has further led to foundations to computing with intelligent trees. Intelligent game trees are defined with chess playing examples and applications to cyberspace computing. Techniques for generating intelligent models are developed with soundness and completeness theorems abbreviated here with basis in our papers. The techniques can be applied as a basis to authentication on cyberspace computing. The WWW applications are summed by an authentication proposition. Agent computing has been applied by (Nourani 1999) to business and cyberspace commerce. The present approaches have a theoretical basis abbreviated in the following sections. We start with agents, define modules and algebras, and agent and module morphisms. Starting with what are called hysterectic agents (Genesereth&Nilsson 1987). A hysterectic agent has an internal state set I, which the agent can distinguish its membership. The agent can transit from each internal state to another in a single step. Actions by agents are based on I and board observations. There is an external state set K, modulated to a set T of distinguishable subsets from the observation viewpoint. An agent cannot distinguish states in the same partition defined by a congruence relation. A sensory function s:K $\rightarrow$ T maps each state to the partition it belongs. Let A be a set of actions which can be performed by agents. A function action can be defined to characterize an agent activities- action: D x T$\rightarrow$ A. The update function database maps a state and a state partition t into a new internal database- database: D x T $\rightarrow$ D. There is also a memory update function mem: I x T $\rightarrow$ I. To define agent at arbitrary level of activity knowledge level agents are defined. All excess level detail is eliminated. In this abstraction an agent's internal state consists entirely of a database of sentences and the agent's actions are viewed as inferences based on its database. The action function for a knowledge level agent maps a database and a state partition t into the action to be performed by an agent in a state with database and observed state partition t.

A knowledge-level agent is defined as <D,K,T,A,see,do,database,action> as follows: the set D in the tuple is an arbitrary set of predicate calculus databases, S is a set of external states, T is the set of partitions of S, A is a set of actions, see is a function from S into T, do is a function from A S into S, database is a function from D x T into D, and action is a function from D x T into A. Knowledge level agents are example hysterectic agents.

Cryptosiganture Agent Language Processing

Blockchain tranactions are based on immutable strings, encoded with protocol languages expressible on signature tree to process and authenticate on network transactions. The process applies Shared Ledgers and Digital ID's. Trust ledger update on transactions with data partitioning for selective data exposures, while encoding business rules on a business logic layer realizing transactions on cryptocurrencies. Block sequening and data stringing are applied with Hash code distributed transactions on Multisignature cooperative transactions.

The formal basis to the above is charcaterized by an intelligent language (Nourani 1996, 1997). Such languages afford syntactic constructs that allow function symbols and corresponding objects, such that the function symbols are implemented by computing agents. Sentential logic is the standard formal language applied when defining basic models. The language L is a set of sentence symbol closed by finite application of negation and conjunction to sentence symbols. Once quantifier logical symbols are added to the language, the language of first order logic can be defined. A Model for L is a structure 𝕮 with a corresponding set 𝕮 such that for each constant symbol in the language there corresponds a constant in 𝕮. For each function symbol in the language there is a function defined on 𝕮; and for each relation symbol in the language there is a relation defined on 𝕮. For the algebraic theories we are defining for intelligent tree computing in the forthcoming sections the language is defined from signatures as in the logical language is the language of many-sorted equational logic. Since an exposition at MFCS track, Berno on intelligent languages (Nourani 1995). Comparable papers are (Burkhardt 1994) Basic agent computing area briefs are on the DESIRE model (Brazier, F.M.T., Dunin-Keplicz, et.la. A brief here an overview on what the concept is: A set of function symbols in the language,)for example, f is the set modeled in the computing world by AI Agents with across and/or over board capability. Thus the language defined by the signature has designated function symbols called f with specific designation options on structure models. The Agent function symbols define signatures that have specific properties. For example, to state that f is names for only 1-1 function is an *intelligent language function designation*. This is the subject of the following areas where free algebras on intelligent trees that we call cryptosmart in this context. Cryptosmart is an annotation to subsignatures that are mutually designated encrypted. For example that subsignature operations are algebraically closed to the subsignature, or that certain functions must be designated 1-1 respective.

A multi-sorted signature Σ = (Sorts, Ops). There is sort set and Ops is a set of operations on the sorts of form n: s1 × . . . × sk → s. s1, . . ., sk, s ∈ Sorts, k ≥ 0. operation name n. argument sorts s1 × . . . × sk . target sort s. arity s1 × . . . × sk → s. For k = 0: constant n:→ s of sort s.

Definition 2.1 We say that a signature Σ is cryptosmart iff it has an intelligent function symbol subsignature. We say that a language has crsptosmart syntax if the syntax is defined by such signature Σ.

Definition 2.2 A language L is said to be an cryptosmart signature language iff L is defined from an cryptosmart intelligent syntax.

Intelligent languages and signatures (Nourani 1997) allow us to present computational theories with formulas on terms with intelligent function symbols.

Recalling what was the starts to context free grammars for agent computing.

(Nourani 1997) proves that String Intelligent languages are Context-Free-ICF. The above stated theorem can have newer instantiations for cryptosmart signatures in forthcoming papers. Bitcoins, for example, are unforgeable bitstrings "Mined" by the protocol itself. Digital signature keys own and transfer bitcoins. Owners are pseudonymous, e.g., D4hAZeKE7vER2YvmH4yT. Every transaction transfers a bitcoin (fraction) from current to next owner. Such bitcoin now belongs to D4h.... signed by the key of current owner: flow linkable by protocol, and not anonymous when converted to real-world assets. Validation is based on the global history of past transactions. Signer has received the bitcoin before, or Signer has not yet spent the bitcoin. Every operation o appends a "block" of valid transactions (tx) to the log. The log content is verifiable from the most recent element, while the log entries form a hash chain

ht ← Hash([tx1, tx2, ...] ‖ ht-1 ‖ t) .

Agent Authentication

By definitions 2.1 and 2.2 agent signatures are carried by the intelligent signature. Computing with intelligent trees might embed automatic agent signature authentication. The basis for the computing is a signature match to start agent messages. Basic authentication is automatic when the intelligent computing interface to WWW is cranked up. Further encoding can be embedded when the agent signatures are designed. For example, the agent signature can specify what the agent types are with which it can engage exchange at all. The signature might specify the class of messages and or transactions allowed. Basic agent protocol can also be encoded by the agent signatures. Our protocol model starts with A be an alphabet and Σ a signature with $A \subset \Sigma$. Let $P_{\Sigma} = \{p1,\ldots,pn\}$ $n \in \omega$ the natural numbers ordinal, with $p_i \in \Sigma^*$.

Having the above we can begin to reach a mathematics computational basis to address block chain protocol and crypto currency areas, for example, defining transaction processing onto a database or block chain model. Authentication or consensus might be encoded or decided on and/or agent trees. The agent and/or game trees (Nourani 1997) are example tree rewriting on signatured trees.

AND/OR trees (Nilsson 1969) game trees defined to solve an authemtication or check consensus from a stakes player's stand point. are

n an OR node.
/ | \
m an AND node
/__|__\
/ | \

Formally a node problem is said to be solved if one of the following conditions hold.

1. The node is the set of terminal nodes (primitive problem- the node has no successor).
2. The node has AND nodes as successors and the successors are solved.
3. The node has OR nodes as successors and any one of the successors is solved.

A solution to the original problem is given by the subgraph of AND/OR graph sufficient to show that the node is solved. A program which can play a theoretically perfect game would have task like searching and AND/OR tree for a solution to a one person problem to a two-person game. An intelligent AND/OR tree is and AND/OR tree where the tree branches are intelligent trees. The branches compute a Boolean function via agents. The Boolean function is what might satisfy a goal formula on the tree. An intelligent AND/OR tree is solved iff the corresponding Boolean functions solve the AND/OR trees named by intelligent functions on the trees. Thus node m might be f(a1,a2,a3) & g(b1,b2), where f and g are Boolean functions of three and two variables, respectively, and ai's and bi's are Boolean valued agents satisfying goal formulas for f and g.

g is on OR agent
/ | \
b1 | b2
f f is an AND agent
/__|__\
/ | \
a1 a2 a3

Example open trusted team play at blockchain has the following game characteristics:

*There is a common blockchain protocol
*Consensus is distrubuted permissionless
*There is a team leader deciding a goal ledger is closed: i,e, BC game solved.
  ◦   Transations are immutable

Examples: An event processing system blockchain for processing a lottery.
A university network tuition processing system for a univerity group.
Blockchain transactions are based on a team member consensus.No single player possesses all the knowledge. "Portfolio" of access control and stake protocols prevail, regulating the team ``ball passes.´´

Agents, Modules, and Blocks

A digital identity is information on an entity used by computer systems to represent an external agent. That agent may be a person, organisation, application, or device. ISO/IEC 24760-1 denotes identity as "set of attributes related to an entity. The computing enterprise requires more general techniques of model construction and extension, since it has to accommodate dynamically changing world descriptions and theories. The models to be defined are for complex computing phenomena, for which we define generalized diagrams. The techniques in the first author´s over a decade model building as applied to the problem of AI reasoning allows us to build and extend models through diagrams. It required us to define the notion of generalized diagram. Generic diagrams characterize models with prespecified generalized Skolem functions. The specific minimal set of function symbols is the set with which a model for a knowledge base can be defined. The G-diagram techniques allowed us to formulate AI worlds, KB's in a minimal computable manner to be applied to agent computation. The techniques in (Nourani 1991,94a) for model building as applied to the problem of AI reasoning allows us to build and extend models through diagrams. A technical example of algebraic models defined from syntax had appeared in defining initial algebras for equational theories of data types (ADJ 1973) and our research in (Nilsson 1969). In such direction for computing models of equational theories of computing problems are presented by a pair (Σ,E), where is a signature (of many sorts, for a sort set S) (ADJ 1973,Nourani 1995a) and E a set of -equations. Signatures are in the same sense as key signatures in music.

We apply multi-sorted algebras via definition 2.3 to multiagent systems.

Definition 2.3 Let Σ be a multi-sorted signature. A Σ algebra A consists of a set As for each $s \in S$ (called the carrier if A of sort s) and a function $<A>$: $As1 \times As2 \times ....\times Asn \rightarrow As$ for each $\Sigma <w,s>$, with $w=s1s2...sn$ (called the operation named by $\Sigma <w,s>$). For $<,s>$, A As, i,e the (set of names) of constants of sort s.

Briefing on the mathematical basis for where we began to study NLP algorithms since (Nourani-Fähndlich 2014) there are new applications for compound signatures over product languages. The fragment categories (Nourani 1996) can be addressed at several levels: We can consider defining a correspondence to an arbitrary infinitary language where the sets you wish to address with respect to the new signature that are to be the structure for your language are definable: you can call that $L\Sigma$. On $T\Sigma$ we can take well-defined fragments on the $L\Sigma$ language towards techniques for creating models (Nourani 1996, 2014).

Some preliminary definitions are as follows taking for granted structures and languages for at least first order logic with algebraic structures. Though this paper is not so explicit on the mathematics for models when we present tree congruences to check signature validity there are implicit homomorphisms that are model checking for truth assignments to event agenda instantiations.

Definition 2.5 Let M be a structure for a language L, call a subset X of M a generating set for M if no proper substructure of M contains X, i.e. if M is the closure of X U {c(M): c is a constant symbol of L}. An assignment of constants to M is a pair <A,G>, where A is an infinite set of constant symbols in L and G: A → M such that {G(a): a in A} is a set of generators for M. Interpreting a by g(a), every element of M is denoted by at least one closed term of L(A). For a fixed assignment <A,G> of constants to M, the diagram of M, D<A,G>(M) is the set of basic (atomic and negated atomic) sentences of L(A) true in M. (Note that L(A) is L enriched with set A of constant symbols.)

Definition 2.6 We say that a formula is positive iff it is built from atomic formulas using only the connectives &, v and the quantifiers∀, ∃.

Definition 2.7 A formula φ (x1,x2,...,xn) is preserved under homomorphisms iff for any homomorphisms f of a model A onto a model B and all a1,...,an in A if A |= φ[a1,...,an] B |= ω[fa1,...,fan].

Theorem 1 (Nourani 2010) Let L1, L2 be two positive languages. Let L = L1 ∩ L2. Suppose T is a complete theory in L and T1 ⊃ T, T2 ⊃ T are consistent in L1, L2, respectively. Suppose there is model M definable from a positive diagram in the language L1 ∪ L2 such that there are models M1 and M2 for T1 and T2 where M can be homomorphically embedded in M1 and M2. (i) T1 ∪ T2 is consistent. (ii) There is model N for T1 ∪ T2 definable from a positive diagram that homomorphically extends that of M1 and M2.

Theorem 2 (Nourani 2010) Let L1, L2 be two positive languages. Let L = L1 ∩ L2. Suppose T is a complete theory in L and T1 ⊃ T, T2 ⊃ T are consistent in L1, L2, respectively. Then

(i)   T1∪T2 has a model M, that is a positive end extension on Models M1 and M2 for T1, and T2, respectively.
      (ii) M is definable from a positive diagram in the language L1 ∪ L2.

Block Product Signatures Agent Languages

Beginning with the mathematical basis for where we began to study NLP algorithms since (Nourani-Fahndlich 2014) we apply our new techniques for compound signatures over product languages by assigning a signature language to every block. We can consider a correspondence to an arbitrary infinitary language where the sets you wish to address with respect to the new signature that are to be the structure for your language are definable: you can call that L_Σ. The linguistics abstraction techniques developed since 1997 allows us to lift from context. With signature tree languages we can carry on partitions on models for a formal language that factor generic models. Let L1,.....Ln are language fragments n ∈ω Σ1,... Σn Are the fragment natural grammar signatures T<Σ1 >.........T<Σn> are the free trees on the grammar signatures. Each fragment language signature tree T<Σi > can be assigned a fragment semantics whereby to each t ∈ T<Σi > the free well-formed syntax trees ti and tj are ≡ iff there is a context free parse normal form common to both. Let us denote that congruence with ≡ $_{CTF}$ fragment L1, L2,..., Ln Fragments n < ω, i.e. a natural number.

Thereby we have a mathematical characterizations for blocks on a chain signature on a product language

$\Pi \; i \in \omega \; L\Sigma i$

Let us define a product signature filter following the first author's recent product language filters publications, e.g. (Nourani 2018) to present public key signatures for block chain crypto-signatures (refer to crypto literatures).

Definition 2.8 A block chain public key signature for an n-block party with protocol signature languages $\{L\Sigma i \; i <= n \}$ is a signature Ω such that $\Omega \cap \Sigma i$ is $\neq$ ᵉ, i.e. nonempty intersection.

Remark: For arbitrary Σ-trees ti, tk $\in L\Sigma i$. The terms ti, tk are authentic crypto term pairs for the n-block party iff ti $\equiv \Omega$ tk can be ascertained. So each party must have the Ω mathematically reachable its personal scramble to authenticate pairs.

In the following the language products are direct product on the free $T<\Sigma i >$. The basic algebraic signature tree congruences are standard notions since (ADJ 1973).

Theorem 3 Let $\Pi \; i \in \omega \; L\Sigma i$ be a product block chain computation process, then the n-block chain transaction consensus can be computable iff for every pair transaction protocol signature trees ti and tk in $\Pi \; i \in \omega \; L\Sigma i$, ti $\equiv \Omega$ tk .

Hence, the direct product on signature tree algebras is the block party scramble for the public key consensus protocol.

AN AGENT BLOCK CHAIN PROTOCOL

Let A be an alphabet and Σ a signature with A $\subset \Sigma$. Let $P_{\Sigma} = \{p1,\ldots,pn\}$ n$\in\omega$ the natural numbers ordinal, with $p_i \in \Sigma^*$. So each p_i is a Σ-term. We might define on ordering on P_{Σ} as follows on the following paragraph. Let us define a function v: $\Sigma^* \to \Sigma^*$. Now let $p_i > p_{j \; iff} \; p_{i \; = \; v(t,} \; p_{j) \; for \; some} \; t \in \Sigma^*$. Let us define a priority function Top on $P_{\Sigma \; as \; follows: \; Top:} \; P_{\Sigma} \to P_{\Sigma \; defined \; with \; Top \;} (^P \Sigma) = \{pi: for all _{pj} \in P_{\Sigma,} \; p_i > p_j \}$. Now we can define a preliminary cryptosignatured block chain protocol with

BCP = $\{P_{\Sigma:} \; (x,y_{)} \; x \in P_{\Sigma,} \; y \in P_{\Sigma,}$ and x $<y\}$. Having the above we can begin to reach a mathematics computational basis to address block chain protocol and crypto currency areas, for example, defining and a Put or Get on a database block chain model.

Let us consider the following example (Nourani 2001) (O is the Banking) Network,Transfer an example of an action in A, and R has equations listed on Transfer and ETransfer

Object:= A_Sirrius_Function

OPS:= Transfer_Computing_Funds (Amount, To,From) | .... Transfer(Many_Mill-K\$,ID, Vault_Funds) ==> signal an agent to activate a destination vault computer agent; pass authentication signature; pass Name bank number; activate funds transfer completion agents; transfer authentication signature to agent for deposit; signal transaction completion.

Exp:= ETransfer_Computing_Funds (Amount,To, From) | Etransfer_Computing_Funds(Many_Mill-K\$, ID, Vault_Funds) ==>

If Vault_Agent busy signal: try preemptive agent activation; recover from busy waited periods;

If amount exceeds immediate_funds_available:

Activate installment funding agents: set authentication for payments over several years; If Vault_funds all committed, activate agents to transfer from BC Crypto R&D_Funds

Figure 1. A glimpse from IBM research zürich blockchain

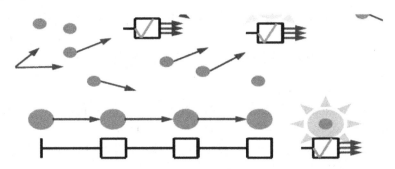

Agent Computing, Events, and Agendas

Competitive model multiagent planning (Nourani 1999, Geneserch Nilsson 1987, Nourani-Schulte 2014) is an important application area to illustrate how event-based distributed computation on blockchain can be modelled. Event based computing is modeled at AI with boards and an agenda for goals to satisfy. Events are modeled with agents that send signals indicating changes to agenda boards towards even updates, or to interim goals. With multiagent systems computing Σ basis event knowledge- level cooperation between autonomous agents has significant benefits for distributed systems engineering. Examples are interoperability, scalability, and reconfigurability Another important direction is designs with intelligent multi-tiers applying agents and intelligent business objects with applications to intelligent WWW interfaces (Nourani 2005)

Block Board Actions on Agendas

Let us partake a glimpse from IBM on Nakamura consensus with block trans actions. Nodes prepare block: the list of valid transactions. There is a lottery race to form a winning valid chain.

vs

A lottery race is carried on a random event- based agenda board. Events are managed by reaching a winning sequence. The mathematical model for the event-based agenda driven block chain protocol is as follows. Block chain with an agent model is accomplished with a what we define as a Block Board $\Sigma = \{\Sigma i,.... \Sigma n\}$ that is agenda driven for block actions. Let us define A block board with a multiagent signature $\Sigma = \{\Sigma i,.... \Sigma n\}$ for Σi an action Ai on the block.

Cryptosigature Block chain consensus protocol Algorithm (Nourani 2017):

For an action, i.e. a block chain transaction, that is carried out with an action Ai, the action Ai blockboard:

The blockboard agenda carries out the action Ai for Σi with arity m iff

1. For every agent term ti on $\Sigma(x1,...,xm)$ every variable x corresponding to the Ai agent is instantiated with an authenticated block player; e,g. a player with the group public key. and
2. Block chain protocol condition BCP is met for the action Ai.

Iterate on i on Ai.

The agenda board fires the transaction iff a &b. are satisfied.

The above is priority consensus block party consensus algorithm realized on product signature terms.

Concluding Comments

A mathematical basis for consensus based block chain computing and trust models is presented. A novel priority-based block chain protocol algorithm based on consensus on agenda event-based computing is developed. Distributed computing for consensus. Novel product language block cryptography for anonymous trusted transactions for ledgers and block chain networks are presented in preliminary format on a multiagent block chain state machine model. Visual data bases and morphic encoding are further areas that this author and authors at the general areas have published on papers.

ACKNOWLEDGMENT

Thanking Prof. Uwe Egbert Wolter, Bergen, for preliminary comments on a draft paper..

REFERENCES

A Preliminary Block Chain Protocol Language Cyrus F Nourani Group Technical brief. (2018). TU Berlin.

Athey, C. (2017). *The Digital Privacy Paradox: Small Money, Small Costs, Small Talk*. Retrieved from https://papers.ssrn.com/sol3/papers2.cfm?abstract_id=2916489

Brazier, F. M. T., Dunin-Keplicz, B., Jennings, N. R., & Treur, J. (1997). DESIRE: modeling mulch-agent systems in a compositional formal framework. International Journal of Cooperative Information Systems, 1(152).

Burkhard, H. D. (1994). On Fair Controls in Multi-Agent Systems. *ECAI 1994, 11th European Conference on Artificial Intelligence*, 254-258.

Cachin, Andrulaki, & Osboren. (2016). *Blockchain, cryptography, and Consensus*. IBM Zürich.

Ernest and Young. (2015). *Sharing ledgers for sharing economies: an exploration of mutual distributed ledgers (aka blockchain technology)*. Retrieved from https://fsinsights.ey.com/thejournalhttps://fsinsights.ey.com/thejournal

Genesereth, M. R., & Nilsson, N. J. (1987). *Logical Foundations of Artificial Intelligence*. Morgan-Kaufmann.

Goguen, Thatcher, Wagner, & Wright. (1973). A Junction Between Computer Science and Category Theory (parts I and II). IBM T.J. Watson Research Center.

Gupta. (2018). Computer and Cyber Security: Principles, Algorithm, Aplications, and Perspectives. CRC Press, Taylor & Francis.

Hai, H., Xie, D. Q., & Ke, Q. (2018). A watermarking-based authentication and image restoration in multimedia sensor networks. *International Journal of High Performance Computing and Networking*, *12*(1), 65–73. doi:10.1504/IJHPCN.2018.093846

Ibtihal, M., Driss, E. O., & Hassan, N. (2017). Homomorphic encryption as a service for outsourced images in mobile cloud computing environment. *International Journal of Cloud Applications and Computing*, *7*(2), 27–40. doi:10.4018/IJCAC.2017040103

Merkle Tree - Eine Basis der Blockchain. (n.d.). Retrieved from https://blockchainwelt.de

Nilsson, N. J. (1969). Searching, problem solving, and game-playing trees for minimal cost solutions. In A. J. Morell (Ed.), *IFIP 1968* (Vol. 2, pp. 1556–1562). Amsterdam: North-Holland.

Nilsson, N. J. (1969). Searching, problem solving, and game-playing trees for minimal cost solutions. In A. J. Morell (Ed.), *IFIP 1968* (Vol. 2, pp. 1556–1562). Amsterdam: North-Holland.

Nourani, C. F. (1996). Slalom Tree Computing- A Computing Theory for Artificial Intelligence. AI Comm., 4(4).

Nourani, C. F. (1997). Modelling,Validation,and Hybrid Design of Intelligent Systems. *8th Workshop Knowledge Engineering Methods and Languages*.

Nourani, C. F. (1998). Intelligent Languages A preliminary Syntactic Theory. *Proceedings of the MFCS'98 satellite workshop on Grammar systems*, 281-287.

Nourani, C. F. (2000). Intelligent Heterogenous Multimedia and Intelligent Active Visual DB and KB. ICCIT 2000, Las Vegas, NV.

Nourani, C. F. (2003). A Sound and Complete Agent Logic Paradigm, 2000. In *Parts and abstract published Fall Symposium*. AAAI Press.

Nourani, C. F. (2003). Versatile Abstract Syntax Meta-Contextual Logic and VR Computing. *36th Lingustische Kolloquium, Austria Proceedings*.

Nourani, C. F. (2005). *Business Planning and Cross Organizational Models Workshop on Collaborative Cross- Organizational Process Design*. Retrieved from http://www.mensch-und-computer.de/mc2005

Nourani, C. F. (2017). *On cryptosigature Protocol Morphic Languages 2017*. Retrieved from https://www.researchgate.net/project/Block-Chain-Protocol-Crypto-Signatures-and-Languages

Nourani & Fähndrich. (2018*). Direct Product Models and Languages- A Preliminary*. Universal Logic, Vichy, France.

Nourani & Fandlich. (2014). *Factors on Signatured Trees and Semantic Language Processing, Abstract*. DAI-TU Berlin.

Nourani & Moudi. (2008). *Fields, Certificates, and Models*. 1039-12-AMS 2008 Spring Western Section Meeting, Claremont, CA.

Nourani & Schulte. (2011). *SFU, Vancouver, Canada Draft February 2011, Revision 1:September 25, 2012 SFU, Vancouver, Canada Computation Logic Lab. Multiagent Decision Trees, Competitive Models, and Goal Satisfiability*. DICTAP.

Nourani & Schulte. (2015). Computing Predictive Analytics, Business Intelligence, and Economics: Modeling Techniques with Start-ups and Incubators. Publisher Apple Academic Press Inc.

Nourani. (1998). Agent Computing, KB For Intelligent Forecasting, and Model 15. In *AAAI Wkshp on Agent Based Systems in the Business Context*. AAAI Press.

Nourani. (2000). Cyberspace Interfaces, CyberSignatures, and Business-Business WWW Computing. *Expert Update- Knowledge Based Systems and Applied AI, 3*(3).

Tewari, A., & Gupta, B. B. (2017). Cryptanalysis of a novel ultra-lightweight mutual authentication protocol for IoT devices using RFID tags. *The Journal of Supercomputing, 73*(3), 1085–1102. doi:10.100711227-016-1849-x

Weber. (2016). *Untrusted Business Process Monitoring and Execution Using Blockchain*. Retrieved from http://link.springer.com/chapter/10.1007/978-3-319-45348-4_19

Zkik, Orhanou, & El Hajji. (2017). Secure mobile multi cloud architecture for authentication and data storage. *International Journal of Cloud Applications and Computing, 7*(2).

Chapter 13
Automate Model Transformation From CIM to PIM up to PSM in Model-Driven Architecture

Yassine Rhazali

https://orcid.org/0000-0003-1488-0216

ISIC Research Team of ESTM, LMMI Laboratory of ENSAM, Moulay Ismail University of Meknes, Morocco

Asma El Hachimi

MISC Laboratory, Ibn Tofail University, Morocco

Idriss Chana

ISIC Research Team of ESTM, LMMI Laboratory of ENSAM, Moulay Ismail University of Meknes, Morocco

Mohammed Lahmer

ISIC Research Team of ESTM, LMMI Laboratory of ENSAM, Moulay Ismail University of Meknes, Morocco

Abdallah Rhattoy

ISIC Research Team of ESTM, LMMI Laboratory of ENSAM, Moulay Ismail University of Meknes, Morocco

ABSTRACT

The CIM, PIM, and PSM models are the main levels of the MDA approach. Model transformation is an important step in the MDA process. Indeed, in MDA there are two elementary transformation kinds: CIM to PIM transformation and PIM to PSM transformation. However, most searches propose approaches transforming PIM to PSM, since there are multiple points in common between PIM and PSM. Nevertheless, transforming CIM to PIM is rarely addressed in research because these two levels are mainly different. However, there is not a synthesis work that makes it possible to carry out a model transformation from CIM to PIM towards PSM until obtaining the code. This synthesis methodology allows controlling models transformation from CIM to PIM to PSM, indeed, up to obtaining code according the MDA. This approach makes it possible to limit the intervention of computer scientists in the life cycle of software development. Indeed, this methodology allows modeling only CIM, the business process, and then obtains the source code through successive semi-automatic transformations.

DOI: 10.4018/978-1-7998-1082-7.ch013

Copyright © 2020, IGI Global. Copying or distributing in print or electronic forms without written permission of IGI Global is prohibited.

INTRODUCTION

MDE (Model Driven Engineering) (Schmidt, 2006) is an alternative approach of software engineering. This approach allows the development of software systems by basing on the models. This approach focuses on the creation of the basic models and transforming them, to multiple levels of abstraction, in order to automatic generation of source code. The objective of this approach is to automate the operation of software development that is realized manually by the software experts. MDE is a general methodology which can be supported by several approaches, indeed, MDA (Model Driven Architecture) (OMG-MDA, 2015) of OMG (Object Management Group) is considered as the most prevalent approach. MDA follows the same fundamentals of MDE; however, it identifies its own bases presented by three levels of abstraction, respect of various requirements, and the recommendation of some standards.

CIM (Computation Independent Model) is the highest level of abstraction and the first into MDA. Indeed, CIM level is independent of computation, for this, the researchers represent only the business process reality into this level. CIM models are made by business experts. The second level of abstraction in MDA is the PIM level that describes models useful to information system analysts and designers. PIM (Platform Independent Model) level contains the conceptual models, and the analysis models, of information system. The lowest level of abstraction in MDA is the PSM (Platform Specific Model) which is constituted by code models; these models are very useful by software developers. The models of PSM level formed of all information related to a specific platform. MDA is a model-based architecture, for this, the textual code does not interpreted as a level in MDA, however, source code is the ultimate goal into MDA.

Model transformation presents the key of MDA. The transformations between different levels of MDA start with the transformations from CIM (Computation Independent Mode) to PIM (Platform Independent Model) that allow to partially obtain the PIM models from the CIM models. The objective is to rewrite technically the information contained in the CIM models into PIM models, which enables to ensure that business information is preserved throughout the MDA process. Then, the transformation from PIM level to PSM (Platform Specific Model) level requires adding into PIM models the technical information related to the target platform.

Our approach based, in CIM level, BPMN (Business Process Model and Notation) (OMG-BPMN, 2011) collaboration diagram and business process diagram which represent standards of business process model. Next, through these latter standards the authors can build rich business models that contain well-concentrated information help us to get PIM models. The first model in the PIM level is the use case diagram model that interprets the functionalities of the system. Then, the sequence diagram model describes information interaction with the system in a dynamic way. Next, the class diagram model allows presenting the system classes and their relationships. Finally, all classes are structured in packages into package diagram model. Then, PIM models can be transformed trough a tool to PSM, indeed, up to code.

CIM, PIM and PSM are the important levels in MDA . Model transformation is the main step in the MDA approach. However, in MDA there are two primary transformation: CIM to PIM transformation and PIM to PSM transformation. Nevertheless, most works offer approaches transforming PIM to PSM, indeed, there are several commonality between PIM and PSM. However, transforming CIM to PIM is rarely broached in research because these two levels are mainly dissimilar. Indeed, there is not a synthesis work which makes it possible to achieve a model transformation from CIM to PIM towards PSM until geting the code. This synthesis research allows mastering models transformation from CIM to PIM to PSM, indeed, up to obtaining code according the MDA. This work makes it possible to limit the intervention of computer scientists in the life cycle of software development, indeed this work allows modeling only CIM, the business process, and then, get the source code through several automatic transformations.

The rest of this paper is organized as follows. In section II, the authors describe the related works of the models transformation .Then, in Section III, the researchers show the approach, specify the construction rules of CIM level, and describe the transformation rules that allow transforming CIM to PIM to PSM up to code. Next, in Section IV, the authors illustrate the proposal in a case study showing the establishment of CIM level and transforming it to PIM level, then, they transform PIM to PSM and finally to code. However, in section V the researchers analyze the contributions of the approach compared with related work. Finally, in Section VI, the authors conclude by specifying the current works and by presenting future works.

RELATED WORK

In this section, the researchers describe the related works concerning model transformation into MDA.

The oriented-service transformation from CIM to PIM presented In (Castro et al., 2011). In this approach the authors establish CIM level with: the BPMN notation for modeling the business process and the value model (Gordijn et al., 2003) for identifying services from the beginning in the business perspective. The authors based on the ATL (atlas transformation language) language for moving toward PIM level which is represented by two extensions of the activity diagram and two extensions of use case diagram.

In (Hahn et al., 2010) the authors propose an approach of engineering services model-driven, they represent the CIM level through BPMN notation. Then, they use ATL language to move to PIM level which is represented by SoaML (OMG-SoaML, 2012) models.

In (Zhang et al., 2005) they authors show a methodology in which the CIM and PIM are respectively represented by features and components. Responsibilities in this approach are considered as connectors between features and components to facilitate the transformation task from CIM to PIM. (Grammel el el., 2010) the authors based on a DSL connection, which allows the management of traceability in general.

A methodology respecting MDA allow transforming model of use case diagram to model of activity diagram is provided by (Gutiérrez et al., 2008). The authors based on QVT for transforming existing use cases diagram model to the activity diagram model.

In (Kherraf et al., 2008) the authors propose a methodology allows transforming the CIM to PIM. For modeling the business perspective in CIM level, the authors use the business process model and the use case diagram, then, the system requirements are modeled by the activity diagram in the CIM level. Next, the system requirements are transformed to components of the system which are presented by the component diagram in the PIM level. Finally, a set of business archetypes facilitate the transformation from the system components to the class diagram model.

In (Kardoš et al., 2010) the authors provide an analytical method for transforming CIM to PIM into MDA. The authors establish CIM models through the data flow diagram. Then, they move to PIM models which are modeled by use case diagram, activity diagram, sequence diagram, and class diagram.

A method for moving to Information system model from business process model is presented in (Mokrys, 2012). Into CIM level the authors establish the business process model by basing on BPMN notation. However, PIM models are presented by UML class diagram and state diagram.

In (Rhazali et al., 2015a) the authors establish a transformation method for moving from CIM to PIM. This method based on BPMN notation for presenting the business process models. Then, PIM models are established by the three classical modeling views. This method focuses on analytic survey that allows moving from CIM level to PIM level through a semi-automatic transformation.

In (Rhazali et al., 2015b) the authors present a methodology for transforming CIM models to PIM models. The authors establish business process through UML 2 activity diagram. However, the PIM models are modeled by class diagram, state diagram and package diagram. This methodology founded on a set of transformation rules for transforming CIM models to PIM models.

In (Rhazali et al., 2016a) the authors propose an approach for transforming business process models to analysis and design model. This approach allows establishing business process in CIM by basing on SoaML models .However, PIM models are presented by UML 2 use case diagram, state diagram, class diagram and web diagram presented by SoaML: software component.

In (Rhazali et al., 2016b) the authors represent an approach to move from CIM to PIM; they define the business process by using BPMN. However, the PIM level is established by UML. This approach founded MVC design pattern.

In (Rhazali et al., 2017) the authors define a method to transform from CIM level to PIM level; they define the business process by using UML activity diagram. However, the PIM level by UML diagrams models. In PIM level this approach is founded also in SoaML and IFML.

In (Rhazali et al., 2018) the authors represent an approach to shift from CIM to PIM; they define the business process by using BPMN. However, the PIM level is established by the three UML view point. This approach founded also in web model to define PIM level.

After this overview on related works, we can arrange the works into four classes. We find works that use model requirements (such as the use case diagram) in the CIM level, to facilitate the transformation to PIM (Gutiérrez et al., 2008; Kherraf et al., 2008). Then, other researches (Castro et al., 2011; Hahn, et al., 2010), even if they define the business processes in CIM level, do not represent the structural view (usually through the class diagram) in the PIM level. There are also methods such as (Kardoš et al., 2010) which represent the structural view in the PIM level, but the authors do not specify transformation rules. Finally, there are methods (Zhang et al., 2005; Grammel et al., 2010) that define exactly the transformation rules and do not have the models used in the CIM and PIM level.

So we can say that the main contributions of our study compared with others as follows: a business process model is used in CIM level; then, we define the structural view in PIM level; next we propose an approach of generic transformation that has clear rules to achieve the maximum possible automatic transformation from CIM to PIM up to PSM.

PROPOSED METHOD FOR TRANSFORMING CIM TO PIM up to PSM

A business process model is the abstraction of the real business process inside enterprise. In accordance with our modeling objectives the authors can establish different models to present the same reality. The researchers can model for controlling the business process, for improving the communication process with partners and customers, or for establishing initial models in the process of software development. In this proposal, our objective is to design business process models as a first stage in the process of software system development. In the last case there are two possibilities: either establish business models destined to be transformed, manually through the analysts and the software designers, toward design models, or establish business models automatically transformable toward the design models. The second choice was considered in this methodology, because this work founded on the MDA. For this, the proposal

Figure 1. Our CIM to PIM up to PSM Transformation proposal

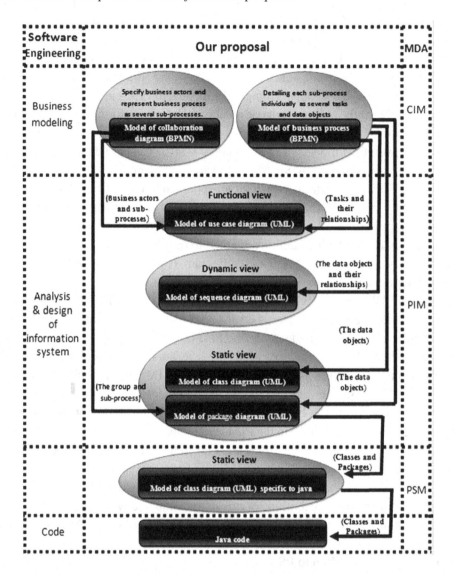

allows to model real business models, contain useful information, which facilitate the transformation from CIM to PIM to PSM up to code.

Our methodology presents the business perspective in the CIM level, through business process models, for preserving the business knowledge during the transformation toward the PIM models in order to achieve a quality information system.

In this Methodology (cf. Figure 1), the researchers use the two standards of modeling business processes, the BPMN collaboration diagram and BPMN business process diagram, for taking advantage of each standard in order to achieve rich models into CIM level, for facilitating the transformation to PIM to PSM up to code.

MDA advocates the use of UML diagrams for modeling the PIM level. Indeed, in our proposal the authors define use case diagram to present functional view of the system, however, the sequence diagram interpret the system behavioral view, then, the class diagram shows the structural view of the system. However, the authors structure all classes in packages into package diagram. Then, PIM models can be transformed trough a tool to PSM, indeed, up to code. Indeed, All PIM and PSM models are obtained through an automatic or semi-automatic transformation from CIM models, via well-defined transformation rules and tools.

Below, the researchers represent the construction rules of CIM models, and the transformation rules that allow transforming CIM models to the PIM models, and propose to facilitate transformation from PIM to the PSM level, then, up to obtaining code.

Construction Rules of the CIM Level

The rules for constructing the model of BPMN collaboration diagram (cf. Figure 2):

- Establish an average sub-processes (not complexes sub-processes). In order to each sub-process must be comprised between 4 task and 12 tasks.
- If a sub-process provides a complementary operation to other sub-processes or contains less than four tasks, the authors can merge several sub-processes into one, on condition that the sub-process merged do not surpasses 10 tasks.
- Present manual tasks and do not show other kind of the tasks.
- Represent general business process and avoid the details
- Focus only on sub-processes and their sequences.
- Specify the maximum of the collaborators which interact in achieving the business process.
- The sub-processes belonging to the same category must be grouped inside the "Group" notation.

Figure 2. CIM generic models: BPMN generic model

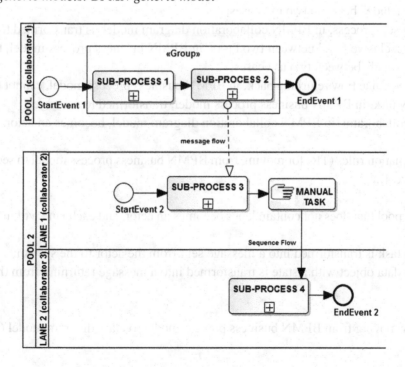

Figure 3. Schema of passage from the CIM level models to use case diagram model.

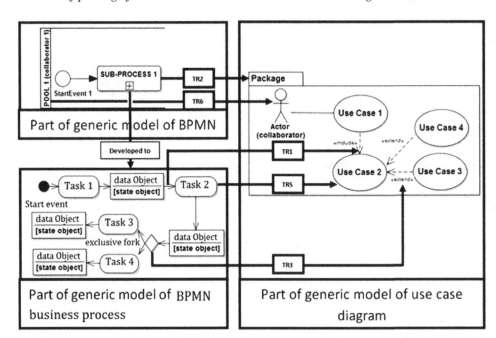

Transformation Rules from the CIM level to PIM level

The transformation rules (TR) of passage from CIM models to use case diagram model (cf. Figure 3):

- TR1: the "sequence flow" between two tasks, in BPMN business process model, becomes a relationship "include" between two use cases;
- TR2: Each sub-process, in BPMN collaboration diagram model, is transformed to a package;
- TR3: the "exclusive fork" between two tasks, in BPMN business process model, becomes a relationship "extend" between two use cases;
- TR4: the sequence flow returning back, in BPMN business process model, cannot be transformed;
- TR5: every task, in BPMN business process model, transformed to use case;
- TR6: the collaborator, in BPMN collaboration diagram model, becomes an actor.

The transformation rules (TR) for moving from BPMN business process model to sequence diagram model (cf. Figure 4):

- TR7: each pool that does not contain lanes becomes an actor, and each lane within a pool becomes an actor;
- TR8: each task is transformed into a message sent from the actor to the system;
- TR9: each data object with a state is transformed into a message returning from the system to the actor.

The rules for moving from BPMN business process model to class diagram model (cf. Figure 5):

Figure 4. Schema of passage from the CIM models to sequence model.

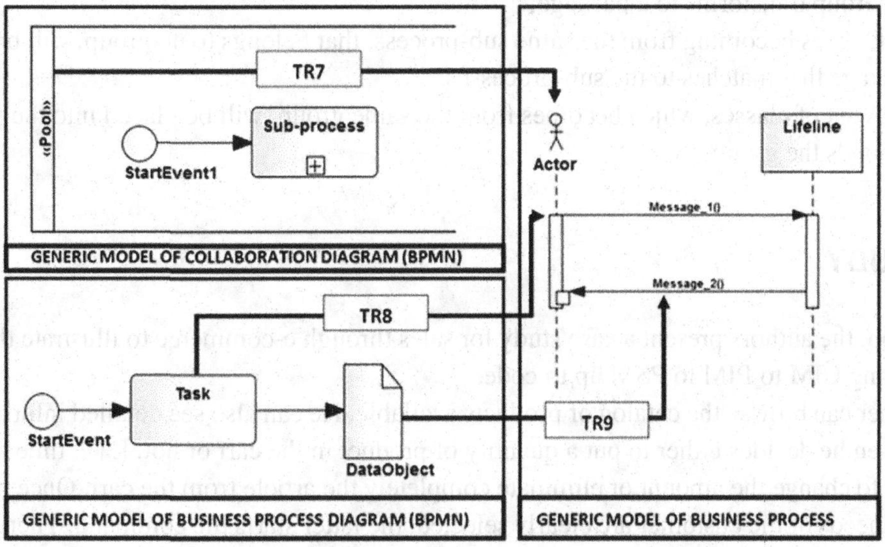

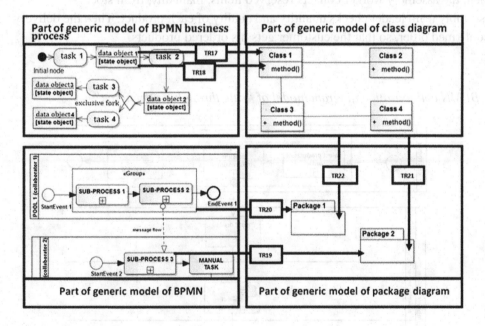

Figure 5. Schema of passage from the CIM models to models of class and package diagram.

- TR17: data object becomes a class;
- TR18: State of a data object becomes a class method.

The rules for moving from the BPMN collaboration diagram model and the class diagram model to the package diagram model (cf. Figure 5):

- TR19: Sub-process that does not belong to any group becomes a package;
- TR20: Group transforms to a package;
- TR21: Classes becoming from the same sub-process, that belongs to no group, will be placed into the package that matches to the sub-processes;
- TR22: A set of classes, which becomes from the same group, will be placed into the package that corresponds the group.

CASE STUDY

In this section, the authors present a case study for sales through e-commerce to illustrate this approach of transforming CIM to PIM to PSM up to code.

A customer can browse the catalog of products available. He can also see detailed information about each item, then he decides either to put a quantity of product in the cart or not. Each time the customer has the right to change the amount or eliminate completely the article from the cart. Once products that satisfied the needs of the customer are clearly selected, the latter starts the command. Then, he presents the payment information, and precise details of delivery.

An order agent begins treating the order, declaring the reservation of products specified by the customer. Then, the assembly worker collects reserved items, manually, from stock.

The assembly team leader checks quantity and quality of each product. Then the delivery agent carries the confirmed order, so that the customer gets his ordered products.

Figure 6. BPMN collaboration diagram model of "sale through e-commerce".

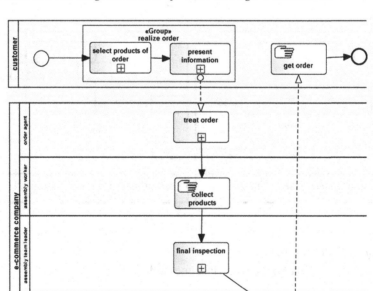

Presentation of the CIM Level

Figure 6 shows the model of the business process represented by BPMN collaboration diagram. In this model the researchers just specified sub-processes and their sequence by avoiding the identification of tasks and connections to present a business process in general. The authors have presented the maximum of collaborators to define a true business process, in which there is collaboration between several business actors. For example, instead of putting a single lane "delivery service", the researchers identified the lanes: "assembly worker", "assembly team leader" and "delivery agent".

Figure 7 shows the second model in CIM level as a model of BPMN business process. Through this model the researchers individually detail each sub-process of the previous model as several actions. However, in this model the sub-processes "select product for order" is analyzed. Also, we have identified all possible ways towards connections. Then the authors presented an object node with its state in the output of each action.

Presentation of the PIM level

Figure 8 shows a diagram use case model. This latter model is transformed from CIM models. Nevertheless, the sub-process "select product for order" becomes a package inside use case diagram model. Next, the collaborator "customer" that realizes the sub-process becomes actor. However, the tasks which detail the sub-process become use cases. Indeed, exclusive fork which connects between two tasks becomes relationship "extend" between two use cases. For example, in the BPMN business process diagram model, there is a decision node that lies between the two tasks "designate product" and "put in cart quantity product ", so the two correspondent use cases are connected by the relationship "extend". Control flow which connects between two tasks becomes relationship "include" between two use cases. Thus, in the BPMN business process diagram model, there is sequence flow between the two tasks "present catalog" and "designate product", indeed, the two corresponding use cases are connected by a relationship "include". Nevertheless, the sequence flow returning backward did not transform as a relationship "include". For example, the relationship between the tasks "put in cart product quantity" and "present catalog" did not interpret in use case diagram model, so as not to complicate the model, and because the use case diagram focuses only on the identification of functionalities and not on the sequence of the functionalities.

Figure 8 presents the sequence model diagram transformed from the BPMN business process diagram of CIM. In this model the tasks are transformed to messages go from actor to system. Indeed, in the data object are transformed to messages returned from system to actor. Then, each pool that does not contain lanes becomes a line life "actor", and each lane within a pool becomes a line life "actor". E.g. the tasks "present catalog" is transformed to messages go from actor to system in sequence diagram model, then, the data object "catalog" with the state "presented" becomes message "catalog presented" returned from system to actor in the sequence diagram. However, pool "customer" that does not contain lanes becomes an actor.

Figure 9 shows the final objective of the PIM level which is the construction of a model of class diagram. This model is transformed from the model of the BPMN business process. In this model the classes are transformed from object nodes. Then the states of an object are transformed to functions of the class. So the object node "order" with state "started" transform to class "order" that contains the "start" method.

Figure 7. BPMN business process diagram model that develops the sub-process: "select product for order".

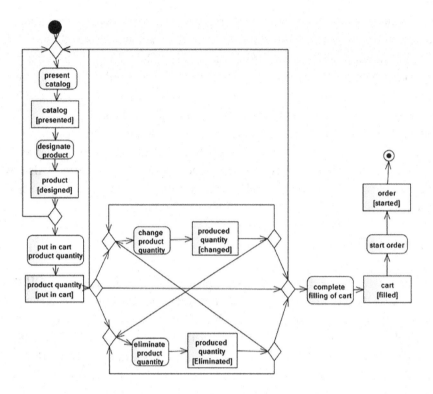

Figure 8. I: use case diagram model of "select product for order", II: sequence diagram model of "select product for order".

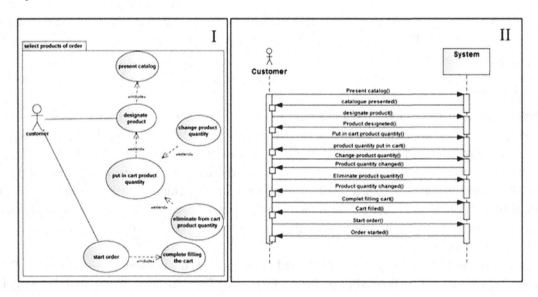

Figure 9. I: class diagram model of "select product for order", II: package diagram model of "sale through e-commerce".

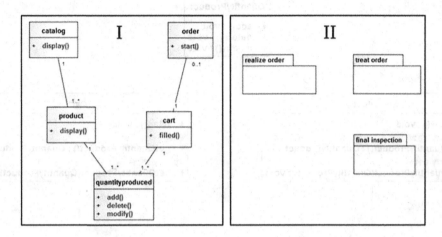

Figure 9 shows a model of the package diagram. So the group "realize order" transform into package. Then the sub-processes that are not belong to any group, such as "treat order" and "final inspection" become packages.

Presentation of the PSM Level

Since there are several proven tools in the market that allow the transformation from the PIM level to the PSM level and from the PSM level to the code, we are not going to try to make a competitor tool, we will be satisfied by using one tool that we consider performing.

In figure 10 it is a java-oriented class diagram that represents the PSM level, this diagram is obtained after an automatic transformation through the tool "enterprise architect" which took as input a xml class diagram model file of the graphical class diagram model (cf. Figure 9).

Presentation Of The Code

In figure 11 it is a java code is obtained after an automatic transformation through "enterprise architect". The java code is grouped into five classes which are: catalog, product, card, order and quantityProduct. As well as the methods that are in each class more than the relations between classes.

ANALYSIS AND DISCUSSION

For presenting the CIM level, there is a current that based only on system requirements models like in (Fatolahi et al., 2008; Gutiérrez et al., 2008; Wu et al., 2007), but CIM level must be independent of computation. Then, there is a hybrid stream that founded on business process and system requirements for modeling the CIM level as in (Kherraf et al., 2008). In these approaches, system requirements presented from the beginning into CIM models in order to facilitate the transformation from CIM to PIM. In our methodology, business processes are modeled into CIM level. Nevertheless, according to OMG

Figure 10. I: class diagram model java oriented of "select product for order".

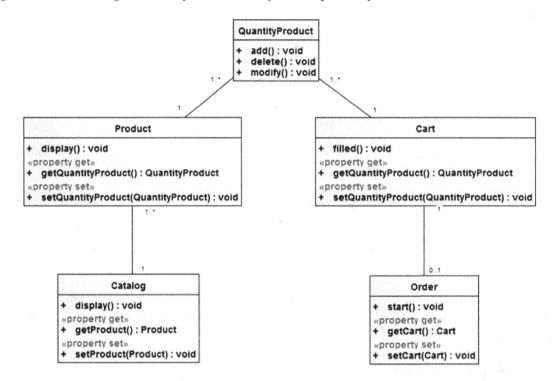

in (OMG-MDA, 2014), the CIM level contains business process models, which are independent of computation. Indeed, in (OMG-BPMN, 2011), the benefits of most business process standards meet in BPMN, for this, the authors founded on BPMN notation to model business processes.

The researchers divide the PIM models in accordance with the three modeling views (Roques, 2004; Demuth, 1999): dynamic, functional and static. According (Blanc, 2005; Kleppe, 2003; Fowler, 2005) UML is recommended by MDA in the PIM level. However, the intersection between our UML models and the three classical modeling views is showed as follows: the functional view is presented by the use case diagram model, the state diagram model interprets the dynamic view and the static view is presented by the class diagram model.

There is no approach which includes the three modeling views, In PIM, apart (Kardoš et al., 2010; Rhazali et al., 2015c). Nevertheless, several approaches do not model the classes into the PIM level as in (Zhang et al., 2005; Rodríguez et al., 2007; Castro et al., 2011; Mazón et al., 2007; Gutiérrez et al., 2008; Wu et al., 2007), but the code does not easily results by transformation without classes. Our methodology covers the three views of modeling. However, static view is presented by class diagram model and package diagram model.

Most transformation methods, approves their proposals through a case study like in (Kherraf et al., 2008; Zhang et al., 2005; Kardoš et al., 2010; Rodríguez et al., 2007; Rodríguez et al., 2008; Rodríguez et al., 2010; Mazón et al., 2007; Gutiérrez et al., 2008 Mokrys et al., 2012; Bousetta et al., 2013; Rhazali et al., 2016d; Rhazali et al., 2015c, Rhazali et al., 2015d). Then one approach (Wu et al., 2007) has not approved. . Nevertheless, our methodology is approved by a case study of sale through e-commerce.

Figure 11. I: java code class diagram model of "select product for order".

```
/**
 * @author Yassine
 * @version 1.0
 * @created 05-avr.-2019 02:10:52
 */
public class Order {

    private Cart m_Cart;

    public Order(){

    }

    public void finalize() throws Throwable {

    }

    public Cart getCart(){
        return m_Cart;
    }

    /**
     *
     * @param newVal
     */
    public void setCart(Cart newVal){
        m_Cart = newVal;
    }

    public void start(){

    }
}
```

```
/**
 * @author Yassine
 * @version 1.0
 * @created 05-avr.-2019 02:10:52
 */
public class Product {

    private QuantityProduct m_QuantityProduct;

    public Product(){

    }

    public void finalize() throws Throwable {

    }

    public void display(){

    }

    public QuantityProduct getQuantityProduct(){
        return m_QuantityProduct;
    }

    /**
     *
     * @param newVal
     */
    public void setQuantityProduct(QuantityProduct newVal){
        m_QuantityProduct = newVal;
    }
}
```

```
/**
 * @author Yassine
 * @version 1.0
 * @created 05-avr.-2019 02:10:52
 */
public class Cart {

    private QuantityProduct m_QuantityProduct;

    public Cart(){

    }

    public void finalize() throws Throwable {

    }

    public void filled(){

    }

    public QuantityProduct getQuantityProduct(){
        return m_QuantityProduct;
    }

    /**
     *
     * @param newVal
     */
    public void setQuantityProduct(QuantityProduct newVal){
        m_QuantityProduct = newVal;
    }
}
```

```
/**
 * @author Yassine
 * @version 1.0
 * @created 05-avr.-2019 02:10:52
 */
public class Catalog {

    private Product m_Product;

    public Catalog(){

    }

    public void finalize() throws Throwable {

    }

    public void display(){

    }

    public Product getProduct(){
        return m_Product;
    }

    /**
     *
     * @param newVal
     */
    public void setProduct(Product newVal){
        m_Product = newVal;
    }
}
```

```
/**
 * @author Yassine
 * @version 1.0
 * @created 05-avr.-2019 02:10:52
 */
public class QuantityProduct {

    public QuantityProduct(){
    }
    public void finalize() throws Throwable {
    }
    public void add(){
    }
    public void delete(){
    }
    public void modify(){
    }
}
```

Figure 12. CIM meta-models:BPMN meta-model.

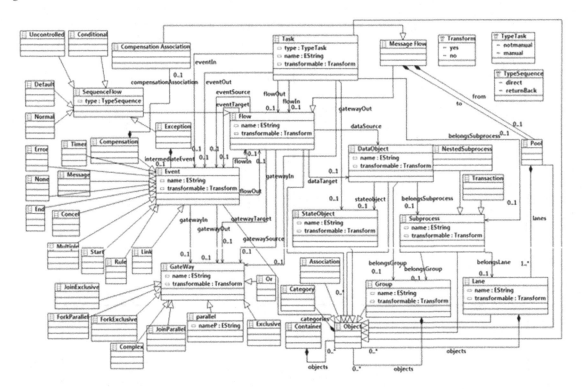

The researchers can classify the related works into five categories. The authors find researches use, early in CIM level, the requirements models which represent the system requirements (through use case diagram) to facilitate the transformation to PIM like in (Kherraf et al., 2008). Then, other studies as in (Castro, 2011), even if they define the business processes in CIM level, do not represent the structural view usually (through the class diagram) that represents the goal of the PIM level.

Then there are methods that target transformation in a particular field, like in (Mazón et al., 2007) the authors move to the PIM that focuses on conceptual modeling of data warehouse, however, this approach only tackles the transformation in the field of data warehouse. There are methods such as (Kardoš et al., 2010) which represent the structural view in the PIM level and are not intended for a particular area, but the authors show a case study of a transformation to the PIM level without mentioning the rules used in the transformation. Finally, there are methods as in (Zhang et al., 2005) that define exactly the transformation rules and do not have the models used in the CIM and PIM level.

So the researchers can say that the main contributions of our study in comparison with related works as follow. Our method based on establishment on construction rules for organizing CIM level in order to facilitate the transformation from CIM to PIM. In this proposal the business process interpreted in CIM models for respecting the MDA approach. Then, the authors define the structural view in PIM models (through using class and package diagram), indeed, in the PIM level, the classes considered as the base for moving toward the code models in PSM. Our goal is not just the realization of the transformation from the CIM to the PIM, but our objective is to obtain a PIM level which can be transformed subsequently to the PSM level. Next, the researchers propose an approach of generic transformation that is not related to a particular field. Indeed, our approach has clear rules to achieve, the maximum possible, automatic transformation from CIM level to PIM level.

Figure 13. PIM meta-models (part I): I: use case meta-model, II: state met-model

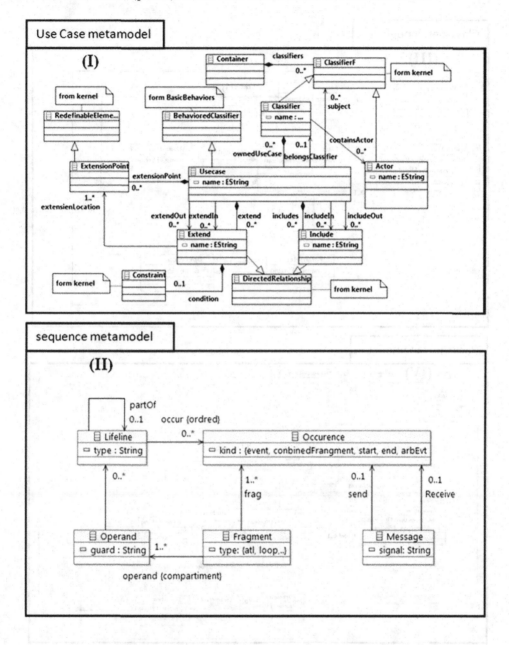

There is no methodology, in related work, which establish CIM and PIM meta-models except (Castro, 2011; Gutiérrez, 2008). But without meta-models, the practical model transformation is impossible. The Figure 12 shows our CIM meta-model, which is represented by BPMN meta-model. However, the Figure 13 and Figure 14 show our PIM meta-model that is interpreted by sequence meta-model, use case meta-model, class meta-model and package meta-model.

There is several models transformation approaches (Bouraoui, 2019; Elmounadi, 2019; Mefteh, 2018; Suratno, 2018) that validate most of the criteria already mentioned in this section but so far there is no methodology that allows proposing an approach ensures the transformation in MDA from the CIM level to the PIM level I up to PSM, even, getting the code.

Figure 14. PIM meta-models (part II): III: class meta-model, IV: package meta-model .

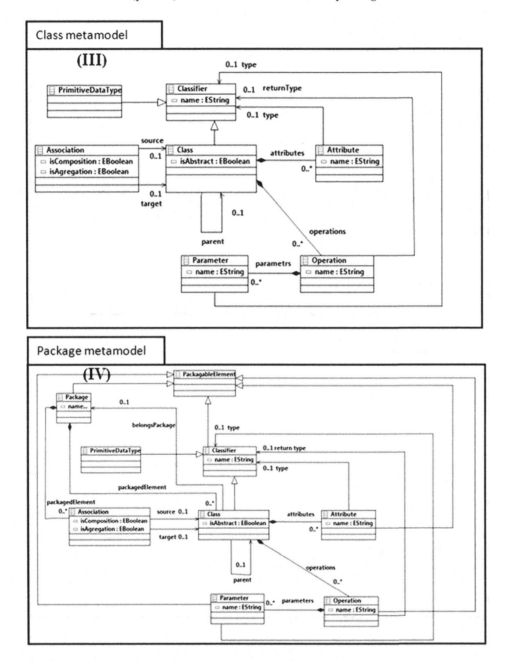

Our approach can be combined in the future with several new technologies, especially with innovative ideas in Iot and cloud computing (Hossain, 2019; Singh, 2019 ; Memos, 2018 ; Elmisery, 2018), as well as with an innovative idea in big data and cyber security (Gupta, 2016; Jiang, 2018; Gupta, 2017; Gupta, 2018; Sahoo, 2019), then we also think about combining our approach to IaaS and cloud computing (Ahuja, 2018; Kashif, 2018).

Our methodology is the unique approach based on construction rules for structuring CIM level for the purpose of automate the transformation to PIM level, indeed, the CIM level structuring must give transformable models to PIM level. However, approaches of related work do not provide a methodology that allows transformation from the CIM level to the PIM level up to the PSM level, so there are approaches that focus either on the transformation from the CIM to the PIM, or the transformation from the PIM to the PSM, . therefor our approach is the only methodology allows mastering models transformation from CIM to PIM to PSM, indeed, up to obtaining code according the MDA. So, This work makes it possible to limit the intervention of computer scientists in the life cycle of software development, indeed this work allows modeling only CIM, the business process, and then, get the source code through several automatic transformations.

Our objective in this methodology is not just the transition from the CIM level to the PIM level to PSM level, but our goal is to limit the intervention of computer scientists in the life cycle of software development, indeed this work allows modeling only CIM, the business process, and then, get the source code through several automatic transformations.

CONCLUSION

One of the major challenges in the software development process is the definition of an approach that allows moving from models that describe the operation of business to models which present the analysis and design of software.

Based on MDA, our approach provides a solution to the problem of transformation of business models represented in CIM level to analysis and design models, modeled in PIM level. This approach results in a set of well organized and useful classes in the process of software development. Our approach also makes it possible to transform analysis and design models into platform-specific models, PSM, and then to source code.

The ongoing work is intended to improve the rules of construction of the CIM and the rules of transformation to the PIM. In our future work, we think to implement a tool allows to design business process model in CIM level and transform this basic model automatically until the source code of the system is obtained.

we tried to propose for the first time an approach that allows to provide the source code from a model provided by non computer scientists, but we cannot affirm the power of our approach as we have not yet implemented in an application and we have not tested it in true true magnitude, so the usefulness of our methodology will be highlighted during the development of the tool supporting our approach.

REFERENCES

Ahuja, S. P., & Deval, N. (2018). On the Performance Evaluation of IaaS Cloud Services With System-Level Benchmarks. *International Journal of Cloud Applications and Computing*, 8(1), 80–96. doi:10.4018/IJCAC.2018010104

Blanc, X. (2005). *MDA en action*. Paris, France: Ed. Eyrolles.

Bouraoui, A., & Gharbi, I. (2019). Model driven engineering of accessible and multi-platform graphical user interfaces by parameterized model transformations. *Science of Computer Programming*, *172*, 63–101. doi:10.1016/j.scico.2018.11.002

Bousetta, B., El Beggar, O., & Gadi, T. (2013). A methodology for CIM modeling and its transformation to PIM. *Journal of Information Engineering and Applications*, *2*(3), 1–21.

De Castro, V., Marcos, E., & Vara, J. M. (2011). Applying CIM-to-PIM model transformations for the service-oriented development of information systems. *Journal of Information and Software Technology*, *53*(1), 87–105. doi:10.1016/j.infsof.2010.09.002

Demuth, B., & Hussmann, H. (1999), Using OCL Constraints for Relational Database Design. In *Proceedings, The Unified Modeling Language, Second Int. Conference* (pp. 598-613). Academic Press. 10.1007/3-540-46852-8_42

Elmisery, A. M., Sertovic, M., & Gupta, B. B. (2018). Cognitive Privacy Middleware for Deep Learning Mashup in Environmental IoT. *IEEE Access: Practical Innovations, Open Solutions*, *6*, 8029–8041. doi:10.1109/ACCESS.2017.2787422

Elmounadi, A., El Moukhi, N., Berbiche, N., & Sefiani, N. (2019). A new PHP discoverer for Modisco. *International Journal of Advanced Computer Science and Applications*, *10*(1), 169–174. doi:10.14569/IJACSA.2019.0100122

Fatolahi, A., Somé, S. S., & Lethbridge, T. C. (2008). Towards a semi-automated model-driven method for the generation of web-based applications from use cases. In *Proceedings, 4th Model Driven Web Engineering Workshop* (pp. 31-45). Toulouse, France: Academic Press.

Fowler, M. (2005). *Language Workbenches and Model Driven Architecture*. Retrieved January 11, 2015, from http://www.martinfowler.com/articles /mdaLanguageWorkbench.html

Gordijn, J., & Akkermans, J. M. (2003). Value based requirements engineering: Exploring innovative e-commerce idea. *Requirements Engineering Journal*, *8*(2), 114–134. doi:10.100700766-003-0169-x

Grammel, B., & Kastenholz, S., A. (2010). generic traceability framework for facet-based traceability data extraction in model-driven software development. In *Proceedings, 6th ECMFA Traceability Workshop held in conjunction ECMFA* (pp. 7-14). Paris, France: Academic Press. 10.1145/1814392.1814394

Gupta, B. B. (2017). *Computer and Cyber Security: Principles*. Algorithm, Applications and Perspectives.

Gupta, B. B., Agrawal, D. P., & Yamaguchi, S. (2016). *Handbook of Research on Modern Cryptographic Solutions for Computer and Cyber Security*. Hershey, PA: IGI Global. doi:10.4018/978-1-5225-0105-3

Gupta, S., & Gugulothu, N. (2018). Secure NoSQL for the Social Networking and E-Commerce Based Bigdata Applications Deployed in Cloud. *International Journal of Cloud Applications and Computing*, *8*(2), 113–129. doi:10.4018/IJCAC.2018040106

Gutiérrez, J. J., Nebut, C., Escalona, M. J., Mejías, M., & Ramos, I. M. (2008). Visualization of use cases through automatically generated activity diagrams. In *Proceedings, 11th International Conference MoDELS'08* (pp 83-96). Toulouse, France: Academic Press. 10.1007/978-3-540-87875-9_6

Hahn, C., Dmytro, P., & Fischer, K. (2010). A model-driven approach to close the gap between business requirements and agent-based execution. In *Proceedings, 4th Workshop on Agent-based Technologies and applications for enterprise interoperability* (pp. 13–24). Toronto, Canada: Academic Press.

Hossain, K., Rahman, M., & Roy, S. (2019). IoT Data Compression and Optimization Techniques in Cloud Storage: Current Prospects and Future Directions. *International Journal of Cloud Applications and Computing, 9*(2), 43–59. doi:10.4018/IJCAC.2019040103

Jiang, F., Fu, Y., Gupta, B. B., Lou, F., Rho, S., Meng, F., & Tian, Z. (2018). *Deep Learning based Multi-channel intelligent attack detection for Data Security. IEEE Transactions on Sustainable Computing.* doi:10.1109/TSUSC.2018.2793284

Kardoš, M., & Drozdová, M. (2010). Analytical method of CIM to PIM transformation in Model Driven Architecture (MDA). *Journal of Information and Organizational Sciences, 34*(1), 89–99.

Kashif, U. A., Memon, Z. A., Siddiqui, S., Balouch, A. R., & Batra, R. (2018). Architectural Design of Trusted Platform for IaaS Cloud Computing. *International Journal of Cloud Applications and Computing, 8*(2), 47–65. doi:10.4018/IJCAC.2018040103

Kherraf, S., Lefebvre, É., & Suryn, W. (2008). Transformation from CIM to PIM using patterns and Archetypes. In *Proceedings, 19th Australian Software Engineering Conference* (pp. 338 – 346). Perth, Australia: Academic Press. 10.1109/ASWEC.2008.4483222

Kleppe, A., Warmer, G. J., & Bast, W. (2003). *MDA Explained: The Model Driven Architecture: Practice and Promise.* Boston: Addison-Wesley.

Mazón, J., Pardillo, J., & Trujillo, J. (2007), A model-driven goal-oriented requirement engineering approach for data warehouses. In *Proceedings, Conference on Advances in Conceptual Modeling: Foundations and Applications, ER Workshops* (pp. 255–264). Auckland, New Zealand: Academic Press. 10.1007/978-3-540-76292-8_31

Mefteh, M., Bouassida, N., & Ben-Abdallah, H. (2018). Towards naturalistic programming: Mapping language-independent requirements to constrained language specifications. *Science of Computer Programming, 166*, 89–119. doi:10.1016/j.scico.2018.05.006

Memos, V. A., Psannis, K. E., Ishibashi, Y., Kim, B., & Gupta, B. B. (2018). An Efficient Algorithm for Media-based Surveillance System (EAMSuS) in IoT Smart City Framework. *Future Generation Computer Systems, 83*, 619–628. doi:10.1016/j.future.2017.04.039

Miles, R., & Hamilton, K. (2006). *Learning UML 2.0.* Boston: O'Reilly Media.

Mokrys, M. (2012). Possible transformation from Process Model to IS Design Model. *Proceedings, 1th International Virtual Conference*, 71–74.

OMG-BPMN. (2011). *Business Process Model and Notation (BPMN)-Version 2.0.* Boston: OMG.

OMG-MDA. (2014). *Object Management Group Model Driven Architecture (MDA)MDA Guide rev. 2.0.* Boston: OMG.

OMG-QVT. (2015). *Meta Object Facility (MOF) 2.0 Query/View/Transformation Specification, V1.2.* Boston: OMG.

OMG-SoaML. (2012). *Service Oriented Architecture Modeling Language (SoaML) – Specification for the UML Profile and Metamodel for Services (UPMS)*. Boston: OMG.

Rhazali, Y., Hadi, Y., Chana, I., Lahmer, M., & Rhattoy, A. (2018). A model transformation in model driven architecture from business model to web model. *IAENG International Journal of Computer Science*, *45*(1), 104–117.

Rhazali, Y., Hadi, Y., & Mouloudi, A. (2015a). A Methodology of Model Transformation in MDA: From CIM to PIM. *International Review on Computers and Software*, *10*(11). doi: 10.15866/irecos.v10i12.8088

Rhazali, Y., Hadi, Y., & Mouloudi, A. (2015b). A Methodology for Transforming CIM to PIM through UML: From Business View to Information System View. *Proceedings, Third World Conference on Complex Systems*. 10.1109/ICoCS.2015.7483318

Rhazali, Y., Hadi, Y., & Mouloudi, A. (2015c). Disciplined Approach for Transformation CIM to PIM in MDA. In *Proceedings, 3rd International Conference on Model-Driven Engineering and Software Development* (pp. 312 – 320). Angers, France: Academic Press. DOI: 10.5220/0005245903120320

Rhazali, Y., Hadi, Y., & Mouloudi, A. (2015d). Transformation Approach CIM to PIM: From Business Processes Models to State Machine and Package Models. In *Proceedings, the 1st International Conference on Open Source Software Computing*. Amman, Jordan: Academic Press. DOI: 10.1109/OSSCOM.2015.7372686

Rhazali, Y., Hadi, Y., & Mouloudi, A. (2016a). CIM to PIM Transformation in MDA: From Service-Oriented Business Models to Web-Based Design Models. *International Journal of Software Engineering and Its Applications*, *10*(4), 125–142. doi:10.14257/ijseia.2016.10.4.13

Rhazali, Y., Hadi, Y., & Mouloudi, A. (2016b). Model Transformation with ATL into MDA from CIM to PIM Structured through MVC. *Procedia Computer Science*, *83*, 1096–1101. doi:10.1016/j.procs.2016.04.229

Rhazali, Y., Hadi, Y., & Mouloudi, A. (2016c). A Based-Rule Method to Transform CIM to PIM into MDA. *International Journal of Cloud Applications and Computing*, *6*(2), 11–24. doi:10.4018/IJCAC.2016040102

Rhazali, Y., Hadi, Y., & Mouloudi, A. (2016d). A new methodology CIM to PIM transformation resulting from an analytical survey. In *Proceedings, 4th International Conference on Model-Driven Engineering and Software Development (MODELSWARD)* (pp. 266-273). Rome, Italy: Academic Press. DOI: 10.5220/0005690102660273

Rhazali, Y., Hadi, Y., & Mouloudi, A. (2017). A model transformation in MDA from CIM to PIM represented by web models through SoaML and IFML. In *Colloquium in Information Science and Technology, CIST* (pp. 116-121). Tangier, Morocco: Academic Press. DOI: 10.1109/CIST.2016.7805027

Rodríguez, A., & García-Rodríguez de Guzmán, I. (2010). Semi-formal transformation of secure business processes into analysis class and use case models: An MDA approach. *Journal of Information and Software Technology*, *52*(9), 945–971. doi:10.1016/j.infsof.2010.03.015

Roques, P. (2004). *UML in Practice: The Art of Modeling Software Systems Demonstrated through Worked Examples and Solutions*. Wiley.

Sahoo, S. R., & Gupta, B. B. (2019). Classification of various attacks and their defence mechanism in online social networks: A survey. *Enterprise Information Systems*, *13*(6), 832–864. doi:10.1080/17517 575.2019.1605542

Schmidt, D. C. (2006). Guest Editor's Introduction: Model-Driven Engineering. *IEEE Computer*, *39*(2), 25–31. doi:10.1109/MC.2006.58

Singh, N., & Vardhan, M. (2019). Distributed Ledger Technology based Property Transaction System with Support for IoT Devices. *International Journal of Cloud Applications and Computing*, *9*(2), 60–78. doi:10.4018/IJCAC.2019040104

Suratno, B., Ozkan, B., Turetken, O., & Grefen, P. (2018). A Method for Operationalizing Service-Dominant Business Models into Conceptual Process Models. *Lecture Notes in Business Information Processing*, *319*, 133–148. doi:10.1007/978-3-319-94214-8_9

Zhang, W., Mei, H., Zhao, H., & Yang, J. (2005). Transformation from CIM to PIM: A Feature-Oriented Component-Based approach. In *Proceedings, MoDELS* (pp. 248-263). Montego Bay, Jamaica: Academic Press. 10.1007/11557432_18

Compilation of References

A Preliminary Block Chain Protocol Language Cyrus F Nourani Group Technical brief. (2018). TU Berlin.

Abbadi, I. M. & Martin, A. (2011). Trust in the Cloud. *Information Security Technical Report, 16*(3-4), 108-114.

Abghour, N., & Ouzzif, M. (2018). A novel security framework for managing Android permissions using blockchain technology. *International Journal of Cloud Applications and Computing, 8*(1), 55-79.

Aceto, G., Botta, A., de Donato, W., & Pescape, A. (2013, June). Cloud monitoring: A survey. *Elsevier, Computer Networks, 57*(9), 2093–2115. doi:10.1016/j.comnet.2013.04.001

Ackermann, T. (2012). *IT security risks management: perceived IT security risks in the context of Cloud Computing.* Springer Science & Business Media.

Aebischer, B., & Hilty, L. M. (2015). The energy demand of ICT: A historical perspective and current methodological challenges. In *ICT Innovations for Sustainability* (pp. 71–103). Springer International Publishing. doi:10.1007/978-3-319-09228-7_4

Ahuja, S. P., & Deval, N. (2018). On the Performance Evaluation of IaaS Cloud Services With System-Level Benchmarks. *International Journal of Cloud Applications and Computing, 8*(1), 80–96. doi:10.4018/IJCAC.2018010104

Akyildiz, I., McNair, J., Ho, J., Uzunalioglu, H., & Wang, W. (1999). Mobility management in next-generation wireless systems. *Proceedings of the IEEE, 87*(8), 1347–1384. doi:10.1109/5.775420

Al Nuaimi, K., Mohamed, N., Al Nuaimi, M., & Al-Jaroodi, J. (2012, December). A survey of load balancing in cloud computing: Challenges and algorithms. In *Network Cloud Computing and Applications (NCCA), 2012 Second Symposium on* (pp. 137-142). IEEE.

Alam, Q., Malik, S. U. R., Akhunzada, A., Choo, K.-K. R., Tabbasum, S., & Alam, M. (2017). A Cross Tenant Access Control (CTAC) Model for Cloud Computing:Formal Specification and Verification. *IEEE Transactions on Information Forensics and Security, 12*(6), 1259–1268. doi:10.1109/TIFS.2016.2646639

Alangar, V. (2013). Cloud Computing Security and Encryption. *International Journal of Advance Research in Computer Science and Management Studies, 1*(5), 58-63.

Alhanahnah, M., Bertok, P., & Tari, Z. (2017). Trusting cloud service providers: Trust phases and a taxonomy of trust factors. *IEEE Cloud Computing, 4*(1), 44–54. doi:10.1109/MCC.2017.20

Ali, M. (2019a). Multiple Perspective of Cloud Computing Adoption Determinants in Higher Education a Systematic Review. *International Journal of Cloud Applications and Computing, 9*(3), 89–109. doi:10.4018/IJCAC.2019070106

Ali, M. (2019b). Cloud Computing at a Cross Road: Quality and Risks in Higher Education. *Advances in Internet of Things, 9*(3), 33–49. doi:10.4236/ait.2019.93003

Ali, M. (2019c). The Barriers and Enablers of the Educational Cloud: A Doctoral Student Perspective. *Open Journal of Business and Management, 7*(1), 24. doi:10.4236/ojbm.2019.71001

Ali, M., Khan, S. U., & Vasilakos, A. V. (2015, February). Security in cloud computing: Opportunities and challenges. *Elsevier, Information Sciences, 305*, 357–383. doi:10.1016/j.ins.2015.01.025

Ali, M., Wood-Harper, T., & Al-Gahtani, A. S. (2019). Contextual Analysis of Educational Monitoring and Progression as a Service (EMPaaS) System in Higher Education. *Open Journal of Business and Management, 7*(3), 1525–1542. doi:10.4236/ojbm.2019.73105

Almrot, E., & Andersson, S. (2013). *A study of the advantages & dis-advantages of mobile cloud computing versus native environment* (Bachelor Thesis). Blekinge Institute of Technology, Karlskrona.

Alshamaila, Y., Papagiannidis, S., & Li, F. (2013). Cloud computing adoption by SMEs in the north east of England: A multi-perspective framework. *Journal of Enterprise Information Management, 26*(3), 250–275. doi:10.1108/17410391311325225

Al-Somali, S., & Baghabra, H. (2017). Investigating the Determinants of IT Professionals' Intention to Use Cloud-Based Applications and Solutions: An Extension of the Technology Acceptance. *International Journal of Cloud Applications and Computing, 6*(3), 45–62. doi:10.4018/IJCAC.2016070104

Amini, Jamil, Ahmad, & Z`aba. (2015). Threat Modeling Approaches for Securing Cloud Computing. *Journal of Applied Sciences*, 953-967.

Angin, P., Bhargava, B., Ranchal, R., Singh, N., & Linderman, M. (2010). An Entity-centric Approach for Privacy and Identity Management in Cloud Computing. *Proceedings of 29th IEEE International Symposium on Reliable Distributed Systems*. 10.1109/SRDS.2010.28

Ankur Dave, A. J. (2016). GraphFrames: An Integrated API for Mixing Graph and Relational Queries. GRADES 2016, June 24 2016, Redwood Shores, CA.

An, Y. Z., Zaaba, Z. F., & Samsudin, N. F. (2016). Reviews on Security Issues and Challenges in Cloud Computing. *International Engineering Research and Innovation Symposium (IRIS)*, 160. 10.1088/1757-899X/160/1/012106

ApacheT. (n.d.). Retrieved from: http://tomcat.apache.org/

Armbrust, M., Fox, A., Griffith, R., Joseph, A. D., Katz, R., Konwinski, A., ... Stoica, I. (2010). A View of Cloud Computing. *Communications of the ACM, 53*(4), 50–58. doi:10.1145/1721654.1721672

Arora & Parashar. (2013). Secure User Data in Cloud Computing Using Encryption Algorithms. *International Journal of Engineering Research and Applications, 3*(4), 1922-1926.

Arpaci, I. (2017). Antecedents and consequences of cloud computing adoption in education to achieve knowledge management. *Computers in Human Behavior, 70*(1). 382-390.doi.org/10.1016/j.chb.2017.01.024

Ashraf, Kehkashan, Gull, & Moin u Din. (2018). Transparency service model for data security in cloud computing. *2018 International Conference on Computing, Mathematics and Engineering Technologies (iCoMET)*, 1-6. doi: 10.1109/ICOMET.2018.8346365

Assunção, M. D., Calheiros, R. N., Bianchi, S., Netto, M. A., & Buyya, R. (2015). Big Data computing and clouds: Trends and future directions. *Journal of Parallel and Distributed Computing, 79*, 3–15. doi:10.1016/j.jpdc.2014.08.003

Ateniese, G., Fu, K., Green, M., & Hohenberger, S. (2006). Improved proxy re-encryption schemes with applications to secure distributed storage. *ACM Transactions on Information and System Security, 9*(1), 1–30. doi:10.1145/1127345.1127346

Athey, C. (2017). *The Digital Privacy Paradox: Small Money, Small Costs, Small Talk.* Retrieved from https://papers.ssrn.com/sol3/papers2.cfm?abstract_id=2916489

Avram, M. G. (2014). Advantages and Challenges of Adopting Cloud Computing from an Enterprise Perspective. *The 7th International Conference Interdisciplinarity in Engineering, 12,* 529-534.

Azarnik, A., Shayan, J., Alizadeh, M., & Karamizadeh, S. (2013). Associated Risks of Cloud Computing for SMEs. *Open International Journal Informatics, 1*(1), 37–45.

Babu, D. (2013). Honey bee behavior inspired load balancing of tasks in cloud computing environments. *Applied Soft Computing, 13*(5), 2292–2303. doi:10.1016/j.asoc.2013.01.025

Baek, J., Vu, Q. H., Liu, J. K., Huang, X., & Xiang, Y. (2015). A Secure Cloud Computing Based Framework for Big Data Information Management of Smart Grid. IEEE Transactions on Cloud Computing, 3(2).

Bala Chandar, R., Kavitha, M. S., & Seenivasan, K. (2014). A Proficient Model for High End Security in Cloud Computing. *ICTACT Journal on Soft Computing, 4*(2), 698-702.

Banerjee, S., Mukherjee, I., & Mahanti, P. K. (2009). Cloud computing initiative using modified ant colony framework. *World Academy of Science, Engineering and Technology, 56,* 221–224.

Barron, C., Yu, H., & Zhan, J. (2013). Cloud Computing Security Case Studies and Research. *The 2013 International Conference of Parallel and Distributed Computing.*

Băsescu, C. A., Carpen-Amarie, C., Leordeanu, A., & Antoniu, G. (2011). Managing Data Access on Clouds: A Generic Framework for Enforcing Security Policies. *International Conference on Advanced Information Networking and Applications (AINA).* 10.1109/AINA.2011.61

Batalla, J. M., Mastorakis, G., Mavromoustakis, C. X., & Zurek, J. (2016, October). On cohabitating networking technologies with common wireless access for Home Automation Systems purposes. *IEEE Wireless Communications, 23*(5), 76–83. doi:10.1109/MWC.2016.7721745

Beloglazov, A., Buyya, R., Lee, Y. C., & Zomaya, A. (2011). A taxonomy and survey of energy-efficient data centers and cloud computing systems. *Advances in Computers, 82*(2), 47–111. doi:10.1016/B978-0-12-385512-1.00003-7

Ben Arfa Rabai, L., Jouini, M., Ben Aissa, A., & Mili, A. (2012). An economic model of security threats for cloud computing systems. *International Conference on Cyber Security, Cyber Warfare and Digital Forensic (CyberSec),* 100–105. 10.1109/CyberSec.2012.6246112

Bhagat & Sahu. (2013). Cloud Data Security while using Third Party Auditor. *International Journal of Computer Applications, 70*(16), 9-14.

Bhardwaj, Subrahmanyam, Avasthi, & Sastry. (2016). Security Algorithms for Cloud Computing. Elsevier *Procedia Computer Science, 85,* 535 – 542.

Bhattasali, T., Chaki, R., & Chaki, N. (2013). Secure and trusted cloud of things. *Proceedings of INDICON Annual IEEE India Conference.*

Bhushan, K., & Gupta, B. B. (2018). Detecting DDoS Attack using Software Defined Network (SDN) in Cloud Computing Environment. In *2018 5th International Conference on Signal Processing and Integrated Networks (SPIN).* IEEE. 10.1109/SPIN.2018.8474062

Bhushan, K., & Gupta, B. B. (2017). Security challenges in cloud computing: State-of-art. *International Journal of Big Data Intelligence, 4*(2), 81–107. doi:10.1504/IJBDI.2017.083116

Blanc, X. (2005). *MDA en action*. Paris, France: Ed. Eyrolles.

Blei, D. M., Ng, A. Y., & Michael, I. J. (2003). Latent Dirichlet Allocation. *Journal of Machine Learning Research*.

Blog: Follow what's happening at Get Cloud Services. (2014, December 23). Mobile Cloud Com-puting – Pros and Cons. *GetCloud Services*. Available: https://www.getcloudservices.com/blog/mobile-cloud-computing-pros-and-cons/

Bojkovic, Z., & Bakmaz, B. (2012). Smart grid communications architecture: A survey and challenges. *Proc. 11th Int. Conf. Appl. Comput. Appl. Comput. Sci.*, 83–89.

Boldyreva, A., Palacio, A., & Warinschi, B. (2012). Secure proxy signature schemes for delegation of signing rights. *Journal of Cryptology*, 25(1), 57–115. doi:10.100700145-010-9082-x

Boneh, D., Lynn, B., & Shacham, H. (2001). Short signatures from the weil pairing. Advances in Cryptology, 2248, 514-532. doi:10.1007/3-540-45682-1_30

Boneh, D., & Franklin, M. K. (2001). Identity-based encryption from the weil pairing. *Proc. 21st Annu. Int. Cryptol. Conf. Adv. Cryptol.*, 2139, 213–229.

Boneh, D., & Hamburg, M. (2008). Generalized identity based and broadcast encryption schemes. *International Conference on the Theory and Application of Cryptology and Information Security*, 455-470. 10.1007/978-3-540-89255-7_28

Borah, A. D., Muchahary, D., Singh, S. K., & Borah, J. (2015). Power Saving Strategies in Green Cloud Computing Systems. *International Journal of Grid and Distributed Computing*, 8(1), 299–306. doi:10.14257/ijgdc.2015.8.1.28

Botta, A., de Donato, W., Persico, V., & Pescape, A. (2016, March). Integration of Cloud Computing and Internet of Things: A Survey. *Journal of Future Generation Computer Systems*, 56, 1–54. doi:10.1016/j.future.2015.09.021

Bouraoui, A., & Gharbi, I. (2019). Model driven engineering of accessible and multi-platform graphical user interfaces by parameterized model transformations. *Science of Computer Programming*, 172, 63–101. doi:10.1016/j.scico.2018.11.002

Bousetta, B., El Beggar, O., & Gadi, T. (2013). A methodology for CIM modeling and its transformation to PIM. *Journal of Information Engineering and Applications*, 2(3), 1–21.

Bradford, C. (2017). *7 Most Infamous Cloud Security Breaches*. Retrieved from https://blog.storagecraft.com/7-infamous-cloudsecurity-breaches/

Brazier, F. M. T., Dunin-Keplicz, B., Jennings, N. R., & Treur, J. (1997). DESIRE: modeling mulch-agent systems in a compositional formal framework. International Journal of Cooperative Information Systems, 1(152).

Brender, N., & Markov, I. (2013). Risk perception and risk management in cloud computing: Results from a case study of Swiss companies. *International Journal of Information Management*, 33(5), 726–733. doi:10.1016/j.ijinfomgt.2013.05.004

Brito, T. B., Trevisan, E. F., & Booter, R. C. (2011). A Conceptual Comparison Between Discrete and Continuous Simulation to Motivate the Hybrid Simulation Technology. *Proceedings of the 2011 Winter Simulation Conference*, 3915-3927.

Budrienė, D., & Zalieckaitė, L. (2012). Cloud computing application in small and medium-sized enterprises. *Issues of Business and Law*, 4(1), 119–130. doi:10.5200/ibl.2012.11

Burkhard, H. D. (1994). On Fair Controls in Multi-Agent Systems. *ECAI 1994, 11th European Conference on Artificial Intelligence*, 254-258.

Buyya, R., Beloglazov, A., & Abawajy, J. (2010). *Energy-efficient management of data center resources for cloud computing: A vision, architectural elements, and open challenges*. arXiv preprint arXiv:1006.0308

Buyya, R., Yeo, C. S., & Venugopal, S. (2008). Market-oriented cloud computing: Vision, hype, and reality for delivering it services as computing utilities. *Proceeding of 10th IEEE international conference on high performance computing and communications,* 5–13. doi: 10.1109/hpcc.2008.172

Buyya, R., Yeo, C. S., Venugopal, S., Broberg, J., & Brandic, I. (2009). Cloud computing and emerging IT platforms: Vision, hype, and reality for delivering computing as the 5th utility. *Future Generation Computer Systems, 25*(6), 599–616. doi:10.1016/j.future.2008.12.001

Cachin, Andrulaki, & Osboren. (2016). *Blockchain, cryptography, and Consensus.* IBM Zürich.

Calheiros, R. N., Ranjan, R., Beloglazov, A., De Rose, C. A., & Buyya, R. (2011). CloudSim: A toolkit for modeling and simulation of cloud computing environments and evaluation of resource provisioning algorithms. *Software, Practice & Experience, 41*(1), 23–50. doi:10.1002pe.995

Cao, F., & Cao, Z. F. (2010). An identity based proxy signature scheme secure in the standard model. In *Proceeding of GRC 10,* (pp. 67–72). IEEE Computer Society. 10.1109/GrC.2010.174

Cao, H., Zhang, J., Liu, J., & Li, Z.-Y. (2016). A new quantum proxy multisignature scheme using maximally entangled seven-qubit states. *International Journal of Theoretical Physics, 55*(2), 774–780. doi:10.100710773-015-2715-y

Cater-Steel, A. (2008). *Information Systems Research Methods, Epistemology, and Applications.* Information Science Reference.

Chahal, K., & Eldabi, T. (2010). A multi-perspective comparison between system dynamics and discrete event simulation. *Journal of Business Information Systems,* 4-17.

Cha, J. C., & Cheon, J. H. (2003). An identity-based signature from gap Diffie-Hellman groups. In *PKC 2003.* Lecture Notes in Computer Science. Springer Verlag.

Chan, F., Lee, G. K., Lee, E. J., Kubota, C., & Allen, C. A. (2007). Structural equation modeling in rehabilitation counseling research. *Rehabilitation Counseling Bulletin, 51*(1), 44–57. doi:10.1177/00343552070510010701

Chang, V., & Ramachandran, M. (2016). Towards achieving data security with the cloud computing adoption framework. IEEE Transactions on Services Computing, 9(1), 138–151. doi:10.1109/TSC.2015.2491281

Chang, L. X. L. (2015). Efficiently Computing Top-K Shortest Path Join. *18th International Conference on Extending Database Technology (EDBT),* Brussels, Belgium.

Chang, V. (2015). *A proposed cloud computing business framework.* Nova Science Publisher.

Chatterjee & Roy. (2017). Cryptography in Cloud Computing: A Basic Approach to Ensure Security in Cloud. *International Journal of Engineering Science and Computing, 7*(5), 11818-11821.

Chiregi, M. & Jafari Navimipour, N. (2017). Cloud computing and trust evaluation: A systematic literature review of the state-of-the-art mechanisms. *Journal of Electrical Systems and Information Technology.*

Chong, F., Carraro, G., & Wolter, R. (n.d.). *Multi-tenant data architecture.* Retrieved from http://ramblingsofraju.com/wp-content/uploads/2016/08/Multi-Tenant-Data-Architecture.pdf

Chong, R. F. (n.d.). *Designing a database for multi-tenancy on the cloud.* Retrieved from https://developer.ibm.com/tutorials/dm-1201dbdesigncloud/

Chu, C.-K., Liu, J. K., Wong, J. W., Zhao, Y., & Zhou, J. (2013). Privacy preserving smart metering with regional statistics and personal enquiry services. *Proc. 8th ACM SIGSAC Symp. Inf., Comput. Commun. Soc.,* 369–380. 10.1145/2484313.2484362

Chuan Shi, Y. L. (2017). A Survey of Heterogeneous Information Network Analysis. *IEEE Transactions on Knowledge and Data Engineering*, 29(1), 17–37. doi:10.1109/TKDE.2016.2598561

Clark, C., Fraser, K., Hand, S., Hansen, J. G., Jul, E., Limpach, C., . . . Warfield, A. (2005, May). Live migration of virtual machines. In *Proceedings of the 2nd conference on Symposium on Networked Systems Design & Implementation-Volume 2* (pp. 273-286). USENIX Association.

Cloud Security Alliance. (2018). *State of Cloud Security 2018*. Author.

Cochran, W. G. (2007). *Sampling techniques*. John Wiley & Sons.

Cohen, L., Manion, L., & Morrison, K. (2017). *Research Methods in Education*. Taylor & Francis. doi:10.4324/9781315456539

Comer, D. E. (2018). *The Internet book: everything you need to know about computer networking and how the Internet works*. Chapman and Hall/CRC. doi:10.1201/9780429447358

Compuware. (2014). *73% of Companies Fear Cloud Providers Hide Performance Problems*. Available: https://www.cnbc.com/2014/04/30/globe-newswire-73-of-companies-fear-cloud-providers-hide-performance-problems.html

Couch, L. W. II. (2013). *Digital and Analog Communication Systems* (8th ed.). Prentice Hall.

Creswell, J. W., & Clark, V. L. P. (2011). *Designing and Conducting Mixed Methods Research*. SAGE Publications.

Creswell, J. W., & Creswell, J. D. (2018). *Research Design: Qualitative, Quantitative, and Mixed Methods Approaches*. SAGE Publications.

CSA. (2011). *Security Guidance for Critical Areas of Focus in Cloud Computing V3.0*. Cloud Security Alliance (CSA).

Dabbagh, M., Hamdaoui, B., Guizani, M., & Rayes, A. (2015). Toward energy-efficient cloud computing: Prediction, consolidation, and overcommitment. *IEEE Network*, 29(2), 56–61. doi:10.1109/MNET.2015.7064904

Dam, S., Mandal, G., Dasgupta, K., & Dutta, P. (2014). An ant colony based load balancing strategy in cloud computing. In Advanced Computing, Networking and Informatics-Volume 2 (pp. 403-413). Springer International Publishing. doi:10.1007/978-3-319-07350-7_45

Dasgupta, K., Mandal, B., Dutta, P., Mandal, J. K., & Dam, S. (2013). A genetic algorithm (ga) based load balancing strategy for cloud computing. *Procedia Technology*, 10, 340–347. doi:10.1016/j.protcy.2013.12.369

de Bruin, B., & Floridi, L. (2017). The ethics of cloud computing. *Science and Engineering Ethics*, 23(1), 21–39. doi:10.100711948-016-9759-0 PMID:26886482

De Castro, V., Marcos, E., & Vara, J. M. (2011). Applying CIM-to-PIM model transformations for the service-oriented development of information systems. *Journal of Information and Software Technology*, 53(1), 87–105. doi:10.1016/j.infsof.2010.09.002

Demuth, B., & Hussmann, H. (1999), Using OCL Constraints for Relational Database Design. In *Proceedings, The Unified Modeling Language, Second Int. Conference* (pp. 598-613). Academic Press. 10.1007/3-540-46852-8_42

Devadas, S., & Malik, S. (1995, January). A survey of optimization techniques targeting low power VLSI circuits. In *Proceedings of the 32nd annual ACM/IEEE Design Automation Conference* (pp. 242-247). ACM. 10.1145/217474.217536

Dharavath, Mishra, & Edla. (n.d.). Secure Data Storage in Cloud: An e-Stream Cipher-Based Secure and Dynamic Updation Policy. *Arabian Journal for Science and Engineering*, 1-11.

Ding, H., Li, X., & Gong, C. (2015). Trust model research in cloud computing environment. *2015 International Symposium on Computers & Informatics.* 10.2991/isci-15.2015.143

Dinh, H. T., Lee, C., Niyato, D., & Wang, P. (2013). A Survey of Mobile Cloud Computing: Architecture, Applications, and Approaches. *Wirel. Commun. Mob. Comput*, 1–38.

Dinh, T. H., Lee, C., Niyato, D., & Wang, P. (2013). A survey of mobile cloud computing: Architecture, applications, and approaches. *Wireless Communications and Mobile Computing, 13*(18), 1587–1611. doi:10.1002/wcm.1203

Do & Pham. (2018). DW-PathSim: a distributed computing model for topic-driven weighted meta-path-based similarity measure in a large-scale content-based heterogeneous information network. *Journal of Information and Telecommunication*, 1-20.

Dobre, C., & Xhafa, F. (2014, July). Intelligent services for big data science. *Future Generation Computer Systems, 37*, 267–281. doi:10.1016/j.future.2013.07.014

Doelitzscher, F., Sulistio, A., Reich, C., Kuijs, H., & Wolf, D. (2011). Private cloud for collaboration and e-Learning services: From IaaS to SaaS. *Computing, 91*(1), 23–42. doi:10.100700607-010-0106-z

Dorgham, O., Almonani, A., Alauthman, M., Albalas, F., & Obeidat, A. (2018, April). An Online Intrusion Detection System to Cloud Computing Based on Neucube Algorithms. *International Journal of Cloud Applications and Computing, 8*(2), 96–112. doi:10.4018/IJCAC.2018040105

Doukas, C., Pliakas, T., & Maglogiannis, I. (2010). Mobile Healthcare Information Management utilizing Cloud Computing and Android OS. *Proceedings of 32nd Annual International Conference of the IEEE EMBS.* 10.1109/IEMBS.2010.5628061

Dragotti, P. L., Vetterli, M., & Blu, T. (2007). Sampling Moments and Reconstructing Signals of Finite Rate of Innovation: Shannon Meets Strang-Fix. *IEEE Transactions on Signal Processing, 55*(5), 1741–1757. doi:10.1109/TSP.2006.890907

Duff, J. (2009). Smart grid challenges. *Proc. Workshop High Perform. Trans. Syst.* Available: http://www.hpts.ws/papers/2009/session4/duff.pdf

Dutta, A., Peng, G. C., & Choudhary, A. (2013). Risks in enterprise cloud computing: The perspective of IT experts. *Journal of Computer Information Systems, 53*(4), 39–48. doi:10.1080/08874417.2013.11645649

Efthymiou, C., & Kalogridis, G. (2010). Smart grid privacy via anonymization of smart metering data. *Proc. 1st Int. Conf. Smart Grid Commun.*, 238–243. 10.1109/SMARTGRID.2010.5622050

Elmisery, A. M., Sertovic, M., & Gupta, B. B. (2018). Cognitive Privacy Middleware for Deep Learning Mashup in Environmental IoT. *IEEE Access: Practical Innovations, Open Solutions, 6*, 8029–8041. doi:10.1109/ACCESS.2017.2787422

Elmounadi, A., El Moukhi, N., Berbiche, N., & Sefiani, N. (2019). A new PHP discoverer for Modisco. *International Journal of Advanced Computer Science and Applications, 10*(1), 169–174. doi:10.14569/IJACSA.2019.0100122

El-Yahyaoui & Ech-Chrif El Kettani. (2018). Data privacy in cloud computing. *2018 4th International Conference on Computer and Technology Applications (ICCTA)*, 25-28.

Elzeki, O. M., Reshad, M. Z., & Elsoud, M. A. (2012). Improved max-min algorithm in Cloud computing. *International Journal of Computers and Applications, 50*(12).

Encalada, W. L., & Sequera, J. L. C. (2017). Model to Implement Virtual Computing Labs via Cloud Computing Services. *Symmetry, 9*(7), 117. doi:10.3390ym9070117

Ernest and Young. (2015). *Sharing ledgers for sharing economies: an exploration of mutual distributed ledgers (aka blockchain technology).* Retrieved from https://fsinsights.ey.com/thejournalhttps://fsinsights.ey.com/thejournal

Etminani, K., & Naghibzadeh, M. (2007, September). A min-min max-min selective algorihtm for grid task scheduling. In *Internet, 2007. ICI 2007. 3rd IEEE/IFIP International Conference in Central Asia on* (pp. 1-7). IEEE. 10.1109/CANET.2007.4401694

Etro, F. (2015). The economics of cloud computing. In Cloud Technology: Concepts, Methodologies, Tools, and Applications (pp. 2135-2148). IGI Global. doi:10.4018/978-1-4666-6539-2.ch101

Fang, L., Susilo, W., & Wang, J. (2009). Anonymous conditional proxy re-encryption without random oracle. In *International Conference on Provable Security*, (pp. 47-60). Springer Berlin Heidelberg. 10.1007/978-3-642-04642-1_6

Fan, W., Yang, S., Pei, J., & Luo, H. (2012). Building trust into cloud. *International Journal of Cloud Computing and Services Science, 1*(3), 115–122.

Fan, Z., Kulkarni, P., Gormus, S., Efthymiou, C., Kalogridis, G., Sooriyabandara, M., ... Chin, W. (2012, January). Smart grid communications: Overview of research challenges, solutions, and standardization activities. *IEEE Communications Surveys and Tutorials, 15*(1), 21–38. doi:10.1109/SURV.2011.122211.00021

Farhangi, H. (2010, January/February). The path of the smart grid. *IEEE Power & Energy Magazine, 8*(1), 18–28. doi:10.1109/MPE.2009.934876

Fatolahi, A., Somé, S. S., & Lethbridge, T. C. (2008). Towards a semi-automated model-driven method for the generation of web-based applications from use cases. In *Proceedings, 4th Model Driven Web Engineering Workshop* (pp. 31-45). Toulouse, France: Academic Press.

Fernandes, D. A., Soares, L. F., Gomes, J. V., Freire, M. M., & Inácio, P. R. (2014). Security issues in cloud environments: A survey. *International Journal of Information Security, 13*(2), 113–170. doi:10.100710207-013-0208-7

Ferraiolo, D. F., Sandhu, R., Gavrila, S., Kuhn, D. R., & Chandramouli, R. (2001, August). Proposed NIST standard for role-based access control. *ACM Transactions on Information and System Security, 4*(3), 224–274. doi:10.1145/501978.501980

Filali, F. Z., & Yagoubi, B. (2015). Global trust: A trust model for cloud service selection. *International Journal of Computer Network and Information Security, 7*(5), 41–50. doi:10.5815/ijcnis.2015.05.06

Filin, S., Harada, H., Hasegawa, M., & Kato, S. (2008, September). QoS-guaranteed load-balancing dynamic spectrum access algorithm. In *2008 IEEE 19th International Symposium on Personal, Indoor and Mobile Radio Communications* (pp. 1-6). IEEE. 10.1109/PIMRC.2008.4699466

Filiposka, S., Mishev, A., & Juiz, C. (2016). Current Prospects Towards Energy-Efficient Top HPC Systems. *Computer Science and Information Systems, 13*(1), 151–171. doi:10.2298/CSIS150228063F

Fornell, C., & Larcker, D. F. (1981). Structural equation models with unobservable variables and measurement error: Algebra and statistics. *JMR, Journal of Marketing Research, 18*(3), 382–388. doi:10.1177/002224378101800313

Foster, I., Zhao, Y., Raicu, I., & Lu, S. (2008). Cloud computing and grid computing 360-degree compared. In *Grid Computing Environments Workshop (GCE)*, (pp. 1–10). IEEE. 10.1109/GCE.2008.4738445

Fowler, M. (2005). *Language Workbenches and Model Driven Architecture*. Retrieved January 11, 2015, from http://www.martinfowler.com/articles /mdaLanguageWorkbench.html

Fremdt, S., Beck, R., & Weber, S. (2013). Does Cloud Computing Matter? An analysis of the Cloud Model software-as-a-service and its impact on operational agility. *Proceedings of 46th Hawaii International Conference on System Sciences*, 1025-1034. 10.1109/HICSS.2013.182

Fu, Z., Ren, K., Shu, J., Sun, X., & Huang, F. (2015, December). Enabling Personalized Search over Encrypted Outsourced Data with Efficiency Improvement. *IEEE Transactions on Parallel and Distributed Systems*.

Fu, Z., Ren, K., Shu, J., Sun, X., & Huang, F. (2016, September). Enabling Personalized Search over Encrypted Outsourced Data with Efficiency Improvement. *IEEE Transactions on Parallel and Distributed Systems*, 27(9), 2546–2559. doi:10.1109/TPDS.2015.2506573

Garg, S. K., Versteeg, S., & Buyya, R. (2013). A framework for ranking of cloud computing services. *Future Generation Computer Systems*, 29(4), 1012–1023. doi:10.1016/j.future.2012.06.006

Garrison, G., Wakefield, R. L., & Kim, S. (2015). The effects of IT capabilities and delivery model on cloud computing success and firm performance for cloud supported processes and operations. *International Journal of Information Management*, 35(4), 377–393. doi:10.1016/j.ijinfomgt.2015.03.001

Gaurangkumar, K., & Minubhai, C. (2012, January). To Achieve Trust in the Cloud. *Advanced Computing & Communication Technologies (ACCT), 2012 Second International Conference on*, 16-19. 10.1109/ACCT.2012.115

Gençay, E., Sinz, C., & Kuchlin, W. (2008, April). Towards SLA-based optimal workload distribution in SANs. In *NOMS 2008-2008 IEEE Network Operations and Management Symposium* (pp. 755-758). IEEE.

Genesereth, M. R., & Nilsson, N. J. (1987). *Logical Foundations of Artificial Intelligence*. Morgan-Kaufmann.

Gentry, C., & Silverberg, A. (2002). Hierarchical id-based cryptography. *Proceedings of ASiACRYPT '02*, 548-566.

Godse, M., & Mulik, S. (2009, September). An approach for selecting software-as-a-service (SaaS) product. *Cloud Computing, 2009, CLOUD'09. IEEE International Conference on*, 155-158.doi: 10.1109/cloud.2009.74

Goguen, Thatcher, Wagner, & Wright. (1973). A Junction Between Computer Science and Category Theory (parts I and II). IBM T.J. Watson Research Center.

Gordijn, J., & Akkermans, J. M. (2003). Value based requirements engineering: Exploring innovative e-commerce idea. *Requirements Engineering Journal*, 8(2), 114–134. doi:10.100700766-003-0169-x

Gou, Z., Yamaguchi, S., & Gupta, B. B. (2017). Analysis of various security issues and challenges in cloud computing environment: a survey. In Identity Theft: Breakthroughs in Research and Practice (pp. 221-247). IGI Global. doi:10.4018/978-1-5225-0808-3.ch011

Gou, Z., Yamaguchi, S., & Gupta, B. B. (2017). Analysis of Various Security Issues and Challenges in Cloud Computing Environment: A Survey. In *Handbook of Research on Modern Cryptographic Solutions for Computer and Cyber Security* (pp. 221–247). IGI Global.

Grammel, B., & Kastenholz, S., A. (2010). generic traceability framework for facet-based traceability data extraction in model-driven software development. In *Proceedings, 6th ECMFA Traceability Workshop held in conjunction ECMFA* (pp. 7-14). Paris, France: Academic Press. 10.1145/1814392.1814394

Green, M., & Ateniese, G. (2007). Identity-based proxy re-encryption. *Proc. 5th Int. Conf. Appl. Cryptograph. Netw. Security*, 4521, 288–306. 10.1007/978-3-540-72738-5_19

Grobauer, B., Walloschek, T., & Stocker, E. (2011). Understanding cloud computing vulnerabilities. *IEEE Security and Privacy*, 9(2), 50–57. doi:10.1109/MSP.2010.115

Grozev, N., & Buyya, R. (2014, March). Inter-cloud architectures and application brokering: Taxonomy and survey. *Software, Practice & Experience*, 44(3), 369–390. doi:10.1002pe.2168

Gu, C. X., & Zhu, Y. F. (2006). *An efficient id-based proxy signature scheme from pairings.* Retrieved from IACR ePrint Archive: http://eprint.iacr.org/2006/158

Gu, K., Jia, W., Chen, R., & Liu, X. (2013). Secure and efficient proxy signature scheme in the standard model. *Chinese Journal of Electronics*, 22(4), 666–670.

Gu, K., Jia, W., & Jiang, C. (2015). Efficient identity-based proxy signature in the standard model. *The Computer Journal*, 58(4), 792–807. doi:10.1093/comjnl/bxt132

Gunarathne, T., Wu, T. L., Qiu, J., & Fox, G. (2010, November). MapReduce in the Clouds for Science. In *Cloud Computing Technology and Science (CloudCom), 2010 IEEE Second International Conference on* (pp. 565-572). IEEE. 10.1109/CloudCom.2010.107

Gunjan, Tiwari, & Sahoo. (2013). *Towards Securing APIs in Cloud Computing.* arXiv preprint arXiv:1307.6649

Guo, P., & Liu, Z. (2012). An Ant System based on Moderate Search for TSP. *Computer Science and Information Systems*, 9(4), 1533–1552. doi:10.2298/CSIS120302057G

Gupta Brij, B. (2018). *Computer and Cyber Security: Principles, Algorithm, Applications, and Perspectives.* CRC Press, Taylor & Francis.

Gupta, B. B., Agrawal, D. P., & Yamaguchi, S. (2016). Handbook of Research on Modern Cryptographic Solutions for Computer and Cyber Security. IGI Global. doi:10.4018/978-1-5225-0105-3

Gupta, Beri, & Behal. (2016). Cloud Computing: A Survey on Cloud Simulation Tools. *International Journal for Innovative Research in Science & Technology*, 2(11), 430-434.

Gupta. (2018). Computer and Cyber Security: Principles, Algorithm, Aplications, and Perspectives. CRC Press, Taylor & Francis.

Gupta, B. B. (2017). *Computer and Cyber Security: Principles.* Algorithm, Applications and Perspectives.

Gupta, B. B. (Ed.). (2018). *Computer and cyber security: principles, algorithm, applications, and perspectives.* CRC Press.

Gupta, B. B., & Badve, O. P. (2017). Taxonomy of DoS and DDoS attacks and desirable defense mechanism in a cloud computing environment. *Neural Computing & Applications*, 28(12), 3655–3682. doi:10.100700521-016-2317-5

Gupta, B. B., & Badve, O. P. (2017, December). Taxonomy of DoS and DDoS attacks and desirable defence mechanism in a Cloud computing environment. *Springer, Neural Computing and Applications*, 28(12), 3665–3682.

Gupta, P., Seetharaman, A., & Raj, J. R. (2013). The usage and adoption of cloud computing by small and medium businesses. *International Journal of Information Management*, 33(5), 861–874. doi:10.1016/j.ijinfomgt.2013.07.001

Gupta, S., & Gugulothu, N. (2018). Secure NoSQL for the Social Networking and E-Commerce Based Bigdata Applications Deployed in Cloud. *International Journal of Cloud Applications and Computing*, 8(2), 113–129. doi:10.4018/IJCAC.2018040106

Gururaj, R., Mohsin, I., & Farrukh, A. (2017). A Comprehensive Survey on Security in Cloud Computing. *FNC/MobiSPC 2017*, 110, 465-472.

Gutierrez-Garcia, J. O., & Ramirez-Nafarrate, A. (2013, June). Policy-based agents for virtual machine migration in cloud data centers. In *Services Computing (SCC), 2013 IEEE International Conference on* (pp. 603-610). IEEE. 10.1109/SCC.2013.55

Gutierrez-Garcia, J. O., & Ramirez-Nafarrate, A. (2015). Agent-based load balancing in Cloud data centers. *Cluster Computing*, *18*(3), 1041–1062. doi:10.100710586-015-0460-x

Gutiérrez, J. J., Nebut, C., Escalona, M. J., Mejías, M., & Ramos, I. M. (2008). Visualization of use cases through automatically generated activity diagrams. In *Proceedings, 11th International Conference MoDELS'08* (pp 83-96). Toulouse, France: Academic Press. 10.1007/978-3-540-87875-9_6

Habib, S. M., Ries, S., & Muhlhauser, M. (2011). Towards a Trust Management System for Cloud Computing. *Proceedings of IEEE International Joint Conference TrustCom-11/IEEE ICESS-11/FCST-11*. 10.1109/TrustCom.2011.129

Hada, P. S., Singh, R., & Meghwal, M. M. (2011, December). Security Agents: A Mobile Agent based Trust Model for Cloud Computing. *International Journal of Computers and Applications*, *36*(12), 12–15.

Haghighat, M., Zonouz, S., & Abdel-Mottaleb, M. (2015, November). CloudID: Trustworthy cloud-based and cross-enterprise biometric identification. *Expert Systems with Applications*, *42*(21), 7905–7916. doi:10.1016/j.eswa.2015.06.025

Hahn, C., Dmytro, P., & Fischer, K. (2010). A model-driven approach to close the gap between business requirements and agent-based execution. In *Proceedings, 4th Workshop on Agent-based Technologies and applications for enterprise interoperability* (pp. 13–24). Toronto, Canada: Academic Press.

Hai, H., Qing, X. D., & Ke, Q. (2018). A watermarking-based authentication and image restoration in multimedia sensor networks. *International Journal of High Performance Computing and Networking*, *12*(1), 65–73. doi:10.1504/IJHPCN.2018.093846

Hai-Jew, S. (2014). *Enhancing Qualitative and Mixed Methods Research with Technology*. IGI Global.

Hair, J. F., Anderson, R. E., Tatham, R. L., & Black, W. C. (1998). Multivariate data analysis. Academic Press.

Hamlen, K., Kantarcioglu, M., Khan, L., & Thuraisingham, B. (2010). Security issues for Cloud Computing. *International Journal of Information Security and Privacy*, *4*(2), 39–51. doi:10.4018/jisp.2010040103

Hamza & Omar. (2013). Cloud computing security: Abuse and nefarious use of cloud computing. *Int. J. Comput. Eng. Res.*, 22-27.

Hamza, Y. A., & Omar, M. D. (2013). Cloud computing security: Abuse and nefarious use of cloud computing. *Int. J. Comput. Eng. Res*, *3*(6), 22–27.

Hashizume, K., Rosado, D. G., Fernández-Medina, E., & Fernandez, E. B. (2013). Fernández-Medina E, & Fernandez E. B, An analysis of security issues for cloud computing. *Journal of Internet Services and Applications*, *4*(1), 1–13. doi:10.1186/1869-0238-4-5

Hashizume, K., Rosado, D. G., Fernandez-Medina, E., & Fernandez, E. B. (2013, December). An analysis of security issues for cloud computing. *Journal of Internet Services and Applications*, *4*(5), 1–13.

Hassan, H. A., Kashkoush, M. S., Azab, M., & Sheta, W. M. (2019). Impact of using multi-levels of parallelism on HPC applications performance hosted on Azure cloud computing. *International Journal of High Performance Computing and Networking*, *13*(3), 251–260. doi:10.1504/IJHPCN.2019.098579

Hayes, B. (2008). Cloud computing. *Communications of the ACM*, *51*(7), 9–11. doi:10.1145/1364782.1364786

He, H., Feng, Y., Li, Z., Zhu, Z., Zhang, W., & Cheng, A. (2015). Dynamic Load Balancing Technology for Cloud-oriented CDN. *Computer Science and Information Systems*, *12*(2), 765–786. doi:10.2298/CSIS141104025H

Hesarlo, P. S. (2014). Security, Privacy and Trust Challenges in Cloud Computing and Solutions. *International Journal of Computer Network and Information Security*, *6*(8), 34–40. doi:10.5815/ijcnis.2014.08.05

He, W., Yan, G., & Xu, L. D. (2014, May). Developing vehicular data cloud services in the IoT environment. *IEEE Transactions on Industrial Informatics*, *10*(2), 1587–1595. doi:10.1109/TII.2014.2299233

He, X., Ren, Z., Shi, C., & Fang, J. (2016). A novel load balancing strategy of software-defined cloud/fog networking in the Internet of Vehicles. *China Communications*, *13*(Supplement2), 140–149. doi:10.1109/CC.2016.7833468

Hilbert, M., & López, P. (2011). The World's Technological Capacity to Store, Communicate, and Compute Information. *Science*, *332*(6025), 60–65. doi:10.1126cience.1200970 PMID:21310967

Horrigan, J. B. (2008). *Use of cloud computing applications and services*. PEW Internet & American Life Project.

Hossain, K., Rahman, M., & Roy, S. (2019). IoT Data Compression and Optimization Techniques in Cloud Storage: Current Prospects and Future Directions. *International Journal of Cloud Applications and Computing*, *9*(2), 43–59. doi:10.4018/IJCAC.2019040103

Hossain, M. S., Muhammad, G., Abdul, W., Song, B., & Gupta, B. B. (2018). Cloud-assisted secure video transmission and sharing framework for smart cities. *Future Generation Computer Systems*, *83*, 596–606. doi:10.1016/j.future.2017.03.029

Hsu, P. F., Ray, S., & Li-Hsieh, Y. Y. (2014). Examining cloud computing adoption intention, pricing mechanism, and deployment model. *International Journal of Information Management*, *34*(4), 474–488. doi:10.1016/j.ijinfomgt.2014.04.006

Hu, J., Gu, J., Sun, G., & Zhao, T. (2010, December). A scheduling strategy on load balancing of virtual machine resources in cloud computing environment. In *2010 3rd International symposium on parallel architectures, algorithms and programming* (pp. 89-96). IEEE.

Hu, X., Lu, H., & Xu, H. (2015). An efficient identity-based proxy signature scheme in the standard model with tight reduction. In *Proceedings of International Joint Conference, Advances in Intelligent Systems and Computing*, (pp. 309–319). Springer International Publishing. 10.1007/978-3-319-19713-5_27

Huang, D., Zhang, X., Kang, M., & Luo, J. (2010). MobiCloud: building secure cloud framework for mobile computing and communication. In *2010 fifth IEEE international symposium on service oriented system engineering*, (pp. 27-34). IEEE. 10.1109/SOSE.2010.20

Huang, D. (2011, October). Mobile cloud computing. *IEEE COMSOC Multimedia Communications Technical Committee (MMTC). E-Letter*, *6*(10), 27–31.

Huang, J., & Nicol, D. M. (2013). Trust mechanisms for cloud computing. *Journal of Cloud Computing: Advances. Systems and Applications*, *2*(1), 9.

Hu, B. (2018). Leveraging Meta-path based Context for Top-N Recommendation with A Neural Co-Attention Mode. *KDD: Proceedings / International Conference on Knowledge Discovery & Data Mining. International Conference on Knowledge Discovery & Data Mining.*

Hu, X., Wang, J., & Xu, H. (2015). An improved efficient identity based proxy signature in the standard model. *International Journal of Computer Mathematics*, *58*(4), 1–18.

Hu, X., Zhang, X., Wang, J., Xu, H., Tan, W., & Yang, Y. (2016). Secure and Efficient Identity-Based Proxy Signature Scheme in the Standard Model Based on Computational Diffie–Hellman Problem. *Arabian Journal for Science and Engineering*, 1–11.

Hu, Y., Wu, W., & Cheng, D. (2012). Towards law-aware semantic cloud policies with exceptions for data integration and protection. *2nd International Conference on Web Intelligence, Mining and Semantics*. 10.1145/2254129.2254162

Ibtihal, M., & Hassan, N. (2017). Homomorphic encryption as a service for outsourced images in mobile cloud computing environment. *International Journal of Cloud Applications and Computing, 7*(2), 27–40. doi:10.4018/IJCAC.2017040103

IEEE. (2011). *P2030/D7.0 draft guide for smart grid interoperability of energy technology and information technology operation with the electric power system (EPS), and end-user applications and loads.* P2030/D670.

Indu, Anand, & Bhaskar. (2018). Identity and access management in cloud environment: mechanisms and challenges. *Engineering Science and Technology, an International Journal, 21*(4), 574-588.

Intel Security. (2017). *Building Trust in a Cloudy Sky: The State of Cloud Adoption and Security.* Retrieved from http://usdatavault.com/library/Building-Trust-in-a-Cloudy-Sky.pdf

Islam, Manivannan, & Zeadally. (2016). A classification and characterization of security threats in cloud computing. *Int. J. Next-Gener.Comput, 7*(1).

Islam, N. (2017, July). Analysis of Various Encryption Algorithms in Cloud Computing. *International Journal of Computer Science and Mobile Computing, 6*(7), 90–97.

Ismail, U. M., Islam, S., Ouedraogo, M., & Weippl, E. (2016). A framework for security transparency in cloud computing. *Future Internet, 8*(1), 5. doi:10.3390/fi8010005

Jabir, R. M. (2016). Analysis of cloud computing attacks and countermeasures. In *2016 18th International Conference on Advanced Communication Technology (ICACT).* IEEE.

Jain, N., Deshpande, A. V., Raghu, B., & Khanaa, V. (2017). *A eficácia dos bancos de dados em nuvem. In 2017 Conferência Internacional sobre Algoritmos, Metodologia, Modelos e Aplicações em Tecnologias Emergentes (ICAMMAET)* (pp. 1–3). IEEE.

Jawad, Z. M., Ajlan, I. K., & Abdulameer, Z. D. (2017). Cloud Computing Adoption by Higher Education Institutions of Iraq: An Empirical Study. *Journal of Education College Wasit University, 1*(28), 591–608. doi:10.31185/eduj.Vol1.Iss28.24

Jeba, J. A., Roy, S., Rashid, M. O., Atik, S. T., & Whaiduzzaman, M. (2019). Towards Green Cloud Computing an Algorithmic Approach for Energy Minimization in Cloud Data Centers. *International Journal of Cloud Applications and Computing, 9*(1), 59–81. doi:10.4018/IJCAC.2019010105

Jiang, F., Fu, Y., Gupta, B. B., Lou, F., Rho, S., Meng, F., & Tian, Z. (2018). *Deep Learning based Multi-channel intelligent attack detection for Data Security. IEEE Transactions on Sustainable Computing.* doi:10.1109/TSUSC.2018.2793284

Jiang, Q., Ma, J., & Wei, F. (2018, June). On the Security of a Privacy-Aware Authentication Scheme for Distributed Mobile Cloud Computing Services. *IEEE Systems Journal, 12*(2), 2039–2042. doi:10.1109/JSYST.2016.2574719

Jin, H., Gao, W., Wu, S., Shi, X., Wu, X., & Zhou, F. (2011). Optimizing the live migration of virtual machine by CPU scheduling. *Journal of Network and Computer Applications, 34*(4), 1088–1096. doi:10.1016/j.jnca.2010.06.013

Jouini, M., & Ben Arfa Rabai, L. (2014). Surveying and Analyzing Security Problems in Cloud Computing Environments. *The 10th International Conference on Computational Intelligence and Security (CIS 2014),* 689–493.

Jouini, M., Ben Arfa Rabai, L., & Ben Aissa, A. (2014). Classification of security threats in information systems. *ANT/SEIT 2014.*

Jouini, M., Ben Arfa Rabai, L., & Khedri, R. (2015). A Multidimensional Approach Towards a Quantitative Assessment of Security Threats. *ANT/SEIT 2015,* 507-514.

Jouini, M., & Ben Arfa Rabai, L. (2016). Security Framework for Secure Cloud Computing Environments. *International Journal of Cloud Applications and Computing, 6*(3), 32–44. doi:10.4018/IJCAC.2016070103

Jouini, M., Ben Arfa Rabai, L., Ben Aissa, A., & Mili, A. (2012). Towards quantitative measures of information security: A cloud computing case study. *International Journal of Cyber-Security and Digital Forensics, 1*(3), 265–279.

Jouini, M., Ben Arfa Rabai, L., Ben Aissa, A., & Mili, A. (2013). A cyber security model in cloud computing environments. *Journal of King Saud University-Computer and Information Sciences, 25*(1), 63–75. doi:10.1016/j.jksuci.2012.06.002

Jun, C. (2011). IPv6 virtual machine live migration framework for cloud computing. *Energy Procedia, 13*, 5753–5757.

Kadhim, Q. K., Yusof, R., Mahdi, H. S., Ali Al-shami, S.S., & Selamat, S. R. (2018). A Review Study on Cloud Computing Issues. *1st International Conference on Big Data and Cloud Computing (ICoBiC 2017)*. 10.1088/1742-6596/1018/1/012006

Kalogridis, G., Efthymiou, C., Denic, S., Lewis, T., & Cepeda, R. (2010). Privacy for smart meters: Towards undetectable appliance load signatures. *Proc. 1st Int. Conf. Smart Grid Commun.*, 232–237. 10.1109/SMARTGRID.2010.5622047

Kalpana, P., & Singaraju, S. (2012). Data Security in Cloud Computing using RSA Algorithm. *International Journal of Research in Computer and Communication technology, 1*(4), 143-146.

Kalra, M., & Singh, S. (2015). A review of metaheuristic scheduling techniques in cloud computing. *Egyptian Informatics Journal, 16*(3), 275–295. doi:10.1016/j.eij.2015.07.001

Kardoš, M., & Drozdová, M. (2010). Analytical method of CIM to PIM transformation in Model Driven Architecture (MDA). *Journal of Information and Organizational Sciences, 34*(1), 89–99.

Kashif, U. A. (2019). *Architectural design of trusted platform for IaaS cloud computing. In Cloud Security: Concepts, Methodologies, Tools, and Applications* (pp. 393–411). IGI Global.

Kashif, U. A., Memon, Z. A., Siddiqui, S., Balouch, A. R., & Batra, R. (2018). Architectural Design of Trusted Platform for IaaS Cloud Computing. *International Journal of Cloud Applications and Computing, 8*(2), 47–65. doi:10.4018/IJCAC.2018040103

Katz, J., & Wang, N. (2003). Efficiency improvements for signature schemes with tight security reductions. In *Proceedings of CCS'03*, (pp. 1–10). ACM Press. 10.1145/948109.948132

Kaur, R., & Kinger, S. (2014, March). Analysis of Security Algorithms in Cloud Computing. *International Journal of Application or Innovation in Engineering & Management, 3*(3), 171–176.

Keil, M. (1995). Pulling the plug: Software project management and the problem of project escalation. *Management Information Systems Quarterly, 19*(4), 421–447. doi:10.2307/249627

Kenyon, H. (2010). Closing an overlooked vulnerability. *Government Computer News*. Retrieved from https://www.drivesaversdatarecovery.com/images/pdf/GCN+09_06_10.pdf

Keskin, T., & Taskin, N. (2014). A pricing model for cloud computing service. *Proceedings of 47th Hawaii International Conference on System Science*, 699-707. 10.1109/HICSS.2014.94

Khadilkar, V., Gupta, A., Kantarcioglu, M., Khan, L., & Thuraisingham, B. (2010). Secure Data Storage and Retrieval in the Cloud. *COLLABORATECOM Proceedings of the 2010, 6th International Conference on Collaborative Computing: Networking, Applications and Worksharing (CollaborateCom 2010)*, 1-8.

Khalil, I., Khreishah, A., & Azeem, M. (2014, March). Consolidated Identity Management System for secure mobile cloud computing. *Elsevier, Computer Networks, 99*, 99–110. doi:10.1016/j.comnet.2014.03.015

Khan, S., & Sharma, N. (2014). Effective scheduling algorithm for load balancing (SALB) using ant colony optimization in cloud computing. *International Journal of Advanced Research in Computer Science and Software Engineering, 4*.

Khan, A. N., Kiah, M. M., Khan, S. U., & Madani, S. A. (2013). Towards secure mobile cloud computing: A survey. *Future Generation Computer Systems*, *29*(5), 1278–1299. doi:10.1016/j.future.2012.08.003

Khanagha, S., Volberda, H., Sidhu, J., & Oshri, I. (2013). Management innovation and adoption of emerging technologies: The case of cloud computing. *European Management Review*, *10*(1), 51–67. doi:10.1111/emre.12004

Khan, K. M., & Malluhi, Q. (2010). Establishing trust in cloud computing. *IT Professional*, *12*(5), 20–27. doi:10.1109/MITP.2010.128

Kherraf, S., Lefebvre, É., & Suryn, W. (2008). Transformation from CIM to PIM using patterns and Archetypes. In *Proceedings, 19th Australian Software Engineering Conference* (pp. 338 – 346). Perth, Australia: Academic Press. 10.1109/ASWEC.2008.4483222

Khurana, H., Hadley, M., Lu, N., & Frincke, D. (2010). Smart-grid security issues. *Security Privacy*, *8*(1), 81–85. doi:10.1109/MSP.2010.49

Kim, M., & Park, S. O. (2013, December). Trust management on user behavioral patterns for a mobile cloud computing. *Springer, Cluster Computing*, *16*(4), 725–731. doi:10.100710586-013-0248-9

Kim, W. (2009). Cloud computing: Today and tomorrow. *Journal of Object Technology*, *8*(1), 65–72. doi:10.5381/jot.2009.8.1.c4

Kleppe, A., Warmer, G. J., & Bast, W. (2003). *MDA Explained: The Model Driven Architecture: Practice and Promise*. Boston: Addison-Wesley.

Ko, R. K., Jagadpramana, P., Mowbray, M., Pearson, S., Kirchberg, M., Liang, Q., & Lee, B. S. (2011). TrustCloud: A framework for accountability and trust in cloud computing. In *Services (SERVICES), 2011 IEEE World Congress on, 2011*. IEEE.

Kokilavani, T., & Amalarethinam, D. D. G. (2011). Load balanced min-min algorithm for static meta-task scheduling in grid computing. *International Journal of Computers and Applications*, *20*(2), 43–49.

Kolb, L., Thor, A., & Rahm, E. (2012, April). Load balancing for mapreduce-based entity resolution. In *2012 IEEE 28th international conference on data engineering* (pp. 618-629). IEEE. 10.1109/ICDE.2012.22

Kong, P. S. (2012). Meta Path-Based Classification in Heterogeneous Information Networks. *CIKM'12*.

Koomey, J. (2011). *Growth in data center electricity use 2005 to 2010*. A report by Analytical Press.

Kord, N., & Haghighi, H. (2013, May). An energy-efficient approach for virtual machine placement in cloud based data centers. In *Information and Knowledge Technology (IKT), 2013 5th Conference on* (pp. 44-49). IEEE. 10.1109/IKT.2013.6620036

Kouatli, I. (2016). Managing Cloud Computing Environment: Gaining Customer Trust with Security and Ethical Management. *Procedia Computer Science*, 91412–91421.

Kozuch, M., & Satyanarayanan, M. (2002). Internet suspend/resume. In *Mobile Computing Systems and Applications, 2002. Proceedings Fourth IEEE Workshop on* (pp. 40-46). IEEE.

Kryftis, Y., Mastorakis, G., Mavromoustakis, C., Mongay Batalla, J., Pallis, E., & Kormentza G. (2016). Efficient Entertainment Services Provision over a Novel Network Architecture. *IEEE Wireless Communications Magazine*.

Kumar, Munjal, & Sharma. (2011). Comparison of Symmetric and Asymmetric Cryptography with Existing Vulnerabilities and Countermeasures. *International Journal of Computer Science and Management Studies, 11*(3).

Lane, D. C. (2000). *You Just Don't Understand Me*. Working Paper, London School of Economics, Operational Research Group.

Lang, W., Patel, J. M., & Naughton, J. F. (2010). On energy management, load balancing and replication. *SIGMOD Record*, *38*(4), 35–42. doi:10.1145/1815948.1815956

Lao, N. W. W. (2010). Fast Query Execution for Retrieval Models Based on Path-Constrained Random Walks. KDD'10, Washington, DC.

Leavitt, N. (2009). Is cloud computing really ready for prime time? Computer, 42(1), 15–25. doi:10.1109/MC.2009.20

Lee, R., & Jeng, B. (2011, October). Load-balancing tactics in cloud. In *Cyber-Enabled Distributed Computing and Knowledge Discovery (CyberC), 2011 International Conference on* (pp. 447-454). IEEE. 10.1109/CyberC.2011.79

Lee, S. G., Chae, S. H., & Cho, K. M. (2013). Drivers and inhibitors of SaaS adoption in Korea. *International Journal of Information Management*, *33*(3), 429–440. doi:10.1016/j.ijinfomgt.2013.01.006

Liang, H., Huang, D., Cai, L. X., Shen, X. S., & Peng, D. (2011). Resource Allocation for Security Services in Mobile Cloud Computing. *Proceedings of IEEE Conference on Computer Communications Workshops INFOCOM WKSHPS 2011*. 10.1109/INFCOMW.2011.5928806

Liang, Z. (2014). *Cloud Data Management*. doi:10.1007/978-3-319-04765-2__2

Liao, X., Jin, H., & Liu, H. (2012). Towards a green cluster through dynamic remapping of virtual machines. *Future Generation Computer Systems*, *28*(2), 469–477. doi:10.1016/j.future.2011.04.013

Li, C., Zhang, Z., & Zhang, L. (2018). A Novel Authorization Scheme for Multimedia Social Networks Under Cloud Storage Method by Using MA-CP-ABE. *International Journal of Cloud Applications and Computing*, *8*(3), 32–47. doi:10.4018/IJCAC.2018070103

Li, H., Dai, Y., Tian, L., & Yang, H. (2009). Identity-based authentication for cloud computing. *Proc. 1st Int. Conf. Cloud Comput.*, *5931*, 157–166. 10.1007/978-3-642-10665-1_14

Li, H., Mao, R., Lai, L., & Qiu, R. (2010). Compressed meter reading for delay-sensitive and secure load report in smart grid. *Proc. 1st Int. Conf. Smart Grid Commun.*, 114–119. 10.1109/SMARTGRID.2010.5622027

Li, J., Huang, L., Zhou, Y., He, S., & Ming, Z. (2017, January). Computation partitioning for mobile cloud computing in big data environment. *IEEE Transactions on Industrial Informatics*, *11*.

Lim, H., & Paterson, K. G. (2011). Identity-based cryptography for grid security. *International Journal of Information Security*, *10*(1), 15–32. doi:10.100710207-010-0116-z

Lin, A., & Chen, N. C. (2012). Cloud computing as an innovation: Percepetion, attitude, and adoption. *International Journal of Information Management*, *32*(6), 533–540. doi:10.1016/j.ijinfomgt.2012.04.001

Li, P., & Xie, W. (2012). A strategic framework for determining e-commerce adoption. *Journal of Technology Management in China*, *7*(1), 22–35. doi:10.1108/17468771211207321

Liu, C. J. (2018.). Finding top-k shortest paths withdiversity. *TKDE, 30*(3), 488–502.

Liu, Z., & Wang, X. (2012, June). A PSO-based algorithm for load balancing in virtual machines of cloud computing environment. In *International Conference in Swarm Intelligence* (pp. 142-147). Springer Berlin Heidelberg. 10.1007/978-3-642-30976-2_17

Liu, H., Xia, F., Yang, Z., & Cao, Y. (2011). An Energy-Efficient Localization Strategy for Smartphones. *Computer Science and Information Systems*, 8(4), 1117–1128. doi:10.2298/CSIS110430065L

Lohman, T. (2011). *DDoS is cloud's security achilles heel.* Retrieved from http://www.computerworld.com.au/article/401127/ddos_cloud_security_achilles_heel/

Low, C., Chen, Y., & Wu, M. (2011). Understanding the determinants of cloud computing adoption. *Industrial Management & Data Systems*, 111(7), 1006–1023. doi:10.1108/02635571111161262

Lu, X., & Gu, Z. (2011, September). A load-adapative cloud resource scheduling model based on ant colony algorithm. In *2011 IEEE International Conference on Cloud Computing and Intelligence Systems* (pp. 296-300). IEEE. 10.1109/CCIS.2011.6045078

Madhavaiah, C., Bashir, I., & Shafi, S. I. (2012). Defining cloud computing in business perspective: A review of Research. *Vision: The Journal of Business Perspective*, 16(3), 163–173. doi:10.1177/0972262912460153

Mahmood, Z. (2011). Data location and security issues in cloud computing. In *Emerging Intelligent Data and Web Technologies (EIDWT), 2011 International Conference on.* IEEE. 10.1109/EIDWT.2011.16

Malarvizhi, N., & Uthariaraj, V. R. (2009, December). Hierarchical load balancing scheme for computational intensive jobs in Grid computing environment. In *2009 First International Conference on Advanced Computing* (pp. 97-104). IEEE. 10.1109/ICADVC.2009.5378268

Malik & Kumar. (2015). Cloud Computing Security Improvement using Diffie Hellman and AES. *International Journal of Computer Applications, 118*(1), 25-28.

Malik, A., & Nazir, M. M. (2012). Security Framework for Cloud Computing Environment: A Review. *Journal of Emerging Trends in Computing and Information Sciences*, 3(3).

Mao, Y., Chen, X., & Li, X. (2014). Max–min task scheduling algorithm for load balance in cloud computing. In *Proceedings of International Conference on Computer Science and Information Technology* (pp. 457-465). Springer India. 10.1007/978-81-322-1759-6_53

Marinescu, D. C. (2017). *Cloud computing: theory and practice.* Morgan Kaufmann.

Marks, A. E., & Lozano, B. (2010). *Executive's guide to cloud computing.* John Wiley & Sons.

Marston, S., Li, Z., Bandyopadhyay, S., Zhang, J., & Ghalsasi, A. (2011). Cloud computing— The business perspective. *Decision Support Systems*, 51(1), 176–189. doi:10.1016/j.dss.2010.12.006

Mathisen, E. (2011). Security challenges and solutions in cloud computing. *5th IEEE International Conference on Digital Ecosystems and Technologies (IEEE DEST 2011).* 10.1109/DEST.2011.5936627

MATLAB and Simulink® Release. (2014a). The MathWorks, Inc.

Matthew, K., & Md, A. (2017). An Effective Way of Evaluating Trust in Inter-cloud Computing. *International Journal of Computer Network and Information Security*, 9(2), 36–42. doi:10.5815/ijcnis.2017.02.05

Mayer, R. C., Davis, J. H., & Schoorman, F. D. (1995). An integrative model of organizational trust. *Academy of Management Review*, 20(3), 709–734. doi:10.5465/amr.1995.9508080335

Mazón, J., Pardillo, J., & Trujillo, J. (2007), A model-driven goal-oriented requirement engineering approach for data warehouses. In *Proceedings, Conference on Advances in Conceptual Modeling: Foundations and Applications, ER Workshops* (pp. 255–264). Auckland, New Zealand: Academic Press. 10.1007/978-3-540-76292-8_31

McAfee. (2018). *Navigating a Cloudy Sky: Practical Guidance and the State of Cloud Security*. Retrieved from https://www.mcafee.com/enterprise/en-us/assets/executive-summaries/es-navigating-cloudy-sky.pdf

McKenty, J. (n.d.). *Nebula's implementation of role based access control (RBAC)*. Retrieved from http://nebula.nasa.gov/blog/2010/06/03/nebulas-implementation-role-based-access-control-rbac/,2010

Mefteh, M., Bouassida, N., & Ben-Abdallah, H. (2018). Towards naturalistic programming: Mapping language-independent requirements to constrained language specifications. *Science of Computer Programming*, *166*, 89–119. doi:10.1016/j.scico.2018.05.006

Mell, P., & Grance, T. (2011). NIST Definition of Cloud Computing - Recommendations of the National Institute of Standards and Technology. National Institute of Standards and Technology Special Publication.

Mell, P., & Grance, T. (2011). *The NIST definition of cloud computing*. Available: https://www.nist.gov/sites/default/files/documents/itl/cloud/cloud-def-v15.pdf

Melland & Grance. (2009). The nist definition of cloud computing. National Institute of Standards and Technology.

Mell, P., & Grance, T. (2009). The NIST definition of cloud computing. *National Institute of Standards and Technology*, *53*(6), 50.

Mell, P., & Grance, T. (2010). The nist definition of cloud computing. *Communications of the ACM*, *53*(6), 50.

Mell, P., & Grance, T. (2010). The NIST definition of cloud computing. *Communications of the ACM*, *53*(6).

Memos, V. A., Psannis, K. E., Ishibashi, Y., Kim, B., & Gupta, B. B. (2018). An Efficient Algorithm for Media-based Surveillance System (EAMSuS) in IoT Smart City Framework. *Future Generation Computer Systems*, *83*, 619–628. doi:10.1016/j.future.2017.04.039

Meng, C. R. C. (2015). Discovering Meta-Paths in Large Heterogeneous Information Networks. WWW 2015, Florence, Italy.

Merkle Tree - Eine Basis der Blockchain. (n.d.). Retrieved from https://blockchainwelt.de

Metheny, M. (2017). *Federal Cloud Computing: The Definitive Guide for Cloud Service Providers*. Elsevier Science.

Michael, S., & Malak, R. E. (2016). *GraphX in Action*. Manning.

Miki, N., Ino, F., & Hagihara, K. (2019). PACC: A directive-based programming framework for out-of-core stencil computation on accelerators. *International Journal of High Performance Computing and Networking*, *13*(1), 19–34. doi:10.1504/IJHPCN.2019.097046

Miles, R., & Hamilton, K. (2006). *Learning UML 2.0*. Boston: O'Reilly Media.

Mishra, S. K., Sahoo, B., & Parida, P. P. (2018). Load balancing in cloud computing: a big picture. *Journal of King Saud University-Computer and Information Sciences*.

Mohammed Banu, A., Trevor, W.-H., & Mostafa, M. (2018). Benefits and Challenges of Cloud Computing Adoption and Usage in Higher Education: A Systematic Literature Review. *International Journal of Enterprise Information Systems*, *14*(4), 64–77. doi:10.4018/IJEIS.2018100105

Mokrys, M. (2012). Possible transformation from Process Model to IS Design Model. *Proceedings, 1th International Virtual Conference*, 71–74.

Mollah, M. B., Azad, M., & Vasilakos, A. (2017, April). Security and privacy challenges in mobile cloud computing: Survey and way ahead. *Journal of Network and Computer Applications*, *84*, 38–54. doi:10.1016/j.jnca.2017.02.001

Mondal, H. S. (2017). Enhancing secure cloud computing environment by Detecting DDoS attack using fuzzy logic. In *2017 3rd International Conference on Electrical Information and Communication Technology (EICT)*. IEEE. 10.1109/EICT.2017.8275211

Mondal, B., Dasgupta, K., & Dutta, P. (2012). Load balancing in cloud computing using stochastic hill climbing-a soft computing approach. *Procedia Technology*, 4, 783–789. doi:10.1016/j.protcy.2012.05.128

Morgan, L., & Conboy, K. (2013).Factors Affecting The Adoption Of Cloud Computing: An Exploratory Study. *Proceedings of the 21st European Conference on Information Systems*, 34(1), 28-36.

Mosco, V. (2015). *To the cloud: Big data in a turbulent world*. Routledge.

Moyano, F., Fernandez-Gago, C., & Lopez, J. (2013). A framework for enabling trust requirements in social cloud applications. *Requirements Engineering*, 18(4), 321–341. doi:10.100700766-013-0171-x

Muangprathub, J. (2014). A Novel Algorithm for Building Concept Lattice. *Applied Mathematical Sciences*, 8(11), 507–515. doi:10.12988/ams.2014.312682

Muchahari, M. K., & Sinha, S. K. (2012). A new trust management architecture for cloud computing environment. In *Cloud and Services Computing (ISCOS), 2012 International Symposium on, 2012*. IEEE.

Muriithi, P., Horner, D. & Pemberton, L. (2016). Factors contributing to adoption and use of information and communication technologies within research collaborations in Kenya. *Information Technology for Development, 22*(sup1), 84-100.

Musa, F. A., & Sani, S. M. (2016). Security Threats and Countermeasures In Cloud Computing. *International Research Journal of Electronics and Computer Engineering*, 2(4), 22–27.

Muttalib Khan, Haroon Khan, & Ahmad. (2008). Security in Cloud by Diffie Hellman Protocol. *International Journal of Engineering and Innovative Technology, 4*(5), 125-128.

Naqvi, S. A. A., Javaid, N., Butt, H., Kamal, M. B., Hamza, A., & Kashif, M. (2018, September). Metaheuristic optimization technique for load balancing in cloud-fog environment integrated with smart grid. In *International Conference on Network-Based Information Systems* (pp. 700-711). Springer, Cham.

Negi, P., Mishra, A., & Gupta, B. B. (2013). *Enhanced CBF packet filtering method to detect DDoS attack in cloud computing environment*. arXiv preprint arXiv:1304.7073

Negi, P., Mishra, A., & Gupta, B. B. (2013). Enhanced CBF Packet Filtering Method to Detect DDoS Attack in Cloud Computing Environment. *Cryptography and Security*. arXiv preprint arXiv:1304.7073

Nelson, M., Lim, B. H., & Hutchins, G. (2005). Fast transparent migration for virtual machines. *USENIX Annual Technical Conference*, 391–394.

Neves, F. T., Marta, F. C., Correia, A. M. R., & Neto, M. D. C. (2011).The adoption of cloud computing by SMEs: identifying and coping with external factors. *Conference Proceedings*.

Ni, J., Huang, Y., Luan, Z., Zhang, J., & Qian, D. (2011, December). Virtual machine mapping policy based on load balancing in private cloud environment. In *Cloud and Service Computing (CSC), 2011 International Conference on* (pp. 292-295). IEEE. 10.1109/CSC.2011.6138536

Nilsson, N. J. (1969). Searching, problem solving, and game-playing trees for minimal cost solutions. In A. J. Morell (Ed.), *IFIP 1968* (Vol. 2, pp. 1556–1562). Amsterdam: North-Holland.

Nishant, K., Sharma, P., Krishna, V., Gupta, C., Singh, K. P., & Rastogi, R. (2012, March). Load balancing of nodes in cloud using ant colony optimization. In *Computer Modelling and Simulation (UKSim), 2012 UKSim 14th International Conference on* (pp. 3-8). IEEE. 10.1109/UKSim.2012.11

Nitin Mehrotra et al. (2019, August 10). *What is Apache Hadoop in Azure HDInsight?* Retrieved from Microsoft Azure: https://docs.microsoft.com/en-us/azure/hdinsight/hadoop/apache-hadoop-introduction

Nkhoma, M., & Dang, D. (2013). Contributing factors of cloud computing adoption: A technology-organisation-environment framework approach. *International Journal of Information Systems and Engineering, 1*(1), 38–49.

Nourani & Fähndrich. (2018*). Direct Product Models and Languages- A Preliminary*. Universal Logic, Vichy, France.

Nourani & Fandlich. (2014). *Factors on Signatured Trees and Semantic Language Processing, Abstract*. DAI-TU Berlin.

Nourani & Moudi. (2008). *Fields, Certificates, and Models*. 1039-12-AMS 2008 Spring Western Section Meeting, Claremont, CA.

Nourani & Schulte. (2011). *SFU, Vancouver, Canada Draft February 2011, Revision 1:September 25, 2012 SFU, Vancouver, Canada Computation Logic Lab. Multiagent Decision Trees, Competitive Models, and Goal Satisfiability*. DICTAP.

Nourani & Schulte. (2015). Computing Predictive Analytics, Business Intelligence, and Economics: Modeling Techniques with Start-ups and Incubators. Publisher Apple Academic Press Inc.

Nourani, C. F. (1996). Slalom Tree Computing- A Computing Theory for Artificial Intelligence. AI Comm., 4(4).

Nourani, C. F. (1998). Intelligent Languages A preliminary Syntactic Theory. *Proceedings of the MFCS'98 satellite workshop on Grammar systems*, 281-287.

Nourani, C. F. (2000). Intelligent Heterogenous Multimedia and Intelligent Active Visual DB and KB. ICCIT 2000, Las Vegas, NV.

Nourani, C. F. (2003). A Sound and Complete Agent Logic Paradigm, 2000. In *Parts and abstract published Fall Symposium*. AAAI Press.

Nourani, C. F. (2003). Versatile Abstract Syntax Meta-Contextual Logic and VR Computing. *36th Lingustische Kolloquium, Austria Proceedings*.

Nourani, C. F. (2005). *Business Planning and Cross Organizational Models Workshop on Collaborative Cross- Organizational Process Design*. Retrieved from http://www.mensch-und-computer.de/mc2005

Nourani, C. F. (2017). *On cryptosigature Protocol Morphic Languages 2017*. Retrieved from https://www.researchgate.net/project/Block-Chain-Protocol-Crypto-Signatures-and-Languages

Nourani. (1998). Agent Computing, KB For Intelligent Forecasting, and Model 15. In *AAAI Wkshp on Agent Based Systems in the Business Context*. AAAI Press.

Nourani. (2000). Cyberspace Interfaces, CyberSignatures, and Business-Business WWW Computing. *Expert Update-Knowledge Based Systems and Applied AI, 3*(3).

Nourani, C. F. (1997). Modelling,Validation,and Hybrid Design of Intelligent Systems. *8th Workshop Knowledge Engineering Methods and Languages*.

Odeh, M., Garcia-Perez, A., & Warwick, K. (2017). Cloud Computing Adoption at Higher Education Institutions in Developing Countries: A Qualitative Investigation of Main Enablers and Barriers. *International Journal of Information and Education Technology (IJIET), 7*(12), 921–927. doi:10.18178/ijiet.2017.7.12.996

OMG-BPMN. (2011). *Business Process Model and Notation (BPMN)-Version 2.0.* Boston: OMG.

OMG-MDA. (2014). *Object Management Group Model Driven Architecture (MDA)MDA Guide rev. 2.0.* Boston: OMG.

OMG-QVT. (2015). *Meta Object Facility (MOF) 2.0 Query/View/Transformation Specification, V1.2.* Boston: OMG.

OMG-SoaML. (2012). *Service Oriented Architecture Modeling Language (SoaML) – Specification for the UML Profile and Metamodel for Services (UPMS).* Boston: OMG.

Ouf, S., & Nasr, M. (2015). Cloud Computing: The Future of Big Data Management. *International Journal of Cloud Applications and Computing, 5*(2), 53–61. doi:10.4018/IJCAC.2015040104

Pacinia, E., Mateosb, C., & Garinoa, C. G. (2014). Balancing Throughput and Response Time in Online Scientific Clouds via Ant Colony Optimization. *Advances in Engineering Software, 84*, 31-47.

Padilha, R., Iano, Y., Moschim, E., & Loschi, H. J. (2017). Computational Simulation Performance Based In Hybrid Model For Broadcasting Systems, in Set. *International Journal Of Broadcast Engineering, 3.*

Padilha, R., Iano, Y., Moschim, E., Monteiro, A. C. B., & Loschi, H. J. (2017a). Computational Simulation Performance based in Hybrid Model for Telecommunication Systems. *BTSym'17, 3.*

Padilha, R., Iano, Y., Moschim, E., Monteiro, A. C. B., & Loschi, H. J. (2017b). Computational Performance of An Hybrid Model for Wireless Telecommunication Systems with Multipath Rayleigh. *BTSym'17, 3.*

Padilha, R., Martins, I. B., & Moschim, E. (2016). Discrete Event Simulation and Dynamical Systems: A study of art. BTSym'16, Campinas, SP, Brazil.

Padilha, R. (2018). Proposta de Um Método Complementar de Compressão de Dados Por Meio da Metodologia de Eventos Discretos Aplicada. In *Um Baixo Nível de Abstração. Dissertação (Mestrado em Engenharia Elétrica).* Campinas, SP, Brasil: Faculdade de Engenharia Elétrica e de Computação, Universidade Estadual de Campinas.

Pan, K., & Chen, J. (2015, September). Load balancing in cloud computing environment based on an improved particle swarm optimization. In *Software Engineering and Service Science (ICSESS), 2015 6th IEEE International Conference on* (pp. 595-598). IEEE. 10.1109/ICSESS.2015.7339128

Pan, J. S., Wang, H., Zhao, H., & Tang, L. (2015). Interaction artificial bee colony based load balance method in cloud computing. In *Genetic and Evolutionary Computing* (pp. 49–57). Springer International Publishing. doi:10.1007/978-3-319-12286-1_6

Patel, G., Mehta, R., & Bhoi, U. (2015). Enhanced Load Balanced Min-min Algorithm for Static Meta Task Scheduling in Cloud Computing. *Procedia Computer Science, 57*, 545–553. doi:10.1016/j.procs.2015.07.385

Patel, P., Bansal, D., Yuan, L., Murthy, A., Greenberg, A., Maltz, D. A., ... Kim, C. (2013, August). Ananta: Cloud scale load balancing. *Computer Communication Review, 43*(4), 207–218. doi:10.1145/2534169.2486026

Pearson, S., & Benameur, A. (2010). Privacy, security and trust issues arising from cloud computing. In *Cloud Computing Technology and Science (CloudCom), 2010 IEEE Second International Conference on, 2010.* IEEE.

Peter, J. P. (1981). Construct validity: A review of basic issues and marketing practices. *JMR, Journal of Marketing Research, 18*(2), 133–145. doi:10.1177/002224378101800201

Peterson, R. A., & Kim, Y. (2013). On the relationship between coefficient alpha and composite reliability. *The Journal of Applied Psychology, 98*(1), 194–198. doi:10.1037/a0030767 PMID:23127213

Pettey, C. (2007). *Gartner estimates ICT industry accounts for 2 percent of global CO2 emissions.* Dostupno na: https://www. gartner. com/newsroom/id/503867

Pfarr, F., & Buckel, T. (2014). Cloud Computing Data Protection – A Literature Review and Analysis. *Proceedings of 47th Hawaii International Conference on System Sciences*, 5018-5027. 10.1109/HICSS.2014.616

Pham, P., & Do, P. (2019). W-MetaPath2Vec: The topic-driven meta-path-based model for large-scaled content-based heterogeneous information network representation learning. *Expert Systems with Applications*, *123*, 328–344. doi:10.1016/j. eswa.2019.01.015

Phuc, D. (2019). A System for Natural language Interaction With the heterogeneous information network. In B. B. Gupta (Ed.), *Handbook of Research on Cloud Computing and Big Data Applications in IoT*. IGI Global.

Plageras, A. P., Psannis, K. E., Stergiou, C., Wang, H., & Gupta, B. B. (2018). Efficient IoT-based sensor BIG Data collection–processing and analysis in smart buildings. *Future Generation Computer Systems*, *82*, 349–357. doi:10.1016/j. future.2017.09.082

Plageras, A. P., Stergiou, C. L., & Psannis, K. E. (2017). Solutions for Inter-connectivity and Security in a Smart Hospital Building. *Proceedings of 15th IEEE International Conference on Industrial Informatics (INDIN 2017)*. 10.1109/INDIN.2017.8104766

Pointcheval, D., & Stern, J. (2000). Security arguments for digital signatures and blind signatures. *Cryptology*, *13*(3), 361–396. doi:10.1007001450010003

Popa, D., Cremene, M., Borda, M., & Boudaoud, K. (2013). A Security Framework for Mobile Cloud Applications. *Proceedings of 11th RoEduNet International Conference*. 10.1109/RoEduNet.2013.6511724

Prasad, M. R., Gyani, J., & Murti, P. R. K. (2012, October). Mobile Cloud Computing: Implications and Challenges. *Journal of Information Engineering and Applications*, *2*(7), 7–15.

Priyadarshinee, P., Raut, R. D., Jha, M. K., & Gardas, B. B. (2017). Understanding and predicting the determinants of cloud computing adoption: A two staged hybrid SEM-Neural Networks Approach. *Computers in Human Behavior*, *76*(1), 341–362. doi:10.1016/j.chb.2017.07.027

Priyadharshini, A. (2013). A survey on security issues and countermeasures in cloud computing storage and a tour towards multi-clouds. *International Journal of Research in Engineering & Technology*, *1*(2), 1–10.

Procaccianti, G., Lago, P., & Bevini, S. (2015). A systematic literature review on energy efficiency in cloud software architectures. *Sustainable Computing: Informatics and Systems*, *7*, 2–10.

Puthal, D., Obaidat, M. S., Nanda, P., Prasad, M., Mohanty, S. P., & Zomaya, A. Y. (2018). Secure and sustainable load balancing of edge data centers in fog computing. *IEEE Communications Magazine*, *56*(5), 60–65. doi:10.1109/MCOM.2018.1700795

Qaisar, S., & Khawaja, K. F. (2012). Cloud computing: Network/ security threats and countermeasures. *Interdisciplinary Journal of Contemporary Research in Business*, *3*(9).

Radhan, T., Patidar, M., Reddy, K., & Asha, A. (2012). *Understanding Shared Technology in Cloud Computing and Data Recovery Vulnerability.* Retrieved from www.ijcst.com

Radojević, B., & Žagar, M. (2011, May). Analysis of issues with load balancing algorithms in hosted (cloud) environments. In *MIPRO, 2011 Proceedings of the 34th International Convention* (pp. 416-420). IEEE.

Ragmani, A., El Omri, A., Abghour, N., Moussaid, K., & Rida, M. (2018). A performed load balancing algorithm for public Cloud computing using ant colony optimization. *Recent Patents on Computer Science, 11*(3), 179–195. doi:10.2174/2213275911666180903124609

Rahimi, M. R., Ren, J., Liu, C. H., Vasilakos, A. V., & Venkatasubramanian, N. (2014, April). Mobile Cloud Computing: A survey, State of Art and Future Directions. *Mobile Networks and Applications, 19*(2), 133–143. doi:10.100711036-013-0477-4

Rai, P. K., & Bunkar, R. K. (2014). Study of security risk and vulnerabilities of cloud computing. *Int. J. Comput. Sci. Mobile Comput., 3*, 490–496.

Rajesh, K., & Sharma, S. (2015). Security Challenges and Issues in Cloud Computing – The Way Ahead. *Int. J. Innov. Res. Adv. Eng., 2*(9), 32–35.

Rakesh, D. H., Bhavsar, R. R., & Thorve, A. S. (2012). Data security over cloud. *International Journal of Computers and Applications*, (5), 11–14.

Rama Krishna, A., Chakravarthy, A. S. N. & Sastry, A. S. C. S. (2016). Variable Modulation Schemes for AWGN Channel based Device to Device Communication. *Indian Journal of Science and Technology, 9*(20).

Ramachandra, G., Iftikar, M., & Khan, F. A. (2017). A Comprehensive Survey on Security in Cloud Computing. *Procedia Computer Science, 110*, 465–472. doi:10.1016/j.procs.2017.06.124

Ramezani, F., Lu, J., & Hussain, F. (2014). Task based system load balancing approach in cloud environments. In *Knowledge Engineering and Management* (pp. 31–42). Springer Berlin Heidelberg. doi:10.1007/978-3-642-37832-4_4

Ramezani, F., Lu, J., & Hussain, F. K. (2014). Task-based system load balancing in cloud computing using particle swarm optimization. *International Journal of Parallel Programming, 42*(5), 739–754. doi:10.100710766-013-0275-4

Rani, B. K., Rani, B. P., & Babu, A. V. (2015). Cloud computing and inter-clouds–types, topologies and research issues. *Procedia Computer Science, 50*, 24–29. doi:10.1016/j.procs.2015.04.006

Rao, B. B. P., Saluia, P., Sharma, N., Mittal, A., & Sharma, S. V. (2012). Cloud computing for Internet of Things & sensing based applications. *Proceedings of IEEE 6th International Conference on Sensing Technology (ICST 2012)*, 374–380. 10.1109/ICSensT.2012.6461705

Rao, R. V., & Selvamani, K. (2015). Data Security Challenges and Its Solutions in Cloud Computing. *Procedia Computer Science*, 48204–48209.

Rathi, K., Kumari, S., & Student, M. (2015). A Survey on Trust in Cloud Computing. *International Journal of Engineering Technology. Management and Applied Sciences, 3*(1), 175–181.

Ren, X., Lin, R., & Zou, H. (2011, September). A dynamic load balancing strategy for cloud computing platform based on exponential smoothing forecast. In *2011 IEEE International Conference on Cloud Computing and Intelligence Systems* (pp. 220-224). IEEE. 10.1109/CCIS.2011.6045063

Rhazali, Y., Hadi, Y., & Mouloudi, A. (2017). A model transformation in MDA from CIM to PIM represented by web models through SoaML and IFML. In *Colloquium in Information Science and Technology, CIST* (pp. 116-121). Tangier, Morocco: Academic Press. DOI: 10.1109/CIST.2016.7805027

Rhazali, Y., Hadi, Y., Chana, I., Lahmer, M., & Rhattoy, A. (2018). A model transformation in model driven architecture from business model to web model. *IAENG International Journal of Computer Science, 45*(1), 104–117.

Rhazali, Y., Hadi, Y., & Mouloudi, A. (2015a). A Methodology of Model Transformation in MDA: From CIM to PIM. *International Review on Computers and Software, 10*(11). doi: 10.15866/irecos.v10i12.8088

Rhazali, Y., Hadi, Y., & Mouloudi, A. (2015b). A Methodology for Transforming CIM to PIM through UML: From Business View to Information System View. *Proceedings, Third World Conference on Complex Systems.* 10.1109/ICoCS.2015.7483318

Rhazali, Y., Hadi, Y., & Mouloudi, A. (2015c). Disciplined Approach for Transformation CIM to PIM in MDA. In *Proceedings, 3rd International Conference on Model-Driven Engineering and Software Development* (pp. 312 – 320). Angers, France: Academic Press. DOI: 10.5220/0005245903120320

Rhazali, Y., Hadi, Y., & Mouloudi, A. (2015d). Transformation Approach CIM to PIM: From Business Processes Models to State Machine and Package Models. In *Proceedings, the 1st International Conference on Open Source Software Computing.* Amman, Jordan: Academic Press. DOI: 10.1109/OSSCOM.2015.7372686

Rhazali, Y., Hadi, Y., & Mouloudi, A. (2016a). CIM to PIM Transformation in MDA: From Service-Oriented Business Models to Web-Based Design Models. *International Journal of Software Engineering and Its Applications, 10*(4), 125–142. doi:10.14257/ijseia.2016.10.4.13

Rhazali, Y., Hadi, Y., & Mouloudi, A. (2016b). Model Transformation with ATL into MDA from CIM to PIM Structured through MVC. *Procedia Computer Science, 83*, 1096–1101. doi:10.1016/j.procs.2016.04.229

Rhazali, Y., Hadi, Y., & Mouloudi, A. (2016c). A Based-Rule Method to Transform CIM to PIM into MDA. *International Journal of Cloud Applications and Computing, 6*(2), 11–24. doi:10.4018/IJCAC.2016040102

Rhazali, Y., Hadi, Y., & Mouloudi, A. (2016d). A new methodology CIM to PIM transformation resulting from an analytical survey. In *Proceedings, 4th International Conference on Model-Driven Engineering and Software Development (MODELSWARD)* (pp. 266-273). Rome, Italy: Academic Press. DOI: 10.5220/0005690102660273

Rittinghouse, J. W., & Ransome, J. F. (2009). *Cloud Computing: Implementation, Management, and Security.* CRC Press.

Rittinghouse, J. W., & Ransome, J. F. (2016). *Cloud computing: implementation, management, and security.* CRC Press.

Rodríguez, A., & García-Rodríguez de Guzmán, I. (2010). Semi-formal transformation of secure business processes into analysis class and use case models: An MDA approach. *Journal of Information and Software Technology, 52*(9), 945–971. doi:10.1016/j.infsof.2010.03.015

Rogers, K., Klump, R., Khurana, H., Aquino-Lugo, A., & Overbye, T. (2010, June). An authenticated control framework for distributed voltage support on the smart grid. *IEEE Transactions on Smart Grid, 1*(1), 40–47. doi:10.1109/TSG.2010.2044816

Roques, P. (2004). *UML in Practice: The Art of Modeling Software Systems Demonstrated through Worked Examples and Solutions.* Wiley.

Rouse, M. (2009). *Virtual machine escape.* Retrieved from http://whatis.techtarget.com/definition/virtual-machine-escape

Rusitschka, S., Eger, K., & Gerdes, C. (2010). Smart grid data cloud: A model for utilizing cloud computing in the smart grid domain. *Proc. 1st Int. Conf. Smart Grid Commun.,* 483–488. 10.1109/SMARTGRID.2010.5622089

Sahoo, S. R., & Gupta, B. B. (2019). Classification of various attacks and their defence mechanism in online social networks: A survey. *Enterprise Information Systems, 13*(6), 832–864. doi:10.1080/17517575.2019.1605542

Sambrekar, K., & Rajpurohit, V. S. (2019). Fast and Efficient Multiview Access Control Mechanism for Cloud Based Agriculture Storage Management System. *International Journal of Cloud Applications and Computing, 9*(1), 33–49. doi:10.4018/IJCAC.2019010103

Sapuntzakis, C. P., Chandra, R., Pfaff, B., Chow, J., Lam, M. S., & Rosenblum, M. (2002). Optimizing the migration of virtual computers. *ACM SIGOPS Operating Systems Review, 36*(SI), 377-390.

Sarddar, D., Sen, P., & Sanyal, M. K. (2016). Central Controller Framework for Mobile Cloud Computing. *International Journal of Grid and Distributed Computing, 9*(4), 233–240. doi:10.14257/ijgdc.2016.9.4.21

Sarkar & Chatterjee. (2014). Enhancing Data Storage Security in Cloud Computing Through Steganography. *ACEEE Int. J. on Network Security, 5*(1), 13-19.

Satyanarayanan, M., Bahl, V., Caceres, R., & Davies, N. (2009). The case for vm-based cloudlets in mobile computing. *IEEE Pervasive Computing, 8*(4), 14–23. doi:10.1109/MPRV.2009.82

Sayler, A., Keller, E., & Grunwald, D. (2013). Jobber: Automating inter-tenant trust in the cloud. *5th USENIX Workshop Hot Topics Cloud Comput.*

Schmidt, D. C. (2006). Guest Editor's Introduction: Model-Driven Engineering. *IEEE Computer, 39*(2), 25–31. doi:10.1109/MC.2006.58

Schneider, S., & Sunyaev, A. (2016). Determinant factors of cloud-sourcing decisions: Reflecting on the IT outsourcing literature in the era of cloud computing. *Journal of Information Technology, 31*(1), 1–31. doi:10.1057/jit.2014.25

Schuldt, J. C. N., Matsuura, K., & Paterson, K. G. (2008). Proxy signatures secure against proxy key exposure. In *Proc. PKC2008*, (pp. 141– 161). Springer. 10.1007/978-3-540-78440-1_9

Sengupta, S., Kaulgud, V., & Sharma, V. S. (2011). Cloud computing security–trends and research directions. *2011 IEEE World Congress on Services*, 524–531. 10.1109/SERVICES.2011.20

Sethi, S., & Sruti, S. (2016). *Cloud security issues and challenges*. Resource Management and Efficiency in Cloud Computing Environments.

Shah, M. A., Swaminathan, R., & Baker, M. (2008). Privacy preserving audit and extraction of digital contents. IACR Cryptology EPrint Archive, 186.

Shahzad, A., & Hussain, M. (2013). Security Issues and Challenges of Mobile Cloud Computing. *International Journal of Grid and Distributed Computing, 6*(6), 37–50. doi:10.14257/ijgdc.2013.6.6.04

Shamir, A. (1984). Identity-based cryptosystems and signature schemes. *Proc. CRYPTO Adv. Cryptol., 196*, 47–53.

Shao, J., Wei, G., Ling, Y., & Xie, M. (2011). Identity-based conditional proxy re-encryption. In *Communications (ICC), 2011 IEEE International Conference on*, (pp. 1-5). IEEE. 10.1109/icc.2011.5962419

Shi, C. X. K. (2013). *HeteSim: A General Framework for Relevance Measure in Heterogeneous Networks*. Retrieved October 31, 2018, from https://arxiv.org/abs/1309.7393

Shi, E., Niu, Y., Jakobsoon, M., & Chow, R. (2010). Implicit Authentica-tion through Learning User Behavior. *Proceedings of ISC'10 13th International Conference on Information Security*, 99-113.

Shiraz, M., Gani, A., Khokhar, R. H., & Buyya, R. (2012, November). A Review on Distributed Application Processing Frameworks in Smart Mobile Devices for Mobile Cloud Computing. *IEEE Communications Surveys and Tutorials, 15*(3), 1294–1313. doi:10.1109/SURV.2012.111412.00045

Sidhu & Mahajan. (2014). Enhancing Security in Cloud Computing Structure by Hybrid Encryption. *International Journal of Recent Scientific Research, 5*(1), 128-132.

Sidhu, M. S., Thulasiraman, P., & Thulasiram, R. K. (2013, April). A load-rebalance PSO heuristic for task matching in heterogeneous computing systems. In *Swarm Intelligence (SIS), 2013 IEEE Symposium on* (pp. 180-187). IEEE. 10.1109/SIS.2013.6615176

Simmhan, Y., Kumbhare, A. G., Cao, B., & Prasanna, V. (2011). An analysis of security and privacy issues in smart grid software architectures on clouds. *Proceedings of IEEE 4th International Conference on Cloud Computing*, 582–589. 10.1109/CLOUD.2011.107

Singh, G., & Kinger, S. (2013). Integrating AES, DES, and 3-DES Encryption Algorithms for Enhanced Data Security. *International Journal of Scientific & Engineering Research, 4*(7).

Singh, A., Juneja, D., & Malhotra, M. (2015). Autonomous agent based load balancing algorithm in cloud computing. *Procedia Computer Science, 45*, 832–841. doi:10.1016/j.procs.2015.03.168

Singh, N., & Vardhan, M. (2019). Distributed Ledger Technology based Property Transaction System with Support for IoT Devices. *International Journal of Cloud Applications and Computing, 9*(2), 60–78. doi:10.4018/IJCAC.2019040104

Singla & Singh. (2013). Cloud Data Security using Authentication and Encryption Technique. *International Journal of Advanced Research in Computer Engineering & Technology, 2*(7), 2232-2235.

Single Sign-On with SAML on force.com. (2013). Retrieved from http://wiki.developerforce.com/page/SingleSign-OnwithSAMLonForce.com

Skourletopoulos, G., Mavromoustakis, C. X., Mastorakis, G., Batalla, J. M., & Sahalos, J. N. (2017, August). An Evaluation of Cloud-Based Mobile Services with Limited Capacity: A Linear Approach. *Springer, Soft Computing, 21*(16), 4523–4530. doi:10.100700500-016-2083-4

Soares, L. F. B., Fernandes, D. A. B., Freire, M. M., & Inacio, P. R. M. (2013). Secure user authentication in cloud computing management interfaces. *Proceedings of the IEEE 32nd International Performance Computing and Communications Conference*, 1-2. 10.1109/PCCC.2013.6742763

Sobragi, C. G., Maçada, A. C. G., & Oliveira, M. (2014). Cloud computing adoption: A multiple case study. *BASE-Revista de Administração e Contabilidade da Unisinos, 11*(1), 75–91.

Soofi, A. A., Khan, M. I., & Amin, F. (2014). Encryption Techniques for Cloud Data Confidentiality. *International Journal of Grid and Distributed Computing, 7*(4), 11–20. doi:10.14257/ijgdc.2014.7.4.02

Sotomayor, B., Montero, R. S., Llorente, I. M., & Foster, I. (2009). Virtual infrastructure management in private and hybrid clouds. *IEEE Internet Computing, 13*(5), 14–22. doi:10.1109/MIC.2009.119

Stergiou, C., Psannis, K. E., Plageras, A. P., Xifilidis, T., & Gupta, B. B. (2018c). Security and Privacy of Big Data for Social Networking Services in Cloud. *Proceedings of IEEE conference on Computer Communications (IEEE INFOCOM 2018)*. 10.1109/INFCOMW.2018.8406831

Stergiou, C., & Psannis, K. E. (2016, May). Recent advances delivered by Mobile Cloud Computing and Internet of Things for Big Data applications: A survey. *International Journal of Network Management*, 1–12.

Stergiou, C., & Psannis, K. E. (2017). Recent advances delivered by Mobile Cloud Computing and Internet of Things for Big Data applications: A survey. *International Journal of Network Management, 27*(3), e1930. doi:10.1002/nem.1930

Stergiou, C., & Psannis, K. E. (2017a). Algorithms for Big Data in Advanced Communication Systems and Cloud Computing. *Proceedings of 19th IEEE Conference on Business Informatics 2017 (CBI2017)*. 10.1109/CBI.2017.28

Stergiou, C., & Psannis, K. E. (2017b, November). Efficient and Secure Big Data delivery in Cloud Computing. *Springer, Multimedia Tools and Applications, 76*(21), 22803–22822. doi:10.100711042-017-4590-4

Stergiou, C., Psannis, K. E., & Gupta, B. B. (2018f). Advanced Media-based Smart Big Data on Intelligent Cloud Systems. *IEEE Transaction on Sustainable Computing.*

Stergiou, C., Psannis, K. E., Gupta, B. B., & Ishibashi, Y. (2018). Security, privacy & efficiency of sustainable cloud computing for big data & IoT. *Sustainable Computing: Informatics and Systems, 19*, 174–184.

Stergiou, C., Psannis, K. E., Gupta, B. B., & Ishibashi, Y. (2018, September). Security, privacy & efficiency of sustainable Cloud Computing for Big Data & IoT. *Sustainable Computing: Informatics and Systems, 19*, 174–184.

Stergiou, C., Psannis, K. E., Gupta, B., & Ishibashi, Y. (2018e, June). Security, Privacy & Efficiency of Sustainable Cloud Computing for Big Data & IoT. *Elsevier, Sustainable Computing, Informatics and Systems.*

Stergiou, C., Psannis, K. E., Kim, B.-G., & Gupta, B. (2018a, January). Secure integration of IoT and Cloud Computing. *Elsevier, Future Generation Computer Systems, 78*(3), 964–975. doi:10.1016/j.future.2016.11.031

Stergiou, C., Psannis, K. E., Plageras, A. P., Ishibashi, Y., & Kim, B.-G. (2018b, March). Algorithms for efficient digital media transmission over IoT and cloud networking. *Journal of Multimedia Information System, 5*(1), 27–34.

Straub, D. W. (1989). Validating instruments in MIS research. *Management Information Systems Quarterly, 13*(2), 147–169. doi:10.2307/248922

Straub, D., Boudreau, M. C., & Gefen, D. (2004). Validation guidelines for IS positivist research. *Communications of the Association for Information Systems, 13*(1), 380–427.

Subashini, S., & Kavitha, V. (2011, January). A survey on security issues in service delivery models of cloud computing. *Journal of Network and Computer Applications, 34*(1), 1–11. doi:10.1016/j.jnca.2010.07.006

Sultan, N. (2010). Cloud computing for education: A new dawn? *International Journal of Information Management, 30*(2), 109–116. doi:10.1016/j.ijinfomgt.2009.09.004

Sun, Y. J. H. (2011). Path-Sim: Meta path-based top-k similarity search in heterogeneous information networks. VLDB, 992–1003.

Sun, D., Chang, G., Sun, L., & Wang, X. (2011). Surveying and analyzing security, privacy and trust issues in cloud computing environments. *Procedia Engineering*, 152852–152856.

Sun, Y., Han, J., Yan, X., Yu, P., & Wu, T. (2011). *Path-Sim: Meta path-based top-k similarity search in heterogeneous information networks.* VLDB.

Sun, Y., Yu, Y., Zhang, X., & Chai, J. (2013). On the security of an identity based proxy signature scheme in the standard model. *IEICE Transactions on Fundamentals of Electronics, Communications and Computer Science, E96–A*(3), 721–723. doi:10.1587/transfun.E96.A.721

Sun, Y., Zhang, J., Xiong, Y., & Zhu, G. (2014). Data Security and Privacy in Cloud Computing. *International Journal of Distributed Sensor Networks*, 1–9.

Suo, H., Liu, Z., Wan, J., & Zhou, K. (2013). Security and Privacy in Mobile Cloud Computing. *Proceedings of 9th International Conference on Wireless Communications and Mobile Computing (IWCMC 2013)*. 10.1109/IWCMC.2013.6583635

Suratno, B., Ozkan, B., Turetken, O., & Grefen, P. (2018). A Method for Operationalizing Service-Dominant Business Models into Conceptual Process Models. *Lecture Notes in Business Information Processing, 319*, 133–148. doi:10.1007/978-3-319-94214-8_9

Tang, L., Pan, J. S., Hu, Y., Ren, P., Tian, Y., & Zhao, H. (2015, August). A Novel Load Balance Algorithm for Cloud Computing. In *International Conference on Genetic and Evolutionary Computing* (pp. 21-30). Springer International Publishing.

Tariq, M. I., Tayyaba, S., Rasheed, H., & Ashraf, M. W. (2017). Factors influencing the Cloud Computing adoption in Higher Education Institutions of Punjab, Pakistan. In *Communication, Computing and Digital Systems (C-CODE), International Conference on, 2017*. IEEE.

Tewari, A., & Gupta, B. B. (2017). Cryptanalysis of a novel ultra-lightweight mutual authentication protocol for IoT devices using RFID tags. *The Journal of Supercomputing, 73*(3), 1085–1102. doi:10.100711227-016-1849-x

Thanh, Ho., & Phuc, Do. (2018). *Social Network Analysis Based on Topic Model with Temporal Factor. International Journal of Knowledge and Systems Science (IJKSS)*.

The Guardian. (2018). *University Research Excellence Framework 2014 – the full rankings*. Available: https://www.theguardian.com/news/datablog/ng-interactive/2014/dec/18/university-research-excellence-framework-2014-full-rankings

The Open Group. (2009). *Risk Taxonomy*. The Open Group.

Thilakarathne, A., & Wijayanayake, J. I. (2014). Security Challenges Of Cloud Computing. *International Journal of Scientific & Technology Research, 3*(11), 200–203.

Tomasz Drabas, D. L. (2017). *Learning PySpark*. Packt.

Tozer, E. P. (2012). *Broadcast Engineer's Reference Book* (1st ed.). Focal Press.

Trivedi, H. (2013). *Cloud Computing Adoption Model for Governments and Large Enterprises (Master of Science in Management)*. MIT School of Engineering.

Ukil, A., Jana, D., & De Sarkar, A. (2013). A security framework in cloud computing infrastructure. *International Journal of Network Security & Its Applications, 5*(5), 11–24. doi:10.5121/ijnsa.2013.5502

Utterback, J. M. (1971). The process of technological innovation within the firm. *Academy of Management Journal, 14*(1), 75–88. doi: 10.2307/254712

Velumadhava Rao, R., & Selvamani, K. (2015). Data Security Challenges and Its Solutions in Cloud Computing. *Elsevier Procedia Computer Science, 48*, 204 – 209.

Velumadhava Raoa, R., & Selvamanib, K. (2015). Data Security Challenges and Its Solutions in Cloud Computing. *International Conference on Computer, Communication and Convergence (ICCC 2015), 48*, 204-209.

Venters, W., & Whitley, E. A. (2012). A critical review of cloud computing: Researching desires and realities. *Journal of Information Technology, 27*(3), 179–197. doi:10.1057/jit.2012.17

Verburg, P. H., Dearing, J. A., Dyke, J. G., van der Leeuw, S., Seitzinger, S., Steffen, W., & Syvitski, J. (2016). Methods and approaches to modelling the anthropocene. *Global Environmental Change, 39*, 328–340. doi:10.1016/j.gloenvcha.2015.08.007

Verma, S., & Sharma, B. (2013). An efficient proxy signature scheme based on RSA cryptosystem. *Int. J. Adv. Sci. Technol., 51*, 121–126.

Viswanathan, P. (2012). *Cloud Computing – Is it Really All That Beneficial?* Available: http://mobiledevices.about.com/od/additionalresources/a/Cloud-Computing-Is-It-Really-All-That-Beneficial.htm

Walterbusch, M., Martens, B., & Teuteberg, F. (2013). Exploring Trust. In *Cloud Computing: A Multi-Method Approach* (p. 145). ECIS.

Wang, S. C., Yan, K. Q., Liao, W. P., & Wang, S. S. (2010, July). Towards a load balancing in a three-level cloud computing network. In *Computer Science and Information Technology (ICCSIT), 2010 3rd IEEE International Conference on* (Vol. 1, pp. 108-113). IEEE.

Wang, T., Liu, Z., Chen, Y., Xu, Y., & Dai, X. (2014, August). Load balancing task scheduling based on genetic algorithm in cloud computing. In *Dependable, Autonomic and Secure Computing (DASC), 2014 IEEE 12th International Conference on* (pp. 146-152). IEEE. 10.1109/DASC.2014.35

Wang, C., Ren, K., Lou, W., & Li, J. (2010, July). Toward publicly auditable secure cloud data storage services. *IEEE Network*, *24*(4), 19–24. doi:10.1109/MNET.2010.5510914

Wang, H. (2013). Proxy provable data possession in public clouds. *IEEE Transactions on Services Computing*, *6*(4), 551–559. doi:10.1109/TSC.2012.35

Wang, H., Han, H., Wang, X., Fang, R., & Mei, W. (2019). A high efficient map-matching algorithm for the GPS data processing intended for the highways. *IJHPCN*, *13*(2), 132–140. doi:10.1504/IJHPCN.2019.097504

Wang, J., Guo, Q., & Wang, Y. (2015). Security analysisi of a designated verifier proxy signature scheme. *Xibei Shifan Daxue Xuebao. Ziran Kexue Ban*, *51*(5), 55–58.

Wang, Q., Wang, C., Ren, K., Lou, W., & Li, J. (2011). Enabling Public Auditability and Data Dynamics for Storage Security in Cloud Computing. *IEEE Transactions on Parallel and Distributed Systems*, *22*(5), 847–859. doi:10.1109/TPDS.2010.183

Wang, T., & Wei, Z. (2016). Analysis of forgery attack on one-time proxy signature and the improvement. *International Journal of Theoretical Physics*, *55*(2), 743–745. doi:10.100710773-015-2711-2

Wang, W., Xu, Y., & Khanna, M. (2011). A survey on the communication architectures in smart grid. *Computer Networks*, *55*(15), 3604–3629. doi:10.1016/j.comnet.2011.07.010

Wasilah, N. L. E., Santosa, P. I., & Ferdiana, R. (2017). Recommendation of cloud computing use for the academic data storage in University in Lampung Province, Indonesia. *2017 7th International Annual Engineering Seminar (InAES)*, 1-5.

Weber. (2016). *Untrusted Business Process Monitoring and Execution Using Blockchain*. Retrieved from http://link.springer.com/chapter/10.1007/978-3-319-45348-4_19

Wei, J., Yang, G., & Mu, Y. (2014). Anonymous proxy signature with restricted traceability. In *Proceedings of 2014 IEEE 13th International Conference on Trust, Security and Privacy in Computing and Communications*, (pp. 575–581). IEEE Press. 10.1109/TrustCom.2014.73

Wei, D., Lu, Y., Jafari, M., Skare, P., & Rohde, K. (2010). An integrated security system of protecting smart grid against cyber attacks. *Proc. Eur. Conf. Innovative Smart Grid Technol.*, 1–7.

Weis, J., & Alves-Foss, J. (2011). Securing database as a service: Issues and compromises. *IEEE Security and Privacy*, *9*(6), 49–55. doi:10.1109/MSP.2011.127

Whaiduzzaman, M., Sookhak, M., Gani, A., & Buyya, R. (2014, April). A survey on vehicular cloud computing. *Journal of Network and Computer Applications*, *40*, 325–344. doi:10.1016/j.jnca.2013.08.004

Whaiduzzaman, Md., & Haque, M. N. (2014, June). A Study on Strategic Provision of Cloud Computing Services. *The Scientific World Journal*, 1–8.

What is a Cloud Provider? (n.d.). Retrieved from: https://azure.microsoft.com/en-in/overview/what-is-a-cloud-provider/

Whitaker, A., Cox, R. S., Shaw, M., & Gribble, S. D. (2004, March). Constructing Services with Interposable Virtual Hardware. In NSDI (pp. 169-182). Academic Press.

Willcocks, L. P., Sauer, C., & Lacity, M. C. (2016). *Enacting Research Methods in Information Systems* (Vol. 2). Palgrave Macmillan.

Willcocks, L., Venters, W., & Whitley, E. (2014). *Moving to the Cloud Corporation*. Palgrave Macmillan. doi:10.1057/9781137347473

Wu, T. Y., Lee, W. T., Lin, Y. S., Lin, Y. S., Chan, H. L., & Huang, J. S. (2012, January). Dynamic load balancing mechanism based on cloud storage. In *Computing, Communications and Applications Conference (ComComAp)*, 2012 (pp. 102-106). IEEE. 10.1109/ComComAp.2012.6154011

Wu, W. W. (2011). Mining significant factors affecting the adoption of SaaS using the rough set approach. *Journal of Systems and Software*, *84*(3), 435–441. doi:10.1016/j.jss.2010.11.890

Wu, W., Mu, Y., Susilo, W., Seberry, J., & Huang, X. Y. (2007). Identity based proxy signature from pairings. In *Proceeding of ATC 2007*, (pp. 22–31). Springer.

Yadav, R. (2015). *Spark Cookbook*. Packt Publishing.

Yadav, V., & Aggarwal, P. (2014). Fingerprinting Based Recursive Information Hiding Strategy in Cloud Computing Environment. *International Journal of Computer Science and Mobile Computing, 3*(5), 702 – 707.

Yaokumah, W., & Amponsah, R. A. (2017). Examining the Contributing Factors for Cloud Computing Adoption in a Developing Country. *International Journal of Enterprise Information Systems, 13*(1), 17–37. doi:10.4018/IJEIS.2017010102

Yassa, S., Chelouah, R., Kadima, H., & Granado, B. (2013). Multi-objective approach for energy-aware workflow scheduling in cloud computing environments. The Scientific World Journal. PubMed.

Yin, H., Zhao, Q., Xu, D., Chen, X., Chang, Y., Yue, H., & Zhao, N. (2019). 1.25 Gbits/s-message experimental transmission utilising chaos-based fibre-optic secure communications over 143 km. *International Journal of High Performance Computing and Networking, 14*(1), 42–51. doi:10.1504/IJHPCN.2019.099738

Yuvaraj, M. (2016). Determining factors for the adoption of cloud computing in developing countries: A case study of Indian academic libraries. *The Bottom Line (New York, N.Y.), 29*(4), 259–272. doi:10.1108/BL-02-2016-0009

Zapata, B. C., Fernández-Alemán, J. L., & Toval, A. (2015). Security in Cloud Computing: A Mapping Study. *Computer Science and Information Systems, 12*(1), 161–184. doi:10.2298/CSIS140205086C

Zargari, S. A. & Smith, A. (2014). Policing as a service in the cloud. *Information Security Journal: A Global Perspective, 23*(4-6), 148-158.

Zhang, Z., & Zhang, X. (2010, May). A load balancing mechanism based on ant colony and complex network theory in open cloud computing federation. In *Industrial Mechatronics and Automation (ICIMA), 2010 2nd International Conference on* (Vol. 2, pp. 240-243). IEEE. 10.1109/ICINDMA.2010.5538385

Zhang, F., & Kim, K. (2003). Efficient id-based blind signature and proxy signature from bilinear pairings. In *Proceedings of ACISP 2003*, (pp. 312–323). Springer. 10.1007/3-540-45067-X_27

Zhang, J., & Mao, J. (2011). Another efficient proxy signature scheme in the standard model. *Journal of Information Science and Engineering, 27*, 1249–1264.

Zhang, J., Tang, W., & Mao, J. (2014). Efficient public verification proof of retrievability scheme in cloud. *Cluster Computing, 17*(4), 1401–1411. doi:10.100710586-014-0394-8

Zhang, T., Lin, W., Wang, Y., Deng, S., Shi, C., & Chen, L. (2010). The design of information security protection framework to support smart grid. *Proc. Int. Conf. Power Syst. Technol.*, 1–5. 10.1109/POWERCON.2010.5666681

Zhang, W., Mei, H., Zhao, H., & Yang, J. (2005). Transformation from CIM to PIM: A Feature-Oriented Component-Based approach. In *Proceedings, MoDELS* (pp. 248-263). Montego Bay, Jamaica: Academic Press. 10.1007/11557432_18

Zhang, Y., Chen, X., Wong, D. S., Li, H., & You, I. (2017). *Ensuring attribute privacy protection and fast decryption for outsourced data security in mobile cloud computing. Elsevier, Information Sciences, 379*, 42–61.

Zheng, Q., Wang, X., Khan, M. K., Zhang, W., Gupta, B. B., & Guo, W. (2018). A lightweight authenticated encryption scheme based on chaotic scml for railway cloud service. *IEEE Access: Practical Innovations, Open Solutions, 6*, 711–722. doi:10.1109/ACCESS.2017.2775038

Zhou, F., Goel, M., Desnoyers, P., & Sundaram, R. (2013). Scheduler vulnerabilities and coordinated attacks in cloud computing. *Journal of Computer Security, 21*(4), 533–559. doi:10.3233/JCS-130474

Zhu, Z. R. C. (2018). Evaluating Top-k Meta Path Queries on Large Heterogeneous Information Networks. IEEE ICDM 2018.

Zhu, S., & Han, Y. (2018, January). Secure data outsourcing scheme in cloud computing with attribute-based encryption. *International Journal of High Performance Computing and Networking, 12*(2), 128–136. doi:10.1504/IJHPCN.2018.094363

Ziebell, R. C., Albors-Garrigos, J., Schoeneberg, K. P., & Marin, M. R. P. (2019). Adoption and Success of e-HRM in a Cloud Computing Environment: A Field Study. *International Journal of Cloud Applications and Computing, 9*(2), 1–27. doi:10.4018/IJCAC.2019040101

Zissis, D., & Lekkas, D. (2012). Addressing cloud computing security issues. *Future Generation Computer Systems, 28*(3), 583–592. doi:10.1016/j.future.2010.12.006

Zkik, Orhanou, & El Hajji. (2017). Secure mobile multi cloud architecture for authentication and data storage. *International Journal of Cloud Applications and Computing, 7*(2).

Zkik, K., Orhanou, G., & El Hajji, S. (2017). Secure mobile multi cloud architecture for authentication and data storage. *International Journal of Cloud Applications and Computing, 7*(2), 62–76. doi:10.4018/IJCAC.2017040105

Related References

To continue our tradition of advancing information science and technology research, we have compiled a list of recommended IGI Global readings. These references will provide additional information and guidance to further enrich your knowledge and assist you with your own research and future publications.

Abbas, R., Michael, K., & Michael, M. G. (2017). What Can People Do with Your Spatial Data?: Socio-Ethical Scenarios. In A. Marrington, D. Kerr, & J. Gammack (Eds.), *Managing Security Issues and the Hidden Dangers of Wearable Technologies* (pp. 206–237). Hershey, PA: IGI Global. doi:10.4018/978-1-5225-1016-1.ch009

Abulaish, M., & Haldar, N. A. (2018). Advances in Digital Forensics Frameworks and Tools: A Comparative Insight and Ranking. *International Journal of Digital Crime and Forensics*, 10(2), 95–119. doi:10.4018/IJDCF.2018040106

Ahmad, F. A., Kumar, P., Shrivastava, G., & Bouhlel, M. S. (2018). Bitcoin: Digital Decentralized Cryptocurrency. In G. Shrivastava, P. Kumar, B. Gupta, S. Bala, & N. Dey (Eds.), *Handbook of Research on Network Forensics and Analysis Techniques* (pp. 395–415). Hershey, PA: IGI Global. doi:10.4018/978-1-5225-4100-4.ch021

Ahmed, A. A. (2017). Investigation Approach for Network Attack Intention Recognition. *International Journal of Digital Crime and Forensics*, 9(1), 17–38. doi:10.4018/IJDCF.2017010102

Akhtar, Z. (2017). Biometric Spoofing and Anti-Spoofing. In M. Dawson, D. Kisku, P. Gupta, J. Sing, & W. Li (Eds.), Developing Next-Generation Countermeasures for Homeland Security Threat Prevention (pp. 121-139). Hershey, PA: IGI Global. doi:10.4018/978-1-5225-0703-1.ch007

Akowuah, F. E., Land, J., Yuan, X., Yang, L., Xu, J., & Wang, H. (2018). Standards and Guides for Implementing Security and Privacy for Health Information Technology. In Y. Maleh (Ed.), *Security and Privacy Management, Techniques, and Protocols* (pp. 214–236). Hershey, PA: IGI Global. doi:10.4018/978-1-5225-5583-4.ch008

Akremi, A., Sallay, H., & Rouached, M. (2018). Intrusion Detection Systems Alerts Reduction: New Approach for Forensics Readiness. In Y. Maleh (Ed.), *Security and Privacy Management, Techniques, and Protocols* (pp. 255–275). Hershey, PA: IGI Global. doi:10.4018/978-1-5225-5583-4.ch010

Aldwairi, M., Hasan, M., & Balbahaith, Z. (2017). Detection of Drive-by Download Attacks Using Machine Learning Approach. *International Journal of Information Security and Privacy*, *11*(4), 16–28. doi:10.4018/IJISP.2017100102

Alohali, B. (2017). Detection Protocol of Possible Crime Scenes Using Internet of Things (IoT). In M. Moore (Ed.), *Cybersecurity Breaches and Issues Surrounding Online Threat Protection* (pp. 175–196). Hershey, PA: IGI Global. doi:10.4018/978-1-5225-1941-6.ch008

AlShahrani, A. M., Al-Abadi, M. A., Al-Malki, A. S., Ashour, A. S., & Dey, N. (2017). Automated System for Crops Recognition and Classification. In N. Dey, A. Ashour, & S. Acharjee (Eds.), *Applied Video Processing in Surveillance and Monitoring Systems* (pp. 54–69). Hershey, PA: IGI Global. doi:10.4018/978-1-5225-1022-2.ch003

Anand, R., Shrivastava, G., Gupta, S., Peng, S., & Sindhwani, N. (2018). Audio Watermarking With Reduced Number of Random Samples. In G. Shrivastava, P. Kumar, B. Gupta, S. Bala, & N. Dey (Eds.), *Handbook of Research on Network Forensics and Analysis Techniques* (pp. 372–394). Hershey, PA: IGI Global. doi:10.4018/978-1-5225-4100-4.ch020

Anand, R., Sinha, A., Bhardwaj, A., & Sreeraj, A. (2018). Flawed Security of Social Network of Things. In G. Shrivastava, P. Kumar, B. Gupta, S. Bala, & N. Dey (Eds.), *Handbook of Research on Network Forensics and Analysis Techniques* (pp. 65–86). Hershey, PA: IGI Global. doi:10.4018/978-1-5225-4100-4.ch005

Aneja, M. J., Bhatia, T., Sharma, G., & Shrivastava, G. (2018). Artificial Intelligence Based Intrusion Detection System to Detect Flooding Attack in VANETs. In G. Shrivastava, P. Kumar, B. Gupta, S. Bala, & N. Dey (Eds.), *Handbook of Research on Network Forensics and Analysis Techniques* (pp. 87–100). Hershey, PA: IGI Global. doi:10.4018/978-1-5225-4100-4.ch006

Antunes, F., Freire, M., & Costa, J. P. (2018). From Motivation and Self-Structure to a Decision-Support Framework for Online Social Networks. In V. Ahuja & S. Rathore (Eds.), *Multidisciplinary Perspectives on Human Capital and Information Technology Professionals* (pp. 116–136). Hershey, PA: IGI Global. doi:10.4018/978-1-5225-5297-0.ch007

Atli, D. (2017). Cybercrimes via Virtual Currencies in International Business. In M. Moore (Ed.), *Cybersecurity Breaches and Issues Surrounding Online Threat Protection* (pp. 121–143). Hershey, PA: IGI Global. doi:10.4018/978-1-5225-1941-6.ch006

Baazeem, R. M. (2018). The Role of Religiosity in Technology Acceptance: The Case of Privacy in Saudi Arabia. In J. McAlaney, L. Frumkin, & V. Benson (Eds.), *Psychological and Behavioral Examinations in Cyber Security* (pp. 172–193). Hershey, PA: IGI Global. doi:10.4018/978-1-5225-4053-3.ch010

Bailey, W. J. (2017). Protection of Critical Homeland Assets: Using a Proactive, Adaptive Security Management Driven Process. In M. Dawson, D. Kisku, P. Gupta, J. Sing, & W. Li (Eds.), Developing Next-Generation Countermeasures for Homeland Security Threat Prevention (pp. 17-50). Hershey, PA: IGI Global. doi: 10.4018/978-1-5225-0703-1.ch002

Bajaj, S. (2018). Current Drift in Energy Efficiency Cloud Computing: New Provocations, Workload Prediction, Consolidation, and Resource Over Commitment. In S. Aljawarneh & M. Malhotra (Eds.), *Critical Research on Scalability and Security Issues in Virtual Cloud Environments* (pp. 283–303). Hershey, PA: IGI Global. doi:10.4018/978-1-5225-3029-9.ch014

Balasubramanian, K. (2018). Hash Functions and Their Applications. In K. Balasubramanian & M. Rajakani (Eds.), *Algorithmic Strategies for Solving Complex Problems in Cryptography* (pp. 66–77). Hershey, PA: IGI Global. doi:10.4018/978-1-5225-2915-6.ch005

Balasubramanian, K. (2018). Recent Developments in Cryptography: A Survey. In K. Balasubramanian & M. Rajakani (Eds.), *Algorithmic Strategies for Solving Complex Problems in Cryptography* (pp. 1–22). Hershey, PA: IGI Global. doi:10.4018/978-1-5225-2915-6.ch001

Balasubramanian, K. (2018). Secure Two Party Computation. In K. Balasubramanian & M. Rajakani (Eds.), *Algorithmic Strategies for Solving Complex Problems in Cryptography* (pp. 145–153). Hershey, PA: IGI Global. doi:10.4018/978-1-5225-2915-6.ch012

Balasubramanian, K. (2018). Securing Public Key Encryption Against Adaptive Chosen Ciphertext Attacks. In K. Balasubramanian & M. Rajakani (Eds.), *Algorithmic Strategies for Solving Complex Problems in Cryptography* (pp. 134–144). Hershey, PA: IGI Global. doi:10.4018/978-1-5225-2915-6.ch011

Balasubramanian, K. (2018). Variants of the Diffie-Hellman Problem. In K. Balasubramanian & M. Rajakani (Eds.), *Algorithmic Strategies for Solving Complex Problems in Cryptography* (pp. 40–54). Hershey, PA: IGI Global. doi:10.4018/978-1-5225-2915-6.ch003

Balasubramanian, K., & K., M. (2018). Secure Group Key Agreement Protocols. In K. Balasubramanian, & M. Rajakani (Eds.), *Algorithmic Strategies for Solving Complex Problems in Cryptography* (pp. 55-65). Hershey, PA: IGI Global. doi: 10.4018/978-1-5225-2915-6.ch004

Balasubramanian, K., & M., R. (2018). Problems in Cryptography and Cryptanalysis. In K. Balasubramanian, & M. Rajakani (Eds.), *Algorithmic Strategies for Solving Complex Problems in Cryptography* (pp. 23-39). Hershey, PA: IGI Global. doi: 10.4018/978-1-5225-2915-6.ch002

Balasubramanian, K., & Abbas, A. M. (2018). Integer Factoring Algorithms. In K. Balasubramanian & M. Rajakani (Eds.), *Algorithmic Strategies for Solving Complex Problems in Cryptography* (pp. 228–240). Hershey, PA: IGI Global. doi:10.4018/978-1-5225-2915-6.ch017

Balasubramanian, K., & Abbas, A. M. (2018). Secure Bootstrapping Using the Trusted Platform Module. In K. Balasubramanian & M. Rajakani (Eds.), *Algorithmic Strategies for Solving Complex Problems in Cryptography* (pp. 167–185). Hershey, PA: IGI Global. doi:10.4018/978-1-5225-2915-6.ch014

Balasubramanian, K., & Mathanan, J. (2018). Cryptographic Voting Protocols. In K. Balasubramanian & M. Rajakani (Eds.), *Algorithmic Strategies for Solving Complex Problems in Cryptography* (pp. 124–133). Hershey, PA: IGI Global. doi:10.4018/978-1-5225-2915-6.ch010

Balasubramanian, K., & Rajakani, M. (2018). Secure Multiparty Computation. In K. Balasubramanian & M. Rajakani (Eds.), *Algorithmic Strategies for Solving Complex Problems in Cryptography* (pp. 154–166). Hershey, PA: IGI Global. doi:10.4018/978-1-5225-2915-6.ch013

Balasubramanian, K., & Rajakani, M. (2018). The Quadratic Sieve Algorithm for Integer Factoring. In K. Balasubramanian & M. Rajakani (Eds.), *Algorithmic Strategies for Solving Complex Problems in Cryptography* (pp. 241–252). Hershey, PA: IGI Global. doi:10.4018/978-1-5225-2915-6.ch018

Barone, P. A. (2017). Defining and Understanding the Development of Juvenile Delinquency from an Environmental, Sociological, and Theoretical Perspective. In S. Egharevba (Ed.), *Police Brutality, Racial Profiling, and Discrimination in the Criminal Justice System* (pp. 215–238). Hershey, PA: IGI Global. doi:10.4018/978-1-5225-1088-8.ch010

Beauchere, J. F. (2018). Encouraging Digital Civility: What Companies and Others Can Do. In R. Luppicini (Ed.), *The Changing Scope of Technoethics in Contemporary Society* (pp. 262–274). Hershey, PA: IGI Global. doi:10.4018/978-1-5225-5094-5.ch014

Behera, C. K., & Bhaskari, D. L. (2017). Malware Methodologies and Its Future: A Survey. *International Journal of Information Security and Privacy*, *11*(4), 47–64. doi:10.4018/IJISP.2017100104

Benson, V., McAlaney, J., & Frumkin, L. A. (2018). Emerging Threats for the Human Element and Countermeasures in Current Cyber Security Landscape. In J. McAlaney, L. Frumkin, & V. Benson (Eds.), *Psychological and Behavioral Examinations in Cyber Security* (pp. 266–271). Hershey, PA: IGI Global. doi:10.4018/978-1-5225-4053-3.ch016

Berbecaru, D. (2018). On Creating Digital Evidence in IP Networks With NetTrack. In G. Shrivastava, P. Kumar, B. Gupta, S. Bala, & N. Dey (Eds.), *Handbook of Research on Network Forensics and Analysis Techniques* (pp. 225–245). Hershey, PA: IGI Global. doi:10.4018/978-1-5225-4100-4.ch012

Berki, E., Valtanen, J., Chaudhary, S., & Li, L. (2018). The Need for Multi-Disciplinary Approaches and Multi-Level Knowledge for Cybersecurity Professionals. In V. Ahuja & S. Rathore (Eds.), *Multidisciplinary Perspectives on Human Capital and Information Technology Professionals* (pp. 72–94). Hershey, PA: IGI Global. doi:10.4018/978-1-5225-5297-0.ch005

Bhardwaj, A. (2017). Ransomware: A Rising Threat of new age Digital Extortion. In S. Aljawarneh (Ed.), *Online Banking Security Measures and Data Protection* (pp. 189–221). Hershey, PA: IGI Global. doi:10.4018/978-1-5225-0864-9.ch012

Bhattacharjee, J., Sengupta, A., Barik, M. S., & Mazumdar, C. (2018). An Analytical Study of Methodologies and Tools for Enterprise Information Security Risk Management. In M. Gupta, R. Sharman, J. Walp, & P. Mulgund (Eds.), *Information Technology Risk Management and Compliance in Modern Organizations* (pp. 1–20). Hershey, PA: IGI Global. doi:10.4018/978-1-5225-2604-9.ch001

Bruno, G. (2018). Handling the Dataflow in Business Process Models. In V. Ahuja & S. Rathore (Eds.), *Multidisciplinary Perspectives on Human Capital and Information Technology Professionals* (pp. 137–151). Hershey, PA: IGI Global. doi:10.4018/978-1-5225-5297-0.ch008

Carneiro, A. D. (2017). Defending Information Networks in Cyberspace: Some Notes on Security Needs. In M. Dawson, D. Kisku, P. Gupta, J. Sing, & W. Li (Eds.), Developing Next-Generation Countermeasures for Homeland Security Threat Prevention (pp. 354-375). Hershey, PA: IGI Global. doi: 10.4018/978-1-5225-0703-1.ch016

Chakraborty, S., Patra, P. K., Maji, P., Ashour, A. S., & Dey, N. (2017). Image Registration Techniques and Frameworks: A Review. In N. Dey, A. Ashour, & S. Acharjee (Eds.), *Applied Video Processing in Surveillance and Monitoring Systems* (pp. 102–114). Hershey, PA: IGI Global. doi:10.4018/978-1-5225-1022-2.ch005

Chaudhari, G., & Mulgund, P. (2018). Strengthening IT Governance With COBIT 5. In M. Gupta, R. Sharman, J. Walp, & P. Mulgund (Eds.), *Information Technology Risk Management and Compliance in Modern Organizations* (pp. 48–69). Hershey, PA: IGI Global. doi:10.4018/978-1-5225-2604-9.ch003

Cheikh, M., Hacini, S., & Boufaida, Z. (2018). Visualization Technique for Intrusion Detection. In Y. Maleh (Ed.), *Security and Privacy Management, Techniques, and Protocols* (pp. 276–290). Hershey, PA: IGI Global. doi:10.4018/978-1-5225-5583-4.ch011

Chen, G., Ding, L., Du, J., Zhou, G., Qin, P., Chen, G., & Liu, Q. (2018). Trust Evaluation Strategy for Single Sign-on Solution in Cloud. *International Journal of Digital Crime and Forensics, 10*(1), 1–11. doi:10.4018/IJDCF.2018010101

Chen, J., & Peng, F. (2018). A Perceptual Encryption Scheme for HEVC Video with Lossless Compression. *International Journal of Digital Crime and Forensics, 10*(1), 67–78. doi:10.4018/IJDCF.2018010106

Chen, K., & Xu, D. (2018). An Efficient Reversible Data Hiding Scheme for Encrypted Images. *International Journal of Digital Crime and Forensics, 10*(2), 1–22. doi:10.4018/IJDCF.2018040101

Chen, Z., Lu, J., Yang, P., & Luo, X. (2017). Recognizing Substitution Steganography of Spatial Domain Based on the Characteristics of Pixels Correlation. *International Journal of Digital Crime and Forensics, 9*(4), 48–61. doi:10.4018/IJDCF.2017100105

Cherkaoui, R., Zbakh, M., Braeken, A., & Touhafi, A. (2018). Anomaly Detection in Cloud Computing and Internet of Things Environments: Latest Technologies. In K. Munir (Ed.), *Cloud Computing Technologies for Green Enterprises* (pp. 251–265). Hershey, PA: IGI Global. doi:10.4018/978-1-5225-3038-1.ch010

Chowdhury, A., Karmakar, G., & Kamruzzaman, J. (2017). Survey of Recent Cyber Security Attacks on Robotic Systems and Their Mitigation Approaches. In R. Kumar, P. Pattnaik, & P. Pandey (Eds.), *Detecting and Mitigating Robotic Cyber Security Risks* (pp. 284–299). Hershey, PA: IGI Global. doi:10.4018/978-1-5225-2154-9.ch019

Cortese, F. A. (2018). The Techoethical Ethos of Technic Self-Determination: Technological Determinism as the Ontic Fundament of Freewill. In R. Luppicini (Ed.), *The Changing Scope of Technoethics in Contemporary Society* (pp. 74–104). Hershey, PA: IGI Global. doi:10.4018/978-1-5225-5094-5.ch005

Crosston, M. D. (2017). The Fight for Cyber Thoreau: Distinguishing Virtual Disobedience from Digital Destruction. In M. Korstanje (Ed.), *Threat Mitigation and Detection of Cyber Warfare and Terrorism Activities* (pp. 198–219). Hershey, PA: IGI Global. doi:10.4018/978-1-5225-1938-6.ch009

da Costa, F., & de Sá-Soares, F. (2017). Authenticity Challenges of Wearable Technologies. In A. Marrington, D. Kerr, & J. Gammack (Eds.), *Managing Security Issues and the Hidden Dangers of Wearable Technologies* (pp. 98–130). Hershey, PA: IGI Global. doi:10.4018/978-1-5225-1016-1.ch005

Dafflon, B., Guériau, M., & Gechter, F. (2017). Using Physics Inspired Wave Agents in a Virtual Environment: Longitudinal Distance Control in Robots Platoon. *International Journal of Monitoring and Surveillance Technologies Research*, 5(2), 15–28. doi:10.4018/IJMSTR.2017040102

Dash, S. R., Sheeraz, A. S., & Samantaray, A. (2018). Filtration and Classification of ECG Signals. In C. Pradhan, H. Das, B. Naik, & N. Dey (Eds.), *Handbook of Research on Information Security in Biomedical Signal Processing* (pp. 72–94). Hershey, PA: IGI Global. doi:10.4018/978-1-5225-5152-2.ch005

Dhavale, S. V. (2018). Insider Attack Analysis in Building Effective Cyber Security for an Organization. In J. McAlaney, L. Frumkin, & V. Benson (Eds.), *Psychological and Behavioral Examinations in Cyber Security* (pp. 222–238). Hershey, PA: IGI Global. doi:10.4018/978-1-5225-4053-3.ch013

Dixit, P. (2018). Security Issues in Web Services. In G. Shrivastava, P. Kumar, B. Gupta, S. Bala, & N. Dey (Eds.), *Handbook of Research on Network Forensics and Analysis Techniques* (pp. 57–64). Hershey, PA: IGI Global. doi:10.4018/978-1-5225-4100-4.ch004

Doraikannan, S. (2018). Efficient Implementation of Digital Signature Algorithms. In K. Balasubramanian & M. Rajakani (Eds.), *Algorithmic Strategies for Solving Complex Problems in Cryptography* (pp. 78–86). Hershey, PA: IGI Global. doi:10.4018/978-1-5225-2915-6.ch006

E., J. V., Mohan, J., & K., A. (2018). Automatic Detection of Tumor and Bleed in Magnetic Resonance Brain Images. In C. Pradhan, H. Das, B. Naik, & N. Dey (Eds.), *Handbook of Research on Information Security in Biomedical Signal Processing* (pp. 291-303). Hershey, PA: IGI Global. doi: 10.4018/978-1-5225-5152-2.ch015

Escamilla, I., Ruíz, M. T., Ibarra, M. M., Soto, V. L., Quintero, R., & Guzmán, G. (2018). Geocoding Tweets Based on Semantic Web and Ontologies. In M. Lytras, N. Aljohani, E. Damiani, & K. Chui (Eds.), *Innovations, Developments, and Applications of Semantic Web and Information Systems* (pp. 372–392). Hershey, PA: IGI Global. doi:10.4018/978-1-5225-5042-6.ch014

Farhadi, M., Haddad, H. M., & Shahriar, H. (2018). Compliance of Electronic Health Record Applications With HIPAA Security and Privacy Requirements. In Y. Maleh (Ed.), *Security and Privacy Management, Techniques, and Protocols* (pp. 199–213). Hershey, PA: IGI Global. doi:10.4018/978-1-5225-5583-4.ch007

Fatma, S. (2018). Use and Misuse of Technology in Marketing: Cases from India. *International Journal of Technoethics*, 9(1), 27–36. doi:10.4018/IJT.2018010103

Fazlali, M., & Khodamoradi, P. (2018). Metamorphic Malware Detection Using Minimal Opcode Statistical Patterns. In Y. Maleh (Ed.), *Security and Privacy Management, Techniques, and Protocols* (pp. 337–359). Hershey, PA: IGI Global. doi:10.4018/978-1-5225-5583-4.ch014

Filiol, É., & Gallais, C. (2017). Optimization of Operational Large-Scale (Cyber) Attacks by a Combinational Approach. *International Journal of Cyber Warfare & Terrorism*, 7(3), 29–43. doi:10.4018/IJCWT.2017070103

Forge, J. (2018). The Case Against Weapons Research. In R. Luppicini (Ed.), *The Changing Scope of Technoethics in Contemporary Society* (pp. 124–134). Hershey, PA: IGI Global. doi:10.4018/978-1-5225-5094-5.ch007

G., S., & Durai, M. S. (2018). Big Data Analytics: An Expedition Through Rapidly Budding Data Exhaustive Era. In D. Lopez, & M. Durai (Eds.), *HCI Challenges and Privacy Preservation in Big Data Security* (pp. 124-138). Hershey, PA: IGI Global. doi: 10.4018/978-1-5225-2863-0.ch006

Gammack, J., & Marrington, A. (2017). The Promise and Perils of Wearable Technologies. In A. Marrington, D. Kerr, & J. Gammack (Eds.), *Managing Security Issues and the Hidden Dangers of Wearable Technologies* (pp. 1–17). Hershey, PA: IGI Global. doi:10.4018/978-1-5225-1016-1.ch001

Gamoura, S. C. (2018). A Cloud-Based Approach for Cross-Management of Disaster Plans: Managing Risk in Networked Enterprises. In S. Aljawarneh & M. Malhotra (Eds.), *Critical Research on Scalability and Security Issues in Virtual Cloud Environments* (pp. 240–268). Hershey, PA: IGI Global. doi:10.4018/978-1-5225-3029-9.ch012

Gao, L., Gao, T., Zhao, J., & Liu, Y. (2018). Reversible Watermarking in Digital Image Using PVO and RDWT. *International Journal of Digital Crime and Forensics*, *10*(2), 40–55. doi:10.4018/IJDCF.2018040103

Geetha, S., & Sindhu, S. S. (2016). Audio Stego Intrusion Detection System through Hybrid Neural Tree Model. In B. Gupta, D. Agrawal, & S. Yamaguchi (Eds.), *Handbook of Research on Modern Cryptographic Solutions for Computer and Cyber Security* (pp. 126–144). Hershey, PA: IGI Global. doi:10.4018/978-1-5225-0105-3.ch006

Geethanjali, P. (2018). Bio-Inspired Techniques in Human-Computer Interface for Control of Assistive Devices: Bio-Inspired Techniques in Assistive Devices. In D. Lopez & M. Durai (Eds.), *HCI Challenges and Privacy Preservation in Big Data Security* (pp. 23–46). Hershey, PA: IGI Global. doi:10.4018/978-1-5225-2863-0.ch002

Ghany, K. K., & Zawbaa, H. M. (2017). Hybrid Biometrics and Watermarking Authentication. In S. Zoughbi (Ed.), *Securing Government Information and Data in Developing Countries* (pp. 37–61). Hershey, PA: IGI Global. doi:10.4018/978-1-5225-1703-0.ch003

Hacini, S., Guessoum, Z., & Cheikh, M. (2018). False Alarm Reduction: A Profiling Mechanism and New Research Directions. In Y. Maleh (Ed.), *Security and Privacy Management, Techniques, and Protocols* (pp. 291–320). Hershey, PA: IGI Global. doi:10.4018/978-1-5225-5583-4.ch012

Hadlington, L. (2018). The "Human Factor" in Cybersecurity: Exploring the Accidental Insider. In J. McAlaney, L. Frumkin, & V. Benson (Eds.), Psychological and Behavioral Examinations in Cyber Security (pp. 46-63). Hershey, PA: IGI Global. doi: 10.4018/978-1-5225-4053-3.ch003

Haldorai, A., & Ramu, A. (2018). The Impact of Big Data Analytics and Challenges to Cyber Security. In G. Shrivastava, P. Kumar, B. Gupta, S. Bala, & N. Dey (Eds.), *Handbook of Research on Network Forensics and Analysis Techniques* (pp. 300–314). Hershey, PA: IGI Global. doi:10.4018/978-1-5225-4100-4.ch016

Hariharan, S., Prasanth, V. S., & Saravanan, P. (2018). Role of Bibliographical Databases in Measuring Information: A Conceptual View. In J. Jeyasekar & P. Saravanan (Eds.), *Innovations in Measuring and Evaluating Scientific Information* (pp. 61–71). Hershey, PA: IGI Global. doi:10.4018/978-1-5225-3457-0.ch005

Hore, S., Chatterjee, S., Chakraborty, S., & Shaw, R. K. (2017). Analysis of Different Feature Description Algorithm in object Recognition. In N. Dey, A. Ashour, & P. Patra (Eds.), *Feature Detectors and Motion Detection in Video Processing* (pp. 66–99). Hershey, PA: IGI Global. doi:10.4018/978-1-5225-1025-3.ch004

Hurley, J. S. (2017). Cyberspace: The New Battlefield - An Approach via the Analytics Hierarchy Process. *International Journal of Cyber Warfare & Terrorism*, 7(3), 1–15. doi:10.4018/IJCWT.2017070101

Hussain, M., & Kaliya, N. (2018). An Improvised Framework for Privacy Preservation in IoT. *International Journal of Information Security and Privacy*, 12(2), 46–63. doi:10.4018/IJISP.2018040104

Ilahi-Amri, M., Cheniti-Belcadhi, L., & Braham, R. (2018). Competence E-Assessment Based on Semantic Web: From Modeling to Validation. In V. Ahuja & S. Rathore (Eds.), *Multidisciplinary Perspectives on Human Capital and Information Technology Professionals* (pp. 246–267). Hershey, PA: IGI Global. doi:10.4018/978-1-5225-5297-0.ch013

Jambhekar, N., & Dhawale, C. A. (2018). Cryptography in Big Data Security. In D. Lopez & M. Durai (Eds.), *HCI Challenges and Privacy Preservation in Big Data Security* (pp. 71–94). Hershey, PA: IGI Global. doi:10.4018/978-1-5225-2863-0.ch004

Jansen van Vuuren, J., Leenen, L., Plint, G., Zaaiman, J., & Phahlamohlaka, J. (2017). Formulating the Building Blocks for National Cyberpower. *International Journal of Cyber Warfare & Terrorism*, 7(3), 16–28. doi:10.4018/IJCWT.2017070102

Jaswal, S., & Malhotra, M. (2018). Identification of Various Privacy and Trust Issues in Cloud Computing Environment. In S. Aljawarneh & M. Malhotra (Eds.), *Critical Research on Scalability and Security Issues in Virtual Cloud Environments* (pp. 95–121). Hershey, PA: IGI Global. doi:10.4018/978-1-5225-3029-9.ch005

Jaswal, S., & Singh, G. (2018). A Comprehensive Survey on Trust Issue and Its Deployed Models in Computing Environment. In S. Aljawarneh & M. Malhotra (Eds.), *Critical Research on Scalability and Security Issues in Virtual Cloud Environments* (pp. 150–166). Hershey, PA: IGI Global. doi:10.4018/978-1-5225-3029-9.ch007

Javid, T. (2018). Secure Access to Biomedical Images. In C. Pradhan, H. Das, B. Naik, & N. Dey (Eds.), *Handbook of Research on Information Security in Biomedical Signal Processing* (pp. 38–53). Hershey, PA: IGI Global. doi:10.4018/978-1-5225-5152-2.ch003

Jeyakumar, B., Durai, M. S., & Lopez, D. (2018). Case Studies in Amalgamation of Deep Learning and Big Data. In D. Lopez & M. Durai (Eds.), *HCI Challenges and Privacy Preservation in Big Data Security* (pp. 159–174). Hershey, PA: IGI Global. doi:10.4018/978-1-5225-2863-0.ch008

Jeyaprakash, H. M. K., K., & S., G. (2018). A Comparative Review of Various Machine Learning Approaches for Improving the Performance of Stego Anomaly Detection. In G. Shrivastava, P. Kumar, B. Gupta, S. Bala, & N. Dey (Eds.), Handbook of Research on Network Forensics and Analysis Techniques (pp. 351-371). Hershey, PA: IGI Global. doi: 10.4018/978-1-5225-4100-4.ch019

Jeyasekar, J. J. (2018). Dynamics of Indian Forensic Science Research. In J. Jeyasekar & P. Saravanan (Eds.), *Innovations in Measuring and Evaluating Scientific Information* (pp. 125–147). Hershey, PA: IGI Global. doi:10.4018/978-1-5225-3457-0.ch009

Jones, H. S., & Moncur, W. (2018). The Role of Psychology in Understanding Online Trust. In J. McAlaney, L. Frumkin, & V. Benson (Eds.), *Psychological and Behavioral Examinations in Cyber Security* (pp. 109–132). Hershey, PA: IGI Global. doi:10.4018/978-1-5225-4053-3.ch007

Jones, H. S., & Towse, J. (2018). Examinations of Email Fraud Susceptibility: Perspectives From Academic Research and Industry Practice. In J. McAlaney, L. Frumkin, & V. Benson (Eds.), *Psychological and Behavioral Examinations in Cyber Security* (pp. 80–97). Hershey, PA: IGI Global. doi:10.4018/978-1-5225-4053-3.ch005

Joseph, A., & Singh, K. J. (2018). Digital Forensics in Distributed Environment. In G. Shrivastava, P. Kumar, B. Gupta, S. Bala, & N. Dey (Eds.), *Handbook of Research on Network Forensics and Analysis Techniques* (pp. 246–265). Hershey, PA: IGI Global. doi:10.4018/978-1-5225-4100-4.ch013

K., I., & A, V. (2018). Monitoring and Auditing in the Cloud. In K. Munir (Ed.), *Cloud Computing Technologies for Green Enterprises* (pp. 318-350). Hershey, PA: IGI Global. doi: 10.4018/978-1-5225-3038-1.ch013

Kashyap, R., & Piersson, A. D. (2018). Impact of Big Data on Security. In G. Shrivastava, P. Kumar, B. Gupta, S. Bala, & N. Dey (Eds.), *Handbook of Research on Network Forensics and Analysis Techniques* (pp. 283–299). Hershey, PA: IGI Global. doi:10.4018/978-1-5225-4100-4.ch015

Kastrati, Z., Imran, A. S., & Yayilgan, S. Y. (2018). A Hybrid Concept Learning Approach to Ontology Enrichment. In M. Lytras, N. Aljohani, E. Damiani, & K. Chui (Eds.), *Innovations, Developments, and Applications of Semantic Web and Information Systems* (pp. 85–119). Hershey, PA: IGI Global. doi:10.4018/978-1-5225-5042-6.ch004

Kaur, H., & Saxena, S. (2018). UWDBCSN Analysis During Node Replication Attack in WSN. In C. Pradhan, H. Das, B. Naik, & N. Dey (Eds.), *Handbook of Research on Information Security in Biomedical Signal Processing* (pp. 210–227). Hershey, PA: IGI Global. doi:10.4018/978-1-5225-5152-2.ch011

Kaushal, P. K., & Sobti, R. (2018). Breaching Security of Full Round Tiny Encryption Algorithm. *International Journal of Information Security and Privacy*, *12*(1), 89–98. doi:10.4018/IJISP.2018010108

Kavati, I., Prasad, M. V., & Bhagvati, C. (2017). Search Space Reduction in Biometric Databases: A Review. In M. Dawson, D. Kisku, P. Gupta, J. Sing, & W. Li (Eds.), Developing Next-Generation Countermeasures for Homeland Security Threat Prevention (pp. 236-262). Hershey, PA: IGI Global. doi:10.4018/978-1-5225-0703-1.ch011

Kaye, L. K. (2018). Online Research Methods. In J. McAlaney, L. Frumkin, & V. Benson (Eds.), *Psychological and Behavioral Examinations in Cyber Security* (pp. 253–265). Hershey, PA: IGI Global. doi:10.4018/978-1-5225-4053-3.ch015

Kenekar, T. V., & Dani, A. R. (2017). Privacy Preserving Data Mining on Unstructured Data. In S. Tamane, V. Solanki, & N. Dey (Eds.), *Privacy and Security Policies in Big Data* (pp. 167–190). Hershey, PA: IGI Global. doi:10.4018/978-1-5225-2486-1.ch008

Khaire, P. A., & Kotkondawar, R. R. (2017). Measures of Image and Video Segmentation. In N. Dey, A. Ashour, & S. Acharjee (Eds.), *Applied Video Processing in Surveillance and Monitoring Systems* (pp. 28–53). Hershey, PA: IGI Global. doi:10.4018/978-1-5225-1022-2.ch002

Knibbs, C., Goss, S., & Anthony, K. (2017). Counsellors' Phenomenological Experiences of Working with Children or Young People who have been Cyberbullied: Using Thematic Analysis of Semi Structured Interviews. *International Journal of Technoethics*, 8(1), 68–86. doi:10.4018/IJT.2017010106

Ko, A., & Gillani, S. (2018). Ontology Maintenance Through Semantic Text Mining: An Application for IT Governance Domain. In M. Lytras, N. Aljohani, E. Damiani, & K. Chui (Eds.), *Innovations, Developments, and Applications of Semantic Web and Information Systems* (pp. 350–371). Hershey, PA: IGI Global. doi:10.4018/978-1-5225-5042-6.ch013

Kohler, J., Lorenz, C. R., Gumbel, M., Specht, T., & Simov, K. (2017). A Security-By-Distribution Approach to Manage Big Data in a Federation of Untrustworthy Clouds. In S. Tamane, V. Solanki, & N. Dey (Eds.), *Privacy and Security Policies in Big Data* (pp. 92–123). Hershey, PA: IGI Global. doi:10.4018/978-1-5225-2486-1.ch005

Korstanje, M. E. (2017). English Speaking Countries and the Culture of Fear: Understanding Technology and Terrorism. In M. Korstanje (Ed.), *Threat Mitigation and Detection of Cyber Warfare and Terrorism Activities* (pp. 92–110). Hershey, PA: IGI Global. doi:10.4018/978-1-5225-1938-6.ch005

Korstanje, M. E. (2018). How Can World Leaders Understand the Perverse Core of Terrorism?: Terror in the Global Village. In C. Akrivopoulou (Ed.), *Global Perspectives on Human Migration, Asylum, and Security* (pp. 48–67). Hershey, PA: IGI Global. doi:10.4018/978-1-5225-2817-3.ch003

Krishnamachariar, P. K., & Gupta, M. (2018). Swimming Upstream in Turbulent Waters: Auditing Agile Development. In M. Gupta, R. Sharman, J. Walp, & P. Mulgund (Eds.), *Information Technology Risk Management and Compliance in Modern Organizations* (pp. 268–300). Hershey, PA: IGI Global. doi:10.4018/978-1-5225-2604-9.ch010

Ksiazak, P., Farrelly, W., & Curran, K. (2018). A Lightweight Authentication and Encryption Protocol for Secure Communications Between Resource-Limited Devices Without Hardware Modification: Resource-Limited Device Authentication. In Y. Maleh (Ed.), *Security and Privacy Management, Techniques, and Protocols* (pp. 1–46). Hershey, PA: IGI Global. doi:10.4018/978-1-5225-5583-4.ch001

Kukkuvada, A., & Basavaraju, P. (2018). Mutual Correlation-Based Anonymization for Privacy Preserving Medical Data Publishing. In C. Pradhan, H. Das, B. Naik, & N. Dey (Eds.), *Handbook of Research on Information Security in Biomedical Signal Processing* (pp. 304–319). Hershey, PA: IGI Global. doi:10.4018/978-1-5225-5152-2.ch016

Kumar, G., & Saini, H. (2018). Secure and Robust Telemedicine using ECC on Radix-8 with Formal Verification. *International Journal of Information Security and Privacy*, 12(1), 13–28. doi:10.4018/IJISP.2018010102

Kumar, M., & Bhandari, A. (2017). Performance Evaluation of Web Server's Request Queue against AL-DDoS Attacks in NS-2. *International Journal of Information Security and Privacy*, 11(4), 29–46. doi:10.4018/IJISP.2017100103

Kumar, M., & Vardhan, M. (2018). Privacy Preserving and Efficient Outsourcing Algorithm to Public Cloud: A Case of Statistical Analysis. *International Journal of Information Security and Privacy*, *12*(2), 1–25. doi:10.4018/IJISP.2018040101

Kumar, R. (2018). A Robust Biometrics System Using Finger Knuckle Print. In G. Shrivastava, P. Kumar, B. Gupta, S. Bala, & N. Dey (Eds.), *Handbook of Research on Network Forensics and Analysis Techniques* (pp. 416–446). Hershey, PA: IGI Global. doi:10.4018/978-1-5225-4100-4.ch022

Kumar, R. (2018). DOS Attacks on Cloud Platform: Their Solutions and Implications. In S. Aljawarneh & M. Malhotra (Eds.), *Critical Research on Scalability and Security Issues in Virtual Cloud Environments* (pp. 167–184). Hershey, PA: IGI Global. doi:10.4018/978-1-5225-3029-9.ch008

Kumari, R., & Sharma, K. (2018). Cross-Layer Based Intrusion Detection and Prevention for Network. In G. Shrivastava, P. Kumar, B. Gupta, S. Bala, & N. Dey (Eds.), *Handbook of Research on Network Forensics and Analysis Techniques* (pp. 38–56). Hershey, PA: IGI Global. doi:10.4018/978-1-5225-4100-4.ch003

Lapke, M. (2018). A Semiotic Examination of the Security Policy Lifecycle. In Y. Maleh (Ed.), *Security and Privacy Management, Techniques, and Protocols* (pp. 237–253). Hershey, PA: IGI Global. doi:10.4018/978-1-5225-5583-4.ch009

Liang, Z., Feng, B., Xu, X., Wu, X., & Yang, T. (2018). Geometrically Invariant Image Watermarking Using Histogram Adjustment. *International Journal of Digital Crime and Forensics*, *10*(1), 54–66. doi:10.4018/IJDCF.2018010105

Liu, Z. J. (2017). A Cyber Crime Investigation Model Based on Case Characteristics. *International Journal of Digital Crime and Forensics*, *9*(4), 40–47. doi:10.4018/IJDCF.2017100104

Loganathan, S. (2018). A Step-by-Step Procedural Methodology for Improving an Organization's IT Risk Management System. In M. Gupta, R. Sharman, J. Walp, & P. Mulgund (Eds.), *Information Technology Risk Management and Compliance in Modern Organizations* (pp. 21–47). Hershey, PA: IGI Global. doi:10.4018/978-1-5225-2604-9.ch002

Long, M., Peng, F., & Gong, X. (2018). A Format-Compliant Encryption for Secure HEVC Video Sharing in Multimedia Social Network. *International Journal of Digital Crime and Forensics*, *10*(2), 23–39. doi:10.4018/IJDCF.2018040102

M., S., & M., J. (2018). Biosignal Denoising Techniques. In C. Pradhan, H. Das, B. Naik, & N. Dey (Eds.), *Handbook of Research on Information Security in Biomedical Signal Processing* (pp. 26-37). Hershey, PA: IGI Global. doi: 10.4018/978-1-5225-5152-2.ch002

Mahapatra, C. (2017). Pragmatic Solutions to Cyber Security Threat in Indian Context. In R. Kumar, P. Pattnaik, & P. Pandey (Eds.), *Detecting and Mitigating Robotic Cyber Security Risks* (pp. 172–176). Hershey, PA: IGI Global. doi:10.4018/978-1-5225-2154-9.ch012

Majumder, A., Nath, S., & Das, A. (2018). Data Integrity in Mobile Cloud Computing. In K. Munir (Ed.), *Cloud Computing Technologies for Green Enterprises* (pp. 166–199). Hershey, PA: IGI Global. doi:10.4018/978-1-5225-3038-1.ch007

Maleh, Y., Zaydi, M., Sahid, A., & Ezzati, A. (2018). Building a Maturity Framework for Information Security Governance Through an Empirical Study in Organizations. In Y. Maleh (Ed.), *Security and Privacy Management, Techniques, and Protocols* (pp. 96–127). Hershey, PA: IGI Global. doi:10.4018/978-1-5225-5583-4.ch004

Malhotra, M., & Singh, A. (2018). Role of Agents to Enhance the Security and Scalability in Cloud Environment. In S. Aljawarneh & M. Malhotra (Eds.), *Critical Research on Scalability and Security Issues in Virtual Cloud Environments* (pp. 19–47). Hershey, PA: IGI Global. doi:10.4018/978-1-5225-3029-9.ch002

Mali, A. D. (2017). Recent Advances in Minimally-Obtrusive Monitoring of People's Health. *International Journal of Monitoring and Surveillance Technologies Research*, *5*(2), 44–56. doi:10.4018/IJMSTR.2017040104

Mali, A. D., & Yang, N. (2017). On Automated Generation of Keyboard Layout to Reduce Finger-Travel Distance. *International Journal of Monitoring and Surveillance Technologies Research*, *5*(2), 29–43. doi:10.4018/IJMSTR.2017040103

Mali, P. (2018). Defining Cyber Weapon in Context of Technology and Law. *International Journal of Cyber Warfare & Terrorism*, *8*(1), 43–55. doi:10.4018/IJCWT.2018010104

Malik, A., & Pandey, B. (2018). CIAS: A Comprehensive Identity Authentication Scheme for Providing Security in VANET. *International Journal of Information Security and Privacy*, *12*(1), 29–41. doi:10.4018/IJISP.2018010103

Manikandakumar, M., & Ramanujam, E. (2018). Security and Privacy Challenges in Big Data Environment. In G. Shrivastava, P. Kumar, B. Gupta, S. Bala, & N. Dey (Eds.), *Handbook of Research on Network Forensics and Analysis Techniques* (pp. 315–325). Hershey, PA: IGI Global. doi:10.4018/978-1-5225-4100-4.ch017

Manogaran, G., Thota, C., & Lopez, D. (2018). Human-Computer Interaction With Big Data Analytics. In D. Lopez & M. Durai (Eds.), *HCI Challenges and Privacy Preservation in Big Data Security* (pp. 1–22). Hershey, PA: IGI Global. doi:10.4018/978-1-5225-2863-0.ch001

Mariappan, P. B. P., & Teja, T. S. (2016). Digital Forensic and Machine Learning. In S. Geetha & A. Phamila (Eds.), *Combating Security Breaches and Criminal Activity in the Digital Sphere* (pp. 141–156). Hershey, PA: IGI Global. doi:10.4018/978-1-5225-0193-0.ch009

Marques, R., Mota, A., & Mota, L. (2016). Understanding Anti-Forensics Techniques for Combating Digital Security Breaches and Criminal Activity. In S. Geetha & A. Phamila (Eds.), *Combating Security Breaches and Criminal Activity in the Digital Sphere* (pp. 233–241). Hershey, PA: IGI Global. doi:10.4018/978-1-5225-0193-0.ch014

Mbale, J. (2018). Computer Centres Resource Cloud Elasticity-Scalability (CRECES): Copperbelt University Case Study. In S. Aljawarneh & M. Malhotra (Eds.), *Critical Research on Scalability and Security Issues in Virtual Cloud Environments* (pp. 48–70). Hershey, PA: IGI Global. doi:10.4018/978-1-5225-3029-9.ch003

McAvoy, D. (2017). Institutional Entrepreneurship in Defence Acquisition: What Don't We Understand? In K. Burgess & P. Antill (Eds.), *Emerging Strategies in Defense Acquisitions and Military Procurement* (pp. 222–241). Hershey, PA: IGI Global. doi:10.4018/978-1-5225-0599-0.ch013

McKeague, J., & Curran, K. (2018). Detecting the Use of Anonymous Proxies. *International Journal of Digital Crime and Forensics, 10*(2), 74–94. doi:10.4018/IJDCF.2018040105

Meitei, T. G., Singh, S. A., & Majumder, S. (2018). PCG-Based Biometrics. In C. Pradhan, H. Das, B. Naik, & N. Dey (Eds.), *Handbook of Research on Information Security in Biomedical Signal Processing* (pp. 1–25). Hershey, PA: IGI Global. doi:10.4018/978-1-5225-5152-2.ch001

Menemencioğlu, O., & Orak, İ. M. (2017). A Simple Solution to Prevent Parameter Tampering in Web Applications. In M. Korstanje (Ed.), *Threat Mitigation and Detection of Cyber Warfare and Terrorism Activities* (pp. 1–20). Hershey, PA: IGI Global. doi:10.4018/978-1-5225-1938-6.ch001

Minto-Coy, I. D., & Henlin, M. G. (2017). The Development of Cybersecurity Policy and Legislative Landscape in Latin America and Caribbean States. In M. Moore (Ed.), *Cybersecurity Breaches and Issues Surrounding Online Threat Protection* (pp. 24–53). Hershey, PA: IGI Global. doi:10.4018/978-1-5225-1941-6.ch002

Mire, A. V., Dhok, S. B., Mistry, N. J., & Porey, P. D. (2016). Tampering Localization in Double Compressed Images by Investigating Noise Quantization. *International Journal of Digital Crime and Forensics, 8*(3), 46–62. doi:10.4018/IJDCF.2016070104

Mohamed, J. H. (2018). Scientograph-Based Visualization of Computer Forensics Research Literature. In J. Jeyasekar & P. Saravanan (Eds.), *Innovations in Measuring and Evaluating Scientific Information* (pp. 148–162). Hershey, PA: IGI Global. doi:10.4018/978-1-5225-3457-0.ch010

Mohan Murthy, M. K., & Sanjay, H. A. (2018). Scalability for Cloud. In S. Aljawarneh & M. Malhotra (Eds.), *Critical Research on Scalability and Security Issues in Virtual Cloud Environments* (pp. 1–18). Hershey, PA: IGI Global. doi:10.4018/978-1-5225-3029-9.ch001

Moorthy, U., & Gandhi, U. D. (2018). A Survey of Big Data Analytics Using Machine Learning Algorithms. In D. Lopez & M. Durai (Eds.), *HCI Challenges and Privacy Preservation in Big Data Security* (pp. 95–123). Hershey, PA: IGI Global. doi:10.4018/978-1-5225-2863-0.ch005

Mountantonakis, M., Minadakis, N., Marketakis, Y., Fafalios, P., & Tzitzikas, Y. (2018). Connectivity, Value, and Evolution of a Semantic Warehouse. In M. Lytras, N. Aljohani, E. Damiani, & K. Chui (Eds.), *Innovations, Developments, and Applications of Semantic Web and Information Systems* (pp. 1–31). Hershey, PA: IGI Global. doi:10.4018/978-1-5225-5042-6.ch001

Moussa, M., & Demurjian, S. A. (2017). Differential Privacy Approach for Big Data Privacy in Healthcare. In S. Tamane, V. Solanki, & N. Dey (Eds.), *Privacy and Security Policies in Big Data* (pp. 191–213). Hershey, PA: IGI Global. doi:10.4018/978-1-5225-2486-1.ch009

Mugisha, E., Zhang, G., El Abidine, M. Z., & Eugene, M. (2017). A TPM-based Secure Multi-Cloud Storage Architecture grounded on Erasure Codes. *International Journal of Information Security and Privacy, 11*(1), 52–64. doi:10.4018/IJISP.2017010104

Nachtigall, L. G., Araujo, R. M., & Nachtigall, G. R. (2017). Use of Images of Leaves and Fruits of Apple Trees for Automatic Identification of Symptoms of Diseases and Nutritional Disorders. *International Journal of Monitoring and Surveillance Technologies Research*, *5*(2), 1–14. doi:10.4018/IJMSTR.2017040101

Nagesh, K., Sumathy, R., Devakumar, P., & Sathiyamurthy, K. (2017). A Survey on Denial of Service Attacks and Preclusions. *International Journal of Information Security and Privacy*, *11*(4), 1–15. doi:10.4018/IJISP.2017100101

Nanda, A., Popat, P., & Vimalkumar, D. (2018). Navigating Through Choppy Waters of PCI DSS Compliance. In M. Gupta, R. Sharman, J. Walp, & P. Mulgund (Eds.), *Information Technology Risk Management and Compliance in Modern Organizations* (pp. 99–140). Hershey, PA: IGI Global. doi:10.4018/978-1-5225-2604-9.ch005

Newton, S. (2017). The Determinants of Stock Market Development in Emerging Economies: Examining the Impact of Corporate Governance and Regulatory Reforms (I). In M. Ojo & J. Van Akkeren (Eds.), *Value Relevance of Accounting Information in Capital Markets* (pp. 114–125). Hershey, PA: IGI Global. doi:10.4018/978-1-5225-1900-3.ch008

Nidhyananthan, S. S. A., J. V., & R., S. S. (2018). Wireless Enhanced Security Based on Speech Recognition. In C. Pradhan, H. Das, B. Naik, & N. Dey (Eds.), Handbook of Research on Information Security in Biomedical Signal Processing (pp. 228-253). Hershey, PA: IGI Global. doi: 10.4018/978-1-5225-5152-2.ch012

Norri-Sederholm, T., Huhtinen, A., & Paakkonen, H. (2018). Ensuring Public Safety Organisations' Information Flow and Situation Picture in Hybrid Environments. *International Journal of Cyber Warfare & Terrorism*, *8*(1), 12–24. doi:10.4018/IJCWT.2018010102

Nunez, S., & Castaño, R. (2017). Building Brands in Emerging Economies: A Consumer-Oriented Approach. In Rajagopal, & R. Behl (Eds.), Business Analytics and Cyber Security Management in Organizations (pp. 183-194). Hershey, PA: IGI Global. doi:10.4018/978-1-5225-0902-8.ch013

Odella, F. (2018). Privacy Awareness and the Networking Generation. *International Journal of Technoethics*, *9*(1), 51–70. doi:10.4018/IJT.2018010105

Ojo, M., & DiGabriele, J. A. (2017). Fundamental or Enhancing Roles?: The Dual Roles of External Auditors and Forensic Accountants. In M. Ojo & J. Van Akkeren (Eds.), *Value Relevance of Accounting Information in Capital Markets* (pp. 59–78). Hershey, PA: IGI Global. doi:10.4018/978-1-5225-1900-3.ch004

P., P., & Subbiah, G. (2016). Visual Cryptography for Securing Images in Cloud. In S. Geetha, & A. Phamila (Eds.), *Combating Security Breaches and Criminal Activity in the Digital Sphere* (pp. 242-262). Hershey, PA: IGI Global. doi: 10.4018/978-1-5225-0193-0.ch015

Pandey, S. (2018). An Empirical Study of the Indian IT Sector on Typologies of Workaholism as Predictors of HR Crisis. In V. Ahuja & S. Rathore (Eds.), *Multidisciplinary Perspectives on Human Capital and Information Technology Professionals* (pp. 202–224). Hershey, PA: IGI Global. doi:10.4018/978-1-5225-5297-0.ch011

Pattabiraman, A., Srinivasan, S., Swaminathan, K., & Gupta, M. (2018). Fortifying Corporate Human Wall: A Literature Review of Security Awareness and Training. In M. Gupta, R. Sharman, J. Walp, & P. Mulgund (Eds.), *Information Technology Risk Management and Compliance in Modern Organizations* (pp. 142–175). Hershey, PA: IGI Global. doi:10.4018/978-1-5225-2604-9.ch006

Prachi. (2018). Detection of Botnet Based Attacks on Network: Using Machine Learning Techniques. In G. Shrivastava, P. Kumar, B. Gupta, S. Bala, & N. Dey (Eds.), *Handbook of Research on Network Forensics and Analysis Techniques* (pp. 101-116). Hershey, PA: IGI Global. doi: 10.4018/978-1-5225-4100-4.ch007

Pradhan, P. L. (2017). Proposed Round Robin CIA Pattern on RTS for Risk Assessment. *International Journal of Digital Crime and Forensics*, *9*(1), 71–85. doi:10.4018/IJDCF.2017010105

Prentice, S., & Taylor, P. J. (2018). Psychological and Behavioral Examinations of Online Terrorism. In J. McAlaney, L. Frumkin, & V. Benson (Eds.), *Psychological and Behavioral Examinations in Cyber Security* (pp. 151–171). Hershey, PA: IGI Global. doi:10.4018/978-1-5225-4053-3.ch009

Priyadarshini, I. (2017). Cyber Security Risks in Robotics. In R. Kumar, P. Pattnaik, & P. Pandey (Eds.), *Detecting and Mitigating Robotic Cyber Security Risks* (pp. 333–348). Hershey, PA: IGI Global. doi:10.4018/978-1-5225-2154-9.ch022

R., A., & D., E. (2018). Cyber Crime Toolkit Development. In G. Shrivastava, P. Kumar, B. Gupta, S. Bala, & N. Dey (Eds.), *Handbook of Research on Network Forensics and Analysis Techniques* (pp. 184-224). Hershey, PA: IGI Global. doi: 10.4018/978-1-5225-4100-4.ch011

Raghunath, R. (2018). Research Trends in Forensic Sciences: A Scientometric Approach. In J. Jeyasekar & P. Saravanan (Eds.), *Innovations in Measuring and Evaluating Scientific Information* (pp. 108–124). Hershey, PA: IGI Global. doi:10.4018/978-1-5225-3457-0.ch008

Ramadhas, G., Sankar, A. S., & Sugathan, N. (2018). The Scientific Communication Process in Homoeopathic Toxicology: An Evaluative Study. In J. Jeyasekar & P. Saravanan (Eds.), *Innovations in Measuring and Evaluating Scientific Information* (pp. 163–179). Hershey, PA: IGI Global. doi:10.4018/978-1-5225-3457-0.ch011

Ramani, K. (2018). Impact of Big Data on Security: Big Data Security Issues and Defense Schemes. In G. Shrivastava, P. Kumar, B. Gupta, S. Bala, & N. Dey (Eds.), *Handbook of Research on Network Forensics and Analysis Techniques* (pp. 326–350). Hershey, PA: IGI Global. doi:10.4018/978-1-5225-4100-4.ch018

Ramos, P., Funderburk, P., & Gebelein, J. (2018). Social Media and Online Gaming: A Masquerading Funding Source. *International Journal of Cyber Warfare & Terrorism*, *8*(1), 25–42. doi:10.4018/IJCWT.2018010103

Rao, N., & Srivastava, S., & K.S., S. (2017). PKI Deployment Challenges and Recommendations for ICS Networks. *International Journal of Information Security and Privacy*, *11*(2), 38–48. doi:10.4018/IJISP.2017040104

Rath, M., Swain, J., Pati, B., & Pattanayak, B. K. (2018). Network Security: Attacks and Control in MANET. In G. Shrivastava, P. Kumar, B. Gupta, S. Bala, & N. Dey (Eds.), *Handbook of Research on Network Forensics and Analysis Techniques* (pp. 19–37). Hershey, PA: IGI Global. doi:10.4018/978-1-5225-4100-4.ch002

Ricci, J., Baggili, I., & Breitinger, F. (2017). Watch What You Wear: Smartwatches and Sluggish Security. In A. Marrington, D. Kerr, & J. Gammack (Eds.), *Managing Security Issues and the Hidden Dangers of Wearable Technologies* (pp. 47–73). Hershey, PA: IGI Global. doi:10.4018/978-1-5225-1016-1.ch003

Rossi, J. A. (2017). Revisiting the Value Relevance of Accounting Information in the Italian and UK Stock Markets. In M. Ojo & J. Van Akkeren (Eds.), *Value Relevance of Accounting Information in Capital Markets* (pp. 102–113). Hershey, PA: IGI Global. doi:10.4018/978-1-5225-1900-3.ch007

Rowe, N. C. (2016). Privacy Concerns with Digital Forensics. In R. Cropf & T. Bagwell (Eds.), *Ethical Issues and Citizen Rights in the Era of Digital Government Surveillance* (pp. 145–162). Hershey, PA: IGI Global. doi:10.4018/978-1-4666-9905-2.ch008

Sabillon, R., Serra-Ruiz, J., Cavaller, V., & Cano, J. J. (2017). Digital Forensic Analysis of Cybercrimes: Best Practices and Methodologies. *International Journal of Information Security and Privacy*, *11*(2), 25–37. doi:10.4018/IJISP.2017040103

Sample, C., Cowley, J., & Bakdash, J. Z. (2018). Cyber + Culture: Exploring the Relationship. In J. McAlaney, L. Frumkin, & V. Benson (Eds.), *Psychological and Behavioral Examinations in Cyber Security* (pp. 64–79). Hershey, PA: IGI Global. doi:10.4018/978-1-5225-4053-3.ch004

Sarıgöllü, S. C., Aksakal, E., Koca, M. G., Akten, E., & Aslanbay, Y. (2018). Volunteered Surveillance. In J. McAlaney, L. Frumkin, & V. Benson (Eds.), *Psychological and Behavioral Examinations in Cyber Security* (pp. 133–150). Hershey, PA: IGI Global. doi:10.4018/978-1-5225-4053-3.ch008

Shahriar, H., Clincy, V., & Bond, W. (2018). Classification of Web-Service-Based Attacks and Mitigation Techniques. In Y. Maleh (Ed.), *Security and Privacy Management, Techniques, and Protocols* (pp. 360–378). Hershey, PA: IGI Global. doi:10.4018/978-1-5225-5583-4.ch015

Shet, S., Aswath, A. R., Hanumantharaju, M. C., & Gao, X. (2017). Design of Reconfigurable Architectures for Steganography System. In N. Dey, A. Ashour, & S. Acharjee (Eds.), *Applied Video Processing in Surveillance and Monitoring Systems* (pp. 145–168). Hershey, PA: IGI Global. doi:10.4018/978-1-5225-1022-2.ch007

Shrivastava, G., Sharma, K., Khari, M., & Zohora, S. E. (2018). Role of Cyber Security and Cyber Forensics in India. In G. Shrivastava, P. Kumar, B. Gupta, S. Bala, & N. Dey (Eds.), *Handbook of Research on Network Forensics and Analysis Techniques* (pp. 143–161). Hershey, PA: IGI Global. doi:10.4018/978-1-5225-4100-4.ch009

Singh, N. (2016). Cloud Crime and Fraud: A Study of Challenges for Cloud Security and Forensics. In S. Geetha & A. Phamila (Eds.), *Combating Security Breaches and Criminal Activity in the Digital Sphere* (pp. 68–84). Hershey, PA: IGI Global. doi:10.4018/978-1-5225-0193-0.ch005

Singh, N., Mittal, T., & Gupta, M. (2018). A Tale of Policies and Breaches: Analytical Approach to Construct Social Media Policy. In M. Gupta, R. Sharman, J. Walp, & P. Mulgund (Eds.), *Information Technology Risk Management and Compliance in Modern Organizations* (pp. 176–212). Hershey, PA: IGI Global. doi:10.4018/978-1-5225-2604-9.ch007

Singh, R., & Jalota, H. (2018). A Study of Good-Enough Security in the Context of Rural Business Process Outsourcing. In J. McAlaney, L. Frumkin, & V. Benson (Eds.), *Psychological and Behavioral Examinations in Cyber Security* (pp. 239–252). Hershey, PA: IGI Global. doi:10.4018/978-1-5225-4053-3.ch014

Sivasubramanian, K. E. (2018). Authorship Pattern and Collaborative Research Productivity of Asian Journal of Dairy and Food Research During the Year 2011 to 2015. In J. Jeyasekar & P. Saravanan (Eds.), *Innovations in Measuring and Evaluating Scientific Information* (pp. 213–222). Hershey, PA: IGI Global. doi:10.4018/978-1-5225-3457-0.ch014

Somasundaram, R., & Thirugnanam, M. (2017). IoT in Healthcare: Breaching Security Issues. In N. Jeyanthi & R. Thandeeswaran (Eds.), *Security Breaches and Threat Prevention in the Internet of Things* (pp. 174–188). Hershey, PA: IGI Global. doi:10.4018/978-1-5225-2296-6.ch008

Sonam, & Khari, M. (2018). Wireless Sensor Networks: A Technical Survey. In G. Shrivastava, P. Kumar, B. Gupta, S. Bala, & N. Dey (Eds.), *Handbook of Research on Network Forensics and Analysis Techniques* (pp. 1-18). Hershey, PA: IGI Global. doi: 10.4018/978-1-5225-4100-4.ch001

Soni, P. (2018). Implications of HIPAA and Subsequent Regulations on Information Technology. In M. Gupta, R. Sharman, J. Walp, & P. Mulgund (Eds.), *Information Technology Risk Management and Compliance in Modern Organizations* (pp. 71–98). Hershey, PA: IGI Global. doi:10.4018/978-1-5225-2604-9.ch004

Sönmez, F. Ö., & Günel, B. (2018). Security Visualization Extended Review Issues, Classifications, Validation Methods, Trends, Extensions. In Y. Maleh (Ed.), *Security and Privacy Management, Techniques, and Protocols* (pp. 152–197). Hershey, PA: IGI Global. doi:10.4018/978-1-5225-5583-4.ch006

Srivastava, S. R., & Dube, S. (2018). Cyberattacks, Cybercrime and Cyberterrorism. In G. Shrivastava, P. Kumar, B. Gupta, S. Bala, & N. Dey (Eds.), *Handbook of Research on Network Forensics and Analysis Techniques* (pp. 162–183). Hershey, PA: IGI Global. doi:10.4018/978-1-5225-4100-4.ch010

Stacey, E. (2017). Contemporary Terror on the Net. In *Combating Internet-Enabled Terrorism: Emerging Research and Opportunities* (pp. 16–44). Hershey, PA: IGI Global. doi:10.4018/978-1-5225-2190-7.ch002

Sumana, M., Hareesha, K. S., & Kumar, S. (2018). Semantically Secure Classifiers for Privacy Preserving Data Mining. In Y. Maleh (Ed.), *Security and Privacy Management, Techniques, and Protocols* (pp. 66–95). Hershey, PA: IGI Global. doi:10.4018/978-1-5225-5583-4.ch003

Suresh, N., & Gupta, M. (2018). Impact of Technology Innovation: A Study on Cloud Risk Mitigation. In M. Gupta, R. Sharman, J. Walp, & P. Mulgund (Eds.), *Information Technology Risk Management and Compliance in Modern Organizations* (pp. 229–267). Hershey, PA: IGI Global. doi:10.4018/978-1-5225-2604-9.ch009

Survey, A. K. Balasubramanian & M. Rajakani (Eds.), *Algorithmic Strategies for Solving Complex Problems in Cryptography* (pp. 111–123). Hershey, PA: IGI Global. doi:10.4018/978-1-5225-2915-6.ch009

Tank, D. M. (2017). Security and Privacy Issues, Solutions, and Tools for MCC. In K. Munir (Ed.), *Security Management in Mobile Cloud Computing* (pp. 121–147). Hershey, PA: IGI Global. doi:10.4018/978-1-5225-0602-7.ch006

Thackray, H., & McAlaney, J. (2018). Groups Online: Hacktivism and Social Protest. In J. McAlaney, L. Frumkin, & V. Benson (Eds.), *Psychological and Behavioral Examinations in Cyber Security* (pp. 194–209). Hershey, PA: IGI Global. doi:10.4018/978-1-5225-4053-3.ch011

Thandeeswaran, R., Pawar, R., & Rai, M. (2017). Security Threats in Autonomous Vehicles. In N. Jeyanthi & R. Thandeeswaran (Eds.), *Security Breaches and Threat Prevention in the Internet of Things* (pp. 117–141). Hershey, PA: IGI Global. doi:10.4018/978-1-5225-2296-6.ch006

Thota, C., Manogaran, G., Lopez, D., & Vijayakumar, V. (2017). Big Data Security Framework for Distributed Cloud Data Centers. In M. Moore (Ed.), *Cybersecurity Breaches and Issues Surrounding Online Threat Protection* (pp. 288–310). Hershey, PA: IGI Global. doi:10.4018/978-1-5225-1941-6.ch012

Thukral, S., & Rodriguez, T. D. (2018). Child Sexual Abuse: Intra- and Extra-Familial Risk Factors, Reactions, and Interventions. In R. Gopalan (Ed.), *Social, Psychological, and Forensic Perspectives on Sexual Abuse* (pp. 229–258). Hershey, PA: IGI Global. doi:10.4018/978-1-5225-3958-2.ch017

Tidke, S. (2017). MonogDB: Data Management in NoSQL. In S. Tamane, V. Solanki, & N. Dey (Eds.), *Privacy and Security Policies in Big Data* (pp. 64–91). Hershey, PA: IGI Global. doi:10.4018/978-1-5225-2486-1.ch004

Tierney, M. (2018). #TerroristFinancing: An Examination of Terrorism Financing via the Internet. *International Journal of Cyber Warfare & Terrorism*, 8(1), 1–11. doi:10.4018/IJCWT.2018010101

Topal, R. (2018). A Cyber-Psychological and Behavioral Approach to Online Radicalization. In J. McAlaney, L. Frumkin, & V. Benson (Eds.), *Psychological and Behavioral Examinations in Cyber Security* (pp. 210–221). Hershey, PA: IGI Global. doi:10.4018/978-1-5225-4053-3.ch012

Tripathy, B. K., & Baktha, K. (2018). Clustering Approaches. In *Security, Privacy, and Anonymization in Social Networks: Emerging Research and Opportunities* (pp. 51–85). Hershey, PA: IGI Global. doi:10.4018/978-1-5225-5158-4.ch004

Tripathy, B. K., & Baktha, K. (2018). De-Anonymization Techniques. In *Security, Privacy, and Anonymization in Social Networks: Emerging Research and Opportunities* (pp. 137–147). Hershey, PA: IGI Global. doi:10.4018/978-1-5225-5158-4.ch007

Tripathy, B. K., & Baktha, K. (2018). Fundamentals of Social Networks. In *Security, Privacy, and Anonymization in Social Networks: Emerging Research and Opportunities* (pp. 1–22). Hershey, PA: IGI Global. doi:10.4018/978-1-5225-5158-4.ch001

Tripathy, B. K., & Baktha, K. (2018). Graph Modification Approaches. In *Security, Privacy, and Anonymization in Social Networks: Emerging Research and Opportunities* (pp. 86–115). Hershey, PA: IGI Global. doi:10.4018/978-1-5225-5158-4.ch005

Tripathy, B. K., & Baktha, K. (2018). Social Network Anonymization Techniques. In *Security, Privacy, and Anonymization in Social Networks: Emerging Research and Opportunities* (pp. 36–50). Hershey, PA: IGI Global. doi:10.4018/978-1-5225-5158-4.ch003

Tsimperidis, I., Rostami, S., & Katos, V. (2017). Age Detection Through Keystroke Dynamics from User Authentication Failures. *International Journal of Digital Crime and Forensics*, *9*(1), 1–16. doi:10.4018/IJDCF.2017010101

Wadkar, H. S., Mishra, A., & Dixit, A. M. (2017). Framework to Secure Browser Using Configuration Analysis. *International Journal of Information Security and Privacy*, *11*(2), 49–63. doi:10.4018/IJISP.2017040105

Wahlgren, G., & Kowalski, S. J. (2018). IT Security Risk Management Model for Handling IT-Related Security Incidents: The Need for a New Escalation Approach. In Y. Maleh (Ed.), *Security and Privacy Management, Techniques, and Protocols* (pp. 129–151). Hershey, PA: IGI Global. doi:10.4018/978-1-5225-5583-4.ch005

Wall, H. J., & Kaye, L. K. (2018). Online Decision Making: Online Influence and Implications for Cyber Security. In J. McAlaney, L. Frumkin, & V. Benson (Eds.), *Psychological and Behavioral Examinations in Cyber Security* (pp. 1–25). Hershey, PA: IGI Global. doi:10.4018/978-1-5225-4053-3.ch001

Xylogiannopoulos, K. F., Karampelas, P., & Alhajj, R. (2017). Advanced Network Data Analytics for Large-Scale DDoS Attack Detection. *International Journal of Cyber Warfare & Terrorism*, *7*(3), 44–54. doi:10.4018/IJCWT.2017070104

Yan, W. Q., Wu, X., & Liu, F. (2018). Progressive Scrambling for Social Media. *International Journal of Digital Crime and Forensics*, *10*(2), 56–73. doi:10.4018/IJDCF.2018040104

Yang, L., Gao, T., Xuan, Y., & Gao, H. (2016). Contrast Modification Forensics Algorithm Based on Merged Weight Histogram of Run Length. *International Journal of Digital Crime and Forensics*, *8*(2), 27–35. doi:10.4018/IJDCF.2016040103

Yassein, M. B., Mardini, W., & Al-Abdi, A. (2018). Security Issues in the Internet of Things: A Review. In S. Aljawarneh & M. Malhotra (Eds.), *Critical Research on Scalability and Security Issues in Virtual Cloud Environments* (pp. 186–200). Hershey, PA: IGI Global. doi:10.4018/978-1-5225-3029-9.ch009

Yassein, M. B., Shatnawi, M., & l-Qasem, N. (2018). A Survey of Probabilistic Broadcast Schemes in Mobile Ad Hoc Networks. In S. Aljawarneh, & M. Malhotra (Eds.), *Critical Research on Scalability and Security Issues in Virtual Cloud Environments* (pp. 269-282). Hershey, PA: IGI Global. doi: 10.4018/978-1-5225-3029-9.ch013

Yue, C., Tianliang, L., Manchun, C., & Jingying, L. (2018). Evaluation of the Attack Effect Based on Improved Grey Clustering Model. *International Journal of Digital Crime and Forensics*, *10*(1), 92–100. doi:10.4018/IJDCF.2018010108

Zhang, P., He, Y., & Chow, K. (2018). Fraud Track on Secure Electronic Check System. *International Journal of Digital Crime and Forensics*, *10*(2), 137–144. doi:10.4018/IJDCF.2018040108

Zhao, J., Wang, Q., Guo, J., Gao, L., & Yang, F. (2016). An Overview on Passive Image Forensics Technology for Automatic Computer Forgery. *International Journal of Digital Crime and Forensics*, *8*(4), 14–25. doi:10.4018/IJDCF.2016100102

Zhao, X., Zhu, J., & Yu, H. (2016). On More Paradigms of Steganalysis. *International Journal of Digital Crime and Forensics*, *8*(2), 1–15. doi:10.4018/IJDCF.2016040101

Zhou, L., Yan, W. Q., Shu, Y., & Yu, J. (2018). CVSS: A Cloud-Based Visual Surveillance System. *International Journal of Digital Crime and Forensics*, *10*(1), 79–91. doi:10.4018/IJDCF.2018010107

Zhu, J., Guan, Q., Zhao, X., Cao, Y., & Chen, G. (2017). A Steganalytic Scheme Based on Classifier Selection Using Joint Image Characteristics. *International Journal of Digital Crime and Forensics*, *9*(4), 1–14. doi:10.4018/IJDCF.2017100101

Zoughbi, S. (2017). Major Technology Trends Affecting Government Data in Developing Countries. In S. Zoughbi (Ed.), *Securing Government Information and Data in Developing Countries* (pp. 127–135). Hershey, PA: IGI Global. doi:10.4018/978-1-5225-1703-0.ch008

Zubairu, B. (2018). Security Risks of Biomedical Data Processing in Cloud Computing Environment. In C. Pradhan, H. Das, B. Naik, & N. Dey (Eds.), *Handbook of Research on Information Security in Biomedical Signal Processing* (pp. 177–197). Hershey, PA: IGI Global. doi:10.4018/978-1-5225-5152-2.ch009

About the Contributors

Brij B. Gupta received PhD degree from Indian Institute of Technology Roorkee, India in the area of information security. He has published more than 200 research papers in international journals and conferences of high repute. He has visited several countries to present his research work. His biography has published in the Marquis Who's Who in the World, 2012. At present, he is working as an Assistant Professor in the Department of Computer Engineering, National Institute of Technology Kurukshetra, India. His research interest includes information security, cyber security, cloud computing, web security, intrusion detection, computer networks and phishing.

* * *

Mohammed Ali is an assistant professor who is currently affiliated with the Alliance Manchester business school, The University of Manchester. His research interests includes Digital Strategy and Technological innovation adoption in Organisations. He has publications in the area of Cloud Computing, ERP systems, Internet of The Things, Social Media and Cyber Security. He has contributed to several co-author publications. Mohammed has also published in the International Journal of Enterprise Information Systems IGI-Global, British Academic of Management, AJBM and the International Journal of Cloud Application and Computing (IJCAC). Mohammed is currently involved with valorous projects in the area of Digital Business and submitted chapter of books and journal papers which are under review expected to publish soon.

Rangel Arthur holds a degree in Electrical Engineering from the Paulista State University Júlio de Mesquita Filho (1999), a Master's degree in Electrical Engineering (2002) and a PhD in Electrical Engineering (2007) from the State University of Campinas. Over the years from 2011 to 2014 he was Coordinator and Associate Coordinator of Technology Courses in Telecommunication Systems and Telecommunication Engineering of FT, which was created in its management. From 2015 to 2016 he was Associate Director of the Technology (FT) of Unicamp. He is currently lecturer and advisor to the Innovation Agency (Inova) of Unicamp. He has experience in the area of Electrical Engineering, with emphasis on Telecommunications Systems, working mainly on the following topics: computer vision, embedded systems and control systems

Rabindra K. Barik is currently working as an Assistant Professor in the School of Computer Applications, Kalinga Institute of Industrial Technology, Bhubaneswar, India. He has received his both M.Tech and Ph.D. in Geoinformatics from Motilal Nehru National Institute of Technology, Allahabad, India. His research area includes Geospatial Database, SOA, Cloud Computing, Fog computing, IPR and Geoinformatics. He is a member of IEEE and IAENG.

Suparna Biswas is working as an Assistant Professor at the Department of Computer Science and Engineering in Maulana Abul Kalam Azad University of Technology, WB since 2005. She completed her ME and PhD from Jadavpur University, West Bengal in 2004 and 2013 respectively. She was an ERASMUS MUNDUS PostDoctoral Research Fellow in cLINK project in Northembria University, Newcastle, UK from 5 September 2014 to 3 July 2015. Her areas of research interests are internet of things, wireless body area network (WBAN), network security and remote healthcare.

Chandreyee Chowdhury is a faculty in the department of Computer Science and Engineering at Jadavpur University, India. She received Ph. D in Engineering from Jadavpur University in 2013 and M. E in Computer Science and Engineering from Jadavpur University in 2005. Her research interests include routing issues of Wireless Sensor Networks and its variants, mobile crowd-sensing, and offloading computation. She has more than 50 publications in journals and conferences. She is a member of IEEE and IEEE Computer Society.

Phuc Do is currently an Associate Professor of the University of Infor-mation Technology (UIT), Viet Nam National University, Ho Chi Minh city, Vi-etnam. His research interests include data mining, text mining, information net-work analysis, big data analysis, distributed computing on cloud environment and applications.

Reinaldo França has a B.Sc. in Computer Engineering in 2014. Currently, he is an Ph.D. degree candidate by Department of Semiconductors, Instruments and Photonics, Faculty of Electrical and Computer Engineering at the LCV-UNICAMP working with technological and scientific research as well as in programming and development in C / C ++, Java and .NET languages. His main topics of interest are simulation, operating systems, software engineering, wireless networks, internet of things, broadcasting and telecommunications systems

Neena Gupta received her Ph.D degree from Gurukul Kangri Vishwavidyalaya, Haridwar in the year 2005. Currently, she is working as Associate Professor in the Computer Sciences Department of Gurukul Kangri Vishwavidyalaya, Dehradun Campus. Her research interest includes optimization techniques, Cloud Computing, Security and image processing. She has published much research in International Journals and Conferences of high repute including IEEE, Elsevier, ACM, Springer, Wiley Inderscience, etc. Special Interest: Image Processing, Security, Cloud Computing.

Yuzo Iano. B.Sc. (1972), M.Sc. (1974) and Ph.D. degrees (1986) in Electrical Eng. at UNICAMP, Brazil. Since then he has been working in the technological production field, with 1 patent granted, 8 filed patent applications and 36 projects completed with research and development agencies. He has supervised 29 doctoral theses, 49 master's dissertations, 74 undergraduate and 48 scientific initiation works. He has participated in 100 master's examination boards, 50 doctoral degrees, author of 2 books and more than 250 published articles. He is currently Professor at UNICAMP, Editor-in-Chief of the SET International Journal of Broadcast Engineering and General Chair of the Brazilian Symposium on Technology (BTSym). He has experience in Electrical Engineering, with knowledge in Telecommunications, Electronics and Information Technology, mainly in the field of audio-visual communications and multimedia.

Mouna Jouini received the B.S. degree on computer science applied to management in 2008 from the University of Tunis in the Higher School of Economics and Management of Tunis (ESSECTT), University of Tunis, Tunis, Tunisia. She has obtained the M.S. degree in 2010 in computer science in the Higher Institute of Management (ISG), Tunis University, Tunisia. She also received the Ph.D. degree in computer science applied to management within the optimization strategies and intelligent computing laboratory (SOIE), High Institute of Management of Tunis, University of Tunis on December 30th, 2016. Her research interest includes software engineering metrics, cloud computing, cyber security and security measurement and quantification. She has published. She has participated in several international conferences including topics related to the computer science, cloud computing, cyber security.

Mohammed Lahmer is currently associate Professor at the Ecole Supérieure de Technologie (EST) Moulay Ismaili University, Meknes, Morocco since 2003. He received his PhD degree in computer science, Architecture of information and communication systems from the Mohamed V university, Rabat in 2008. He received his Engineer's degree in Computer Science from ENSIAS (Ecole Nationale Supérieure d'Informatique et d'Analyse des Systemes) in 1996. His research interests lie with the field optimization and model engineering. Doctor Mohammed Lahmer is member of L2MI Lab in ISIC Research Group.

Anupama Mishra has received M.Tech in Computer Science Engineering, India in the area of Computer Science Engineering in 2010. She has published much research in International Journals and Conferences of high repute including IEEE, Elsevier, ACM, Springer, Wiley Inderscience, etc. She is also serving as a reviewer for Journals of IEEE, Springer and many reputed journals. Special Interest: Network Security, Cloud Computing, Cyber Security, Information Security, Cluster Computing ISTE Membership, IBM RAD V6.0 Certification.

Brojo Kishore Mishra is currently working as a Professor in the Department of CSE, School of Engineering, GIET University, Gunupur-765022, Odisha, India. Received M.Tech and Ph.D. degrees in Computer Science from the Berhampur University in 2008 and 2012 respectively. Currently he is guiding 03nos. of Ph.D research scholar under Biju Pattnaik University of Technology, Odisha. His research interests include Data mining and big data analysis, machine learning, Soft computing, Evolutionary computation. He has already published more than 55 research papers in internationally reputed journals and referred conferences, 15 book chapters, has edited 03 books, has authored 02 books and is acting as a member of the editorial board/associate editor / Guest editor of various International journals. He served in the capacity of Keynote Speaker, Plenary Speaker, Program Chair, Proceeding chair, Publicity chair, Special session chairperson and as member of programme committees of many international conferences also. He was associated with a CSI funded research project as a Principal Investigator. He is a life member of ISTE, CSI, and member of IEEE, ACM, IAENG, UACEE, and ACCS.

Rahul Mishra presently perusing his Ph.D. degree from Indian Institute of Technology (ISM) (formerly known as Indian School of Mines), Dhanbad, India. He received his B.Tech degree from Guru Jambheshwar University of Science and Technology, Hissar, India, in 2013 and M.Tech degree from Indian Institute of Technology (ISM) (formerly known as Indian School of Mines), Dhanbad, India in 2016. He works and publishes widely in the areas of Cloud Computing issues and Security, signature scheme and Big Data.

Ana Carolina Borges Monteiro has a B.Sc. in Biomedicine in 2015, holds a Master's degree in Engineering, she is currently a Ph.D. Candidate by the DECOM, Faculty of Electrical and Computer Engineering (FEEC) at UNICAMP, and a researcher at the Laboratory of Visual Communications (LCV), developing research related to Digital Image Processing related to medical areas. Has affinity and expertise in Health and Clinical Analysis, with development in Matlab, C/C++, with topics of interest in Hematology, Medical Informatics, Cell Biology, Cell Pathology, Telecommunications, Broadcasting and Deep Learning.

Cyrus F. Nourani commenced his university degrees at MIT where he became interested in algebraic semantics. He pursued with a category theorist at the University of California on research followed on by IBM Watson labs and TU Berlin, during a brief time to completion. Dr. Nourani's dissertation on computing models and categories proved to have mathematical foundations developments that were published from the postdoctoral times on at AMS ASL, and ETCS. Past 5 year he has been engaged a research professor with TU Berlin since SFU Canda, Vancouver & Burnaby, Burnaby, Canada since 2012. In 2003, he was in R&D at Berlin, IMK Bonn and Munich. He was also a Faculty in Computer Science, Management Science, Mathematics, and Information Sciences at MIT, UCLA, University of Michigan-Ann Arbor, University of Pennsylvania, and University of Southern California and in 1996 at the University of California, Santa Barbara. He was also a Visiting Professor at Edith Cowan University, Perth, Australia and a Lecturer of Management Science and IT at the University of Auckland, New Zealand. He has written over 75 mathematics publications and international reputation in Computer Science and Mathematics, with over 250 publications in AI, EC, IT Management Science, decision trees, and predictive economics game modeling. He has also authored 5 volumes and is the volume editor for Apple Academic Press on Innovations management with 2-3 volumes publishing.

Venkataratnam P. is currently working as an Professor at VTU Extension Centre, UTL Technologies Ltd., Bengaluru. He obtained his MS & Ph.D from Indian Institute of Science (IISc), Bangalore. He has 39 years industrial experience in various R&D organizations. In addition, he has 13 years for teaching experience in various engineering colleges.

Pramod Pillai completed his Bachelor of Engineering degree in Electronics and Communication engineering. He is currently pursuing his Master's in Digital Electronics from VTU Extension Centre, UTL Technologies Ltd, India. His research interest include the application security, web security and cloud security.

Pragati Priyadarshinee received her BE from Biju Patnaik University of Technology (BPUT) and M.Tech (SE) degree from Indian Institute of Information Technology, Allahabad (IIITA). Her research interests include Big-data Analytics, Cloud Computing, Internet of Things, Knowledge Management and Software Architecture. She received her Ph.D. from National Institute of Industrial Engineering (NITIE) and her area of Ph.D. thesis is in IT & Systems. Currently she is working as Associate Professor at BVRIT Hyderabad Engineering College for Women.

Rojalina Priyadarshini has completed her M.Tech in Computer Science and Data Processing in the year 2010. She has more than 10 years of academic experience. Currently she is continuing her Ph. D in the area of Cloud Computing and Machine learning. Her research interest includes data mining, Pattern classification, Bioinformatics, Machine learning and Cloud Computing.

Kostas E. Psannis was born in Thessaloniki, Greece. Kostas received a degree in Physics from Aristotle University of Thessalo-niki (Greece), and the Ph.D. degree from the Department of Elec-tronic and Computer Engineering of Brunel University (UK). From 2001 to 2002 he was awarded the British Chevening scholarship sponsored by the Foreign & Commonwealth Office (FCO), British Government. He was awarded, in the year 2006, a research grant by IISF (Grant No. 2006.1.3.916). Since 2004 he has been a (Visit-ing) Assistant Professor in the Department of Applied Informatics, University of Macedonia, Greece, where currently he is Assistant Professor (& Departmental LLP/Erasmus-Exchange Students Co-ordinator and Higher Education Mentor) in the Department of Ap-plied Informatics, School of Information Sciences. He is also joint Researcher in the Department of Scientific and Engineering Simula-tion, Graduate School of Engineering, Nagoya Institute of Technol-ogy, Japan. He has extensive research, development, and consult-ing experience in the area of telecommunications technologies. Since 1999 he has participated in several R&D funded projects in the area of ICT (EU and JAPAN). Kostas Psannis was invited to speak on the EU-Japan Co-ordinated Call Preparatory meeting, Green & Content Centric Networking (CCN), organized by Europe-an Commission (EC) and National Institute of Information and Communications Technology (NICT)/ Ministry of Internal Affairs and Communications (MIC), Japan (in the context of the upcoming ICT Work Programme 2013) and International Telecommunication Un-ion (ITU) SG13 meeting on DAN/CCN, July 2012, amongst other invited speakers. He has several publications in international Con-ferences, books chapters and peer reviewed journals. His profes-sional interests are: Multimodal Data Communications Systems, Haptic Communication between Humans and Robots, Cloud Transmission/ Streaming/Synchronization, Future Media-Internet of Things, Experiments on International Connections (E- ICONS) over TEIN3 (Pan-Asian), Science Information Network (SINET, Japan), GRNET (Greece)-Okeanos Cloud, and GEANT (European Union) dedicated high capacity connectivity. He is Guest Editor for the Special Issue on Architectures and Algorithms of High Efficiency Video Coding (HEVC) Standard for Real-Time Video Applications (2014), Journal of Real Time Image Processing (Special Issue). He is Guest Editor for the Special Issue on Emerging Multimedia Tech-nology for Smart Surveillance System with IoT Environment (2016), The Journal of Supercomputing (Special Issue). He is Guest Editor for the Special Issue on Emerging Multimedia Technology for Multi-media-centric Internet of Things (mm-IoT) (2016), Multimedia Tools and Applications (Special Issue). He is currently GOLD member committee of IEEE Broadcast Technology Society (BTS) and a member of the IEEE Industrial Electronics Society (IES). From 2017 Prof. Kostas E. Psannis serving as an ASSOCIATE EDITOR for IEEE ACCESS and IEEE Communications Letters. He is also a member of the European Commission (EC) EURAXESS Links JA-PAN and member of the EU-JAPAN Centre for Industrial Cooperation.

Dharavath Ramesh received the B.Tech degree from Kakatiya University, Warangal, India, in 2004 and M.Tech degree from the Jawaharlal Nehru Technological University, Hyderabad, India, in 2009. He received Ph.D degree from Indian Institute of Technology (ISM) (formerly known as Indian School of Mines), Dhanbad, India in 2015. He is currently an assistant professor at the Department of Computer Science and Engineering, Indian Institute of Technology (ISM), Dhanbad, India. He works and publishes widely in the areas of Distributed databases, Cloud Computing Security, and Big Data. He is a professional member of the ACM and Senior member of IEEE.

Ronnie Ramlogan is a Senior Lecturer at the Alliance Manchester Business School, University of Manchester. After gaining his PhD from Manchester in 1995 he worked in the private sector before returning to academia. Ronnie is an experienced researcher who uses qualitative and quantitative methods in his research. He has broad interests in innovation systems and focuses on such issues as the emergence of new sectors, economic growth and productivity, health innovations, and science and technology.

Edla Reddy received the M.Sc degree from Hyderabad Central University, Hyderabad, India, in 2006 and M.Tech degree from the Indian Institute of Technology (ISM) (formerly known as Indian School of Mines), Dhanbad, India in 2009. He received Ph.D.degree from Indian Institute of Technology (ISM) (formerly known as Indian School of Mines), Dhanbad, India in 2013. He is currently an assistant professor at the Department of Computer Science and Engineering, National Institute of Technology Goa, India. He works and publishes widely in the areas of Data Mining, Cloud Computing, and Big Data. He is a member of the ACM and IEEE

Yassine Rhazali is a doctor and a professor of computer science at the University of Moulay Ismail, he obtained his doctorate in software engineering, he proposed tens validated approaches in scientific publications published in scientific conferences and scientific reviews. He is a member of international committees in several conferences and scientific reviews.

Sathi Roy is doing research work towards Ph.D. in the department of Computer Science & Engineering, Jadavpur University. her research interests include cloud computing, Wireless sensor networks, security etc.

Madhu Sake received the Ph. D degree from Jawaharlal Nehru Technological University, Anantapur, India in 2018 and, M.Tech degree from the Jawaharlal Nehru Technological University, Hyderabad, India. He received the B.Tech from Sree Vidyanikethan Engineering College Affiliated to JNTUH. He has 16 years of teaching experience. His areas of interest are wireless networks, Computer Networks, Network Security and Compiler Design. He is currently working as Professor in Guru Nanak Institutions Technical Campus (Autonomous), Hyderabad. He is a Life member of CSI.

Sayani Sen is a Full-time lecturer in Sarojini Naidu College for Women, Dumdum. She obtained her M.Tech in Computer Science & Engineering from University of Kalyani in the year 2015, M.Sc in Computer Science from St. Xavier's College, Kolkata in the year 2013 and B.Sc. Computer Science(Hons) -Gold Medalist from University of Kalyani in the year 2011. She is currently working in the area of Wireless Network & Security.

Christos Stergiou is currently a PhD student in the Department of Applied Informatics, School of Information Sciences, University of Macedonia, Greece. His main research interests include Algorithms for Cloud Computing, Big Data and Wireless Communication. In 2017, he was awarded by the conference committee of 19th IEEE Conference on Business Informatics (CBI) for Doctoral Student Work titled "Algorithms for Big Data in Advanced Communication Systems and Cloud Computing".

Trevor Wood-Harper holds a Chair of Information Systems (IS) and Systemic Change at the Manchester Business School (MBS) having been recruited in 2003 to lead Information Systems & Management research and Doctoral Education at the new University of Manchester. He has held visiting chairs at universities, such as Oslo; South Australia; Australian National (ANU); Cape Town and Napier, Edinburgh; Georgia State and Copenhagen Business School. He has acted as an external examiner for many BSc, MSc and MBA courses including LSE and Warwick. For 10 years he was a member of the British Computer Society (BCS) Validation Panel for undergraduate degrees. Also he has acted, as an advisor on university periodic review panels with the most recent was Henley Business School, Reading. Recently, Wood-Harper was an Associate Editor of the European Journal of Information Systems and continues as a foundation member, from 1991, of the Editorial Board of the Information Systems Journal. Both of these are rated in the top six world-class IS journals. Wood-Harper researches and publishes with the recent editors-in-chief of both journals. In 2008 he was awarded the prize for outstanding research from the International Federation for Information Processing (IFIP). Also he is still a member of the United Kingdom Academy for Information Systems since 1993. Trevor Wood-Harper's broad research areas are: Socio-Technical Systems; Systemic Change, Research Ethics and Action Research. He has published over 250 research articles and co-authored or co-edited 20 books. Since 2001, 25 journal papers and 7 texts were published on a wide range of topics including: the Multiview Methodology; Social Informatics; Information Systems Evolution for Developing Countries; Electronic Governance, Commerce and Communities; Action Research; Ethical Considerations in Systems Development and Doctoral Education.

Siva Yellampalli is currently working as Professor of Practice in School of Engineering and Applied Sciences, SRM University AP, Amaravati He obtained his MS & Ph.D from Louisiana State University. His area of research is system level design for power optimization. His area of research encompasses different research fields such as VLSI, mixed signal circuits/systems development, security, MEMS and CNT sensors. He has published a book in the area of mixed-signal design, and edited two books on carbon nano tubes. He published 70 plus International Journal papers & IEEE Conference papers. In addition he has delivered keynote speeches at International conferences held in Canada, Dubai & Spain including tutorials at various IEEE International Conferences. He has been a consultant to a variety of industries and acts as a reviewer for technical journals and book publishers.

Index

Purchase Print, E-Book, or Print + E-Book

IGI Global's reference books are available in three unique pricing formats:
Print Only, E-Book Only, or Print + E-Book.
Shipping fees may apply.

www.igi-global.com

Recommended Reference Books

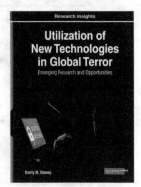

ISBN: 978-1-5225-8876-4
© 2019; 141 pp.
List Price: $135

ISBN: 978-1-5225-8100-0
© 2019; 321 pp.
List Price: $235

ISBN: 978-1-5225-7847-5
© 2019; 306 pp.
List Price: $195

ISBN: 978-1-5225-6313-6
© 2019; 349 pp.
List Price: $215

ISBN: 978-1-5225-7628-0
© 2019; 281 pp.
List Price: $220

ISBN: 978-1-5225-5855-2
© 2019; 337 pp.
List Price: $185

Do you want to stay current on the latest research trends, product announcements, news and special offers?
Join IGI Global's mailing list today and start enjoying exclusive perks sent only to IGI Global members.
Add your name to the list at **www.igi-global.com/newsletters.**

Publisher of Peer-Reviewed, Timely, and Innovative Academic Research

www.igi-global.com   ✉ Sign up at www.igi-global.com/newsletters   **f** facebook.com/igiglobal   **t** twitter.com/igiglobal   **t** linkedin.com/igiglobal

Ensure Quality Research is Introduced to the Academic Community

Become an IGI Global Reviewer for Authored Book Projects

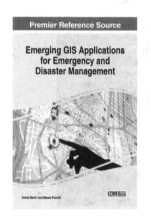
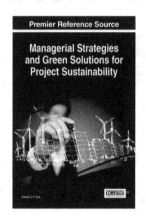

The overall success of an authored book project is dependent on quality and timely reviews.

In this competitive age of scholarly publishing, constructive and timely feedback significantly expedites the turnaround time of manuscripts from submission to acceptance, allowing the publication and discovery of forward-thinking research at a much more expeditious rate. Several IGI Global authored book projects are currently seeking highly-qualified experts in the field to fill vacancies on their respective editorial review boards:

Applications and Inquiries may be sent to:
development@igi-global.com

Applicants must have a doctorate (or an equivalent degree) as well as publishing and reviewing experience. Reviewers are asked to complete the open-ended evaluation questions with as much detail as possible in a timely, collegial, and constructive manner. All reviewers' tenures run for one-year terms on the editorial review boards and are expected to complete at least three reviews per term. Upon successful completion of this term, reviewers can be considered for an additional term.

If you have a colleague that may be interested in this opportunity, we encourage you to share this information with them.

IGI Global Proudly Partners With eContent Pro International

Receive a 25% Discount on all Editorial Services

Editorial Services

IGI Global expects all final manuscripts submitted for publication to be in their final form. This means they must be reviewed, revised, and professionally copy edited prior to their final submission. Not only does this support with accelerating the publication process, but it also ensures that the highest quality scholarly work can be disseminated.

English Language Copy Editing

Let eContent Pro International's expert copy editors perform edits on your manuscript to resolve spelling, punctuaion, grammar, syntax, flow, formatting issues and more.

Scientific and Scholarly Editing

Allow colleagues in your research area to examine the content of your manuscript and provide you with valuable feedback and suggestions before submission.

Figure, Table, Chart & Equation Conversions

Do you have poor quality figures? Do you need visual elements in your manuscript created or converted? A design expert can help!

Translation

Need your documjent translated into English? eContent Pro International's expert translators are fluent in English and more than 40 different languages.

Hear What Your Colleagues are Saying About Editorial Services Supported by IGI Global

"The service was very fast, very thorough, and very helpful in ensuring our chapter meets the criteria and requirements of the book's editors. I was quite impressed and happy with your service."

– Prof. Tom Brinthaupt,
Middle Tennessee State University, USA

"I found the work actually spectacular. The editing, formatting, and other checks were very thorough. The turnaround time was great as well. I will definitely use eContent Pro in the future."

– Nickanor Amwata, Lecturer,
University of Kurdistan Hawler, Iraq

"I was impressed that it was done timely, and wherever the content was not clear for the reader, the paper was improved with better readability for the audience."

– Prof. James Chilembwe,
Mzuzu University, Malawi

Email: customerservice@econtentpro.com   www.igi-global.com/editorial-service-partners

www.igi-global.com

Celebrating Over 30 Years of Scholarly
Knowledge Creation & Dissemination

InfoSci®-Books

A Database of Over 5,300+ Reference Books Containing Over
100,000+ Chapters Focusing on Emerging Research

GAIN ACCESS TO **THOUSANDS** OF
REFERENCE BOOKS AT **A FRACTION**
OF THEIR INDIVIDUAL LIST **PRICE**.

InfoSci®-Books Database

The **InfoSci®-Books** database is a collection of
over 5,300+ IGI Global single and multi-volume
reference books, handbooks of research, and
encyclopedias, encompassing groundbreaking
research from prominent experts worldwide that
span over 350+ topics in 11 core subject areas
including business, computer science, education,
science and engineering, social sciences and more.

Open Access Fee Waiver (Offset Model) Initiative

For any library that invests in IGI Global's InfoSci-Journals and/
or InfoSci-Books databases, IGI Global will match the library's
investment with a fund of equal value to go toward **subsidizing
the OA article processing charges (APCs) for their students,
faculty, and staff** at that institution when their work is submitted
and accepted under OA into an IGI Global journal.*

INFOSCI® PLATFORM FEATURES

- No DRM
- No Set-Up or Maintenance Fees
- A Guarantee of No More Than a 5% Annual Increase
- Full-Text HTML and PDF Viewing Options
- Downloadable MARC Records
- Unlimited Simultaneous Access
- COUNTER 5 Compliant Reports
- Formatted Citations With Ability to Export to RefWorks and EasyBib
- No Embargo of Content (Research is Available Months in Advance of the Print Release)

*The fund will be offered on an annual basis and expire at the end of
the subscription period. The fund would renew as the subscription is
renewed for each year thereafter. The open access fees will be waived
after the student, faculty, or staff's paper has been vetted and accepted
into an IGI Global journal and the fund can only be used toward
publishing OA in an IGI Global journal. Libraries in developing countries
will have the match on their investment doubled.

To Learn More or To Purchase This Database:
www.igi-global.com/infosci-books

eresources@igi-global.com • Toll Free: 1-866-342-6657 ext. 100 • Phone: 717-533-8845 x100   www.igi-global.com

IGI Global
DISSEMINATOR OF KNOWLEDGE
www.igi-global.com

Publisher of Peer-Reviewed, Timely, and
Innovative Academic Research Since 1988

IGI Global's Transformative Open Access (OA) Model:
How to Turn Your University Library's Database Acquisitions Into a Source of OA Funding

In response to the OA movement and well in advance of Plan S, IGI Global, early last year, unveiled their OA Fee Waiver (Offset Model) Initiative.

Under this initiative, librarians who invest in IGI Global's InfoSci-Books (5,300+ reference books) and/or InfoSci-Journals (185+ scholarly journals) databases will be able to subsidize their patron's OA article processing charges (APC) when their work is submitted and accepted (after the peer review process) into an IGI Global journal.*

How Does it Work?

1. When a library subscribes or perpetually purchases IGI Global's InfoSci-Databases including InfoSci-Books (5,300+ e-books), InfoSci-Journals (185+ e-journals), and/or their discipline/subject-focused subsets, IGI Global will match the library's investment with a fund of equal value to go toward subsidizing the OA article processing charges (APCs) for their patrons.

   Researchers: Be sure to recommend the InfoSci-Books and InfoSci-Journals to take advantage of this initiative.

2. When a student, faculty, or staff member submits a paper and it is accepted (following the peer review) into one of IGI Global's 185+ scholarly journals, the author will have the option to have their paper published under a traditional publishing model or as OA.

3. When the author chooses to have their paper published under OA, IGI Global will notify them of the OA Fee Waiver (Offset Model) Initiative. If the author decides they would like to take advantage of this initiative, IGI Global will deduct the US$ 1,500 APC from the created fund.

4. This fund will be offered on an annual basis and will renew as the subscription is renewed for each year thereafter. IGI Global will manage the fund and award the APC waivers unless the librarian has a preference as to how the funds should be managed.

Hear From the Experts on This Initiative:

"I'm very happy to have been able to make one of my recent research contributions, 'Visualizing the Social Media Conversations of a National Information Technology Professional Association' featured in the *International Journal of Human Capital and Information Technology Professionals*, freely available along with having access to the valuable resources found within IGI Global's InfoSci-Journals database."

– Prof. Stuart Palmer,
Deakin University, Australia

For More Information, Visit:
www.igi-global.com/publish/contributor-resources/open-access or contact IGI Global's Database Team at eresources@igi-global.com.